ADVANCES IN PERSONALITY ASSESSMENT
Volume 8

ADVANCES IN PERSONALITY ASSESSMENT
Volume 8

Edited by
James N. Butcher
University of Minnesota

Charles D. Spielberger
University of South Florida

LAWRENCE ERLBAUM ASSOCIATES, PUBLISHERS

1990   Hillsdale, New Jersey   Hove and London

Lawrence Erlbaum Associates, Inc., Publishers
365 Broadway
Hillsdale, New Jersey 07642

ISSN: 0278-2367
ISBN 0-8058-0503-6

Printed in the United States of America
10 9 8 7 6 5 4 3 2 1

Contents

4. **An Epigenetic Approach to the Assessment of Personality: The Study of Instability in Stable Personality Organizations**   **63**
    Arnold Wilson, Steven D. Passik, and M. F. Kuras

5. **The Role of Self-Prediction in Psychological Assessment**   **97**
    Timothy M. Osberg and J. Sidney Shrauger

6. **Rorschach Measures of Psychoanalytic Theories of Defense**   **121**
    Paul Lerner and Howard Lerner

Preface

The field of personality assessment continues to grow and expand at a rapid rate. Developments within the field are reflected by the ever increasing numbers of new books, the recent initiation of several journals on assessment, and the seemingly continuous expansion of empirical research on a plethora of assessment-related topics. The field is, indeed, expanding so rapidly that it is difficult for the personality researcher and clinical practitioner to keep abreast of the many new methods of assessment, and the broad ranging applications of assessment techniques.

The present volume, the eighth in this *Advances in Personality Assessment* Series, is a continuation of our effort to bring together significant original papers representing diverse theoretical perspectives, critical methodological issues, and a variety of assessment techniques. Our major goal has been to solicit creative and unique contributions to the field, and to provide a publication format that permits more extensive and detailed reports of research findings, than is generally possible in a journal article. Authors are also encouraged to speculate about the implications of their work. A second goal has been to provide mental health professionals and researchers with a broad spectrum of personality assessment topics "under one roof" with the hope that the field will benefit from the cross-fertilization of ideas from divergent theoretical perspectives and methodological orientations.

In keeping with the Series goal of encompassing a broad spectrum of assessment approaches, this volume includes a variety of topics, ranging from insightful theoretical analyses, such as Dana's evaluations of multi-ethnic assessment, to sophisticated methodological papers such as Ben-Porath's discussion of the use of factor analysis in the cross-cultural validation of personality inventories. Detailed descriptions of empirical research findings, such as those reported by Clark on the assessment of personality disorder, are also included.

A diversity of assessment approaches are also considered in the present volume. These vary from traditional assessment approaches, such as the Rorschach (Lerner and Lerner) and the MMPI (Savasir and Erol), to newer instruments such as Strelau's Temperament Inventory, which was developed in Europe and only recently introduced in America. We are especially pleased with the opportunity the Series gives us to bring to the attention of our American colleagues important advances in personality assessment that have taken place in other countries.

It is our hope that Volume 8 will provide mental health professionals with new insights and information about important directions in which the field of personality assessment is going. We also hope that the contents of this volume will encourage psychologists and mental health providers whose practice involves psychodiagnosis and personality assessment to contribute to evaluating the adequacy of new interpretations of traditional assessment instruments, and to explore the utility of recently developed measures, in their professional work.

James N. Butcher
Charles D. Spielberger

1 Cross-Cultural and Multi-Ethnic Assessment

Richard H. Dana
University of Arkansas

In 1988 we have glasnost and the imperative that psychology is bound to what Lifton (1987) has referred to as "shared fate," the beginnings of a sense of species self, of being inextricably connected with all other persons on this planet, both individually and collectively. Realization of shared fate has been minimized among professional psychologists, not as an apparent result of racism or malice (Abramowitz & Murray, 1983; López, 1988), but because of unverbalized assumptions about themselves and other persons, a Eurocentric world view.

More than 22% of the population of the United States is of minority composition (U. S. Department of Commerce, Bureau of the Census, 1986) and composed of four major groups: Afro-Americans, Asian Americans, Hispanic Americans, and Native Americans. Early in the next century these groups will compose approximately one third of the population. These persons have historically underutilized available services (e.g., Sue, 1977) in spite of demonstrations that culture-compatible services can be provided by persons who share language and cultural values (Flaskerud, 1986), or use indigenous case-managers whenever they lack facility in the first language of their clients (e.g., Kinsie, 1985; Mollica, Wyshak, & Lavelle, 1987).

Despite recent increases in the numbers of service provider doctoral candidates of minority origins (Howard et al., 1986), these professionals could not address the service needs of the populations they represent even if they limited their practices to persons sharing a common cultural heritage. Nor has appropriate curriculum and training for multicultural services existed in most accredited graduate or internship programs (Bernal & Padilla, 1982; Wyatt & Parham, 1985) in spite of exhortation by the American Psychological Association and the National Council of Schools of Professional Psychology. Furthermore, in the

1

continued absence of major changes in training, there is no doubt that White, middle-class, Anglo psychologists will continue to provide the insensitive services characterized by Sue and Zane (1987) as "a series of frustrations, misunderstandings, distortions and defensive reactions" that include "language, role ambiguities, misinterpretations of behavior, differences in priorities of treatment" (p. 44). If culture-compatible services are ever to be provided by the majority of psychologist service providers, an adequate understanding of culture-specific assessment is required. This chapter outlines an agenda for a serious commitment to a culture-compatible assessment technology and service delivery style.

COMPONENTS OF
CROSS-CULTURAL/MULTI-CULTURAL ASSESSMENT

Table 1.1 presents the components of this agenda in summary form and includes moderators, tests, methods, interpretation, personality theory, service delivery, training, and ethics. This table deliberately begins with moderator variables in order to emphasize the current priority of existing tests and the desire to modify their interpretations for particular groups. These moderator variables are designed to provide measures of the effects of culture on use of standard measures, particularly acculturation scales. However, moderator variables merely provide potential "correction factors" and thereby reaffirm the legitimacy and appropriateness of existing etic instruments (Dana, 1988). Etic refers to an emphasis on universals by looking at a particular culture from the outside, often from a middle-class Anglo-American perspective. Any use of moderators by assessors will not affect the utilization of services by underserved populations, although research in this area can extend knowledge of existing tests, and particularly their limitations for interpretation with diverse cultural groups.

Emic refers to a culture-specific perspective, and five areas are emic in focus: tests, methods, interpretation, personality/personality theory, and service delivery. Although these areas can impact favorably on utilization of services by cultural minorities, any impact will be restricted if used only by indigenous service providers.

New tests include racial identity measures for Afro-Americans, especially the Developmental Inventory of Black Consciousness (DIB-C) (Milliones, 1980), and the Racial Identity Attitude Scale (RIAS) (Parham & Helms, 1981). These tests derive from attempts to understand the cultural conversion experiences, or psychological nigrescence of Afro-Americans in this country (Cross, 1978). These new tests not only suggest parameters of a unique culture-personality interface, but are necessary ingredients of culture-specific personality theory. Other new tests have origins in practice with specific groups (e.g., TEMAS, Malgady, Costantino, & Rogler, 1984) and will not be considered at this time.

TABLE 1.1
Components of Cross-Cultural/Multi-Ethnic Assessment

Components	Description	Example	Reference
Moderators	Culture-specific effects on standard measures	Acculturation scales	Dana (1988)
Tests	Measures derived from culture specific theory	Racial identity/ Black consciousness scales	Milliones (1980) Parham & Helms (1981)
Methods	Interview-derived collaborative narration	Accounts	Jones & Thorne (1987)
Interpretation	Focus on world view/reality construction	Ethnic validity	Tyler et al. (1985)
Personality	Culture-specific theory of self and person	Afro-American Asian American Hispanic American	Jenkins (1982) Hsu (1985) Ramirez (1983)
Service delivery	Culture-specific knowledge of etiquette, social behavior	Interpersonal orientation Credibility/giving Relationship Cultural Script	Gibbs (1985) Sue & Zane (1987) Dana (1986a) Triandis et al. (1985)
Training	Culture-general and culture-specific content with affective, cognitive, behavior goals	Consciousness-raising via courses, seminars, workshops Integration via practica, clerkship, internship language learning, borrowed technology, and inter-disciplinary cooperation	J. M. Bennett (1986)
Ethics	Ethnocentric bias and neglect of cross-cultural issues in APA guidelines	Values, qualifications for service providers, perceptions of services	Pedersen & Marsella (1982)

New methods represent culture-appropriate ways of data collection by tapping an oral tradition that is a less formalized and more natural form of expression for many persons. The accounts method is essentially an interview, or case study, for representation of personality that is inherently emic (Jones & Thorne, 1987). Most published examples of case studies, however, have omitted persons of culturally diverse origins (e.g., Bellah, Madsen, Sullivan, Swidler, & Tipton, 1985; Block, 1986; Josselson, 1987; Rychlak, 1982).

Interpretation of assessment findings from minority and ethnic clients generally proceeds from an implicit Eurocentric world view and reality construction. This world view constitutes a self-contained individualism, or egocentrism (Sampson, 1988), that accepts a unique and intrinsically valued self as separate from others and of primary importance. A more frequent world view among other cultures and American minorities is what Sampson calls an ensembled individualism, or sociocentrism in which the self is inextricably tied to relationships that favor the wellbeing of other persons. Interpretation thus requires what has been called "ethnic validity" (Tyler, Sussewell, & Williams-McCoy, 1985), or awareness and acceptance of many alternative constructions of reality.

Personality theories have not included cross-cultural hermeneutics, but have been the ebullient fantasies of several generations of White male theorists. Psychology is indebted to Monte (1987) for investing these theories with the personal lives of their authors. There are beginnings of personality theory, and more particularly expositions of the self, that are culture-specific, although these emic approaches have not as yet become part of the interpretation practices of professional psychologists (Marsella, DeVos, & Hsu, 1985). Smith (1985) has asserted that the self must always be understood in a context of culture and history.

Service delivery is also culture-specific with an etiquette and social behavior that permits the process to be sanctioned by the client. For many persons affective and empathic responses determine the quality of any relationship, including the engagement with potential service providers. For example, Afro-Americans, Asian Americans, Hispanic Americans, and Native Americans prefer styles that have been called "interpersonal orientation," "credibility and giving," "cultural script," and "relationship," respectively, as indicated in Table 1.1. A culture-compatible service delivery stance must include relevant interpretation in a context of social etiquette and ethnographic knowledge. The ability to use this awareness and relevant knowledge is predicated upon intercultural sensibility as evidenced by ethnorelativism, or unconditional acceptance of culturally different persons (M. J. Bennett, 1986).

Training for cross-cultural/multi-ethnic assessment should include culture-general and culture-specific content available on an interdisciplinary basis, using borrowed technology, including language skills and interdisciplinary cooperation. Ridley (1985) has appropriately emphasized that ethnic and cultural information must be systematically presented in training programs. He suggests a three-dimensional model with population, intervention, and curriculum targets. An explicit training policy for each program is recommended.

Similarly, ethical issues should be addressed in order to protect consumers and providers. The allegation of ethnocentric bias in APA ethical guidelines (Pedersen & Marsella, 1982) should focus attention on the development of culture-specific ethical codes, examination of critical incidents, and a task force to clarify complex ethical dilemmas inherent in cross-cultural service delivery. The remainder of this chapter supplements this introduction by summaries of the eight areas described in Table 1.1 and discussion of the following major issues: (a) ethnorelativism; (b) a refocus of attention on the self; (c) a humane and responsible science.

Moderator Variables

Moderator variables for etic tests provide potential correction that permits cultural variance to be used in interpretation. These variables include acculturation measures, new F tests for the MMPI, and willingness to be self-disclosing or to receive feedback. Acculturation measures are discussed as the major representatives of this component at the present time.

Berry (1980) has described acculturation as a complex process that includes the nature of cultural contact, the course of group relationships, group/individual levels, and measurement. Acculturation can occur by loss of original cultural identity by assimilation or deculturation and with maintenance of original cultural identity by integration or rejection of the dominant society. Traditional language, cognitive style, personality, identity, and attitudes are all affected in the adaptations of individuals and groups. Culture-responsible assessment cannot be accomplished without careful attention to these areas, preferably using independent test data for degree of acculturation in addition to experience/knowledge of the particular culture.

Historically, although some authors have used single indices such as language to estimate degree of acculturation, any single dimension will oversimplify the phenomenon of acculturation. Olmedo (1979) has identified three dimensions by factor analysis: language, "culture-specific attitudes and value orientations" (p. 1069), and educational level/occupational status. Many multidimensional measures of acculturation exist, particularly for Native American tribes, although these are one-way or unilevel avenues to describe whatever remains of cultural heritage (Mendoza, 1984).

The effects of sociocultural interaction constitute a bilevel or two-way process. As a result it is necessary to assess relevant components of the original culture as well as the extent to which the values and behaviors of the dominant society have been incorporated. These bilevel instruments vary greatly in richness of theoretical context, psychometric adequacy, and reliance on empirical data. Two instruments for Chinese Americans (Yao, 1979) were used with well-educated, affluent Taiwan immigrants and a 13% response rate in urban samples (Table 1.2). Although the measures are simple and of adequate reliability, little is known about the generalization of these traits to other Asian groups, or to more representative Taiwan immigrants who currently report less than half of the average annual income of these samples (U. S. Department of Commerce, Bureau of the Census, 1986).

Brown's *Conflicts Resolution Chart* (1982) for Native Americans is creative and unique in using a structured interview with representative behaviors at four points, labeled as generations, on an acculturation/continuum in several areas: spiritual/religious; social/recreational; training/education; and family/self. To the extent that these are core areas for all Native Americans, this method of collecting acculturation information should be useful with many different tribes. No psychometric data are available.

The most engaging and psychometrically sophisticated instruments have been developed for Hispanic Americans as a result of careful thinking about the process of acculturation. Ramirez (1984) has been critical of the presumed generality across groups of a conflict-replacement or distress-adaptation model of acculturation. His *Multicultural Experience Inventory* identifies bicultural, traditional, and atraditional persons using broad base sampling of Mexican-Americans, with impressive reliabilities, and validation using psychohistories, and leadership behaviors. Mendoza and Martinez (1981) developed a multidimensional model of acculturation delineating affective, cognitive, and behavioral adaptations and recognizing that assimilation may be uneven across modalities. A distinction between degrees of assimilation and extinction of cultural practices enabled cultural resistance, cultural shift, cultural incorporation and cultural transmutation to be identified. From this model of acculturation, the *Cultural Life Style Inventory* was constructed in Spanish and English versions, with dimensions of intra-family and extra-family language usage, social affiliations/activities, cultural familiarity/activities, and cultural identification/pride. Evidences of construct validity were provided by hypothesis testing and concordance of profiles with profiles generated by relatives.

Table 1.3 presents selected bilevel, cross-cultural measures that have had cross-cultural applications with two or more distinct cultural groups. Two of these measures have used self-reported behaviors and values (Szapocznik, Scopetta, Kurtines, & Aranalde, 1978; Wong-Rieger & Quintana, 1987). Pictures have been used to provide scores on cultural values (Pierce, Clark, & Kiefer, 1972). This approach is similar to tests of knowledge of particular Native American tribes developed as part of training workshops for White teachers of Native American children (Hornby & Dana, 1980). However, the most distinctive method related psychological dimensions of role taking to willingness to acculturate (Smither & Rodriguez-Giegling, 1982).

There are three choices of moderator variables in the form of acculturation

TABLE 1.2

Selected Bilevel Acculturation Measures for Asian Americans (I), Hispanic Americans (II), and Native Americans (III)

Group/Source	Measure	Commentary
I Yao (1979)	What do I Believe? Intrinsic cultural traits (24 items): attitudes toward family relations, sex education, women's status, social-economic/political issues, America/American people How do I Feel about Living in the United States? External cultural traits (16 items): social isolation, English proficiency, adaptation to American lifestyle, future prospects	1. Alpha reliability = 58/.75 2. Urban sample: Houston/Los Angeles 3. 81% Taiwan immigrants 4. 13.3% response rate (N = 133) 5. Education mean = 19.4 6. Income mean = $32,589
II Ramirez (1984)	Multicultural Experience Inventory. Demographics, personal history data, multicultural participation (57 items). Identifies biculturals, traditionals, atraditionals.	1. Split-half reliability = .79/.68 2. 1046 subjects: Texas/California 3. Life-history interviews from 129 with accurate identification of 125 4. Leadership behavior: multi-culturals flexible, active, tactful, personable.
II Mendoza (in press)	Cultural Life Style Inventory. Orthogonal dimensions: intrafamily language usage; social affiliations/activities; cultural familiarity/activities; cultural identification/pride. Estimates of cultural resistence, incorporation, and shift. Identification of dominant/nondominant lifestyles.	1. Sophisticated construction, content validity, item discrimination analyses, factor analysis, reliability (Alpha; test-retest; parallel form) 2. Correlational evidence of construct validity: hypothesis testing, concordence of porfiles with profiles generated by relatives 3. English and Spanish versions with equivalence data.
III Brown (1982)	Conflicts/Resolution Chart. Areas: spiritual/religious; social/recreational; training/ education; family/self.	1. 4 generations, or points on acculturation continuum, used as weighted scores. 2. No psychometric data.

TABLE 1.3
Selected Bilevel Acculturation Measures with Cross-Cultural Applications

Source	Groups	Measure	Description
Pierce et al. (1972)	Japanese and Mexican Americans	Acculturation Balance Scale	Identification of pictures with American, Mexican, and Japanese cultural values
Smither and Rodriguez-Giegling (1982)	Vietnamese and Nicaraguan refugees	Scales for psychological dimensions of role-taking and willing-ness to accul-turate	Relationship of psycholgoical dimensions (ambition, intelligence, consci-entiousness, like-ability, mental health) to willing-ness to acculturate
Szapocznik et al. (1978)	Cuban and White Americans	Behavioral and Value Accultu-ration Scales	Scales for self-reported behaviors and value orientations
Wong-Rieger and Quintana (1987)	Hispanic Americans Southeast Asians, "foreign students"	Multiculturea1 Acculturation Scale	Self-report of cog-nition, behavior and self-identity. Values orientation items.

measures: unilevel, bilevel, and bilevel/cross-cultural. Unilevel measures de-scribe what remains of an original culture, perhaps under the assumption that total assimilation is desirable, or that these remnants are to be examined. These measures can be used to correct scales of the MMPI (e.g., Hoffmann, Dana, & Bolton, 1985; Montgomery & Orozco, 1985). Because there remains some controversy with regard to cultural bias on the MMPI (Dahlstrom, Lachar, & Dahlstrom, 1986; Dana, 1988; Greene, 1987; Jones & Thorne, 1987), until there is research that clarifies, for example, the nature of item differences across cultural groups, attempts to alter scale scores on the basis of statistical weights may be premature. Providing correction factors per se may be part of the current problem in assessment of minority persons, as Mercer (1986) has noted. The problem may lie in the assumption that differences must be reduced or minimized because somehow these differences are inimical to participation of various groups in American culture (Dana, 1988). Bilevel measures of acculturation for each group seem to offer immediate usefulness because they provide a descriptive context for other assessment data. Although bilevel/cross-cultural measures are of interest, especially when values are included, more work needs to be done on these instruments before they can be recommended for routine assessment use.

Tests

For most groups the cultural component in their lives is part of consciousness from early childhood, a source of strength and identity, and a context of other persons who have shared a similar past. Values shape affects, cognitions, and behaviors into a distinctive world view that provides a basis for the decisions that structure everyday life.

Black Americans, however, have had to painfully reconstruct their past history as a result of an anonymous entry into this country as slaves. This identity has been reconstructed primarily from their African origins, hence the term Afro-American. Because the terms Black, Negro, and Afro-American evoke different perceptions and self-perceptions (Fairchild, 1985), the least prejudicial and most positive image embodies distinctive African cultural origins.

Thomas (1970) used the term negromachy to describe a lack of cultural identity or mental illness in Black Americans. Symptoms of compliance, subservience, repressed rage, and hypersensitivity affected self-concept and reality appreciation. The desire to participate in American society and simultaneous denial of equal opportunity produced conflict, alienation, and symptomatology. Resolution of this conflict was possible as a result of racial identity and growth of personal humanity. Five stages were included by Thomas: verbal anger directed at White society, the pain incurred by self-denial and anxiety concerning change, learning about the cultural heritage, a group process providing linkages to Black experience, and transcendence.

Cross (1971) also described five stages of a Negro-to-Black conversion: pre-encounter, encounter, immersion-emersion, internalization, and internalization-commitment. In the pre-encounter stage, a Eurocentric world view prevails and Blackness is derogated. The encounter stage proceeds from encounter to a cautious reinterpretation of experience. Immersion-emersion occurs at a point of identity acceptance, or "the vortex of psychological metamorphosis" (Cross, 1978, p. 17). Incorporation of ideology and world view is coupled with a sense of racial destiny, intense, exhuberant energy, and exaggerated behaviors. Consolidation of this stage results in internalization, a more balanced perspective. Finally, internalization entails an ongoing and meaningful group activity.

The Thomas and Cross models are similar in the final stage but differ in the degree of focus on transition experiences and preconversion stages. Taylor (in press) examined both ontogenetic models, found agreement on four stages, and selected the Developmental Inventory of Black Consciousness (DIB-C) (Milliones, 1980) to index progress in preconscious, confrontation, internalization, and integration stages. This 80-item instrument, using a 9-point scale, has received considerable psychometric attention, and unpublished studies are reported by Taylor. Norms are available and there are validity data for personal, social, and cultural adjustment. Taylor also elaborates a research agenda that has theoretical and practical consequences.

Parham and Helms (1981; Helms & Parham 1985) constructed three versions of a self-report inventory, the Racial Identity Attitude Scale (RIAS) from Q sort items (Hall, Cross, & Freedle, 1972) to measure the Cross (1971) pre-encounter, encounter, immersion-emersion, and internalization stages. The Negro-to-Black conversion model was modified by considering attitudes or world view present at a particular time to be representative of the identity stages. Interpretation uses patterns of scale elevations and weighted linear combinations of attitudes; however, the encounter items have relatively low reliability (Helms, 1985) and construct validity (Ponterotto & Wise, 1987).

Methods

Leary (1970) anticipated the concern with prefabricated personality constructs and culture-bound medical model categorization in a plea for recognition of a primary role for individual assessees in their own assessment. Assessee and assessor were envisioned as collaborators in a shared process that could result in the creation of personalized assessment devices or procedures. Several persons (e.g., Dana, 1982; Fischer, 1985) proceeded to render the assessment process a collaborative endeavor but did not realize that what was believed on the basis of personal values had an especial poignancy for clients who were culturally different.

Harré and Secord (1972) provided the formal accounts method and Jones and Thorne (1987) described applications to individuals in ethnic and minority groups. This method provides an interview-derived introspective and collaborative narratives. Measures can be constructed with help from members of cultural groups using critical incidents or with Kelly's Role Construct Repertory Test (Jones & Zoppel, 1979). Postassessment narratives by assessees enlarge the cultural context by providing direct feedback to assessors about instruments, items, and the test-taking situation. Assessment findings can also be verified using other members of the same culture as informants (Dana, Hornby, & Hoffmann, in press). The accounts method is at the heart of emic approaches and is congruent with a changing conception of science from positivistic to interpretive (Bruner, 1986) in which ecological validity occurs by expression of individual experience in terms of a still living oral tradition.

Interpretation

Interpretation of assessment data, whether by idiographic or nomothetic means, is ultimately personal and subjective. The professional reality of service-providers is structured by world view, beliefs concerning services/service delivery inculcated during training, the time/place/person conceptions of personality theorists, and knowledge of the multifaceted lives of clients.

An early professional memory entails observation of an assessment by Ed Shneidman during a diplomate exam in which I used projective techniques to examine a White, middle-class male World War II veteran in a Veterans Administration outpatient setting. After the oral exam the next day I was self-congratulatory and never realized that any ostensible success was due to similarities among assessor, observer, and client, all of whom structured a professional service situation within the same idiom from shared expectations and world view. Had the patient been Chicano or Chinese American, the outcome could have been very different.

The interpretation process in service delivery should make explicit the world views and reality constructions of service providers and their clients. White service providers minimize racial or cultural issues (Greene, 1985; Turner & Armstrong, 1981), focus on individual responsibility for problems (Berman, 1979), and perceive personality characteristics differently than non-White therapists (Li-Repac, 1980). (See Table 1.4.)

Attentiveness to cultural differences can be described by an ethnic validity model (Tyler et al., 1985) that accepts differences among persons as authentic ways of being human and requires awareness of the social context for understanding individual lives. Matching service providers and clients by culture-defining and nonculture-defining groups can maximize gains in services. Helms (1985) also has argued for even more elaborate matching in terms of level of identity development for clients and service providers.

Personality and Personality Theory

The culture–personality interface can be described by using either domain as a frame of reference for generating inferences (Klineberg, 1954). American psychology has shifted from using the person as exclusive referent to awareness of Benedict's cultural determinism (e.g., Beit-Hallahmi, 1974; Caplan & Nelson, 1973) and a continuous and subtle interaction between person and environment. The relative contribution of variance in person, setting, and their interaction have been examined and an increasing research knowledge has clinical assessment applications (Kenrick & Funder, 1988). Nonetheless, as a result of present technology and investment in the medical model, many assessors continue to emphasize that personality is largely resident in the person. Implementation of this assumption by instrumentation results in continued minimization of cultural factors. The extent to which individuals are shaped by culture and the particular characteristics affected by particular cultures have not been part and parcel of our personality research tradition.

It is now clear that large segments of the American population cannot receive adequate services unless service providers are able to articulate their problems and dilemmas in culture-relevant terms. If this is not done, there is potential for pathologization, a discrediting of essential ingredients in personal lives and belief systems, and potential distortion of the self or personality.

The self we cherish and study and defend so vigorously (e.g., Perloff, 1987; Spence, 1985) is an American, middle-class, White, and predominantly male self, integumented in a culture that is taken for granted by its inhabitants and credited with being the standard for comparison and emulation worldwide. Understanding of selfhood, or personality theory, however, requires recognition

TABLE 1.4
World View Contributions to Assessment for Major Cultural Groups

Group	Source	Description	Assessment
Afro-Americans	Carter and Helms (1987	Racial identity attitudes as focus for Afro-Euro-American values	Values orientation Racial Identity Attitude Scale
	Jackson (1983)	Black assessment practice model	Components: World view, milieu, situational context
	Mays (1985)	Black ideology	World view
	Rose (1982-83)	Sharing, individual uniqueness affective humanism, diunital existence	Four components account for Black-White personality differences
Asian American	Ho (1985)	Creative synthesis of world views	Collectivism and individualism
	Kinsie (1985)	Value conflicts as basis for different expectations of patients and service providers	Service expectations, values
Hispanic American	Inclan (1985)	Value orientations as guides	Value orientations
Native American	Dana (1986b)	Orientation (self vs. group) and focus of experience (external vs. internal)	Locus of control/locus of responsibility, values, acculturation

that there is a Western concept of self (Johnson, 1985) and cross-cultural hermeneutics (Smith, 1985).

One outcome of a recent debate on individualism has been to differentiate between self-centered individualism and embedded individualism (Sampson, 1988), which differ in self–other boundary characteristics, kinds of power and control exercisable, and the inclusiveness/exclusiveness of the concept of self. American service providers often assume that all clients share with them a belief in self-contained individualism and their personality theory origins serve as context and support. However, many clients experience the self as ensembled as nonpsychologist/psychiatrist personality theorists have suggested (e.g., Etzioni, 1968; Hsu, 1971). An embedded individualism provides more fluid self–other boundaries, a field of personal–social regulatory forces, and an extended range of other persons embraced by the self-concept.

To incorporate awareness of selfhood or personality into the service delivery paradigm, it is necessary that the culture–personality relationship be reexamined by study of different cultural and ethnic groups. Ethnographies, or accounts resulting from fieldwork, are narratives that stay close to everyday life situations, incorporate the point of view (world view) inherent in the culture, and recognize the lack of separation between observer and data (Marcus & Cushman, 1982). Although ethnographic accounts provide useful information, the extent to which the observer is indigenous to the culture is critical, as has been noted in studies of Chicanos (Rosaldo, 1985), in order to minimize mistranslations, failure to recognize figurative speech, double meaning, or humor that misrepresents the culture and unwittingly support stereotypes. Ethnographies can be useful for contextual information on Native American tribes, although tribal informants are increasingly critical of these projects when accomplished by White observers who sojourn on a reservation and then take something away that is only of value to themselves and their discipline.

Only indigenous personality theory and empirical research can provide the knowledge component for a context that permits an increment of understanding on a cross-cultural or cross-ethnic basis. Table 1.5 suggests some sources of culture-specific personality theory. Most of these theories are incomplete and evidence only the beginnings of empirical documentation. For Native Americans, however, there are no such ambitious and psychologized attempts to construct personality theory. The presence of few psychologists with indigenous origins, the large number of different tribes with different acculturation histories, and the distinctive Native American world view suggest that general personality portraits will continue to be presented in literature (Momaday, 1977) or communicated in art form (Highwater, 1981). The large numbers of acculturation instruments, especially for unilevel delineation of traditionalism (Hoffmann, 1983) and the tribe-specific nature of these instruments (Dana, 1986a), attest to the complexity and unevenness of the culture–personality interface.

TABLE 1.5
Culture-Specific Personaltiy Theory for Afro-Americans,
Asian Americans, and Hispanic Americans

Group	Source	Description
Afro-American	Jenkins (1982)	Humanistic theory emphasizing self-concept, competence, pluralism and identity.
Asian American	Hsu (1985)	Applications of general theory (Hsu, 1971) to Chinese and Japanese.
	Sue and Morishima (1982)	Personality, family, sex-role conflict and identity from mental health perspective.
	Tseng and Wu (1985)	Components of culture and personality, including child training, family, traits, and temperament for mainland China, application to Australian, Hawaii, Hong Kong, Singapore, and Taiwan Chinese, with mental health emphasis.
Hispanic American	Diaz-Guerrero (1977)	Sociocultural psychology of personality.
	Ramirez (1983)	Mestizo theory: historical, cultural, ecological, and genetic sources of world view, adaptation, and coping, emphasizing identity and multicultural development.

Service Delivery

In Table 1.1 service delivery was defined by culture-specific knowledge of etiquette and social behavior, but it is the manner in which feeling is used to incorporate awareness into behavior that is critical for the client. The presence of an intercultural sensibility is communicated by transactions of feeling that may be expressed nonverbally (Vogelaar & Silverman, 1984). Although few attempts have been made to put intercultural sensibility into words, Stewart (1981) has used a holographic model to illustrate the indirectness of human connection in a service delivery setting: A cultural groundbase is established by means of empathy. Empathy, as a source of understanding, derives from the culturally conceived concept of self as well as from internal sources of feeling, imagination, and memory that may become salient in the process of relating to another person.

Intercultural sensibility may only be expressible in the presence of ethnorelativism. Ethnorelativism is an attitude toward other persons that accepts differences. M. J. Bennett (1986) has described a series of stages that moves from ethnocentric thinking characterized by denial of differences (Stage 1), defense against differences (Stage 2), and minimization of differences (Stage 3) to progressively greater ethnorelativistic thinking evidenced by acceptance of differences (Stage 4), adaptation or cultural pluralism (Stage 5), and integration or multicultural identity (Stage 6). Ethnorelativistic thinking begins at Stage 4 functioning with respect for cultural differences.

Expressions of ethnorelativism in service delivery to the major cultural groups are summarized in Table 1.6. All of these expressions of sensibility are conveyed by feeling-tone, nonverbal behaviors, and appropriate social etiquette. Sue and Zane (1987) provide evidence that trust and competence are related in client perception, that service delivery style may antedate perception of competence, and that the gift of a service provider can include the gift of self that is culturally congruent as well as the gift of meaningful gain.

These qualities of credibility and giving have somewhat different behavioral nuances across cultural groups. Afro-Americans use "sizing up" and "checking out" the service provider to make certain that caring and sensitivity to their culture and identity are present. If the service provider passes tests of authenticity and equalitarianism, and is identified as a bona fide change agent, then acceptance of the service provider permits performance, or cooperation in the assessment process and any accompanying procedures or tests. Gibbs developed a consultation model (1980) applicable to assessment or treatment relationships (1985) that included these stages of interpersonal orientation.

Native Americans are also suspicious of the intentions of White service providers, but they may be more cautious and withholding during their interpersonal negotiations in a service delivery setting. There is preference for an extended personal relationship before any services are provided. In the history of cross-cultural contacts, trust led to repeated and bitter disappointments and an awareness of genocidal intentions on the part of Whites. As a result the stages of a developing relationship may be extended in time and include social exchanges to document common experiences. An expanded consent for services invites shared assessment findings and clearly stated recommendations in the form of genuine and available interventions. A long-term personal follow-up makes continuity of relationship a basis for the reputation of the service provider that is communicated through the extended family and tribal network (Dana, 1986a).

Credibility and giving have a context in cultural scripts for Hispanic Americans. Simpatía refers to interactions with high frequencies of positive behaviors. Ambiente is a warm, accepting atmosphere. Platicando is a friendly informal, leisurely chatting. Personalismo refers to trust in persons, trust in informality. These scripts suggest that a climate for acceptance of services is only developed on the basis of provider personal qualities as expressed in the professional encounter.

Training

The purpose of training is to enhance intercultural sensitivity by development of ethnorelative thinking (Stage 4). Etic instruments (e.g., MMPI) are Stage 3 in

TABLE 1.6

Intercultural Sensibility, or Ethnorelativism, in Practice

Sensibility	Description	Source/Group
Credibility/Giving	Client perception of effective/ trustworthy and gift-giving service provider	Sue and Zane (1987)/general
Cultural Scripts	Client expectations: ambiente, simpatía, platicando, and personalismo	Triandis et al. (1984) Gomez and Cook (1978)/ Hispanics
Interpersonal Orientation	Stages of relationship and criteria for competence evaluation: appraisal (personal authenticity) investigation (egalitarianism) involvement (identification) engagement (acceptance; performance)	Gibbs (1985)/Afro-Americans
Relationship	Prior contact, communality of experience, empathy, expanded consent, shared find- ings, long-term personal follow up	Dana (1986a)/Native Americans

that they minimize differences (Dana, 1988). Similarly, many service providers are probably Stage 3 persons who act toward culturally different persons with good will, belief in minimization of differences through assimilation, and ignorance of world views and attitudes toward service providers that differ from their own. Stage 4 may be an equivalent of Loevinger's (1976) autonomous stage of ego development. If this is a correct supposition, it follows that Stage 4 thinking may be rare since only about 1% of the population function on an autonomous level (Holt, 1980). The next lower stage of ego development, the individualistic, includes between 8% and 9% of the college population. These persons display qualities of responsibility, tolerance, inner control, nurturance, and lack of aggression (White, 1985) and should be well represented in any graduate student population.

However, relevant training for intercultural communication has evolved quite independently of professional psychology (J. M. Bennett, 1986). Content is both culture-general and culture-specific and is mediated by methods that have cognitive, affective, and behavioral goals. For example, T-groups and role plays, culture simulations, and workshops have been used to combine culture-general and affective goals. Culture-general and cognitive goals have been approached by intercultural communication courses. Culture-specific content and affective goals are combined in simulations and bicultural workshops. Culture-specific content and cognitive goals represent a classroom approach that includes the culture assimilator, a paper-and-pencil analysis of incidents reflecting contrast of values or customs. The usefulness of these approaches for training professional psychologists deserves examination.

Using this format, professional psychology programs should draw from courses in other areas for cognitive content that is culture-general and culture-specific. Language skills need to be developed whenever services are to be offered to persons whose first language is not English because communication of feeling is minimized in a second language (Malgady, Rogler, & Costantino, 1987; Suarez, 1987). Programs should explore T group, role play, workshop, and other structured procedures for affective goals in both culture-general and culture-specific applications.

These exercises should probably antedate attempts to provide services to culturally different clients in practica. Practica, clerkship, and specialty internships, or internship rotations can provide for an integration of knowledge and service delivery. For example, specialized internships are available at the Center for Multicultural Training in Psychology (Boston) and the National Asian American Training Center (San Francisco). Specialized training may be found, for example, at Brandeis University (Training Program in Ethnicity and Mental Health), Marylhurst College (Intercultural Communication Institute), and the University of Hawaii (Institute of Behavioral Sciences). Service providers have also received in-service training in a variety of settings (e.g., Anderson, Bass,

Munford, & Wyatt, 1977; Evans, Acosta, Yamamoto, & Skilbeck, 1984; Lefley, 1985).

Pedersen (1983) has indicated that degree-oriented academic programs were being developed at Boston University, University of Miami, Syracuse University, and Western Washington University. Such programs may be required, especially at the post-doctoral level, for specialization in cross-cultural service delivery in the future.

Ethics

Ethics provide a statement of norms or standards for delineating appropriate behaviors. Professional ethics, as promulgated by the APA (1981), express concern with each individual's sense of self-worth and dignity. General principles deal with responsibility, competence, moral and legal standards, public statements, confidentiality, welfare of the consumer, professional relationships, and assessment techniques.

Pedersen and Marsella (1982) cite ethno-cultural biases in those principles that explicitly mention cultural differences. In Principle 1(a) (Responsibility), there is neglect of the multiplicity of cultural values in this society. What constitutes "objectivity" and "appropriate services" must always be culturally defined. In Principle 2(d) (Competence), professional qualifications for multi-cultural services are not stated. In Principle 3(b) (Moral and Legal Standards), the culturally different perceptions of psychological services are secondary to the expectation of service providers.

Although there are some rules that transcend cultures, there are no metaethics (Barnlund, 1979). Morality, however, is variable and culture-specific. Because cultures have unequal power and psychological boundaries that also differ, communication between persons from different cultures always entails risk because the symbols used may not be consistent or understood and different systems of rules governing communication are being used.

Cross-cultural professional settings must be clear on who does what to whom under what circumstances and with what sanctions. In other words, there must be a system of rules and symbols that is shared by service provider and client as has been suggested by culture-specific etiquettes of service delivery. More concretely, culture-specific inventories of ethical codes need to be developed (Asuncion-Lande, 1979) that identify important beliefs, values, ideas, and attitudes, and suggest the rules for appropriate interpersonal conduct. Each code would contain beliefs with ethical implications about those needs, motives, or interests that should be respected by others. An ethical code addresses the different cultural priorities of satisfaction from potentially competing needs. These ethical codes would be cultural and not professional in nature. A second step constitutes application to professional psychological services and service delivery since moral and legal restraints to practice are culturally different.

Pedersen and Marsella (1982) argue for multiple answers to each problem situation with examples and case studies for clarification. Because conflict between cultural groups is inevitable, realistic guides that suggest their own limits are needed. Sanctions must be available using flexible oversight.

Two personal examples are relevant here. Recently, I observed a skilled psychiatrist during a long afternoon of brief medication-oriented interviews with Indochinese women using an ethnic mental health counselor as interpreter. This service provider understood clearly the world view of this population and has been responsible for articulating their values and expectations to professional audiences. Because he was not fluent in the language of these clients, and establishing a personal link to each woman was part of an existential service delivery stance, he used physical contact carefully and sparingly. Each woman was hugged, patted on the arm or shoulder, or had her hand touched in the course of the interview, particularly at leave-taking, and following the normal cultural behavior of hands clasped and bowing. He wanted me to know he was aware that physical contact with Asian women was taboo and that his use of it was a deliberate part of service delivery. Indeed for almost all of these women, these "touching" behaviors appeared to be consistent and an appropriate part of service delivery. The ethical questions here are obvious, however.

A second example comes from my own experiences with Native Americans. Reservation residents see Whites come and go, sojourn, and make spontaneous attempts to share social life. When services are provided, the response to them and the extent of active participation are determined by the history of social relationships. For Native Americans, helping services are contextualized within the culture and traditionally provided by persons whom they respect and have knowledge of their forebears across generations. White service providers have always kept their White clients/patients at arm's length in social situations, relying on their own discomfort if not specific professional ethical prohibitions for guidance. The ethical dilemmas here are also apparent. Both examples suggest the need for developing culture-specific ethical guidelines.

Discussion

Ethnorelativism. This proposal for assessment services may appear at first to be a formidable addition to an already heavy training agenda. However, sensitization to persons as individuals in a training climate of ethnorelativism simply focuses the attention of professional psychologists on individual differences rather than group differences.

In the enthusiasm for professional status with an accepted empirical rationale for practice, the substitution of an etic or pseudo-etic preoccupation was combined with naive zeal for rendering everyone similar, or minimization of cultural differences (Stage 3), in an American dream that was ostensibly in the best interests of the persons whose original cultures were being disregarded or even obliterated. With unremarkable hindsight, it is apparent that any dilution of cultural origins whatsoever diminishes the quality of life. Bellah and colleagues (1985) have argued convincingly for a "commitment of memory" in which people remember their historical sufferings and virtues in concert with future aspirations as a context of meaning for their individual lives.

It is difficult to forge any responsible valuing of other persons, especially persons who are different from oneself, in a climate of diminished influence of the traditional contexts for meaning. These contexts, or collectivity, include family, community, nation, and religion. Sarason (1986) attributed the absence of any coherent concept of public interest to a weakening of the triad of person, collectivity, and meaning of human existence. A sundered fabric of interrelationships cannot readily provide a bridge between the self-contained American individualism of many affluent, White professional psychologists and an ensembled individualism (Sampson, 1988), with more permeable boundaries including others in the conception of self that is characteristic of many culturally diverse clients.

Because students are not being selected for graduate training in terms of any developmental or stage criteria, it will be necessary to provide relevant training and experiences so that students may practice ethnorelative behaviors as part of a repertoire of professional skills. Attitude change, and Stage 4 ethnorelative thinking, can be an outcome of such training.

A Refocus of Attention on the Self. After conspicuous beginnings to the subjective understanding of persons in the writings of David Rappaport, Roy Schafer, Silvan Tomkins, and Robert Holt, among others, assessment technology became salient and the inferential uses of data were relegated to ancillary importance. This shift of attention occurred as the nomothetic-idiographic controversy was resolved in favor of actuarial uses of assessment data. The self is now being resurrected as a legitimate research focus that includes intensive case study and repeated measurements design (Singer & Kolligan, 1987). The self is a product of culture and epoch. The self that professional psychologists cherish is of relatively recent European origins with boundaries and prerogatives that are unfamiliar in the experience of many cultures (Baumeister, 1986). This Western self has isolated psychologists from many of their clients and estranged America from other nations.

Subjectivity can be reemphasized by the methods used, by an interpretation process that emphasizes culturally relevant content, and by service delivery that honors culturally distinctive behavior and etiquette and does not violate expectation for relationship with a service provider. Personality research has cycled back to an Allportian vision of an extended range of legitimate instruments, particularly the interview, coupled with recognition that subjective data may form the cornerstone for understanding whenever the process of data collection is genuinely collaborative.

A Humane Science.   The quest for a human science now includes awareness that the implicit, unrecognized, and unverbalized attitudes of the service provider can determine the quality of services as perceived by a client. Services will continue to be underutilized, regardless of the relevance and meaningfulness of the personality constructions and interventions, unless this new awareness permeates our professional acts.

In the early days of struggling for recognition as a science any combination of psychological science and the art of human service delivery was indeed remote. Now with a research base that needs only transmogrification into practice, and with professional pressure for caring and compassion, the "art," or creative and developmental human interphase with many other persons can be emphasized. With greater security as a respected profession, there is less pressure for emulation of the medical service delivery paradigm and diminished concern with being scientists first, professionals second, and persons last, or not at all in our engagements with clients. Recently there has been an attempt to reinvest assessment technology with what Naisbitt (1982) has referred to as "high touch," a personal quality of caring in the service delivery process that in generalized format is suggestive of interpersonal orientation or simpatía (Dana, 1985).

It now appears that the crucial determinant of our professional reality is found in assumptions of similarities and differences among persons. Wallace Stevens, the poet, provides a perspective:

> Rationalists, wearing square hats,
> Think, in square rooms,
> Looking at the floor,
> Looking at the ceiling.
> They confine themselves
> To right-angled triangles.
> If they tried rhomboids,
> Cones, waving lines, ellipses—
> As, for example, the ellipse of the half moon—
> Rationalists would wear sombreros. (1957, p. 127)

If professional psychology is to fulfill its many promises in a service society, an immediate future occupational domain will include more than tertiary intervention models. The profession must actively prepare for human problem-solving in all phases of everyday life. Technology must address the quagmire of human relations at the local, state, national, and international levels in addition to interventions in the personal lives of individuals. These professional tasks require a service delivery process that maximizes, honors, and understands differences in gender, culture/ethnicity, social class, religion, and other human characteristics. As Rappaport (1981) has counseled, the use of our technology for empowerment of all citizens is a proper activity in which to express the sense of species self that attends the fate that we all share.

REFERENCES

Abramowitz, S. I., & Murray, J. (1983). Race effects in psychotherapy. In J. Murray & P. R. Abramson (Eds.), *Bias in psychotherapy* (pp. 215–255). New York: Praeger.

American Psychological Association. (1981). Ethical principles of psychologists (rev. ed.). *American Psychologist, 36,* 633–638.

Anderson, G., Bass, B. A., Munford, P. R., & Wyatt, G. E. (1977). A seminar on assessment and treatment of black patients. *Professional Psychology, 8,* 340–348.

Asuncion-Lande, N. C. (1979). Ethics in intercultural communication: An introduction. In N. C. Asuncion-Lande (Ed.), *Ethical perspectives and critical issues in intercultural communication* (pp. 3–7). Falls Church, VA: Speech Communication Association.

Barnlund, D. C. (1979). The crosscultural arena: An ethical void. In N. C. Asuncion-Lande (Ed.), *Ethical perspectives and critical issues in intercultural communication* (pp. 8–13). Falls Church, VA: Speech Communication Association.

Baumeister, R. F. (1986). *Identity: Cultural change and the struggle for self.* New York: Oxford.

Beit-Hallahmi, B. (1974). Salvation and its vicissitudes. Clinical psychology and political values. *American Psychologist, 29,* 124–129.

Bellah, R. N., Madsen, R., Sullivan, W. M., Swidler, A., & Tipton, S. M. (1985). *Habits of the heart: Individualism and commitment in American life.* Berkeley, CA: University of California Press.

Bennett, J. M. (1986). Modes of cross-cultural training: Conceptualizing cross-cultural training as education. *International Journal of Intercultural Relations, 10,* 117–134.

Bennett, M. J. (1986). A development approach to training for intercultural sensitivity. *International Journal of Intercultural Relations, 10,* 179–196.

Berman, J. (1979). Counseling skills used by black and white male and female counselors. *Journal of Counseling Psychology, 26,* 81–84.

Bernal, M. E., & Padilla, A. M. (1982). Status of minority curricula and training in clinical psychology. *American Psychologist, 37,* 780–787.

Berry, J. W. (1980). Acculturation as varieties of adaptation. In A. M. Padilla (Ed.), *Acculturation: Theory, models and some new findings.* Boulder, CO: Westview Press.

Block, J. (1986). *Lives through time.* Hillsdale, NJ: Lawrence Erlbaum Associates.

Brown, S. (1982, May). *Native generations diagnosis and placement on the conflicts/resolution chart.* Paper presented at the meeting of the annual school of additions studies, Center for Alcohol and Addiction Studies, University of Alaska-Anchorage.

Bruner, J. (1986). *Actual minds, possible worlds.* Cambridge, MA: Harvard University Press.

Caplan, N., & Nelson, S. (1973). On being useful: The nature and consequences of psychological research on social problems. *American Psychologist, 28,* 199–211.

Carter, R. T., & Helms, J. E. (1987). The relationship of black value-orientations to racial identity attitudes. *Measurement and Evaluation in Counseling and Development, 19,* 185–195.

Cross, W. E. (1971). The Negro-to-Black conversion experience: Toward a psychology of black liberation. *Black World, 20,* 13–37.

Cross, W. E. (1978). The Thomas and Cross models of psychological nigrescence: A review. *Journal of Black Psychology, 5*(1), 13–31.

Dahlstrom, W. G., Lachar, D., & Dahlstrom, L. E. (1986). *MMPI patterns of American minorities.* Minneapolis: University of Minnesota Press.

Dana, R. H. (1982). *A human science model for personality assessment using projective techniques.* Springfield, IL: Thomas.

Dana, R. H. (1985). A service-delivery paradigm for personality assessment. *Journal of Personality Assessment, 49,* 598–604.

Dana, R. H. (1986a). Personality assessment and Native Americans. *Journal of Personality Assessment, 50,* 480–500.

Dana, R. H. (1986b, September). World view and assessment of Native Americans. Invited paper for the Native American National Rehabilitation Research Symposium, *Improving the Quality of Life of Native Americans: Cross-Cultural Assessment Issues*. Scottsdale, AZ.

Dana, R. H. (1988). Culturally diverse groups and MMPI interpretation. *Professional Psychology: Research and Practice, 19*, 490–495.

Dana, R. H., Hornby, R., & Hoffmann, T. (in press). Personality assessment of Rosebud Sioux: A comparison of Rorschach, Millon Clinical Multiaxial Inventory, and 16 PF reports. *White Cloud Journal*.

Diaz-Guerrero, R. (1977). A Mexican psychology. *American Psychologist, 32*, 934–944.

Etzioni, A. (1968). *The active society*. New York: Free Press.

Evans, L. A., Acosta, F. X., Yamamoto, J., & Skilbeck, W. M. (1984). Orienting psychotherapists to better serve low income and minority patients. *Journal of Clinical Psychology, 40*, 90–96.

Fairchild, H. H. (1985). Black, Negro, or Afro-American? The differences are crucial. *Journal of Black Studies, 16*, 47–55.

Fischer, C. T. (1985). *Individualizing psychological assessment*. Monterey, CA: Brooks-Cole.

Flaskerud, J. H. (1986). The effects of culture-compatible intervention on the utilization of mental health services by minority clients. *Community Mental Health Journal, 22*, 127–141.

Gibbs, J. T. (1980). The interpersonal orientation in mental health consultation: Toward a model of ethnic variations in counseling. *Journal of Community Psychology, 8*, 195–207.

Gibbs, J. T. (1985). Establishing a treatment relationship with black clients: Interpersonal vs instrumental strategies. *Advances in Clinical Social Work*. Silver Spring, MD: National Association of Social Workers.

Gomez, E., & Cook, K. (1978). *Chicano culture and mental health: Trees in search of a forest* (Chicano Culture and Mental Health Monograph Series, Monograph No. 1). San Antonio, TX: Our Lady of the Lake University.

Greene, B. A. (1985). Considerations in the treatment of black patients by white therapists. *Psychotherapy, 22*, 389–393.

Greene, R. L. (1987). Ethnicity and MMPI performance: A review. *Journal of Consulting and Clinical Psychology, 55*, 497–512.

Hall, W. S., Cross, W. E., & Freedle, R. (1972). States in the development of Black awareness: An exploratory investigation. In R. L. Jones (Ed.), *Black psychology* (pp. 156–165). New York: Harper & Row.

Harré, R., & Secord, P. F. (1972). *The exploration of social behavior*. Oxford, England: Blackwell Press.

Helms, J. E. (1985). Toward a theoretical explanation of the effects of race on counseling: A black and white model. *Counseling Psychologist, 12*(4), 153–165.

Helms, J., & Parham, T. A. (1985). *The Racial Identity Attitude Scale* (RIAS). Unpublished manuscript.

Highwater, J. (1981). *The primal mind: Vision and reality in Indian America*. New York: Harper & Row.

Ho, D. Y. F. (1985). Cultural values and professional issues in clinical psychology. *American Psychologist, 40*, 1212–1218.

Hoffmann, T. (1983). *Native American acculturation bibliography*. Unpublished manuscript.

Hoffmann, T., Dana, R. H., & Bolton, B. (1985). Measured acculturation and MMPI-168 performance of Native American adults. *Journal of Cross-Cultural Psychology, 16*, 243–256.

Holt, R. R. (1980). Loevinger's measure of ego development: Reliability and national norms for male and female short forms. *Journal of Personality and Social Psychology, 39*, 909–920.

Hornby, R., & Dana, R. H. (1980). *A support group approach to problem solving with Native American children*. Fayetteville, AR: University of Arkansas Printing Services.

Howard, A., Pion, G. M., Flattau, P. E., Oskamp, S., Pfafflin, S. M., Bray, D. W., & Burstein,

A. G. (1986). The changing face of American psychology: A report from the committee on employment and human resources. *American Psychologist, 41,* 1311–1327.

Hsu, F. L. K. (1971). Psycho-social homeostasis and Jen: Conceptual tools for advancing psychological anthropology. *American Anthropologist, 73*(1), 23–44.

Hsu, F. L. K. (1985). The self in cross-cultural perspective. In A. J. Marsella, G. DeVos & F. L. K. Hsu (Eds.), *Culture and self: Asian and Western perspectives* (pp. 24–55). New York: Tavistock.

Inclan, J. (1985). Variations in value orientations in mental health work with Puerto Ricans. *Psychotherapy, 22,* 324–334.

Jackson, A. M. (1983). A theoretical model for the practice of psychotherapy with black populations. *Journal of Black Psychology, 10*(1), 19–27.

Jenkins, A. H. (1982). *The psychology of the Afro-American: A humanistic approach.* New York: Pergamon.

Johnson, F. (1985). The Western concept of self. In A. J. Marsella, G. DeVos, & F. L. K. Hsu (Eds.), *Culture and self: Asian and Western perspectives* (pp. 91–138). New York: Tavistock.

Jones, E. E., & Thorne, A. (1987). Rediscovery of the subject: Intercultural approaches to clinical assessment. *Journal of Consulting and Clinical Psychology, 55,* 488–495.

Jones, E. E., & Zoppel, C. A. (1979). Personality differences among blacks in Jamaica and in the United States. *Journal of Cross-Cultural Psychology, 10,* 435–456.

Josselson, R. (1987). *Finding herself: Pathways to identity development in women.* San Francisco: Jossey-Bass.

Kenrick, D. T., & Funder, D. C. (1988). Profiting from controversy: Lessons from the person-situation debate. *American Psychologist, 43,* 23–34.

Kinsie, J. D. (1985). Cultural aspects of psychiatric treatment with Indochinese refugees. *American Journal of Social Psychiatry, 5,*(1), 47–53.

Klineberg, O. (1954). How far can the society and culture of people be gauged through their personality characteristics? In F. L. K. Hsu (Ed.), *Aspects of culture and personality* (pp. 29–35). New York: Abelard-Schuman.

Leary, T. (1970). The diagnosis of behavior and the diagnosis of experience. In A. Mahrer (Ed.), *New approaches to personality classification* (pp. 211–236). New York: Columbia University Press.

Lefley, H. P. (1985). Impact of cross-cultural training on black and white mental health professionals. *International Journal of Intercultural Relations, 9,* 305–318.

Lifton, R. J. (1987). Shared fate in the nuclear age. *Sane World,* Summer, 18.

Li-Repac, D. (1980). Cultural influences on perception: A comparison between Caucasian and Chinese-American therapists. *Journal of Cross-Cultural Psychology, 11,* 327–342.

Loevinger, J. (1976). *Ego development.* San Francisco: Jossey-Bass.

López, S. (1988). The empirical basis of ethnocultural and linguistic bias in mental health evaluations of Hispanics. *American Psychologist, 43,* 1095–1097.

Malgady, R. G., Costantino, G., & Rogler, L. H. (1984). Development of a Thematic Apperception Test (TEMAS) for urban Hispanic children. *Journal of Consulting and Clinical Psychology, 52,* 986–996.

Malgady, R. G., Rogler, L. H., & Costantino, G. (1987). Ethnocultural and linguistic bias in mental health evaluation of Hispanics. *American Psychologist, 42,* 228–234.

Marsella, A. J., DeVos, G., & Hsu, F. L. K. (Eds.). (1985). *Culture and self: Asian and Western perspectives.* New York: Tavistock.

Marcus, G. E., & Cushman, D. (1982). Ethnographies as texts. *Annual Review of Anthropology, 11,* 25–69.

Mays, V. M. (1985). The Black American and psychotherapy: The dilemma. *Psychotherapy, 22,* 379–387.

Mendoza, R. H. (1984). Acculturation and sociocultural variability. In J. L. Martinez, Jr. & R. H. Mendoza (Eds.), *Chicano psychology* (pp. 61–75). Orlando, FL: Academic Press.

Mendoza, R. H. (in press). An empirical scale to measure type and degree of acculturation in Mexican-American adolescents and adults.

Mendoza, R. H., & Martinez, J. J. (1981). The measurement of acculturation. In A. Baron, Jr. (Ed.), *Explorations in Chicano psychology* (pp. 71–82). New York: Holt, Rinehart & Winston.

Mercer, J. (1986, September). *Overview of major issues in cross-cultural assessment.* Invited paper presented at the Native American Rehabilitation National Research Symposium, Scottsdale, AZ.

Milliones, J. (1980). Construction of a black consciousness measure: Psychotherapeutic implications. *Psychotherapy: Theory, Research and Practice, 17,* 175–182.

Mollica, R. F., Wyshak, G., & Lavelle, J. (1987). The psychosocial impact of war trauma and torture on Southeast Asian refugees. *American Journal of Psychiatry, 14,* 1567–1572.

Momaday, N. S. (1977). *House made of dawn.* New York: Harper & Row.

Monte, C. F. (1987). *Beneath the mask.* New York: Holt, Rinehart & Winston.

Montgomery, G. T., & Orozco, S. (1985). Mexican Americans' performance on the MMPI as a function of level of acculturation. *Journal of Clinical Psychology, 41,* 203–212.

Naisbitt, J. (1982). *Megatrends.* New York: Warner.

Olmedo, E. L. (1979). Acculturation: A psychometric perspective. *American Psychologist, 34,* 1061–1070.

Parham, T. A., & Helms, J. E. (1981). The influence of Black students' racial identity attitudes as preferences for counselors' race. *Journal of Counseling Psychology, 28,* 250–257.

Pedersen, P. B. (1983, August). *Developing interculturally skilled counselors: A training program.* Paper presented at the meeting of the American Psychological Association, Anaheim, CA.

Pedersen, P. B., & Marsella, A. J. (1982). The ethical crisis for cross-cultural counseling and therapy. *Professional Psychology, 13,* 492–500.

Perloff, R. (1987). Self-interest and personal responsibility redux. *American Psychologist, 42,* 3–11.

Pierce, R. C., Clark, M. M., & Kiefer, C. W. (1972). A "bootstrap" scaling technique. *Human Organization, 31,* 403–410.

Ponterotto, J. G., & Wise, S. L. (1987). Construct validity study of the Racial Identity Attitude Scale. *Journal of Counseling Psychology, 34,* 218–223.

Ramirez III, M. (1983). *Psychology of the Americas: Mestizo perspectives on personality and mental health.* New York: Pergamon.

Ramirez III, M. (1984). Assessing and understanding biculturalism-multiculturalism in Mexican-American adults. In J. L. Martinez, Jr. & R. H. Mendoza (Eds.), *Chicano psychology* (pp. 77–94). Orlando: Academic Press.

Rappaport, J. (1981). In praise of paradox: A social policy of empowerment over prevention. *American Journal of Community Psychology, 9,* 1–25.

Ridley, C. R. (1985). Imperatives for ethnic and cultural relevance in psychology training programs. *Professional Psychology: Research and Practice, 16,* 611–622.

Rosaldo, R. (1985). Chicano studies, 1970–1984. *Annual Review of Anthropology, 14,* 405–427.

Rose, L. R. (1982/83). Theoretical and methodological issues in the study of black culture and personality. *Humboldt Journal of Social Relations, 10,* 320–337.

Rychlak, J. F. (1982). *Personality and lifestyles of young male managers.* San Diego, CA: Academic Press.

Sampson, E. E. (1988). The debate on individualism: Indigenous psychologies of the individual and their role in personal and social functioning. *American Psychologist, 43,* 15–22.

Sarason, S. B. (1986). And what is the public interest? *American Psychologist, 41,* 899–905.

Singer, J. L., & Kolligan, Jr., J. (1987). Personality: Developments in the study of private experience. *Annual Review of Psychology, 38,* 533–574.

Smith, M. B. (1985). The metaphorical basis of selfhood. In A. J. Marsella, G. DeVos & F. L. K. Hsu (Eds.), *Culture and self: Asian and Western perspectives* (pp. 56–88). New York: Tavistock.

Smither, R., & Rodriguez-Giegling, M. (1982). Personality, demographics, and acculturation of

Vietnamese and Nicaraguan refugees to the United States. *International Journal of Psychology, 17*, 19–25.

Spence, J. T. (1985). Achievement American style: The rewards and costs of individualism. *American Psychologist, 40*, 1285–1295.

Stevens, W. (1957). Six significant landscapes. In *Harmonium*. New York: Knopf.

Stewart, E. C. (1981). Cultural sensitivities in counseling. In P. B. Pedersen, J. G. Draguns, W. J. Lonner & J. E. Trimble (Eds.), *Counseling across culture* (pp. 61–86). Honolulu: University Press of Hawaii.

Suarez, M. G. (1987, August). *Implications of Spanish-English bilingualism on the TAT stories*. Paper presented at the meeting of the American Psychological Association, New York.

Sue, S. (1977). Community mental health services to minority groups—some optimism, some pessimism. *American Psychologist, 32*, 616–624.

Sue, S., & Morishima, J. K. (1982). *The mental health of Asian Americans: Contemporary issues in identifying and treating mental problems*. San Francisco: Jossey-Bass.

Sue, S., & Zane, N. (1987). The role of culture and cultural techniques in psychotherapy: A critique and reformulation. *American Psychologist, 42*, 37–45.

Szapocznik, J., Scopetta, M. A., Kurtines, W., & Aranalde, M. A. (1978). Theory and measurement of acculturation. *Interamerican Journal of Psychology, 12*, 113–130.

Taylor, J. (in press). Cultural conversion experience: Implications for mental health research and treatment. In R. L. Jones (Ed.), *Advances in black psychology*. Richmond, CA: Cobb & Henry.

Thomas, C. (1970). Different strokes for different folks. *Psychology Today, 4*(4), 48–53; 78–80.

Triandis, H. C., Marin, G., Lisansky, J., & Betancourt, H. (1984). Simpatía as a cultural script of Hispanics. *Journal of Personality and Social Psychology, 47*, 1363–1375.

Tseng, W-S, & Wu, D. Y. H. (Eds.). (1985). *Chinese culture and mental health*. Orlando, FL: Academic Press.

Turner, S., & Armstrong, S. (1981). Cross-racial psychotherapy: What the therapists say. *Psychotherapy: Theory, Practice and Research, 18*, 375–378.

Tyler, F. B., Sussewell, D. R., & Williams-McCoy, J. (1985). Ethnic validity in psychotherapy. *Psychotherapy, 22*, 311–320.

U. S. Department of Commerce, Bureau of the Census. (1986). *National data book and guide to sources. Statistical abstract of the United States*. Washington, DC: U.S. Government Printing Office.

Vogelaar, L. M., & Silverman, M. S. (1984). Nonverbal communication in cross-cultural counseling: A literature review. *Journal for the Advancement of Counseling, 7*, 41–57.

White, M. S. (1985). Ego development in adult women. *Journal of Personality, 53*, 561–575.

Wong-Rieger, D., & Quintana, D. (1987). Comparative acculturation of Southeast Asian and Hispanic immigrants and sojourners. *Journal of Cross-Cultural Psychology, 18*, 345–362.

Wyatt, G. E., & Parham, W. D. (1985). The inclusion of culturally sensitive course materials in graduate school and training programs. *Psychotherapy, 22*, 461–468.

Yao, E. L. (1979). The assimilation of contemporary Chinese immigrants. *Journal of psychology, 101*, 107–113.

2 Cross-Cultural Assessment of Personality: The Case for Replicatory Factor Analysis

Yossef S. Ben-Porath
University of Minnesota

The use of factor analysis in cross-cultural studies of personality is gradually becoming common practice. In this chapter I survey the use of this methodology and explore its strengths and pitfalls. The already voluminous literature in this area, to be cited later, indicates the importance authors and researchers attach to studying their personality measuring instruments in this manner, and suggests the timeliness of a review. This review will not be exhaustive, but selective, focusing on five representative personality questionnaires: the Eysenck Personality Questionnaire (EPQ), the 16 Personality Factors Questionnaire (16 PF), the Comrey Personality Scales (CPS), the Minnesota Multiphasic Personality Inventory (MMPI), and the California Psychological Inventory (CPI).

There are essentially three non-mutually exclusive objectives of cross-cultural studies of personality. Butcher (1985) suggests that the most notable reason for cross-cultural adoption of personality scales is to provide useful clinical assessment techniques for the second culture. Similarly, adopted instruments may serve useful research purposes in their new culture. Brislin (1983) points out that this is a mutually rewarding endeavor in that cross-cultural research may also lead to the discovery of universals. Thus, the second purpose of cross-cultural studies of personality is to investigate the extent to which personality constructs postulated as the result of research in one culture can be applied universally. Though universality cannot actually be proven, demonstrating invariance of personality constructs across many and diverse cultures can strengthen its plausibility. A third possible purpose for cross-cultural studies of personality is the comparison of "typical" personalities in two or more cultures by comparing mean scale scores across cultures. As noted, these three objectives are in no way mutually exclusive. It is the intent of this chapter to show that all of them can be addressed with proper use of factor analysis.

By way of introduction, the purpose and importance of cross-cultural research in personality is first discussed. Next, the role of factor analysis in these studies is considered and a method termed replicatory factor analysis is highlighted. Its use in cross-cultural studies of some of the major personality inventories today is then reviewed. The final section of this chapter integrates the findings to date, addresses some of the methodological issues raised in these studies, and offers suggestions for their resolution.

WHY CROSS-CULTURAL?

Butcher (1982) has pointed out that the robustness of its constructs is critical to the advancement of personality theory. Butcher and Pancheri (1976) state that cross-cultural research is essential to ascertaining the generality and universality of psychological concepts. Together, these two statements define the issue at hand: If we are only interested in developing personality measures that will enable us to deal with particular prediction and/or classification problems, the applicability of these instruments to other cultures would not necessarily be of interest to us. Stated differently, if in developing measuring instruments in the field of personality we were interested only in predictive or concurrent validity, we would not be obliged to study those instruments in other cultures. Each culture could conceivably develop its own optimal empirically keyed instruments. If, on the other hand, we wish to understand psychologically what a given instrument measures, that is, if we are interested in construct validity, then we may well want to broaden and deepen this understanding by finding out whether the meanings and interpretations associated with an inventory developed in one culture can validly accompany its use in another (see Loevinger, 1957, for a compelling case for the central role of construct validity relative to that of predictive or concurrent validity).

Cross-cultural validation of a measuring instrument enables us to answer the following question: To what extent is the validity of constructs developed to characterize personality in one culture, linked to that culture (the constructs themselves, perhaps products of cultural influences), and to what extent do they actually represent universal entities which are applicable to human beings qua human beings? This is not an either/or question. As noted, universality cannot actually be proven; however its plausibility can be strengthened by demonstrating invariance across many and diverse cultures. If we should discover that the structure of personality is cross-culturally stable, we will be able to go beyond the study of individual differences within a given culture and make meaningful cross-cultural comparisons and generalizations.

WHY FACTOR ANALYSIS?

Many authors have discussed the role of factor analysis in personality research in general, and the cross-cultural study of personality in particular. Though it is not the only method for assessing the invariance of measures across cultures (multidimensional scaling might also prove useful for research of this type), it has undoubtedly been the method of choice. As such, it will be the focus of this discussion. In their text *Cross-Cultural Research Methods,* Brislin, Lonner, and Thorndike (1973) devote a full chapter to factor analysis. They recommend applying confirmatory maximum likelihood methods (Joreskog, 1969) in cross-cultural studies. Buss and Royce (1975) point out that cross-cultural commonalities versus differences can be detected through factor analysis. They consider it crucial to establish the boundaries of factor invariance. Only if structural invariance across cultures has been demonstrated is it methodologically defensible to make cross-cultural comparisons of factor levels. Butcher and Bemis (1984) likewise state that one approach to validating a measure to be adopted in a new culture is its factorial validation to ensure that items and/or scales maintain generally the same psychological meaning in the new culture. In discussing cross-national application of psychological tests, Butcher and Garcia (1978) emphasized that factorial equivalence across cultures cannot be assumed, but should rather be demonstrated by factor analysis. In the *Handbook of Cross-National MMPI Research,* Butcher and Pancheri (1976) discuss the importance of establishing the equivalence of factor structure in assessing the adequacy of a translated instrument. Replication of the factor structure is thus taken to be an indication of adequate translation. The cross-cultural factorial structure of the MMPI is the topic of a full chapter in this handbook. Cattell (1973) regrets that most investigators proceeded to conduct cross-cultural comparisons without first establishing structural equivalence via factor analysis. Unfortunately, as is shown later, this short-coming also characterizes some of the research carried out with Cattell's own instruments. Eysenck and Eysenck (1982a) have also emphasized the importance of factor analysis in cross-cultural studies of personality, pointing out that factor analysis can be used to define the dimensions on which cross-cultural comparisons may be made. Irvine and Carroll (1980) maintain that factor analysis has been the major multivariate tool used in studying paper and pencil tests across cultures and propose a stringent requirement that structure be found invariant across cultures when subjected to a number of factor analytic methods.

As indicated earlier, three main objectives of cross-cultural studies of personality assessment are: (1) the use of personality assessment instruments developed in one culture for clinical and research purposes in a different culture; (2) assessing the universal stability of personality constructs; and (3) comparing "typical" personalities across cultures. In order to achieve objectives one and three, objective two must first be met. Generalizability of a construct to a culture different from the one in which it was developed must be demonstrated first. Failure to do so may result in something analogous to trying to describe a circle in terms of measures of width and length, as if it were a rectangle. Without first showing that the structures to be compared are both rectangles or both circles we have no way of knowing which, if any, dimensions they may have in common. A meaningful way to achieve objective two is factor analysis. Demonstrating factorial invariance of the structure of an instrument developed in culture A, when it is translated and administered adequately to a large representative sample of culture B, is a first and necessary step toward achieving all three objectives of cross-cultural personality research. Demonstrating factorial stability among many and diverse cultures is an essential step toward establishing the potential for a universal structure of personality.

A Note of Caution

The use of factor analysis in personality research in general, and in cross-cultural research in particular, is not without its critics. Brislin (1980) remarks on the lack of consensus concerning the choice of rotation method, estimation of communalities, determining the number of factors, choice of factor model, and so forth. He concludes that it is dangerous to apply this methodology mechanically. In his discussion of factor analysis in personality assessment, Guilford (1975) contends that though this is a powerful and useful technique, the fact that there is no one clear-cut and agreed-upon way to apply it has resulted in different personality structures measured by different inventories. In cross-cultural research this problem can more readily be resolved, in a manner to be outlined later. One important question is when to factor analyze and when not to. Gordon and Kikuchi (1966) argue that empirically keyed tests should not be used for making cross-cultural comparisons. Their rationale is as follows: Factorial invariance must be demonstrated before cross-cultural comparisons can be made. Empirically keyed instruments are not developed in a manner that ensures factorially stable structures. Consequently it is not possible to demonstrate cross-cultural factorial invariance, though such a demonstration is necessary before cross-cultural comparisons can be made. The abundance of cross-cultural research conducted with the empirically keyed MMPI and CPI is evidence that this suggestion was not heeded. Nevertheless, the problem inherent in using factor analysis with empirically developed instruments is real, and has been solved quite differently for the two instruments just mentioned. As is subsequently documented, a substantial body of cross-cultural research data is available on certain aspects of the factorial structure of the MMPI, but a surprising poverty of similar information exists on the CPI, though both have been used extensively in studies across cultures.

These are all valid points of criticism that have been raised against the misapplication of factor-analytic techniques. They serve to remind us that factor analysis, like any other statistical method, will not be useful and may even be misleading if it is employed blindly. For example, though it is argued in this chapter that a replicatory factor analysis should be one of the first steps taken in assessing the validity of cross-culturally adopted measures of personality, as should be in any case in which a factor analysis is conducted, distributions should be examined first in order to detect range restrictions and outliers prior to conducting the analysis. Thus, if members of a particular culture are somewhat restricted on a given construct, this construct is unlikely to be salient in a factor analysis, yet these data do not mean that the trait being assessed does not exist in that culture. What these data do mean is that that particular scale is inappropriate for the purpose of measuring individual differences on that particular trait within that particular culture. This brings up a related point. In the process of cross-culturally adopting a personality inventory, it is possible that only one or a small number of scales will have qualitatively or quantitatively changed in the new culture, while other parts of the instrument remain valid. Thus, if the overall structure of an inventory is found to have changed in a new culture (as would most likely occur in the case of the range restriction previously described), it is important to then examine separately the various components that comprise that instrument prior to determining that it is entirely invalid in the new culture. It may then be found to be the case that some of the scales have maintained their structure across cultures while others have not.

As mentioned earlier, both Brislin (1980) and Guilford (1975) have identified variations in factorial techniques as major obstacles toward assessing the factorial stability of personality measures. Thus, one investigator may choose to perform a principal components analysis, whereas another may prefer to analyze principal factors. Similarly, some investigators have chosen to rotate to oblique solutions, whereas others maintain that in the absence of a specific theory predicting covariation among factors, rotations should be performed so as to achieve orthogonal factor structures. These and other points of controversy surrounding factor analysis have yet to be resolved.

In the following section a method termed replicatory factor analysis is described. This method has the advantage of lending itself equally well to any of the various methods of factor analysis. Its main requirement is that *the same* method be used in both cultures. As is demonstrated, if properly used this method can serve to facilitate cross-cultural studies of personality.

REPLICATORY FACTOR ANALYSIS

Replicatory factor analysis should be conducted in the following manner. A newly translated or adopted instrument should be administered to a large representative sample of the population it will be used with. It should then be factor analyzed with the same methods for estimating communalities and rotating that were used when the instrument was analyzed in the original culture. The number of factors extracted should be restricted to the number found in the original culture. Following this, a direct comparison can be made between the factorial structures found in the two samples. Numerous indices have been suggested for such comparisons (Cattell & Baggaley, 1960; Cattell, Balcar, Horn, & Nesselroade, 1969; Kaiser, Hunka, & Bianchini, 1971; Korth & Tucker, 1975; Korth & Tucker, 1976; Pinneau & Newhouse, 1964; Tucker, 1951), and explanations and evaluations of these indices have been provided (Gorsuch, 1983; Harman, 1976; Muliak, 1972; Rummel, 1970). Empirical studies that have compared these indices (Barrett, 1986; Derogatis, Serio, & Cleary, 1972; Reynolds & Harding, 1983), have shown them to yield generally comparable results. Reynolds and Harding (1983) remark that Cattell and Baggaley's (1960) salient variable similarity index sometimes yields uncomfortably high similarity coefficients when compared to others. There has also been some debate regarding the method of comparison proposed by Kaiser, Hunka, and Bianchini (1971) (cf. Barrett, 1986; Bijen, Van Der Net, & Poortinga, 1986; Eysenck, 1986). As none of these indices appears to be clearly superior to the others, Barrett (1986) recommends employing several of them when comparing factors. Reporting the degree of factor similarity as measured by *several* different methods of comparison (which to date has not been common practice) should strengthen the findings of replicatory factor analysis by avoiding the controversies surrounding one or another of these indices.

Replicatory factor analysis sidesteps the various arguments raised for or against using this or that other method of factor analysis. Its only requirement is that the same method be used in both cultures. Confirmatory factor analysis developed and computerized by Joreskog and Sorbom (1984) could also be used for cross-cultural comparisons. However, as Kline and Barrett (1983) point out, this method has rarely been employed in personality measurement within a single culture. Its use and applicability to personality assessment should be demonstrated first within cultures, before an attempt is made to employ confirmatory factor analysis across cultures.

When we adopt a measuring instrument to a new culture we are also interested in adopting the body of knowledge that has been accumulated on that instrument in the original culture. In other words, we are interested in adopting the external correlates associated with the constructs it purports to measure. (If not, we would be better off developing a new instrument that is perfectly congruent with the idiosyncrasies of the new culture.) In essence, we are interested in adopting the nomological network (Cronbach & Meehl, 1955) in which that instrument's constructs are embedded. The observable part of this nomological net is based on a two-part network of empirical relations: an internal and an external one. The internal network encompasses the interrelationships among the constructs measured by that instrument. Thus, if a personality questionnaire measures n traits or has *n* scales, its internal network of relations is composed of $n(n-1)/2$ correlations among those scales. The external part of the network is made up of the relationships among all the "external" variables associated with the instrument's constructs. If there are m such correlates, then the external net is made up of $m(m-1)/2$ correlations among them. The entire relational network between questionnaire and non-questionnaire variables is made up of $(n+m)$ $(n+m-1)/2$ intercorrelations within and between the two parts of the network.

In the process of establishing an adopted instrument's cross-cultural validity these relationships must be shown to be invariant across cultures. Replicatory factor analysis, when conducted as just described, indicates whether such a laborious project is worthwhile. It provides an immediate comparison between the $n(n-1)/2$ relationships that make up the instrument's internal relational network in each culture. Should these two structures differ significantly, the investigator is alerted that a qualitative change has occurred in the instrument and chances are that the external correlates will also have changed in the new culture. If this indeed is the case, he or she may be better off developing and validating a new instrument that is more appropriate for the new culture. If, on the other hand, the original factorial structure is replicated, the investigator can cautiously proceed to study the validity of the newly adopted instrument and subsequently use it for the purposes and goals that motivated the attempt to export it to a new culture. Thus, replicatory factor analysis provides a time-saving method for initially screening a cross-culturally adopted instrument.

The following review is intended to illustrate the importance of the employment of replicatory factor analysis. Cases are described in which replicatory factor analysis helped provide both a clearer picture of the structure of personality and good personality-measuring instruments for new cultures. Other cases portray the outcome of not applying replicatory factor analysis, or not implementing it as has been prescribed here. As shown, in these cases we are left unclear as to the construct validity of cross-culturally adopted instruments. To reiterate, this review is not exhaustive. The instruments to be reviewed are the most cross-culturally studied representatives of two different philosophies of personality assessment. A structural one represented by factorially derived instruments, and a functional one represented by empirically keyed instruments. The case for replicatory factor analysis is more easily perceived for the former but equally compelling for both.

THE EYSENCK PERSONALITY
QUESTIONNAIRE (EPQ)

The EPQ (Eysenck & Eysenck, 1975) has been submitted to more cross-cultural factor analytical studies than any other personality inventory. This reflects the importance that the Eysencks place upon cross-cultural factorial validation (Eysenck & Eysenck, 1982a, 1982b). Eysenck (1983) pointed out that using the

British scoring key in a different culture without first demonstrating factorial invariance could give rise to misleading results.

In all of the cross-cultural factor analytic studies of the EPQ, male and female data were submitted separately to principal component factor analyses. The procedure was to extract and rotate four factors to simple structure using the PROMAX algorithm of Hendrickson and White (1964) for obtaining oblique simple structure. The four factors expected to emerge from these analyses are termed Extraversion (E), Neuroticism (N), Psychoticism (P) and Lie (L). The next step in these studies was a comparison of the structure found in the new culture with that of the original British sample by the method for assessing factor similarity developed and described by Kaiser, et al. (1971). Eysenck (1983) presented the results of these comparisons in Australia, Bangladesh, Brazil, Bulgaria, Egypt, France, Germany, Greece, Hong Kong, Hungary, Iceland, India, Iran, Israel, Japan, Nigeria, Puerto Rico, Sicily, Singapore, Spain, Sri Lanka, Uganda, and Yugoslavia. The only significant failures to replicate involved factor P in women in Greece and Japan. Similar comparisons were presented by Eysenck (1983) for the adolescent counterpart of the EPQ, the JEPQ. These comparisons were made in Canada, Denmark, Greece, Hong Kong, Hungary, Japan, New Zealand, Spain, and Yugoslavia. Here too, the British structure was overwhelmingly replicated except for factors P and L for Japanese men, factor L in Japanese women and factor P in Hungarian women. The number of subjects in all of these studies was satisfactory except for the Japanese JEPQ study and the Iranian and Nigerian female EPQ sample, all of which numbered fewer than 300 subjects. Only after replicatory factor analysis had demonstrated an invariant factorial structure were cross-cultural comparisons conducted. The results of these comparisons are summarized by Barrett and Eysenck (1984), Eysenck and Eysenck (1985), and Kline and Barrett (1983).

These studies concerning the cross-cultural stability of the EPQ illustrate well the meaning and importance of replicatory factor analysis; however, a note of caution is in order. A recent paper by Bijen et al. (1986) has raised serious questions regarding the findings in these studies. The authors artificially constructed a 40-item pure simple structure using a pseudorandom number generator. They then extracted four factors applying the same technique as was employed in all of the cross-cultural EPQ studies. Finally, they compared the obtained four-factor structure with the original EPQ structure using the Kaiser et al. (1971) method employed in all of the EPQ studies. Thus, other than the actual collection of data, the investigators used the exact same methods that were used in all of the studies previously described. The resulting similarity indices between the British structure and the random structures are alarmingly high; many of them would meet the criteria set by the Eysencks for establishing factorial equivalence across cultures. The implications of these findings are as yet unclear. They call into question both the method used in the cross-cultural EPQ studies and its findings; however, they do *not* refute them. Recently, Barrett

(1986) has proposed a possible solution for the problems associated with this index. Eysenck (1986) has claimed that the points of criticism raised by Bijen et al. (1986) are invalid for homologous scales such as those that comprise the EPQ. Further studies of the cross-cultural invariance of the EPQ in which several methods for assessing underlying factorial similarity are employed may serve to clarify this issue.

THE 16 PERSONALITY FACTORS QUESTIONNAIRE (16PF)

The 16PF (Cattell & Eber, 1964) is another factor analytically derived personality inventory that has received extensive cross-cultural attention. In *Personality and Mood by Questionnaire,* Cattell (1973) pointed out that most investigators tend to proceed with cross-cultural comparisons of level without first establishing comparability of structure. He presents results showing that the first-order structure of the 16PF has been well replicated in France, Germany, Czechoslovakia, Italy, and India. Cattell, Eber, and Tatsuoka (1970) conclude that "secondary source traits have been shown to retain their structure across all other cultures for which they have been tried" (p. 120). The following brief review of the cross-cultural literature on the 16PF will show, however, that in some studies the lower- and higher-order structures have indeed been replicated, while in others they have not.

Tsujioka and Cattell (1965) presented results showing that similar primary first-order factors were found in the United States, France, England, Germany, Japan, and Italy. Cross-cultural comparisons of scale scores were conducted only after similarity in structure had been established. Cattell and Warburton (1961) presented results showing second-order stability across British and American subjects. Cattell and Nicholas (1972) used factor analytic data from the United States, Germany, Venezuela, New Zealand, and Brazil to derive an eight-factor higher order structure of the 16PF. Zak (1976) reproduced the primary factor structure for 15 factors in Israel (with the items belonging to factor B, Intelligence, excluded from the analysis). Cattell, Danko, Cattell, and Raymond (1984), using various configurations of item parcels from the adolescent counterpart of the 16PF, the HSPQ, found in Hawaii a primary structure similar to that found in the mainland United States. These studies all tend to indicate cross-cultural stability of the lower and higher order structures of the 16PF. Other investigators, however, have questioned both these structures themselves and their cross-cultural replicability.

Levonian (1961), studying item intercorrelations of the 16PF, determined that correlations among items from the same scale tend to be lower than among items from different scales. This finding is undoubtedly related to the failure to replicate the factorial structure of the 16PF both within and across cultures reported by others. For example, Phillip (1972) was unable to replicate Cattell et al.'s (1970) finding of a similar second-order structure for the 16PF in the United States and England. In this case the results cannot be attributed to faulty translation. Phillip (1972) suggested that the apparent variation in replicability may be the result of Cattell's tendency to assess similarity of structure by sight rather than by some objective index of similarity. Nowakowska (1974) reported findings with a Polish translation of the 16PF. In this study, the second-order structure was replicated but the primary structure was not. Golden (1978) compared the second-order factor structure in subjects of European versus Japanese ancestry in Hawaii. The factor structure of subjects of Japanese origin was found to be significantly different than that of the Europeans.

Other cross-cultural studies using the 16PF illustrate the misuse of personality inventories in cross-cultural research. Andrade, Godey, and Ford (1969) conducted a cross-cultural study comparing American and Brazilian college students using the 16PF. Though they recognized the need to conduct first a replicatory factor analysis, they did not do so and proceeded to conduct cross-cultural comparisons of scale levels. Their findings are unclear, as it is not known whether the 16PF measured the same constructs in the two cultures. Berton and Clasen (1971) performed an analysis of the Spanish version of the 16PF in Venezuela. They compared the scale reliabilities across cultures under the expressed assumption of factorial equivalence. In view of the replication difficulties earlier described, this assumption is unfounded, rendering the interpretation of their findings unclear. Mehryar (1972) compared Americans versus Iranians, and Iranian boys versus Iranian girls, using a translated 16PF. No attempt was made to demonstrate factorial similarity either across cultures or across sexes within the Iranian sample. Again the results are difficult to interpret. Without additional data we know only that the two cultures differ, but we do not know in what way: qualitatively and/or quantitatively. Replicatory factor analysis is the necessary tool to detect the former.

It is clear that the cross-cultural replicability of the 16PF's factor structure is at best controversial. This controversy could at some point be resolved by proper use of replicatory factor analysis. First, however, we must know what structure we are attempting to replicate. The factorial structure of the 16PF must first be agreed upon and replicated by investigators within the United States before any meaningful cross-cultural replicatory factor analyses can be conducted.

COMREY PERSONALITY SCALES (CPS)

The CPS (Comrey, 1970) is a factor-analytically derived instrument that has not received much cross-cultural attention. The CPS is composed of eight factor scales, each scale being made up of five Factor Homogeneous Item Dimensions (FHIDs), each of which consists of four items. The rationale for choosing the 40

FHIDS as the basic units is that they tend to be structurally more stable than single items.

Forbes, Dexter, and Comrey (1974) administered the American version of the CPS to 179 New Zealand university teachers and students. The 40 FHIDs were factor analyzed by a minimum residual method and then submitted to VARIMAX rotation (Kaiser, 1958). In order to enable a direct comparison with the American structure, eight factors were retained. Only three factors were perfectly replicated. Thus, though the structure itself was maintained (i.e., the same basic factors showed up), its content seemed to differ in New Zealand with some FHIDs loading on different factors than in the original structure. This study is a good example of how replicatory factor analysis should be conducted. It is, however, deficient in its small number of subjects. We are left wondering whether the differences found are true cross-cultural differences or the result of an insufficient number of subjects used in the target culture. Another study (Rodrigues & Comrey, 1974) that used more subjects suggests that the latter may be the case. In this study a Portuguese version of the CPS was administered to 684 subjects in Brazil. The eight factors: Trust, Orderliness, Conformity, Activity, Stability, Extraversion, Masculinity, and Empathy were all closely replicated. In a third study (Montag & Comrey, 1982), a Hebrew version was administered to 185 males in Israel. Factor analysis of the 40 FHIDs resulted in confirmation of seven of the eight factors. Conformity failed to replicate, while other factors differed in the quality of their replications. Again, the sample size is to small and we have no way of telling whether these results reflect true differences between the personality structures of Israelis and Americans as defined by the CPS or whether they are simply the result of chance.

To summarize, the CPS has been studied cross-culturally with the correct techniques, though with marginally adequate sample sizes in two out of the three studies cited. Thus, the cross-cultural replication of the structure of personality defined by the CPS has yet to be demonstrated.

THE MINNESOTA MULTIPHASIC
PERSONALITY INVENTORY (MMPI)

The following two sections deal with the two most important empirically keyed measuring instruments in the field of personality, the MMPI and the CPI. It will become evident that there are marked differences in how these instruments have been evaluated cross-culturally.

The MMPI (Hathaway & McKinley, 1967) is internationally the most widely adopted clinical personality test (Butcher, 1985). It has been translated into over 115 languages and is now in use in more than 50 countries for clinical assessment and research purposes (Butcher, personal communication, April, 1986). A general survey of MMPI research in various cultures has been provided by Butcher and Clark (1979). More recent developments are reviewed by various authors in a previous volume of the series on *Advances in Personality Assessment* (Butcher & Spielberger, 1985). Many of these studies include an assessment of the cross-cultural factorial structure of the MMPI.

The MMPI was not constructed by factor analysis. Each scale was derived independently. One approach to replicatory factor analysis would be to assess the intercorrelations among the scales of the MMPI. The majority of factorial studies of the MMPI in the United States has been conducted in this way (Dahlstrom, Welsh, & Dahlstrom, 1975). Generally, these studies have shown that the MMPI scales load on two major factors, which have been given the labels Anxiety or General Psychopathology and Repression or Overcontrol, respectively. Two smaller additional factors have been termed Social Introversion and Masculinity-Femininity. Wakefield, Bradley, Doughtie, and Kraft (1975) maintain that these factors are to a large extent attributable to overlapping items among the scales that reflect the similarity of the criteria against which these scales were validated. Consequently, demonstrating cross-cultural stability on the MMPI scale level would not lend strong support for the construct validity of these scales. Failure to demonstrate cross-cultural invariance, however, *despite* item overlap and its consequences would raise serious questions regarding the applicability of the translated instrument for the new culture. Thus, replicatory factor analysis on the scale level of the MMPI can serve as an important screening mechanism for the adequacy of cross-culturally adopted versions of this instrument.

Butcher and Pancheri (1976) compared the factorial structure of the MMPI in Israel, Pakistan, Mexico, Costa Rica, Italy, Switzerland, and Japan. Scores on the three validity scales and non K-corrected scores on the 10 clinical scales were factor analyzed by principal components followed by a normal VARIMAX rotation (Kaiser, 1958). Four factors were extracted according to the "scree" criterion proposed by Cattell (1966). Only Italian males did not fit the four-factor solution. Overall similarity across genders was good. Though no indices of factor similarity were reported, it is apparent that in these studies replicatory factor analysis of the MMPI has shown positive results. In examining the factorial structure of the Hebrew version of the MMPI, Gur (1974) found remarkable similarity both between genders in Israel and across cultures. Rissetti and Maltes (1985) presented the results of factor analyzing the Chilean version of the MMPI. The factor structure was found to be similar among men and women sampled from both "normal" and clinical populations. It differed, however, from that found in the studies described earlier. It is therefore not recommended to draw inferences from cross-cultural scale profile comparisons with this instrument in Chile, nor is it justified to "export" American interpretations of scale scores and configurations until this question is further looked into. More research must be conducted to ascertain whether this is the result of true differences in the structure of Chilean personalities as measured by the MMPI, or if this reflects inadequacies of translation and/or sampling; the Chilean MMPI has been found to predict well for clinical populations (Rissetti & Maltes, 1985), which suggests that the latter may be the case. Clark (1985) presented the results of research on the newly consolidated Japanese version of the MMPI. Although factor structures were found to be similar between genders in Japan, the Japanese version yielded a three-factor solution in which only the two main factors were found to be similar to the United States structure. The same questions raised regarding the Chilean version are applicable here.

In general, the factorial structure of the MMPI scales has been shown to be relatively stable across cultures; however, this is not enough. In contrast to factorially constructed instruments, the MMPI scales are highly heterogeneous, and due to item overlap, some of them are highly correlated with each other. In such cases, replicatory factor analysis of the scale structure is a necessary but not sufficient condition for concluding general structure similarity across cultures. The optimal solution would be to factor analyze all 550 items; however, this would require tremendous sample sizes and enormous computer expenses. Recent attempts by Johnson, Butcher, Null, and Johnson (1984) and Costa, Zonderman, McCrae, and Williams (1985) to conduct such item factor analyses have yielded conflicting results. Before cross-cultural comparisons can be made at this level, it is necessary to reach agreement regarding the MMPI's full-scale item structure within the United States. A plausible compromise can be to factor analyze each scale's items separately. Conducting both inter- and intra-scale comparisons would ensure that the internal structure of the instrument as a whole has been maintained, as well as that of each scale on its own. Intra-scale comparisons would not be subject to the effects of item overlap. Since MMPI interpretations rely on both single scale elevations and configural relations among the scales, both types of replicatory factor analyses should be conducted. Failure to find a similar structure does not necessarily have to result in discarding the adopted instrument. What it does imply, however, is that the correlates associated with the MMPI in the United States cannot automatically be assumed to apply in the new culture and must be reestablished through empirical research in that culture.

THE CALIFORNIA PSYCHOLOGICAL INVENTORY (CPI)

The CPI (Gough, 1957) is another instrument on which extensive cross-cultural research has been conducted. Unlike the work with its older sibling, the MMPI, however, most of these studies have not been concerned with factor replication. Gough intended, however, that the CPI measure universal dispositions (e.g., Gough, 1965), and cross-cultural research is of course essential to achieving this goal. Unfortunately, the impact of much of this research is weakened for various reasons, cited in the following review.

The CPI scale that has received the largest amount of cross-cultural attention is the Socialization (So) scale. In an early study Gough and Sandhu (1964) attempted to demonstrate the validity of the So scale in India by showing that it significantly differentiates between delinquents and nondelinquents in that country. Similar findings regarding the So scale are reported by Gough (1965) in studies conducted in 10 countries using eight different languages. Another similar study is reported by Gough, De Vos, and Mizushima (1968) on the So scale in Japan. Unfortunately, in none of these studies was the factorial structure of the newly adopted So scale examined.

Cross-cultural validation studies have also been conducted on other scales of the CPI. Gough (1964) reported a study intended to validate the two achievement scales of the CPI in Italy. Here too, no attempt was made to study the factorial structure of the Italian scales. In another cross-cultural study, Gough (1966) reported that the Femininity (Fe) scale of the CPI significantly differentiated between men and women in France, Italy, Turkey, and Venezuela. Again, replicatory factor analyses were not conducted. Similar cross-cultural studies of the CPI are still being carried out today. As an example, Pitariu (1981) presented a validation of the CPI Fe scale in Rumania, where the CPI was loosely translated using Romanian folk concepts. The translated instrument's factorial structure was not investigated.

All of these studies share a common problem that can be illustrated by considering the findings on the Fe scale. These studies typically involved administering the newly adopted Fe scale to men and women in the new culture and testing whether their respective scores were significantly different. As they stand, these studies can only be interpreted to show that the Fe scale successfully differentiates between males and females in those countries. Less sophisticated and more accurate methods for such differentiation can easily be thought of. Obviously, Gough was seeking to validate cross-culturally the assessment of the construct "Femininity," and not biological gender. In other words, he was seeking to "export" the nomological network associated with femininity in the United States to these new cultures. Demonstrating that the newly adopted scale is capable of differentiating between men and women is not enough for this purpose.

One way to approach this problem is to demonstrate through replicatory factor analyses that the structure of the Fe scale and of the other CPI scales, as well as the inter-scale structure of the entire instrument, are all invariant in the new culture. This would show that the internal relational network has "survived" the adoption into a new culture and lend support to the scale's construct validity in the new culture. This is not the only way to demonstrate this. Alternatively, the new CPI scales could be subjected to all the predictive and concurrent validity studies that had been previously carried out in the United States, thus demonstrating that the external network of the instrument has been maintained. To compare just one such relationship, as was done in the studies previously cited, is clearly not enough. As noted earlier in this chapter, when an instrument is made up of n scales and m external correlates associated with them, its entire relational network is made up of $(n+m)(n+m-1)/2$ correlations. The point-biserial correlation between gender and score on the Fe scale is but one of these. Finding it to be significant *does not* justify cross-culturally adopting the entire network of external correlates associated with the Fe scale in the United States. In order to conclude that the same psychological construct is being measured, all m external correlates associated with the Fe scale in the United States must be shown to apply in the new culture. Replicatory factor analysis offers a cost-effective way of initially probing the cross-cultural validity of a newly adopted instrument. If it demonstrates that the $n(n-1)/2$ correlations that make up the instrument's internal relational network are cross-culturally invariant, then further explication of the entire nomological network is in order. It is undoubtedly more informative, though no more time consuming, than assessing just one component of this extensive network.

Most of the studies just cited were conducted in the 1960s, when the means to conduct replicatory factor analyses were not as readily available as they are today. The following studies suggest that it might be worthwhile to review the CPI's factorial structure in those cases where this was not done. These studies indicate that replicatory factor analysis, when conducted, shows good results for the CPI.

Levin and Karni (1970) demonstrated invariance of the CPI in American and Israeli men by using the Guttman Lingoes smallest space analysis. Though a step in the right direction, their study does not include the all-important demonstration of cross-gender invariance in the new culture. As a result, their findings on the cross-cultural validation of the Fe scale in Israel (Levin & Karni, 1971) are difficult to interpret. Schludermann and Schludermann (1970) studied the generalizability of the CPI factors in Canada. Their sample consisted of 177 men and 171 women. They found a factorially similar structure across genders that was similar to the one reported in the United States (Crites, Bechtold, Goodstein, & Heilbrun, 1961; Mitchell & Pierce-Jones, 1960; Nicholas & Schell, 1963; Springob & Struening, 1964). Nishiyama (1973) presented cross-cultural findings indicating invariance of the CPI factorial structure in Japan. As was noted regarding the MMPI, the inter-scale factor structure tells only half the story. The factor structure of each scale should be studied independently in replicatory factor analyses of empirically keyed instruments.

SUMMARY AND INTEGRATION

The foregoing portrayed state of affairs in the use of factor analysis in cross-cultural studies of personality assessment is both discouraging and encouraging. It is discouraging in view of the large number of studies that have ignored questions of structure replication and have consequently generated findings whose interpretation is open to serious question. Research with the CPI provides the best example in this respect. Here, both the scales and their items have yet to be adequately studied by replicatory factor analyses. The few studies cited earlier that have employed this methodology with the CPI have tended to result in positive findings. Thus, it is recommended that replicatory factor analyses be conducted in the numerous cultures that have adopted the CPI, in order to assess its adequacy for the assessment of personality in those countries.

The scale structure of the MMPI has been studied extensively across cultures, though in many cases no formal indices of factor similarity were reported. Several conclusions may be drawn regarding the cross-cultural factorial structure of the MMPI following this review. Most of the studies that have employed cross-cultural replicatory factor analyses in studying the MMPI have concentrated on inter-scale structure. Due to the number of overlapping items on these scales, this is not as strong a test as in cases where there is no item overlap. Nevertheless it is an important test in that failure to replicate, despite the ''advantage'' of overlapping items, constitutes a particularly strong warning that a qualitative change may have occurred in the process of cross-culturally adopting the instrument. The vast majority of the studies that subjected the MMPI to this cross-cultural test have found its inter-scale structure to hold up well across cultures. It is strongly recommended that future studies concentrate on the intra-scale structure of the MMPI scales. Intra-scale replicatory factor analyses would not have the ''benefit'' of overlapping items and would thus constitute a stronger test for the cross-cultural validity of this instrument.

As previously noted, the case for replicatory factor analysis of such empirically keyed instruments as the MMPI or the CPI is less apparent (though in my view equally compelling) than is the case for using this methodology with factorially based instruments such as the EPQ, 16PF, and the CPS. The EPQ has undoubtedly been subjected to more cross-cultural replicatory factor analyses than any other personality measure. Its factorial structure has been found to hold up well across cultures. Recent debate regarding the specific method used to assess cross-cultural invariance (Barrett, 1986; Bijen et al., 1986; Eysenck, 1986) illustrates the importance of using multiple indices of factorial invariance when conducting replicatory factor analyses. Despite these points of contention, and in view of the analyses conducted by Barrett (1986), it appears that replicatory factor analysis has demonstrated that the EPQ has an extremely stable factorial structure across cultures. In view of the diversity of cultures in which they were obtained, these findings lend considerable support to Eysenck's (1986) claim that his personality factors are universal. Thus, replicatory factor analysis in the case of the EPQ has achieved the three objectives outlined in the beginning of this discussion: Providing personality-measuring instruments for new cultures, assessing the cross-cultural stability of personality constructs derived as the result of research in one specific culture, and providing a method for conducting meaningful cross-cultural comparisons. By demonstrating cross-cultural validity, these findings also lend support to Eysenck's theory of personality. Competing instruments and theories should demonstrate similar cross-cultural stability in their attempt to gain empirical support.

Regarding the 16PF, it would seem that its structure within-culture must be agreed upon first, before attempts are made to replicate it across cultures. This conclusion underlines the necessity for adequate studies of the factorial structure of a personality test in its original culture, before attempts are made to adopt it to a new one.

Cross-cultural analyses of the CPS have yielded mixed results. These may partially be due to insufficient sample sizes in those studies that have generated negative results. Further studies with larger sample sizes are in order so that we may assess the cross-cultural factorial stability of this instrument.

The picture portrayed in this chapter is encouraging because studies that did employ replicatory factor analysis have tended to indicate the possibility of a universal structure of personality. The EPQ, and the theory of personality on which it is based, are currently in the best position to make such a claim. As noted, competing theories and instruments should be subjected to similar cross-cultural studies so that adequate comparisons and evaluations may be conducted. To be sure, in some instances factor structures have not been replicated, cautioning us against unwarranted generalizations and possible misuses of personality inventories. Furthermore, and most important, positive findings that are based on measures that are themselves factorially heterogeneous should not be overstated.

Before concluding, I offer three recommendations for future studies in which replicatory factor analyses are conducted. First, this technique should be seen primarily as an initial test of the extent to which a cross-culturally adopted instrument has maintained its structure. As with any statistical method, replicatory factor analysis should not be applied or interpreted blindly. If properly conducted, this method can yield information that is helpful in assessing the cross-cultural validity of a personality measuring instrument and the constructs that it measures. Secondly, theory-based personality inventories are particularly good candidates for cross-cultural studies employing replicatory factor analyses. In the case of the EPQ, this methodology has provided substantial support for the theory of personality on which that instrument is based. Other theory-based instruments, whether competing or complementary, should be studied in a similar manner. Factorially derived instruments such as the Multidimensional Personality Questionnaire (MPQ) (Tellegen, 1982) and the NEO Personality Inventory (Costa & McCrae, 1985) are two good candidates for such research. Finally, to the extent that we are interested in assessing the universality of personality constructs, future studies should evaluate cross-cultural factorial congruence across different instruments. For example, as measured by both the EPQ and the MMPI, a construct termed Extraversion has repeatedly been identified across many and diverse cultures. Similar findings with the MPQ scale of Social Closeness and the NEO scale of Extraversion would further strengthen the contention that social extraversion is a universal dimension of personality.

Replicatory factor analysis is a valuable technique not only for cross-cultural assessment of personality, but for personality theory and assessment in general as well. Any instrument that is claimed to measure universal personality constructs should be subjected to cross-cultural replicatory research to assess the universal stability of its constructs. Though this is not the only method for assessing the cross-cultural stability of personality constructs, the arguments and findings previously cited demonstrate that it is a meaningful and efficient method for such research. Replicatory factor analysis can be a useful technique for any case in which a construct is to be generalized from one population to another; cross-cultural generalization is only one such possibility.

ACKNOWLEDGMENTS

I would like to thank James Butcher, Auke Tellegen, and Niels Waller for their helpful comments and suggestions on earlier drafts of this chapter.

REFERENCES

Andrade, E. M., Godey, A. D., & Ford, J. J. (1969). A comparison of North American and Brazilian college students personality profiles in the 16PF questionnaire. *International Journal of Psychology, 4,* 55–58.

Barrett, P. (1986). Factor comparisons: An examination of three methods. *Personality and Individual Differences, 7,* 327–340.

Barrett, P., & Eysenck, S. B. G. (1984). The assessment of personality factors across 25 countries. *Personality and Individual differences, 5,* 615–632.

Berry, J. W. (1980). Introduction to methodology. In H. C. Triandis & J. W. Berry (Eds.), *Handbook of Cross-Cultural Psychology Methodology, Vol. 2.* Boston: Allyn & Bacon.

Berton, P., & Clasen, R. E. (1971). An analysis of a Spanish translation of the sixteen personality factors test. *The Journal of Experimental Education, 2,* 12–21.

Bijen, E. J., Van Der Net, T. Z. J., & Poortinga, Y. H. (1986). On cross-cultural comparative studies with the Eysenck Personality Questionnaire. *Journal of Cross-Cultural Psychology, 17,* 3–16.

Brislin, R. W. (1980). Translation and content analysis of oral and written materials. In H. C. Triandis & J. W. Berry (Eds.), *Handbook of Cross-Cultural Psychology Methodology, Vol. 2.* Boston: Allyn and Bacon Inc.

Brislin, R. W. (1983). Cross-cultural research in psychology. *Annual Review of Psychology, 34,* 363–400.

Brislin, R. W., Lonner, W. J., & Thorndike, R. M. (1973). *Cross-Cultural Research Methods.* New York: Wiley.

Buss, A. R., & Royce, J. R. (1975). Detecting cross-cultural commonalities and differences: Intergroup factor analysis. *Psychological Bulletin, 82,* 128–136.

Butcher, J. N. (1982). Cross-cultural research methods in clinical psychology. In P. C. Kendall &

J. N. Butcher (Eds.), *Handbook of Research Methods in Clinical Psychology*. New York: Wiley Intersciences.

Butcher, J. N. (1985). Current developments in MMPI use: An international perspective. In J. N. Butcher & C. D. Spielberger (Eds.), *Advances in Personality Assessment, Vol. 4*.Hillsdale, NJ: Lawrence Erlbaum Associates.

Butcher, J. N., & Bemis, K. M. (1984). Abnormal behavior in cultural context. In H. E. Adams & P. Sutker (Eds.), *Comprehensive Handbook of Psychopathology*. New York: Plenum.

Butcher, J. N., & Clark, L. A. (1979). Recent trends in cross-cultural MMPI research. In J. N. Butcher (Ed.), *New Developments in the Use of the MMPI*. Minneapolis: University of Minnesota Press.

Butcher, J. N., & Garcia, R. E. (1978). Cross-national application of psychological tests. *Personnel and Guidance, 56*, 472–475.

Butcher, J. N., & Pancheri, P. (1976). *Handbook of Cross-National MMPI Research*. Minneapolis: University of Minnesota Press.

Butcher, J. N., & Spielberger, C. D. (1985). *Advances in Personality Assessment, Vol. 4*. Hillsdale, NJ: Lawrence Erlbaum Associates.

Cattell, R. B. (1966). The scree test for the number of factors. *Multivariate Behavioral Research, 1*, 245–246.

Cattell, R. B. (1973). *Personality and Mood By Questionnaire*. CA: Jossey-Bass.

Cattell, R. B., & Baggaley, A. R. (1960). The salient variable similarity index for factor matching. *British Journal of Statistical Psychology, 13*, 33–46.

Cattell, R. B., Balcar, K. R., Horn, J. C., & Nesselroade, J. R. (1969). Factor matching procedures: An improvement of the s index. *Educational and Psychological Measurement, 29*, 781–792.

Cattell, R. B., Danko, G., Cattell, H., & Raymond, J. S. (1984). A cross-cultural study of primary factor structure in preparation of the Hawaiian High School Personality Scale. *Multivariate Experimental Clinical Research, 7*, 1–23.

Cattell, R. B., & Eber, H. (1964). *Manual for the 16 Personality Factor Test*. IL: Institute for Personality and Ability Testing.

Cattell, R. B., Eber, H. W., & Tatsuoka, M. M. (1970). *Handbook for the 16 Personality Factor Questionnaire (16PF)*. IL: Institute for Personality and Ability Testing.

Cattell, R. B., & Nicholas, E. (1972). An improved definition from 10 researchers of second order personality factors in Q data with cross-cultural checks. *Journal of Social Psychology, 86*, 187–203.

Cattell, R. B., & Warburton, F. W. (1961). A cross-cultural comparison of patterns of extroversion and anxiety. *British Journal of Psychology, 52*, 3–15.

Clark, L. A. (1985). A consolidated version of the MMPI in Japan. In J. N. Butcher & C. D. Spielberger (Eds.), *Advances in Personality Assessment, Vol. 4* (pp. 95–130). Hillsdale, NJ: Lawrence Erlbaum Associates.

Comrey, A. L. (1970). *EDITS Manual for the Comrey Personality Scales*. San Diego: Educational and Industrial Testing Service.

Costa, P. T., & McCrae, R. R. (1985). *The NEO personality inventory manual*. Odesa, FL: Psychological Assessment Resources.

Costa, P. T., Zonderman, A. B., McCrae, R. R., & Williams, R. B. (1985). Content and comprehensiveness in the MMPI: An item factor analysis in a normal adult sample. *Journal of Personality and Social Psychology, 48*, 925–933.

Crites, J. O., Bechtold, H. P., Goodstein, L. D., & Heilbrun, A. R. (1961). A factor analysis of the California Psychological Inventory. *Journal of Applied Psychology, 45*, 408–414.

Cronbach, L. J., & Meehl, P. E. (1955). Construct validity in Psychological tests. *Psychological Bulletin, 52*, 281–302.

Dahlstrom, W. G., Welsh, G. S., & Dahlstrom, C. E. (1975). *An MMPI Handbook, Vol. 2: Research and Applications*. Minneapolis: University of Minnesota Press.

Derogatis, L. R., Serio, J. C., & Cleary, P. A. (1972). An empirical comparison of three indices of factorial similarity. *Psychological Reports, 30*, 791–804.

Eysenck, H. J. (1986). Cross-cultural comparisons: The validity of assessment indices of factor comparisons. *Journal of Cross-Cultural Psychology, 17*, 506–515.

Eysenck, S. B. G. (1983). One approach to cross-cultural studies of personality. *Australian Journal of Psychology, 35*, 381–391.

Eysenck, H. J., & Eysenck, M. W. (1985). *Personality and Individual Differences*. New York: Plenum.

Eysenck, H. J., & Eysenck, S. B. G. (1975). *Manual for the Eysenck Personality Questionnaire*. San Diego: Educational and Industrial Testing Service.

Eysenck, H. J., & Eysenck, S. B. G. (1982a). Culture and personality abnormalities. In I. Al-Issa (Ed.), *Culture and Psychopathology*. Baltimore: University Park Press.

Eysenck, H. J., & Eysenck, S. B. G. (1982b). Recent advances in the cross-cultural study of personality. In J. N. Butcher & C. D. Spielberger (Eds.), *Advances in Personality Assessment, Vol. 2* (pp. 41–69). Hillsdale, NJ: Lawrence Erlbaum Associates.

Forbes, A. R., Dexter, W. R., & Comrey, A. L. (1974). A cross-cultural comparison of personality factors. *Multivariate Behavioral Research, 9*, 383–394.

Golden, C. J. (1978). Second-order factor structures of the 16PF. *Journal of Personality Assessment, 42*, 167–170.

Gordon, L. V., & Kikuchi, A. (1966). American personality tests in cross-cultural research—A caution. *Journal of Social Psychology, 69*, 179–183.

Gorsuch, R. L. (1983). *Factor Analysis* (2nd ed.). Hillsdale, NJ: Lawrence Erlbaum Associates.

Gough, H. G. (1957). *Manual for the California Psychological Inventory*. Los Angeles: Consulting Psychologists.

Gough, H. G. (1964). A cross-cultural study of achievement motivation. *Journal of Applied Psychology, 48*, 191–196.

Gough, H. G. (1965). Cross-cultural validation of a measure of asocial behavior. *Psychological Reports, 17*, 379–387.

Gough, H. G. (1966). A cross-cultural analysis of the CPI femininity scale. *Journal of Consulting Psychology, 30*, 136–141.

Gough, H. G., De Vos, G., & Mizushima, K. (1968). Japanese validation of the CPI social maturity index. *Psychological Reports, 22*, 143–146.

Gough, H. G., & Sandhu, H. S. (1964). Validation of the CPI socialization scale in India. *Journal of Abnormal and Social Psychology, 68*, 544–547.

Guilford, J. P. (1975). Factors and factors of personality. *Psychological Bulletin, 82*, 802–814.

Gur, R. (1974). *A Hebrew Version of the Minnesota Multiphasic Personality Inventory (MMPI): Translation, Validation, Preliminary Standardization, and Cross-Cultural Personality Comparison*. Unpublished doctoral dissertation, University of Minnesota.

Harman, H. H. (1976). *Modern Factor Analysis* (2nd ed.). Chicago: University of Chicago Press.

Hathaway, S. R., & McKinley, J. C. (1967). *The Minnesota Multiphasic Personality Inventory*. New York: Psychological Corporation.

Hendrickson, A. E., & White, P. O. (1964). PROMAX: A quick method for rotation to oblique simple structure. *British Journal of Statistical Psychology, 17*, 65–70.

Irvine, S. H., & Carroll, W. K. (1980). Testing and assessment across cultures: Issues in methodology and theory. In H. C. Triandis & J. W. Berry (Eds.), *Handbook of Cross-Cultural Psychology, Vol. 2: Methodology*. Boston: Allyn & Bacon.

Johnson, J. H., Butcher, J. N., Null, C., & Johnson, K. N. (1984). Replicated item level factor analysis of the full MMPI. *Journal of Personality and Social Psychology, 47*, 105–114.

Joreskog, K. G. (1969). A general approach to confirmatory maximum likelihood factor analysis. *Psychometrika, 34*, 183–202.

Joreskog, K. G., & Sorbom, D. (1984). *LISREL VI analysis of linear structural relationships by the method of maximum likelihood.* Mooresville, IN: Scientific Software.

Kaiser, H. F. (1958). The Varimax criterion for analytic rotation in factor analysis. *Psychometrika, 22,* 187–200.

Kaiser, H. F., Hunka, S., & Bianchini, J. C. (1971). Relating factors between studies based upon different individuals. *Multivariate Behavioral Research, 6,* 409–422.

Kline, P., & Barrett, P. (1983). The factors in personality questionnaires among normal subjects. *Advances in Behavior Research and Theory, 5,* 141–202.

Korth, B., & Tucker, L. R. (1975). The distribution of chance congruence coefficients from simulated data. *Psychometrika, 40* 361–371.

Korth, B., & Tucker, L. R. (1976). Procrustes matching by congruence coefficients. *Psychometrika, 41,* 531–535.

Levin, J., & Karni, E. S. (1970). Demonstration of cross-cultural invariance of the California Psychological Inventory in America and Israel by the Guttman Lingoes smallest space analysis. *Journal of Cross-Cultural Psychology, 1,* 253–260.

Levin, J., & Karni, E. S. (1971). A comparative study on the CPI femininity scale in Israel. *Journal of Cross-Cultural Psychology, 2,* 387–391.

Levonian, E. (1961). A statistical analysis of the 16 Personality Factor Questionnaire. *Educational and Psychological Measurement, 21,* 589–596.

Loevinger, J. (1957). Objective tests as instruments of psychological theory. *Psychological Reports, 3,* 635–694.

Mehryar, A. H. (1972). Personality patterns of Iranian boys and girls in Cattell's 16 Personality Factors test. *British Journal of Social and Clinical Psychology, 1,* 251–264.

Mitchell, J. V., & Pierce-Jones, J. A. (1960). A factor analysis of Gough's California Psychological Inventory. *Journal of Consulting Psychology, 24,* 253–256.

Montag, I., & Comrey, A. L. (1982). Personality construct similarity in Israel and the United States. *Applied Psychological Measurement, 6,* 61–67.

Muliak, S. A. (1972). *The Foundations of Factor Analysis.* New York: McGraw-Hill.

Nicholas, R. C., & Schell, R. R. (1963). Factor scales for the California Psychological Inventory. *Journal of Consulting Psychology, 27,* 228–235.

Nishiyama, T. (1973). Cross-cultural invariance of the California Psychological Inventory. *Psychologia, 16,* 75–84.

Nowakowska, M. (1974). Polish adaptation of the 16 Personality Factor Questionnaire (16PF) of R. B. Cattell as a source of cross-cultural comparisons. *Polish Psychological Bulletin, 5,* 25–33.

Phillip, A. E. (1972). Cross-cultural stability of the second order factors in the 16PF. *British Journal of Social and Clinical Psychology, 11,* 276–283.

Pinneau, S. R., & Newhouse, A. (1964). Measures of invariance and comparability in factor analysis for fixed variables. *Psychometrika, 29,* 271–281.

Pitariu, H. (1981). Validation of the CPI femininity scale in Romania. *Journal of Cross-Cultural Psychology, 12,* 111–118.

Reynolds, C. R., & Harding, R. E. (1983). Outcome in two large sample studies of factorial similarity under six methods of comparison. *Educational and Psychological Measurement, 43,* 723–728.

Rissetti, F. J., & Maltes, S. G. (1985). Use of the MMPI in Chile. In J. N. Butcher & C. D. Spielberger (Eds.), *Advances in Personality Assessment, Vol. 4* (pp. 209–257). Hillsdale, NJ: Lawrence Erlbaum Associates.

Rodrigues, A., & Comrey, A. L. (1974). Personality structure in Brazil and the United States. *Journal of Social Psychology, 92,* 19–26.

Rummel, R. J. (1970). *Applied Factor Analysis.* Evanston, IL: Northwestern University Press.

Schludermann, S., & Schludermann, E. (1970). Generalizability of the California Psychological Inventory factors. *Journal of Psychology, 74,* 43–50.

Springob, H. K., & Struening, E. L. (1964). A factor analysis of the California Psychological Inventory on a high school population. *Journal of Consulting Psychology, 2,* 173–179.

Tellegen, A. (1982). *Brief manual for the Multidimensional Personality Questionnaire.* Unpublished manuscript, University of Minnesota.

Tsujioka, B., & Cattell, R. B. (1965). A cross-cultural comparison of second-stratum questionnaire personality factor structures—anxiety and extroversion—in America and Japan. *Journal of Social Psychology, 65,* 205–219.

Tucker, L. R. (1951). *A method for the synthesis of factor analytic studies.* Personnel Research Report No. 984. Washington, DC: Department of the Army.

Wakefield, J. A., Bradley, P. E., Doughtie, E. B., & Kraft, I. A. (1975). Influence of overlapping and non-overlapping items on the theoretical interrelationships of MMPI scales. *Journal of Consulting and Clinical Psychology, 43,* 851–857.

Zak, I. (1976). A Cross-cultural check of the personality structure of the 16PF. *Multivariate Experimental Clinical Research, 2,* 123–127.

3 The Turkish MMPI: Translation, Standardization and Validation

Işık Savaşır
Hacettepe University

Neşe Erol
Ankara University

The MMPI has been widely used as a clinical assessment and research instrument in Turkey for more than a decade. Although the validity of the original MMPI is well documented by research data in the United States and other countries, systematic information regarding the instrument's adaptability and validity for the Turkish culture have been lacking. The aim of this chapter is to summarize the work done on the Turkish MMPI. First, the translation of the items into Turkish and the standardization of the scales are discussed; second, the validation studies designed to examine differences between normals and psychiatric patients and also the differences among various diagnostic groups are summarized. Finally, the factorial structure of the Turkish MMPI is examined.

TRANSLATION OF THE MMPI INTO TURKISH

The equivalence of the same personality inventory in different languages largely depends on careful translation of the items. Translation of the items is considered to be the most important and complicated aspect of cross-cultural research with objective personality inventories (Butcher & Pancheri, 1976). Several methods to ensure the equivalence of items have been suggested by different authors. One of the best known methods to check the equivalence of a translation is back translation, where the items translated back to the original one (Brislin, 1970). Another approach is the bilingual retest method (Prince & Mombour, 1976). Both the original and the translated version of the inventory are administered to a group of bilinguals who are familiar with both cultures and languages. Discrepancies between the two versions in the endorsements of the same item provide useful cues for modifications.

The MMPI has been translated into Turkish several times independently by psychologists at different institutions. One translation, done by the National Testing Bureau, was reexamined and several changes in the items were made (Savaşir & Turgay, 1970). This version was used at a number of hospitals where it was administered to groups of normals and psychiatric patients for a period of 7 years. Comments made on the MMPI items by both normal subjects and patients were collected. It became obvious that there were difficulties in the comprehension of some items. All of the items were reexamined and rewritten in the light of the accumulated knowledge and experience with the test (Savaşir & Erol, 1978).

Bilingual psychologists and psychiatrists were asked to evaluate items that posed particular difficulties in translation. Culturally inappropriate items were adapted for the Turkish culture, for example, "I liked Alice in Wonderland by Lewis Caroll" was changed to "I like to read tales." Some of the items that were written in the past tense in the original created ambiguity when written in the same tense in Turkish. Such items were rewritten in the present tense: "I like my mother" instead of "I liked my mother." Because 95% of the Turkish population are Moslems, items related to religion were also changed. For example, the item "I go to church every week" was not translated as "I go to mosque every week," because regular attendance is not an essential requirement of the religion. Instead, "I pray regularly" was chosen to be more equivalent.

This revised translation of the Turkish inventory (Savaşir, 1978) and the MMPI in English were then administered to 20 bilinguals. An additional 20 subjects were administered the Turkish version of the test twice, one week apart. Test-retest reliabilities were computed for each validity and clinical scale. These correlations are shown in Table 3.1, together with mean composite correlations from German-English, French-English, and Spanish-English studies, as well as composite correlations from nine retest (English-English) studies. The correlations of the Turkish-English versions ranged from .43 to .85. The correlations for some of the scales compared quite favorably with test-retest correlations of the Turkish MMPI and the composite English correlations. For some of the scales, however, the Turkish-English correlations were considerably lower (F, D, K, Pa, Sc). Item endorsements of subjects who had taken the inventory in Turkish and in English were compared. The examination of the discrepant items showed that most of these items were long sentences that had previously been found difficult to translate. Other discrepant items were the ones that had two alternatives indicated by "or." The equivalent word for "or" is not used so frequently in Turkish as it is in English. All of the discrepant items were rewritten. In order to determine whether the new form had a better reliability, the items in the K scale, which had a Turkish-Turkish reliability coefficient of .88 and an English-Turkish reliability of .59, were rewritten and administered in English

TABLE 3.1
Comparison of Test-Retest Correlations Between Turkish-Turkish
Subjects, Turkish-English Bilinguals, English-English
Subjects, and German, French, and Spanish Bilinguals

Scales	Turkish-Turkish	Turkish-English	Composite of Nine Studies: English-English[a]	Composite of German-English French-English Spanish-English[a]
L	.63	.68	.61	.61
F	.53	.46	.62	.81
K	.88	.59	.69	.88
Hs	.89	.74	.59	.65
D	.77	.43	.74	.82
Hy	.82	.62	.62	.66
Pd	.87	.74	.71	.83
Mf	.81	.83	.80	.75
Pa	.51	.43	.61	.58
Pt	.84	.69	.77	.81
Sc	.86	.59	.63	.71
Ma	.70	.77	.70	.74
Si	.89	.89	−	.83

[a]Source: Butcher and Pancheri (1976) p. 85.

and in Turkish to a further sample of 20 bilinguals. The coefficient was found to be .80. This final form of the inventory was printed and used in the standardization study (Savaşir, 1978).

STANDARDIZATION OF THE TURKISH MMPI

The standardization sample consisted of 663 females and 1003 males between the ages of 16 and 50. Unfortunately, due to difficulties associated with lack of sufficient resources, this sample cannot be considered representative of the Turkish population. Furthermore, large cultural differences exist between urban and rural populations in Turkey which pose special problems in obtaining norms for any psychological test.

The subjects were chosen from urban areas, mostly from capital city of Ankara. A better distribution was obtained, however, when the place where the subjects had spent most of their lives was tabulated; 38% had lived in big cities, 30% in moderate to small cities, 19% in towns, and 11% in villages. The majority of the subjects were between the ages of 16 and 21 (64%). The age group 31–50 was not well represented. Due to the young mean age of our sample, most of the subjects were unmarried (85%). The educational level was higher than that of the general population: 42% had attended university, 54% had secondary and high school education, and 3.5% had only a primary school background. Candidates who had any history of psychiatric help were excluded. The MMPI was administered to groups ranging in size from 20 and 25 subjects.

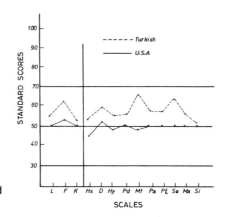

FIG. 3.1. Mean profiles of Turkish and American normal males.

Normative Data

Means and standard deviations were computed separately for males and females for each validity and clinical scale. *T* scores were derived from the formula used in the development of the MMPI. Both *K*-corrected and non *K*-corrected scores were computed (Savaşir, 1981).

Mean Profile Comparisons

The *K*-corrected mean profiles of the Turkish males and females were plotted on the standard MMPI profile forms. Figures 3.1 and 3.2 show the mean scores for the Turkish males and females in comparison with the American norms. As seen in Fig. 3.1, scores on *F*, *Mf*, and *Sc* scales were more than one standard deviation above the American norms. Mean scores for *K* and *Si* were similar for the

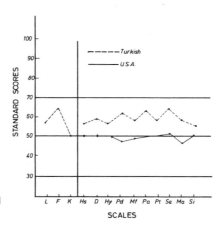

FIG. 3.2. Mean profiles of Turkish and American normal females.

Turkish and American samples. The Turkish males had higher scores than American males (up to one standard deviation) on the remaining scales. In the female sample the highest mean scores were on *F*, *Pa*, and *Sc* (*T* scores ranged between 60 and 70). The mean scores on other were also higher than those of the American norms (*T* scores ranged between 55 and 60).

VALIDATION

In the next section, we describe two studies designed to investigate the validity of the Turkish MMPI. The purpose of the first study was to examine whether the MMPI would discriminate normals from psychiatric patients, and if there were significant differences between different diagnostic groups of patients in a Turkish sample. The second study investigated the factorial structure of the Turkish MMPI.

STUDY 1

Method

Subjects.   The sample was composed of 1000 normals and 1000 psychiatric inpatients. The psychiatric subjects were chosen from inpatients hospitalized at various treatment facilities in Ankara during the years 1978–1980, and consisted of 234 women and 766 men. The criteria used for inclusion of patients in the study were (a) ages between 16 and 50; (b) education of at least primary school level; (c) normal intelligence; (d) hospitalized for at least one week; (e) no history of epilepsy or organic brain syndrome. For subjects who were hospitalized more than once, the first MMPI they completed was included. The normal group was randomly selected from the original standardization sample. Five hundred men and 500 women between the ages of 16 and 50 and educated at least to primary school level were chosen.

Most of the subjects in the normal and psychiatric groups were between the ages of 16 and 30 (93% of normals and 80% of patients). Eighty-five percent of the normals and 60% of the patients were unmarried. The two groups were comparable in terms of educational level. Most of the subjects had secondary or high school education. (More detailed information about the sample can be found in Erol, 1982.)

Procedure.   The MMPI and a short sociodemographic schedule were administered to all subjects. Normals were tested in groups of 20–25. While the patients were individually tested, α sociodemographic schedules were filled in by examiners. The diagnosis of each patient, given independently of the test data, was recorded. Each patient had two diagnoses: (1) a general diagnosis such

as psychosis, neurosis, and so forth, and (2) a specific diagnosis such as schizophrenia or obsessive compulsive neurosis. The general framework of the DSM-II
(APA, 1968) was used for the psychiatric classification. Drug usage could not be
controlled. Most of the patients were receiving medication at the time of the
assessment.

Results and Discussion

Patients were first classified according to their general diagnostic classes to
enhance diagnostic reliability. Furthermore, only inpatients were included in the
study, because interjudge reliability of diagnostic classification for inpatients is
much higher than for outpatients (Feighner, Robins, Guze, Woodruff, Winokur,
& Munoz, 1972).

The distribution of patients across the general diagnostic groups showed that
46.6% of the patients were psychotics, 39.5% were neurotics, and 11.4% were
classified as personality disordered. Only a small percentage (2.5%) were borderlines. The distribution of patients by both general and specific diagnostic
groupings is shown in Table 3.2.

TABLE 3.2
Distribution of Subjects by Diagnositc Groups

General Diagnositc Groups	Male		Female		Total	
	N	%	N	%	N	%
Neurosis	290	37.86	105	44.87	395	39.5
Psychosis	361	47.13	105	44.87	466	46.6
Personality Disorders	95	12.40	19	8.11	114	11.4
Borderlines	20	2.61	5	2.14	25	2.5
Total	766		234		1000	

Specific Diagnostic Groups	Male		Female		Total	
	N	%	N	%	N	%
Anxiety Neurosis	62	8.10	18	7.69	80	8
Depressive Neurosis	165	21.54	49	20.94	214	21.4
Hysterical Neurosis	11	1.44	13	5.55	24	2.4
Obsessive-Compulsive Neurosis	26	3.39	17	7.26	43	4.3
Hypocondriasis	10	1.30	1	0.43	11	1.1
Psychopathy	48	6.26	16	6.84	64	6.4
Schizophrenia (Acute)	115	15.01	55	23.50	170	17
Schizophrenia (Chronic)	128	16.71	27	11.54	155	15.5
Depressive Psychosis	51	6.66	12	5.13	63	6.3
Manic Psychosis	16	2.08	6	2.56	22	2.2
Borderline	20	2.61	5	2.14	25	2.5
Miscellaneous[a]	17	2.22	8	3.42	25	2.5
Invalid	97	12.66	7	2.99	104	10.4
Total	766		234		1000	

[a]alcoholism, drug addiction

Comparison of normal males and females with male and female psychiatric patients. As stated earlier, one of the aims of the study was to examine whether there were significant differences between normal and psychiatric groups on MMPI scores. Thus, a series of two-way analyses of variance (Sex X Psychiatric Status) were calculated separately for each MMPI scale. Significant differences were found between normal and inpatient males on all clinical scales and on all validity scales except scale *L*. Males in the psychiatric group earned higher scores on all clinical scales except *Mf*. The normal male group had higher scores on *Mf* and validity scale *K*. Similar results were obtained with the females. All of the scores on the clinical scales were higher for the psychiatrically ill females. Again, the normal females had higher scores on *K* and no differences were found on *L*.

Sex differences and interaction effects were found for scales *K, Hs, D, Hy, Pt* and *Si*. Normal females had higher scores than normal males on scales *Hs, D, Hy, Pt* and *Si;* however, there were no significant differences on these scale scores between the psychiatrically ill male and females. Normal males had significantly higher scores on *K* than normal females, whereas, there were no significant differences between male and female patients. The finding that psychiatrically ill males and females had higher scores than normals on clinical scales is in accord with our expectations. Higher scores on clinical scores indicate pathology. Likewise, lower *K* scores are expected in patient group since low *K* scores are interpreted as indicative of low ego functioning or inadequate use of defenses.

Comparisons according to general diagnosis. In addition to comparison of normals with psychiatric patients in general, comparisons of males and females were made across different diagnostic groups (psychotic, neurotic, personality disorder, borderline, and normal), and *T* tests were calculated to determine the significant differences on each MMPI scale. Because these results are too detailed to be dealt within this chapter, the following discussion is based on mean profiles of the general and specific diagnostic groups (Erol, 1982).

The neurotic males had the highest scores on scales *Hs, D,* and *Hy*. Similarly, the highest scores earned by the female neurotics were on *D, Hy* and *Hs*. (See Figs. 3.3 and 3.4.) These are the three common scales known as the neurotic triad in MMPI interpretation.

As shown in Fig. 3.5, psychotic males had the highest scores on the clinical scales of *Sc, Pt, Pa, D* and *Hs*. The scores on *F* were highest among the validity scales. Female psychotics earned the highest scores on clinical scales of *Sc, Pa, Pd, Pt, D* and validity scale of *F* (Fig. 3.6). On both profiles the configurations of validity scales were consistent with the common MMPI finding, low *L* and *K* and high *F* scores. Likewise, the so-called psychotic scales were the highest in both males and females.

The highest scales for males who were diagnosed as personality disordered

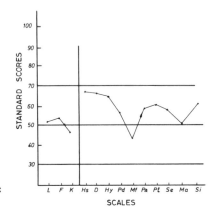

FIG. 3.3. Mean profiles of Turkish neurotic males (N = 200).

were *Pd, Hy, D,* and *Pa* and highest scales for females were *Pd* and *Si*. Males in general had higher scores than females. This might due to sampling errors, because the number of females was much smaller than males. Furthermore, most of the males came from a military hospital where they are more prone to exaggerate their symptoms and thus get out of compulsory military service. This might also explain the fact that personality disordered males had higher scores than psychotics. Elevation of *Si* together with *Pd* for females was an interesting finding since psychopaths in general are found to be extroverts. This finding should be replicated with a larger and carefully selected sample.

There were 104 profiles with *F* raw scores greater than 30 that were considered to be invalid. High scores (higher than *T* score 70) on all clinical scales except *Mf* and *Ma* characterize the invalid profile of males. For females, scores greater than *T* score 70 were *Sc, Pa, Ma, Pt* and *Pd*. Subjects who had invalid

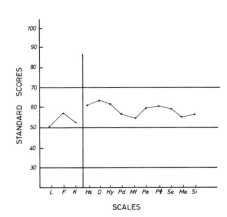

FIG. 3.4. Mean profiles of Turkish neurotic females (N = 105).

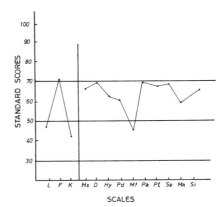

FIG. 3.5. Mean profiles of Turkish psychotic males (N = 361).

profiles in our sample were mostly males ($N = 97$). When these profiles were examined in terms of diagnosis, 53% were diagnosed as schizophrenic, 34% as personality disordered and 12% as neurotics. When invalid profiles are encountered, a diagnosis of either schizophrenia or personality disorder should be considered.

Comparisons according to specific diagnosis.   The inspection of the mean MMPI profile of males diagnosed as hypocondriasis showed that *Hs* was the highest scale, the next highest was *Hy,* and *D* considerably lower than both. This configuration is consistent with the common MMPI profile of somatization. When the mean profiles of 62 male and 18 female patients diagnosed as anxiety neurosis were examined, the highest scores for males were observed on scales *Hs, Hy, Pt,* and *D*. Such a configuration is generally linked to anxiety and

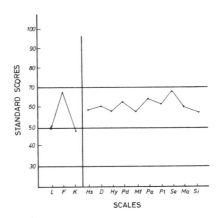

FIG. 3.6. Mean profiles of Turkish psychotic females (N = 105).

somatization. The configuration for females was less clear with moderate elevations on *Pa, Pt, Sc, Hs, D,* and *Hy.* Inspection of the mean profiles of 165 males
and 49 females diagnosed as neurotic depression indicated that the highest scale
for both males and females was *D.* Similar trends were observed for psychotic
depressives. For males, the highest scale was *D* and the next highest *Pt,* both of
which were above a *T* score of 70. Higher elevations were noted for psychotic
depressives when compared to neurotic depressives. For females there seems to
be no significant difference for neurotic or psychotic depression and the configuration is not clear as the male profile. The small sample size for female psychotic
depressives ($N = 12$) may partly account for the difference between the sexes.
The configurations of the mean profiles of males and females diagnosed as
hysterical neurosis showed the typical conversion "V" with high *Hs* and *Hy* and
lower *D* scores. In the mean profiles for both male and female psychopaths the
highest scale was *Pd.* For the males the other scale elevations were on scales *Hy,
D, Hs, Pa,* and *Pt,* and for females on *Ma.* The mean profiles for the males with
the diagnosis of obsessive compulsive neurosis showed elevations in scales *Pt*
and *D.* The highest scales for obsessive compulsive females were *Pt, D,* and *Sc.*
In the mean profiles of acute schizophrenic males and females, the highest scales
for the males were *F, Sc, Pt, Pa,* and *D,* and for the females, *F, Sc, Pa, Pt* and
Ma. High "psychotic scales" and low *K*'s for both males and females are
consistent with the common MMPI profile of schizophrenia. Very similar configurations were also found for chronic schizophrenic males and females. The
highest scales for male diagnosed as manic-psychosis were *Ma, Pa,* and *Hs,* and
for females, *Sc, Pd, Pt,* and *Ma.* The small numbers, especially in the female
group, render it impossible to reach any firm conclusions about the mean profile
of this group.

In conclusion, the above findings and discussions are related to group profiles. A note of caution is necessary because it has been stated that personality
correlates of mean profiles do not necessarily fit the groups as a whole or as some
subset of individuals in the group (Butcher & Tellegen, 1978). These results
need to be further supplemented with studies on code types. Examination of the
group profiles also showed that most of the scale elevations were between *T*
scores of 60 and 70. The finding suggests that clinicians should be sensitive to
scale scores between 60 and 70 in interpreting individual profiles.

STUDY 2

Factor analysis is frequently used in cross-cultural research and is considered a
useful measure of internal validity. Similar factor structures obtained in different
cultures indicate that the instrument can yield comparable findings. This study
was designed to examine the factor structure of the Turkish MMPI.

Method

The data from males and females in the normal sample and also from male and female psychiatric patients were submitted separately to varimax factor solution and orthogonally rotated for three factors. The non-K corrected scores for three validity scales and 10 clinical scales were used in the analysis.

Results and Discussion

Three factors were extracted for normal males and females. Factor loadings on the three factors for normal males and females are shown in Table 3.3. The first factor for the normal males can be labeled psychoticism. It is characterized by high factor loadings on F, Sc, Pt, and Ma, negative loadings on K, and moderate factor loadings on Hs, Pd, and Si. The second factor for normal males has high factor loadings on the neurotic scales Hy, D, and Hs, and can be labeled "neuroticism." Similar results were obtained for normal females. Neuroticism appears as the first factor, with high loadings on Hy, Hs, and D and moderate loadings on L, F, Pd, and Pt. The second factor of psychoticism has high loadings on Sc, Pt, and Si. The third factor is clearly defined in the normal male sample by the high factor loading of Mf and can be labeled masculinity-feminity. In the normal female sample the third factor is less clear with high factor loadings on Ma, Mf, and Pa.

Two factors emerged in the psychiatric male patient sample (Table 3.4).

TABLE 3.3
Factor Loadings for Normal Turkish
Males and Females

Scale	Males			Females		
	F_1	F_2	F_3	F_1	F_2	F_3
L	76	22	15	53	46	-34
F	79	42	-05	52	-58	25
K	-85	07	21	16	84	-15
Hs	51	71	-08	83	-30	01
D	-20	79	-29	76	-35	-14
Hy	17	87	19	88	05	07
Pd	61	57	05	63	-37	32
Mf	04	-00	84	-15	14	64
Pa	58	48	09	33	-37	66
Pt	83	43	-17	51	76	10
Sc	86	44	-11	37	80	33
Ma	76	16	22	08	-31	77
Si	59	37	-39	30	65	07

Percentage of Total Variance

	.52	.14	.08	.43	.18	.09

TABLE 3.4
Factor Loadings for Turkish Male and Female Patients

Scale	Males		Females		
	F_1	F_2	F_1	F_2	F_3
L	00	-72	13	14	70
F	-49	73	24	77	35
K	16	-79	-13	27	77
Hs	82	-29	84	25	15
D	88	-14	86	-08	08
Hy	87	11	87	-06	-15
Pd	60	-51	51	53	22
Mf	-46	-28	32	44	28
Pa	-52	65	32	76	19
Pt	63	68	49	-40	57
Sc	-56	76	43	60	55
Ma	-12	77	-01	79	26
Si	64	-42	56	-10	47

Percentage of Total Variance

	.55	.13	.15	.44	.08

These factors also represent neuroticism and psychoticism. The first factor labeled as neuroticism has high factor loadings on *D*, *Hy*, and *Hs* and moderate loadings on *Pt*, *Pd*, and *Si*. This factor closely resembles the neuroticism factor obtained in the normal male sample. The second factor of psychoticism has high loadings on *F*, *Ma*, *Sc*, *Pt* and *Pa* and high negative loadings on *K* and *L*.

Three factors appeared in the psychiatric female patients (Table 3.4). The first two factors resemble the ones obtained in both normal samples and in the male psychiatric sample. These factors are again labeled neuroticism and psychoticism. The neuroticism factor is characterized by high loadings on *Hy*, *D*, and *Hs* and moderate loadings on *Si* and *Pd*. The psychoticism factor has high loadings on *F*, *Pa*, *Ma*, *Sc* and moderate loadings on *Pd*. The third factor can be labeled "over-control", or defensiveness, as it is defined by high loadings on *L* and *K* and moderate factor loadings on *Pt* and *Sc*. This factor seems to be comparable to the third factor obtained in the 14 national samples reported by Butcher and Pancheri (1976).

In general, the results of factor analysis for both Turkish normal males and females and psychiatric patients yielded clearly interpretable factors. These factors share common features with factors found in other studies carried out in United States and other European countries. Butcher and Pancheri (1976) report factor analytic studies for seven different national groups based on samples of normal males and females and note the overall similarity of the factor structure across these groups. The first factor they labeled as psychoticism (high loadings on *Pd*, *Pa*, *Pt*, *Sc*, and *Ma*) clearly resembles the factor of psychoticism extracted from the normal male and female Turkish sample. The second factor with high loadings on the neurotic scales was labeled neuroticism for the Turkish males and females. A very similar second factor of neuroticism was also obtained in the Turkish psychiatric samples. The second factor for the seven national groups, however, was labeled over-control and was characterized by high loadings on *L* and *K*. A similar factor was obtained only for the Turkish female psychiatric patients. The number of factors extracted might partly account for the differences.

When the factor structure of the Turkish male and female patients were compared to the factor structures obtained in the psychiatric samples of the United States, Italy, and Switzerland as reported by Butcher and Pancheri (1976), the similarities were striking. The first three factors of neuroticism, psychoticism, and over-control were found to be very similar in the Turkish, United States, Italian, and Swiss psychiatric samples with exception of the Turkish male sample where only two factors emerged.

GENERAL CONCLUSIONS

The adaptation and use of psychological inventories or tests that are originally developed in the United States is widespread in many countries. Such instruments, however, must be shown to be reliable, valid, and usable in the target country. The MMPI is one such instrument that has enjoyed world-wide usage and considerable accumulation of cross-cultural research findings.

Our aim was to provide research data on the use of the MMPI in Turkey. The work on the equivalence of the translation, the development of the Turkish norms, the average profile comparisons, differences in average MMPI profiles of various diagnostic groups, and the factor structure of the Turkish MMPI has been summarized. These results suggest that the MMPI can be considered a valid and valuable instrument to be used for research and clinical purposes in Turkey.

REFERENCES

American Psychiatric Association. (1968). *Diagnostic and statistical manual of mental disorders* (2nd ed.). Washington, DC:

Brislin, R. W. (1970). Back translation for cross-cultural research. *Journal of Cross-Cultural Psychology, 1,* 186–216.

Butcher, J. N., & Pancheri, P. A. (1976). *Handbook of Cross-National MMPI Research.* Minneapolis: University of Minnesota Press.

Butcher, J. N., & Tellegen, A. (1978). Common methodological problems in MMPI research. *Journal of Consulting and Clinical Psychology, 46,* 620–628.

Erol, N. (1982). *Ülkemizdeki psikiatrik hastalarda Minnesota Çok Yönlü Kişilik Envanteri'nin geçerlik araştırması.* Unpublished doctoral dissertation, University of Ankara. (Validity study of MMPI with Turkish psychiatric patients.)

Feighner, J. P., Robins, E., Guze, S. B., Woodruff, K. A., Winokur, G., & Munoz, R. (1972). Diagnostic criteria for use in psychiatric research. *Archives of General Psychiatry, 26,* 57–63.

Prince, R., & Mombour, W. (1976). A technique for improving linguistic equivalence in cross-cultural surveys. *International Journal of Social Psychiatry, 13,* 229–237.

Savaşır, I. (1978). Minnesota Çok Yönlü Kişilik Envanterinin (MMPI) Türkçeye uyarlanışı ve standardizasyon projesi. *Psikoloji Dergisi, 1,* 18–25. (Adaptation and standardization project of the Turkish MMPI.)

Savaşır, I. (1981). *Minnesota Çok Yönlü Kişilik Envanteri El Kıtabı.* Ankara: Sevinç Mat. (Handbook of Turkish MMPI.)

Savaşır, I., & Erol, N. (1978). *A revised translation of the Turkish MMPI.* Unpublished report, Ankara.

Savaşır, I., & Turgay, A. (1970). *Translation study of the MMPI on a Turkish sample.* Unpublished report, Ankara.

4

An Epigenetic Approach to the Assessment of Personality: The Study of Instability in Stable Personality Organizations[1]

Arnold Wilson
Steven D. Passik
M. F. Kuras
New School for Social Research

In this chapter, we introduce the EPITAT, an instrument designed to assess epigenetically and psychoanalytically defined levels of dimensions of personality. A vital current in recent psychoanalytic theorizing conceives of personality organization as multileveled and fluid. Some psychoanalysts conceptualize clinical phenomena in this way by focussing upon multiple domains of self experience, modes of self-organization, levels of associative and integrative functioning, and the stepwise developmental acquisition of psychic structure. This view is in contrast to those that portray the personality as composed of static structures and traits. The EPITAT is an instrument that is designed to operationalize many of these theoretical advances that emphasize the unstable, progressive, and regressive aspects of personality. It is also designed to provide empirical referents for certain important clinical concepts. Our use of the EPITAT in this chapter provides a preliminary demonstration that psychic structure is more malleable, in flux, and subject to progressive and regressive influence than has generally been considered, measured, and theoretically depicted.

We have selected 10 particular psychological dimensions in accordance with our view of their clinical and research importance. We expect that it will eventually be demonstrated that an assessment of these dimensions provides predictive and explanatory value for both researchers and clinicians. For example, an EPITAT profile may be able to predict and explain key aspects of

---

[1]A manual explaining and suggesting scoring and training procedures, providing detailed scoring examples, summarizing modal levels for each dimension, and supplying response protocols is available from the senior author. The authors thank Andrew Morrall and Ann Turner for their help throughout the EPITAT project.

psychotherapy, such as the patient's capacity to benefit from some types of intervention at given moments, to participate in transference activity, to form a therapeutic alliance, or to assess the benefits obtained by the patient during and after psychotherapy.

THE EPITAT: THEORETICAL FRAMEWORK AND DEVELOPMENT

The EPITAT aids in explicating a usually implicit clinical inference process. It formalizes and streamlines a clinical inference process based upon psychoanalytic diagnostic and dynamic postulates. As a development in psychological assessment, it leads to inferences quite closely linked to the treatment situation. Many clinicians and researchers have been guided by the above mentioned new ways of psychoanalytic thinking, proceeding to develop multimodal models of personality dynamics and analytic intervention (Gedo, 1979, 1984), levels of integrative failure in diagnosis (Grand, Freedman, Feiner, & Kiersky, in press), object representations (Hartley, Geller, & Behrends, in preparation), the development of multiple domains of self-experience (Stern, 1985), and associative organization (Freedman, Berzofsky, & Passik, in preparation). In developing our clinical instrument rooted in this general approach, we have selected a set of 10 theoretically and clinically relevant variables or, as we will refer to them, dimensions. These dimensions are: affect tolerance, affect expression, uses of an object, empathy, temporality, defensive operation, adaptive needs, centration–decentration, threats to the self, and personal agency. Each one of these dimensions lies along a continuum that we have segregated into five epigenetically defined levels. They are characterized by us in such a way that at least one modal level of each variable can be defined and identified in a narrative based upon its structure and content. We attribute a wide range of meanings to the *way* a story is told in addition to *what* is told. Indeed, the lower levels of an epigenetic continuum impel us to take a broad view of what constitutes telling a story.[2] The EPITAT, then, is an instrument containing 10 psychological dimensions, defined along five modal levels. Although it is applicable to many forms of verbal samples, we have begun by adapting it to Thematic Apperception Test (TAT) narratives.

We are presently exploring the uses of the EPITAT in separate although related idiographic and nomothetic research programs, and with different forms of verbal samples. A typical use of the idiographic or ipsative approach we recommend involves analysis of a profile (10 scores for each of several responses

---

[2]The archaic domains of personality tend to be expressed at times in seemingly irrational ways, integrating psychobiological derivatives that influence language and thought. The EPITAT manual provides a fuller technical discussion of this issue.

to stimuli of varying degrees of provocation or arousal) for a detailed understanding of the constellation of dynamics *within* the individual psyche. We are elsewhere using such an approach to investigate how the instrument contributes to the fine-tuning of the clinical inferences made about an individual. The present chapter is the first representation of the nomothetic or normative side of our research program, intended to introduce the instrument and place it within its theoretical context. In this chapter, this will take the form of: First, attempting to demonstrate its inter-rater reliability and internal clusters; second, highlighting its sensitivity to shifts in the predominant mode of responding in normals from low- to high-arousal conditions (Experiment 1); third, attempting to demonstrate differences between predominant mode of responding between normals and inpatients under both high- and low-arousal conditions (Experiment 2); and fourth, attempting to demonstrate differences between normal, borderline, and psychotic subjects in their predominant mode of responding under both high- and low-arousal conditions and its sensitivity to shifts within each group (Experiment 3). To this end, we present reliability and validity data that have arisen from the between-groups comparisons we have made to date. This normative approach necessitates summarizing and reducing the potential quantity of data available in the full profile, thus sacrificing some of the intricate understanding of each individual subject in an effort to make the instrument amenable to between-groups comparisons. In other words, rather than follow a subject's scores on the 10 dimensions across a number of situations, we average the responses of particular groups chosen by diagnostic criteria across two situations. These two situations are chosen for their high- and low-arousal stimulus value.

Before we move into a discussion of these empirical findings, we will provide a theoretical context for the current work. The EPITAT is predicated upon an intersection of three streams of thought: the principle of epigenesis, the perspective of narration, and psychoanalytic theory. These will now be discussed, along with a discussion of the instrument as it has been prepared for use with TAT narratives.

The Epigenetic Approach

Psychology borrows the principle of epigenesis from general biology, specifically from developmental biology. It has been used by theorists interested in models of human development as a way of conceptualizing a superordinate principle that explains the movement from psychobiological to more explicitly psychological functioning. To briefly summarize the biological view of epigenesis, it has five distinctive features: it postulates a causal sequence of interactions between organism and environment; earlier and more undifferentiated structures in the organism interact with the environment and cause more differentiated structures to unfold in the organism; these structures unfold in a series of levels, stages, or modes; these structures come to possess increased levels of complexity, differentiation, and organization; and particular "emergent" qualities characterize each new level (Kitchener, 1978). A corollary of this view of epigenesis is that a particular level or mode is characterized by a specifiable degree of complexity and differentiation of structure, possesses certain emergent qualities, denotes a particular interplay between an organism and its environment, and is causally related to all past and future modes through the nature of successive transactions that reorganize structure and experience. Werner (1948) and Werner and Kaplan (1963) apply the most clearly developmental posture to these ways of looking at the evolution of personality. After Werner, many theorists interested in human development used the concept of epigenesis in order to understand changes in mental life that are in part qualitatively discontinuous. According to Werner (1948), such changes involve qualities of "gappiness" (a lack of forms characterizing intermediate change states) and "emergence" (nonreducible changes between later and earlier states). Piaget, too, despite his emphasis upon the invariance of logical operations within stages, demonstrates the fantastic and complicated relationship of operation to stage and of operations to each other, developing a model of qualitative and quantitative change in which stability of structure is not assumed.

The principle of epigenesis, when consolidated within the psychoanalytic perspective on human ontogenesis, results in the postulates:

1. The formation of psychic structure is the result of successive reorganizing transactions between the child and the caregiving environment.
2. The form or structuralization of each mode of organization depends on the outcome of each previous mode and the subsequent effects of experience.
3. Each mode integrates previous modes and results in new and more differentiated and articulated levels of organization and regulation.
4. Each mode is defined by its own emergent properties.

Important for the present work are two corollaries: (1) that once a given mode has been integrated by a higher mode, the more archaic form nonetheless continues to exist as a potential endpoint of regression, at which time it can become the overriding organizer of experience; (2) that although having yielded to developmental transformation, lower modes are contained within and can continue to exert influence over higher-order psychological processes. Dimensions of the personality organization are thus subject to more or less constant regressive and progressive influences in response to factors that are both intrapsychic as well as transactional. These qualities that define developmental transformations are captured in the conceptualization of the modal levels for each variable on the EPITAT.

The notion of stable levels of organization (e.g. Kernberg, 1975) viewed from our perspective can be translated into a statement that a person may most often function in certain modes—psychotics in the most primitive, neurotics in the most advanced, and borderlines at various points in between. The concept of level of organization is somewhat limited because it fails to encompass the complicated momentary flux and shifts in intrapsychic and interpersonal functioning. Such a model might insufficiently explain heterogeneity between levels of personality dimensions. An instrument such as ours, deriving its assumptions from psychoanalysis and epigenesis, can locate a person's most frequent mode of functioning or "level of organization" along specified dimensions in a manner consistent with outside indicators, such as a DSM-III diagnosis, and chart a person's upward and downward shifts in mode of functioning along particular dimensions as the environmental transaction at hand (reality demands) varies in the level of arousal produced. In the three studies to be reported, we have targeted these two points as central for the initial establishment of validity for our instrument.

Narration

A second important theoretical influence upon this research is the theory of narration. There has been abundant attention paid to narrative theory in psychoanalytic circles in recent years (Schafer, 1983; Spence, 1982, 1987). Theorists who have tried to characterize psychoanalysis as primarily a hermeneutic science (Ricoeur, 1977; Steele, 1979) have sharpened this controversy. Perhaps more impetus for this line of thinking has emerged from psychologists interested in broad epistemological questions, *how* we know rather than *what* we know. For example, Bruner (1986), persuasively arguing for narrative as a mode of thought, states that humans "construct" their world through active mentation; they are not passive possessors of knowledge that is a "copy" of what is provided from outside. The narratives or "worlds" a person creates cannot help but reflect crucial aspects of their life history and personality organization. A person's narrative productions can be studied for their thematic and structural elements and content, telling us much about their ability to structure and differentiate their experiences (Bruner, in press). In this way, narration can be studied empirically, as opposed to the hermeneutically inspired four truth claims of narration in the psychoanalytic situation put forth by Ricoeur (1977) that eschew any empirical referents.

One major shortcoming of the narrative perspective, from a clinical point of view, has been its primary focus upon the linguistically coded content of its native data base, which is language itself. From our epigenetic and psychoanalytic perspective, information derived from biopsychological (early levels) and psychological (later levels) influences are coded and stored as aspects of the representational world, and are differentially accessible and influential as the various modes surface and recede. These elements also figure prominently in narrativity. Psychoanalytic work on the status of representations (Greenspan, 1979; Horowitz, 1972; Noy, 1969) stresses the early sensorimotor encoding and the later psychological encoding of psychic structure. Clinically, the study of the solely lexical content of a narrative leads to the exclusion of important nonverbal representations, namely those coded in earlier symbolic and presymbolic forms, such as images and actions (Bruner, 1964; Freedman, 1985; Wilson & Malatesta, in press). A major theoretical disjunction occurs when these subjectively accessible contents are not tied to their preverbally coded underpinnings found in repetitions, behavioral enactments, unspoken feeling states, and other clinical phenomena (such as depersonalization) in which symbols are not subjectively accessible (Wilson, 1986). This shortcoming in the clinical utility of narrative theory has rendered the approach especially problematic for those clinicians who commonly work with the severely disturbed, who are profoundly affected by these developmentally early factors. Certain people can be better understood through a complementarity of psychobiological as well as linguistic emphasis on the derivation of meaning. For example, what type of narratives do the thought disordered verbal productions of a schizophrenic patient constitute? These archaic echoes may be part of a hidden, unspoken, or possibly even a prelinguistic narrative, represented in sensorimotor or imagistic forms, that are subject to at best indirect illumination through semantic analysis of spoken content. The schizophrenic with the delusion of thought withdrawal is telling an important preverbal narrative, about feelings of flatness, permeability, loss of autonomy and reversal of agency, inability to create lexical meaning, and poor stimulation regulation rather than simply one of persecutors who may operate bizarre machines that steal his or her thoughts. Of special note in this example is how some preverbal narratives are disguised by having to be communicated through the avenue of lexicality. In our research, we will be conceptualizing modes of organization of content and theme that are beyond or prior to subjectivity and reflective self-awareness (which we later discuss as Modes 1 and 2 in the EPITAT hierarchy). To do this in a manner that is in synchrony with the epigenetic perspective, we will adopt a broad concept of the "narrative creation" that encompasses all of the behaviors, verbalizations, and movements a person makes while narrativizing (along with metaphoric verbal representations of these preverbal forms) during the period allocated for the subject to respond. In addition, inferences about the early modes of the hierarchy—which are characterized by undeveloped psychological structures—will be made when the narratives contain the same undeveloped structural characteristics. We hope to show that these and other inferences about nonverbal elements can be reliably scored from the form (or formlessness) and content of a narrative and the act of a person's construction of a narrative, thereby adding a minor footnote to the theory of narration.

Psychoanalytic Theory

In this section, we briefly discuss some aspects of psychoanalytic theory germane to the construction of our measure. A further discussion of some psychoanalytic implications of this work is found in the Discussion of Empirical

Findings section of this chapter as well. The establishment of an empirically informed developmental basis for theories of structural evolution has become a priority for many psychoanalytic researchers and clinicians. Observers of infants and caregivers, such as Stern (1985) and Greenspan (1979), have approached the study of early ontogeny informed by psychoanalytic theory, and are making an unmistakable mark. In so doing, they have provided us with valuable observations of the human infant's early manners of functioning within the culture of the caregiver–infant matrix. Greenspan has articulated a stage theory, a structural approach that blends cognitive, affective, neurophysiological, behavioral, and social developmental factors in the child. His "developmental structuralist" approach assumes that: (1) the organizational capacity of the child progresses to higher levels as the child matures; and (2) for each phase of development there are certain characteristic tasks the child must accomplish before moving on to the next stage of development. Thus, his developmental structuralist approach proposes a biological-adaptational model of development in which experiential organizations interact with forces of maturational progression and phase-specific environmental interests and influences. A stage theory differs from an epigenetic theory through the former's emphasis upon invariance, phase-specificity that includes critical periods and chronologically normative assumptions, and a relatively undefined relationship between stages.

The complicated and fascinating mechanics around the acquisition of selfhood has been since Freud and continues to be of interest to psychoanalysts. From the direct observation of infants and their caregivers Stern (1985) has inferred a series of "senses of self" on the way to adult selfhood that are hypothesized to exert profound experiential tone on later mental life, although its origins lie in the distant past beyond memorial recollection. These senses of self pivot around such developmental acquisitions as language acquisition, separation responses, and related object relational phenomena. Three senses of self (emergent, core, and self-with-other) precede the lexical self, and determine some aspects of experience that may or may not later be appropriated by the sense of self that can employ the advantages accruing from the use of language. Here, too, can we see a theoretical commentary on how early preverbal mental life exerts a profound impact upon the content and structures of human development. This recognition of self experience as a multilayered phenomenon has important implications for how we view narrative productions. This conception of selfhood led us to select some psychological dimensions on the EPITAT that are bound up with this hierarchical view of self experience. It also is a model of development in many ways similar to the epigenetic model that we propose.

The observationally based theories of Greenspan and Stern are constructed from the bottom up—viewing early development prospectively, with an eye toward what is to come. Psychoanalysts who work only with adults utilize a top down approach—from adulthood reconstructing infancy, with an eye toward what has occurred before. In striving to integrate the findings from both perspectives, defined empirically within each mode, we may arrive at a comprehensive guiding framework for the organization of clinical data and a more empirically sound metapsychological theory. Such an effort can be found in the psychoanalytic model proposed by Gedo and Goldberg (1973) and Gedo (1979, 1984). They have outlined a hierarchically organized model for conceptualizing activities of the mind, composed of five epigenetically defined levels of functioning. Depending upon intrapsychic and environmental demands, from moment to moment any individual is capable of functioning in any of these modes, although certain modes tend to predominate for a particular person over time. With changing conditions, however, any specific mode of organization can emerge as an endpoint for regression in the ubiquitous aim of adaptation. Gedo (1988) has discussed the differing nature of regressive activity. He has noticed that some types of regression only emerge in the clinical situation, while others exist as an aftermath to "actual neuroses". We note that the former would be likely to emerge as a result of some aspect of identification, while the latter provides a window into a characteristic impairment of psychological skills. These are some of the possible roads along which the lower modes can become evident.

Only in more recent writing (1981, 1984, 1988) has Gedo, now intellectually departed from Goldberg, begun discussing particular dimensions along which modal organization can be defined. If these separable dimensions are not conceptualized, then the model is vulnerable to falling victim to the characterization of functioning in terms of global stability or instability, although of five steps rather than two (Freud's neurotic and psychotic) or three (Kernberg's neurotic, borderline, and psychotic). Our specific criteria for each mode differ from those Gedo has described to a greater or lesser extent, and we also systematize particular dimensions by modal level. The specific nuts and bolts of the hierarchical model will, of course, be constantly reevaluated, modified, and updated through the process of empirical investigation, but on the whole this conceptual model will stand or fall on the basis of both its demonstrable clinical utility and how well it holds up to the type of testing we propose in this chapter (Gedo, personal communication).

THE EPITAT

Modal Organization of the EPITAT

The EPITAT has been specifically designed to be sensitive to the manifestations of the more primitive modes of organization. This is one of the unique aspects of the EPITAT that separates it from more traditional assessment techniques, because most assessment instruments empirically standardized employing traditional methods of scaling and test construction are not equipped to adequately assess these archaic dimensions, which are, at best, only indirectly illuminated by a surface analysis of verbal content. There are many problems with self-report instruments that make sophisticated assessment of archaic phenomena problematic (see Wilson, Passik, & Faude, in press).

Investigators employing the EPITAT are able to chart an individual's upward and downward shifts in level of organization along specific dimensions on a moment-to-moment basis as particular intrapsychic and/or environmental demands impinge on the person. Under conditions of low stress, an individual is presumed to be operating in his most frequently preferred modal organization. Under more difficult situations, ones that present integrative challenges, an individual momentarily may regress to a lower modal organization. Charting where regressive and progressive shifts begin and end relative to intrapsychic and environmental conditions—which we have specified as parallel to degree of stress—allows the EPITAT to assess characteristics of diagnostic groups in general and dynamic profiles of individuals in particular.

The EPITAT scale is applied to an individual's narrative productions, that include the verbal as well as the accompanying nonverbal or enactive responses to the stimuli eliciting the narrative response. Important features of this response process exist within both the content of the narrative and the form in which this content is presented. This expanded view of the narrative response is important. By going through the narrative's verbal or lexical form into its underlying meaning structure, we are able to gain access to more primitive modes of organization, which, by definition, are not encoded in verbal expressions. These lower modes exert influence over higher psychological processes as sensorimotor patterns which are difficult for the respondent to articulate in a lexical form. More often, these sensorimotor components of the narrative are seen in repetitions, enactments, and metaphoric expressions. This specific way of analyzing narratives was foreshadowed many years ago by Schafer (1967), in a seminal paper on the TAT called "How Was This Story Told." Crucial diagnostic information was available, Schafer noted, not only in the actual content of the story, but in an analysis of its formal dimensions. Our instrument, which was constructed to be sensitive to both streams of narrative data, in many ways formalizes Schafer's analysis. It also extends it.

We constructed the EPITAT to account for five broadly defined epigenetic modes of personality organization. Briefly, the modes have the following general features, common to all of the 10 psychological dimensions later to be described:

1. Mode 1 is to be understood as a presubjective period of human development. There is a limited distinction between self and other. Information is encoded in sensorimotor or action-oriented forms. The primary feeling states are pleasure and unpleasure. Avoidance of global unpleasure is the predominant defensive activity. Overstimulation is the primary danger.

2. Mode 2 is understood as a transitional period between sensorimotor representations and representations encoded in imagistic forms. Others, especially

significant others, are represented as "separate but attached" because they provide for basic needs, such as soothing. This leads to the other being represented in a polarized fashion—good/bad. Intense attachment to and/or extreme avoidance of others is prominent. The independent volition of others tends to be not understood, and projection is the predominant defensive activity. Separation and issues of autonomy and intrusiveness are the primary danger situations.

3. Mode 3 is a period in which the proper positioning of the self in relationship to the object world is the superordinate developmental task. Self-enhancement and the maintaining of self-esteem are key concerns. A powerful need is the protection of those wishful illusions about both one's and important others' capabilities and capacities, those that support and bolster one's self-esteem. Denial and disavowal are the predominant defensive activities, and the primary danger situation is prohibition from external authority figures. Lexical representational capacities develop and with it a mature communicational ability.

4. Mode 4 is a period of Oedipal level conflicts. Moral anxieties and derivatives of castration fears are the main sources of threat. Subjectively accessible intrapsychic ideational conflict, especially around competition and self-assertion, is the principle danger. There is guilt over sexuality, but genital sexuality is also desired. The predominant defensive activity is repression.

5. Mode 5 is a period characterized by the benevolent resolution of conflict. Creativity and generativity are the basic needs. Aggression is well contained; competition is not a major threat. There is a sense of containment deriving from one's realistic appraisal of a realistic place and role in the object world. The primary dangers come from undistorted reality factors, and the predominant defensive activity is renunciation.

If the five modes are clear, we can now introduce the ten psychological dimensions to be assessed on the EPITAT. Each dimension is to be understood as on a developmental continuum, with epigenetic definition at each modal level. Each dimension has comparable anchor points along the ladder of human development, and can be contrasted with each other in order to help us to understand the personality organization. Each modal level thus defines a particular developmental level of each dimension, and all dimensions are scaled at identical intervals.[3] Comparisons between dimensions can thus present a dynamic profile of progressive and regressive abilities not unlike what Piaget signified with his concepts of vertical and horizontal *decalage*.

---

[3]The specific descriptions of the 10 dimension, 5 mode profile is contained in the EPITAT manual, available from the senior author.

Psychological Dimensions Assessed by the EPITAT

Psychological Dimension 1: Affect Tolerance.   Tolerance is a formal dimension of affective life that is central to the clinical situation (Krystal, 1975). The way in which a person manages their affective arousal can take many forms. Through development and early socialization, a person comes to possess characteristic ways of tolerating emotions. These range from highly unsocialized and immature forms, such as simple avoidance of unpleasure and dedifferentiation and somatization of affects, to a mid-range where one-sided and highly polarized emotional experiences are the rule, to more sophisticated and mature modes in which the nuances of one's emotional life are largely integrated, modulated, and accepted. Depression and anxiety tolerance represent important developmental achievements that are important in assessing a patient's treatability. In the making of a narrative, a subject must confront the affective situations which the stimulus evokes, and the degree of affect tolerance will in part determine the form and content of the narrative.

Psychological Dimension 2: Affect Expression.   Affect expression is a dimension that identifies how an individual's emotions come to play a role in a communicational matrix with important others. As such, it is a key aspect of a person's intrapsychic tendencies toward action. Throughout development, a person's affective experiences are refined and differentiated, usually parallel to formative object relational phenomena, and certain general affective patterns are developed that determine, in part, their typical affective experiences. A central feature of creating a narrative is for the subject to describe what the characters are feeling. A subject's response in this way provides us with clues to conscious and unconscious aspects of their affective life and how affects function as communications or "signals." The affects expressed in the narrative—their intensity and their differentiation (global or specific)—are indicators of a person's modal affective ties to objects.

Psychological Dimension 3: Personal Agency.   Personal Agency is a dimension that identifies a prominent source of self experience. Stern (1985) suggests that preverbal domains of selfhood are laid down in infancy and childhood and that these domains, once in place, contribute to later domains of self-experience that determine the "I" that is motivated. Earliest forms of self-experience are based on action. Later forms are based upon being-with-others, and finally upon more refined and complex verbal representations with a quality of autonomy and self-initiation. Aspects of these self-experiences become represented, and thus come to presage later psychological unfolding. Their integration in the ongoing process of self-experiencing is crucial to adaptation. Problems in integrating these levels of self-experience can lead some patients to function in lower modes to the exclusion of the higher ones. When subjects create narratives, they portray their operative sense of agency in their descriptions of the characters sense of self or in their other behaviors during the response.

Psychological Dimension 4: Centration–Decentration. One of the processes in human development is the steady movement from extreme egocentrism to a more mature sense of one's place in the world, marked by the ability to gauge one's place in a realistic way and appreciate the importance and subtlety of others. This mature understanding is marked by a healthy acceptance of one's strengths, weaknesses, uniqueness, and ordinariness. Thus at the highest level, centration and decentration are well balanced. At lower levels, the self is so expansive and diffuse that it serves to blot out psychological distinctions between self and other, and the expansive self becomes all one can see. The narratives a subject creates will indicate their degree of decentration, in the ways in which their characters are represented and interact with one another.

Psychological Dimension 5: Threats to the Self. Important diagnostic information is to be found in assessing what internal and external dangers are most often perceived as threats by an individual, especially when measured against his or her typical coping mechanisms (see Dimension 6). In addition to objective threats presented by a given situation, there are subjective perceptions of threat that are generated based upon a person's character style, developmental history, and personality organization. An internal or external reality situation will be perceived as more or less threatening to an individual depending upon his or her sense of vulnerability and ability to adaptively cope. In the earliest stages of development, traumatic overstimulation poses a pervasive threat to one's basic identity. This is also true in adulthood for extremely vulnerable people or for people under especially stressful conditions. As one matures, first object loss and then traumatic disillusionment and then failure to live up to expectations emerge as prototypic threats. The nature of the threats to the self can in this way be identified on a continuum.

Psychological Dimension 6: Defenses and Defensive Operations. Defensive operations can be conceptualized along a continuum of increasing sophistication and adaptive value (see Vaillant, 1977). Defensive operations are designed to modify or ward off unpleasure, anxiety, and information that threatens the stability of the self. Defenses are assigned a mode based upon the predominant operations that minimize threatening states in a narrative. Defenses can range from the developmentally earlier action-oriented operations (e.g. avoidance) through a midrange (e.g. projection) to the more sophisticated verbal/symbolic ones (e.g. repression proper).

Psychological Dimension 7: Empathic Knowledge of Others. Throughout development the ability to know other people and empathize with them evolves

(Bergman & Wilson, 1984). Early on, contagion of affect is the basic constituent of empathy (i.e., if one infant in a nursery cries, neighboring ones will cry too). Later, one learns to know and understand others on the basis of stereotypic functions and roles, and later still, as individuals with separate psychologies and perspectives. The narratives a subject creates will reveal his or her level of empathic knowledge of others, by the way the characters understand one another and the way he or she understands them and the story's hero.

Psychological Dimension 8: Use of an Object.   There is a developmental range of object relationships, beginning with the use of another for the sole purpose of stabilization through self-enhancement, through mutual enhancement of both parties, and leading to intimate collaborative relations. Interpersonal relationships evolve during development from basic dependency through mature intimacy. In truly mutual and mature relationships, the lower level functions, the so-called "self-object" functions, are epigenetically subsumed. Under conditions of disturbance or stress, interpersonal relationships can become focussed on lower level uses of the objects in a person's life. The interpersonal relationships in a person's narratives reflect his usual use of objects and patterns of interpersonal contact. Interesting comparisons can be made between the way an individual uses objects and the way he understands them (see Dimension 7).

Psychological Dimension 9: Adaptive Needs.   There are various levels of need which individuals evidence in their attempts to adapt to the exigencies of their environment. At times a person may optimally make use of pacification when overstimulation threatens. On other occasions, confrontation and adaptive feedback are called for. At still other times, interpretation and the generation of insight are helpful when lower level concerns do not serve to derail the higher level ones. The form and content of a person's narratives will help an interpreter to formulate what the storyteller's most pressing needs are.

Psychological Dimension 10: Temporality.   A person's ability to form a continuum of time is an important aspect of his or her cognitive ability to make sense out of the events in his world. This is a developmental acquisition. Time sense proceeds from a timeless and nonsequential beginning to an ordered and sequential stage through the acquisition of language and other cognitive capacities. With a clear and separate sense of past, present, and future, a person can order ambitions, aims, and events easily, and infer causality in an accurate manner. However, when logic is dominated by condensations, wherein distinctions between past, present, and future collapse or are temporarily lost, confusion and panic can follow. A high level of arousal, defensiveness, or wishful thinking can, among other factors, cause an ordered time continuum to be compromised. The degree to which the narrative is structured by a clear time continuum will reflect the subject's ability to construct a temporally ordered world.

VALIDITY AND RELIABILITY OF THE EPITAT

In order to examine the validity of the EPITAT, in this chapter we have limited our attention to narratives produced in response to TAT cards. The TAT is a projective test, consisting of a number of black and white pictures constructed to pull for certain themes. In choosing this type of instrument we are expanding upon the assumptions of the so-called projective hypothesis (Rapaport, Gill, & Schafer, 1968), that in responding to an open-ended or unstructured ambiguous stimulus, an individual through projection onto the stimulus reveals much about his characteristic and conflictual styles of thinking, feeling, and perceiving.

The TAT is an instrument that readily lends itself to the study of narrative construction. From a practical standpoint, the TAT story, outside of a patient's communications in the consulting room, is perhaps the most common form of narrative a clinician encounters and interprets. The TAT story is familiar to most practicing clinicians, accessible, convenient, and due to the structure provided by the TAT card, less ambiguous than an excerpt from a psychotherapy session.[4] It provides an excellent vantage point to study how an individual constructs his or her psychological world, one that can vary relative to changing environment demands and his or her intrapsychic organization. Because each TAT card places certain demands upon a respondent, we may observe how these demands are perceived and how they constrain the psychological construction of the narrative response. In other words, the EPITAT takes the act of constructing a TAT narrative as a model for the way in which the respondent's mind constructs his or her psychological world.

With this in mind, we attempted to construct a controlled situation that hypothetically effected the conditions the individual was faced with in constructing his narrative. A basic assumption of projective testing is that increased arousal is produced by heightened degrees of perceptual ambiguity (both thematic and perceptual) and sexual or aggressive stimuli. A secondary assumption is that heightened arousal results in a regressive mode of responding (Schactel, 1945; Schafer, 1954). We required subjects to respond to specific TAT cards uniformly judged to possess high-arousal or low-arousal stimulus properties. These cards were chosen on the basis of high- and low-arousal rankings of the full set of TAT cards by three senior practicing clinicians. Card 13MF, depicting a man standing with downcast head buried in his arm, while behind him is the figure of a woman, naked to the waist, lying in bed, was chosen unanimously to be the most arousing card. The least arousing card was Card 1, depicting a young boy

---

[4]We have focused on TAT narratives for the purpose of attaining validity and reliability for the EPITAT. Other narrative productions, however, are amenable to analysis by the EPITAT. Autobiographies, descriptions of significant others, and pieces of psychotherapy sessions can also function as narrative responses able to be coded by the EPITAT.

contemplating a violin which rests on the table in front of him. These ratings provided us with an a priori determination of low- and high-arousal situations. This circumvents the potential circularity of defining arousal on the basis of decrements in the respondent's narratives.

By requiring our subjects to respond to high- and low-arousal TAT cards we were able to examine the different ways in which these stimuli were handled, in terms of both the structural and thematic features of the response. As demonstrated in the studies that follow, we observed both regressive and progressive shifts in the individual's narrative constructions along the epigenetic continuum for each dimension included on the EPITAT scale. Our initial hypothesis was that the low arousal condition presented a minimal adaptive challenge; in other words, a situation that theoretically allowed the respondent to function at higher modal levels of organization. Conversely, we hypothesized that the high-arousal condition, replete with difficult integrative challenges, would cause the respondent to regress to a lower modal level of organization. There is some preliminary empirical evidence at hand that lends some support to this hypothesis. In a recent doctoral dissertation, Ehrenreich (1989) examined 5 TAT cards (1, 2, 3BM, 12M, 13MF), and rated them according to directness/intensity of drive experiences and level of defenses exhibited, both of which are theoretically associated with degree of regression. Card 13MF consistently elicited the most drive expressions (2.62 per story), which were also the most consistently "direct-unsocialized" (38.2% of all scoreable responses). Cards 1 and 2 were virtually identical in having the least drive expressions (fewer than 0.75 per card) and also pulled for responses that were primarily "direct-socialized" and secondarily "weak-disguised" (only 10% of the scoreable responses were "direct-unsocialized" on Card 1). A similar pattern held for defenses exhibited, with responses to Card 13MF yielding "lower-level" defenses and those to Card 1 "higher-level" defenses. Although certainly not decisive, these results lend some empirical support to our linkage of level of arousal with degree of regression.

We recognize one potential criticism of this approach, that arousal is in the eyes of the beholder. That is, regardless of the clinician's agreement, the perception of arousal will be subject to varying individual differences. This caveat is perhaps more germane to the ipsative focus upon the single subject. In such cases, where the emphasis is upon the derivation of a more extensive personality profile, the use of several TAT cards may be preferable in order to elicit a wide range of adaptive and maladaptive regressions and progressions. In such cases, specifically arousing situations that serve as triggers to regression can be identified. For our present purposes, we have sacrificed this kind of information in order to study more general between group trends, based on a more objective definition of high and low arousal. A between group analysis of this sort is the preferred design to attain the validity information sought here in our initial introduction of the EPITAT.

Reliability

We now discuss the reliability of the EPITAT in inter-rater form. Inter-rater reliability is the most appropriate form of reliability for our scale. Although all forms of reliability are usually thought of as placing a ceiling on validity, such a relationship will not hold up with a scale such as the EPITAT, in which under-estimation of reliability in other than inter-rater form is built in. Split-half or alternate form reliabilities are not appropriate, because except in overgeneralized terms, one could not predict equivalent halves or forms of TAT stimuli that would hold up across subjects. Internal consistency is not applicable because TAT stimuli present such highly heterogeneous content. Test-retest reliability is likewise not applicable (Atkinson, 1980), because the constellation of themes competing for expression on the TAT changes from Time 1 to Time 2, while nevertheless condensing the same underlying motives. We rely exclusively on inter-rater reliability in our evaluation of the EPITAT because it is the only one that does not lead to automatic underestimation of reliability and, thus, validity, and so is best suited to the type of research involving projective measures we report upon in this chapter.[5]

In our inter-rater reliability trials, raters with relatively limited clinical exposure have been trained to reach a reliability criterion that qualifies them as an expert rater.[6] Reliability trials involving four graduate students in clinical psychology were begun following a series of readings, discussions, and practice protocols supervised by the first author. Of the four students, one was considered "advanced" (internship level), one was considered "intermediate" (predoctoral level), and two were "beginners" (pre-clinical masters level). In addition to the training just mentioned, all had been involved in the preparation of a training manual for the scoring of EPITAT dimensions. Each student was given a 3-card TAT protocol (Cards 5, 10, 15) to score and were blind to the fact that it had been obtained from a hospitalized schizophrenic man. Thus, each student provided 30 judgments (10 per card). We set the criteria for qualification as an expert rater at the following level: 90% of the judgments had to be between +1 and −1 scale point with a minimum of 50% exact matches, all compared with those of an already qualified expert rater. The results of this first trial fell slightly short of our criteria for satisfactory inter-rater reliability. Overall, 82% of the judgments fell between +1 and −1 scale point with 45% exact matches. However, only the two beginning level students had failed to qualify as expert raters.

---

[5]For an elaborate discussion of the multiple problems of establishing forms of reliability on the TAT with psychometric precision, and of the validity claims possible, see Murstein (1973).

[6]This has led us to believe that the EPITAT has didactic value and that it might compare favorably to other forms of teaching psychoanalytically informed principles of interpretation to students at early stages of training. This very hypothesis is under study as part of our ipsative research program.

Following discussion of the protocols, and further training and rewriting of unclear EPITAT items, all the raters were given a similar 3 card TAT protocol (5, 10, 15) of another patient, and were again blind to the diagnostic status of the respondent, in this case a hospitalized borderline patient. The results of this second trial met our criteria for expert rater status for each of the four raters. Pearson Product-Moment correlations of the scores provided by each rater ranged from .85 (the beginning students) to .92 (the advanced students). Final Spearman-Brown Coefficient of Reliability scores were calculated for the entire set of raters, which provides an average of pairwise correlations. This coefficient was .88, supporting the high inter-rater reliability capable of being obtained on the EPITAT after intensive training and immersion in the theory underlying the scale.

We want to reemphasize that inter-rater reliability was achieved with raters who, although novices in a clinical career, had an extensive personal history of working with the concepts contained in the EPITAT. New raters may have difficulty attaining a satisfactory reliability criterion unless extensive educating occurs in the theoretical background informing the inference process captured by the EPITAT. In much the same way as one cannot expect an untrained psychometrician to adequately interpret a Rorschach without training in a guiding theoretical framework to channel inferences (Schafer, 1954), so, too, may the interpreter of the EPITAT require some familiarity with the theoretical/clinical network informing the derivation of this instrument.

In future EPITAT research, we recommend two additional possibilities for obtaining reliability, both of which we are currently investigating. First, using different raters for different dimensions might minimize perseverative tendencies to score modes consistently within subjects. Raters must be very sensitive to subtle distinctions between dimensions, and be careful to score them independently rather then allow one score to bias another for a particular subject. Second, establishing additional checks of reliability after every 10 or 15 subjects rated might prevent bias in the form of drift and guarantee that each rater is consistently using the same internal scale throughout the entire rating procedure. A dummy protocol might be included at intervals in each series to guarantee that there is no idiosyncratic drift taking place.

Validity

The first step in assessing the validity of the EPITAT was to demonstrate that each of the psychological dimensions we have defined are independent and actually measure different components of personality functioning. To this end, we combined the data from the three studies we present in this paper, to form one aggregated data set consisting of 80 subjects. A total of 20 variables, representing the 10 psychological dimensions crossed with the two levels of arousal, were used in a principle components analysis and rotated to Varimax criterion. This analysis showed that each dimension factored relatively independently on a rotated component. That is to say, each dimension appeared with a high loading on one component (between .533 and .886), while all of the other dimensions on a given component appeared with a loading of .366 or less. It is, of course, true that any one dimension in and of itself cannot completely define a factor. Nonetheless, the principle components analysis we employed did yield evidence that the 20 dimensions were largely orthogonal to each other. This is exactly what we had predicted given that we are hypothesizing that there are 20 constructs being measured (10 psychological dimensions by two levels of arousal).

A second test of validity concerns the extent to which the level of arousal affects our results. We set out to determine if partitioning psychological dimensions by level of arousal would lead to meaningful differences in how the data are distributed. An inspection of the correlations within each of the three studies supported the hypothesis that arousal exists as a separate and meaningful entity. If the correlations are broken down by arousal condition, a consistent pattern of results holds up across our three studies. Correlations of low-arousal dimensions with themselves and correlations of high-arousal dimensions with themselves are higher than the correlations obtained when low-arousal dimensions are correlated with high-arousal dimensions. This pattern can be seen by comparing the medians of the correlations of homogenous arousal dimensions with those for heterogenous arousal dimensions within each study. In all three studies there were 45 correlations involving the low-arousal condition, 45 correlations involving the high-arousal conditions, and 100 correlations when high and low arousal were compared. In our first study the medians of the correlations were .447, .654, and .348, for the low-low, high-high, and low-high sets of correlations, respectively. Similarly, in our second study, the median correlations were .730, .718, and .586 for the low-low, high-high, and low-high sets of correlation. Finally, in our third study, the median correlations were .694, .802, and .574 for the low-low, high-high, and low-high sets of correlation. Although the medians of the correlations vary between the studies, the pattern within the studies remains the same. The correlations involving variables of different arousal levels are considerably lower than those involving the same arousal level.

In sum, a principle components analysis and inspection of the correlations within and across arousal for our three studies supports the hypothesis that the EPITAT measures 10 independent dimensions of personality organization that change relative to level of arousal. Further work is thus necessary to establish discriminant and concurrent validity with other and related measures and criteria. These results set the stage for the investigation of: (a) the shifts in these dimensions within normal subjects under different conditions of arousal, wherein we test whether in normal subjects there is flux in personality organization (Experiment 1); (b) the differences in the predominant organization between normal and inpatient subjects relative to level of arousal, wherein we test whether degree of psychopathology broadly defined determines the degree of flux and the predominant mode of organization (Experiment 2); and (c) different modes of responding relative to arousal conditions between normal, inpatient-borderline, and inpatient-psychotic subjects (Experiment 3). A more general Discussion of Experimental Findings section follows the reporting of the Results for all three experiments.

Experiment 1: *Shifts in the Predominant Mode of Responding in Normals From Low- to High-Arousal Conditions*

Hypothesis. In Experiment 1, we hypothesize that, as assessed under low- versus high-arousal condition, normal subjects will be found to score at different modal levels of personality organization on the 10 psychological dimensions on the EPITAT. We expect that subjects in the low-arousal condition will produce higher scores than in the high-arousal condition.

Method

Subjects. The subjects were 40 volunteers, 20 male and 20 female. All were students in an urban university. We refer to them as normals, although they were not formally screened for psychopathology, because they were recruited from classes and are thus undiagnosed. The subjects ranged in age from 23–44, with a mean age of 28 years.

Instrument. The Thematic Apperception Test, scored using the EPITAT rating system.

Procedure. Each subject was given a consent form, explaining that the study involved an examination of how they think and feel, with specific emphasis on happiness, sadness, and ambitiousness. A full set of TAT cards was presented, with a constant order of presentation (1, 5, 15, 14, 10, 13MF, 12M, 3BM, 16). The TAT was administered in the standard manner, as recommended by Allison, Blatt, and Zimet (1968). Trained research assistants administered the TAT cards and recorded the responses verbatim. In addition, the assistants were trained to record significant nonverbal behaviors, including changes of affectivity, tone of voice, movements, posture, and so on, that occurred during the administration.

Following completion of the administration, subjects were debriefed and provided an explanation of the study. As described in the section on Reliability, the TAT cards were then scored by application of the 10 EPITAT dimensions, by trained raters who were blind as to knowledge of the specific hypotheses, group membership, and experimental design. From the complete set of TAT cards, the EPITAT scores for Cards 1 and 13MF were selected to represent the subject's performance under the low- and high-arousal conditions, respectively.

Results and Discussion

A series of paired T-tests, with Alpha set a priori at .05, were used to compare the mean response levels of the normal subjects. Level of arousal was the independent variable. The dependent variable was the mean modal level of responses given by the subjects for each of the dimensions within the high- and low-arousal condition. The mean level of response was computed by summing the scores each subject obtained on the 10 psychological dimensions on the EPITAT and dividing by the total number of dimensions (10) in each arousal condition.

For all of the dependent variables, the low-arousal mean was greater than the high-arousal mean. The one exception was the temporality dimension. The mean scores of subjects on a particular dimension under both arousal conditions are presented in Table 4.1. The results of the paired T-tests are shown in Table 4.2.

The results from this experiment indicate that normal subjects do shift to lower epigenetically defined modes of personality dimensions under a condition of high arousal as compared to under a condition of low arousal. This is important evidence in support of our hypothesis. Normals have generally been thought of as those individuals with the most stable personality organization. We found significant shifts in personality dimensions in response to the arousal conditions they were exposed to. In the low-arousal condition the normal subjects scored at

TABLE 4.1
Results of Normal Subjects on Dimensions
Under High and Low Arousal

	Min	Max	X̄	SD
HiAffExp	1.50	4.00	2.85	.813
LoAffExp	2.00	5.00	3.72	.697
HiAffTol	1.00	4.00	2.67	.863
LoAffTol	2.00	5.00	3.67	.816
HiUseObj	1.00	4.00	2.57	.816
LoUseObj	2.00	5.00	3.57	.674
HiCenDec	2.00	4.00	3.05	.667
LoCenDec	2.00	5.00	3.77	.716
HiPersAg	1.50	4.00	2.87	.666
LoPersAg	2.00	5.00	3.67	.730
HiDefens	1.00	4.00	2.75	.881
LoDefens	2.00	5.00	3.67	.674
HiThreat	1.50	4.00	3.05	.857
LoThreat	3.00	5.00	3.97	.678
HiNeeds	2.00	4.50	3.05	.686
LoNeeds	2.00	5.00	3.77	.803
HiEmp	2.00	4.00	3.00	.743
LoEmp	2.00	5.00	3.45	.724
HiTemp	2.00	5.00	3.27	.786
LoTemp	2.00	5.00	3.57	.748

TABLE 4.2
Paired T-Tests Comparing Psychological Dimensions and Level of Arousal

	$\bar{X}$ Diff	Standard Error	t	p
HiAffExp vs. LoAffExp	-0.875	0.841	4.65	.001
HiAffTol vs. LoAffTol	-1.000	0.778	5.74	.001
HiUseObj vs. LoUseObj	-1.000	0.811	5.51	.001
HiCenDec vs. LoCenDec	-0.725	0.769	4.22	.001
HiPersAg vs. LoPersAg	-0.800	0.715	5.00	.001
HiDefins vs. LoDefens	-0.925	0.893	4.63	.001
HiThreat vs. LoThreat	-0.925	1.055	3.92	.001
HiNeeds vs. LoNeeds	-0.725	1.032	3.14	.005
HiEmp vs. LoEmp	-0.450	0.667	3.01	.007
HiTemp vs. LoTemp	-0.003	0.992	1.35	.197

a mean level just below Mode 4; under high arousal this mean level dropped to Mode 3. The higher Mode 4 was temporarily supplanted by a lower mode of response under a condition of increased arousal.

The data from this experiment concur with epigenetic thinking that predicts, even in a normal population, that the various levels of personality dimensions as defined by the EPITAT appear in response to changing task conditions. That this was shown in a normal population, in which there is expected to be the least amount of flux within dimensions, provides support for our belief that our analysis of the narratives on the TAT allows us to index momentary shifts in response to degrees of arousal. It appears that our instrument, the EPITAT, can measure these shifts.

These shifts lead us to suspect that, under certain conditions, predictable patterns of cognition and emotion characterizing lower modal levels are employed by individuals usually organized at a higher level. The normal subject possesses personality characteristics similar to the disturbed subject when stressed. This is virtually an operational definition of the concept of regression. As such, these findings have important implications for diagnosis and the clinical inference procedure. If normal subjects show systematic changes in their modal level of responses to changes in arousal, then it would be interesting to compare these changes to those observed in an inpatient sample. This was explored in our second experiment.

Experiment 2: *Differences Between Predominant Mode of Responding Between Normals and Inpatients Under High- and Low-Arousal Conditions*

Hypothesis.   In Experiment 2, we compare the modal level of responses of a normal sample versus an inpatient sample relative to degree of arousal. We are specifically concerned with the comparisons between the means of each group under both arousal conditions and whether these mean levels of responses will shift and how far the shift will extend across arousal conditions. We hypothesize that the inpatient sample will exhibit a lower mean modal level of response under both conditions than the mean modal level observed in the normal sample. We further hypothesize that the degree of shift is greater for the inpatient sample across arousal conditions than for the normal sample.

Method

Subjects.   The subjects in this experiment were divided into 2 samples, a normal sample and an inpatient sample. The subjects were 15 males and 15 females, with gender virtually evenly distributed between the samples, each group consisting of 8 males and 7 females. Subjects ranged in age from 16–54, with a mean age of 28. The normal group was composed of 15 students at an urban University, screened for Axis 1 and Axis 2 diagnoses. The inpatient group was composed of an aggregate of 15 hospitalized psychiatric patients, 5 with a DSM-III, Axis 1 (primary) diagnosis of schizophrenia, 5 with a diagnosis of bipolar disorder, and 5 with a diagnosis of schizoaffective disorder. The hospitalized patients were screened for signs of organic pathology and subnormal intelligence, and were not included in the study if such signs were found in their records. The diagnoses were made on the basis of admissions interviews, independent of the administration of the TAT.

Instrument.   The Thematic Apperception Test, scored using the EPITAT rating system.

Procedure.   The EPITAT was administered according to the procedures of Experiment 1.

Results and Discussion

In Experiment 2, we are interested in comparing the modal level of personality organization of normals and inpatients relative to degree of arousal. The design is a 2 by 2 ANOVA: two levels of arousal crossed with the two sample groups. Arousal is a within-subject factor and group membership is a between-subject factor. Means for arousal effects are reported in Table 4.3. Post-hoc tests were done using Fisher's LSD method. The results of this analysis are reported in Table 4.4.

The results show that the responses of normals and inpatients are significantly different from one another on all 10 dimensions, such that normals score significantly higher than inpatients on each dimension. The results also indicate that the responses given by both normals and inpatients significantly differed under the two arousal conditions. In examining the differences between normals and an inpatient sample under high- and low-arousal conditions, we expected to find

TABLE 4.3
Results of Normal Subjects and Inpatients on Dimensions
Under High and Low Arousal

	Min	Max	$\bar{X}$	S.D.
LoAffect Expression				
Normals	3.00	5.00	4.17	.654
Inpatients	2.00	5.00	3.10	.930
HiAffect Expression				
Normals	2.50	5.00	3.67	.699
Inpatients	1.00	3.00	1.73	.623
LoAffect Tolerance				
Normals	3.00	5.00	4.10	.632
Inpatients	1.50	4.00	2.80	.751
HiAffect Tolerance				
Normals	2.00	5.00	3.47	.855
Inpatients	1.00	3.00	1.93	.729
LoUse of Object				
Normals	3.00	5.00	4.03	.581
Inpatients	2.00	4.00	3.03	.611
HiUse of Object				
Normals	2.50	4.50	3.30	.649
Inpatients	1.00	3,00	1.83	.699
LoCentration/Decentration				
Normals	3.00	5.00	4.07	.651
Inpatients	2.00	5.00	3.13	1.125
HiCentration/Decentration				
Normals	2.00	5.00	3.83	.699
Inpatients	1.00	4.00	1.19	.766
LoPersonal Agency				
Normals	3.00	5.00	4.07	.776
Inpatients	2.00	5.00	2.83	.880
HiPersonal Agency				
Normals	2.00	5.00	3.33	.957
Inpatients	1.00	3.00	2.00	.802
LoDefense				
Normals	3.50	5.00	4.23	.530
Inpatients	2.00	5.00	2.83	.880
HiDefense				
Normals	2.00	5.00	3.33	.645
Inpatients	1.00	3.00	1.87	.812
LoThreat				
Normals	3.50	5.00	4.27	.495
Inpatients	1.00	5.00	2.97	1.109
HiThreat				
Normals	2.50	4.50	3.33	.699
Inpatients	1.00	3.00	2.07	.776
LoNeed				
Normals	3.00	5.00	4.23	.594
Inpatients	1.00	5.00	3.03	.972
HiNeed				
Normals	2.00	5.00	3.57	.776
Inpatients	1.00	3.50	1.87	.640
LoEmpathy				
Normals	3.00	5.00	3.90	.573
Inpatients	2.00	5.00	3.60	.849
HiEmpathy				
Normals	1.50	5.00	3.03	.767
Inpatients	1.00	3.00	2.00	.627
LoTemporality				
Normals	1.00	5.00	3.53	.972
Inpatients	2.00	5.00	3.07	1.100
HiTemporality				
Normals	2.00	5.00	3.60	.737
Inpatients	1.00	3.50	2.37	.767

TABLE 4.4
Univariate F-Tests Comparing Normal Subjects' and Inpatients'
Mean Scores on EPITAT Dimensions

	SS	df	MS	F	p
Affexp	33.750	1	33.750	42.792	0.001
Error	22.083	28	0.789		
AffTol	30.104	1	30.104	51.293	0.001
Error	16.433	28	0.587		
UseObj	22.817	1	22.817	44.728	0.001
Error	8.417	28	0.301		
CenDec	30.104	1	30.104	34.034	0.001
Error	24.767	28	0.885		
PersAg	24.704	1	24.704	21.471	0.001
Error	32.217	28	1.151		
Defens	28.107	1	28.107	39.956	0.001
Error	19.633	28	0.701		
Threat	24.704	1	24.704	30.184	0.001
Error	22.917	28	0.818		
Needs	31.538	1	31.538	46.467	0.001
Error	19.000	28	0.679		
Empath	22.817	1	22.817	37.324	0.001
Error	17.117	28	0.611		
Temp	10.838	1	10.838	9.842	0.004
Error	30.833	28	1.101		

differences between the two groups; it was the specific differences in terms of modal shifts that were of primary interest. An inspection of the mean level of response given by the two samples under different levels of arousal show that normals generally score at or around Mode 4 under low-arousal condition and drop to Mode 3 under high arousal. This essentially replicates our first study. Inpatients, on the other hand, generally score at or around Mode 3 under the low-arousal condition and drop to Mode 2 and below under the high-arousal condition. The extent of shift is similar; both drop approximately one mode under the high-arousal condition. However, it is where the shifts begin and end that appear to differentiate the two groups and to be of diagnostic significance.

There were also significant interaction effects between group membership and degree of arousal on three of the dimensions: Affect Expression, Centration/Decentration, and Empathy. The effects were as follows: Affect Expression: $F (2,28) = 9.717$, $p < .005$; Centration/Decentration: $F (2,28) = 6.926$, $p < .014$; Empathy: $F (2,28) = 4.990$, $p < .034$. In all cases the interaction effects are attributable to the drop in the inpatient sample mean under high arousal when contrasted with the lack of a downward shift in the normal sample on these dimensions. For the dimension Affect Expression, the normal sample scored at a mean level of 4.17 for low arousal and 3.67 for high arousal, whereas the inpatient sample scored at a mean level of 3.10 for low arousal and 1.73 for high arousal. For the dimension Centration/Decentration, the normal sample scored at a mean level of 4.07 for low arousal and 3.83 for high arousal, whereas the inpatient sample scored at a mean level of 3.13 for low arousal and 1.93 for high arousal. For the dimension Empathy, the normal sample scored at a mean level of 3.90 for low arousal and 3.60 for high arousal, whereas the inpatient sample scored at a mean level of 3.03 for low arousal and 2.00 for high arousal. For the inpatient sample the shifts on the dimensions that have a significant interaction with arousal level are similar to the shifts on those dimensions that do not. However, for the normal sample, there was no pronounced downward shift in those dimensions involved in the significant interaction effect. This disparity between the two groups is what accounts for the interaction effect. One can thus recognize severe psychopathology most readily by capacities along these dimensions. These dimensions tend to be most stable for normals, yet for inpatients they remain as equally impaired as the other dimensions. Clinically, then, the severely disturbed inpatient displays three particular areas of vulnerability:

1. Under high arousal, inpatients tend to be particularly unable to modulate, control, and express a wide and appropriate affect array, whereas normals retain these capacities.

2. Under high arousal, inpatients lack differentiation of self and other and struggle over enmeshment and issues of internal and external control, whereas normals maintain a sense of differentiation and capacities associated with intact self/other and inner/outer boundaries.

3. Under high arousal, inpatients' knowledge and understanding of others is markedly inefficient and impaired, whereas normals retain a well understood sense of the other as a sentient being.

In sum, our second experiment has shown that the EPITAT is capable of distinguishing between normals and inpatients in terms of level of personality dimensions across arousal conditions. The EPITAT was able to highlight specific dimensions of personality in which normals remain stable while inpatients do not. We attempt to expand upon Experiment 2 by further refining the degree of psychopathology contained within the inpatient sample. In our third experiment we compare normals with two different types of inpatient samples. Specifically, we want to determine if two inpatient groups that differ by diagnosis exhibit different psychological dimensions under a given arousal condition.

Experiment 3: *Differences Between Normal, Inpatient-Borderline, and Inpatient-Psychotic Subjects in Their Predominant Mode of Responding Under High- and Low-Arousal Conditions*

Hypothesis.   In Experiment 3, we compare the modal level of responses between normals, an inpatient-borderline group, and an inpatient group diagnosed with a major psychotic disorder. We hypothesize that the three groups differ in their mean response level under the high- and low-arousal conditions.

Method

Subjects.   The subjects were 30 individuals, falling into three broad diagnostic groups. Ten had a primary Axis 1 diagnosis of psychosis, equally divided between schizophrenia and major affective disorder, 10 had a primary Axis 2 diagnosis of borderline personality disorder, and 10 were normals, students at an urban University. Indication of subnormal intelligence or organic pathology was grounds for exclusion from this study. Diagnoses were made independent of the assessment procedure, as in Experiment 2. These groups were chosen in order to represent a full range (neurotic, borderline, psychotic) of levels of organization (Kernberg, 1975). Males and females were equally distributed throughout the three groups.

Instrument.   The Thematic Apperception Test, scored using the EPITAT rating system.

Procedure.   The EPITAT was administered to the three samples as described in Experiment 1.

Results and Discussion

In this experiment, we are interested in the ability of the EPITAT to distinguish between normal subjects and two independent groups of inpatients diagnosed as either possessing borderline pathology or a major psychotic syndrome. The design was a 2 by 3 ANOVA, two levels of arousal by three groups. Arousal was a repeated measure. Group membership was the between-subject factor. Post-hoc tests were done using Fisher's LSD method.

The results indicate that the EPITAT significantly differentiated normals from the two inpatient samples on all dimensions except for the temporality dimension, essentially replicating Experiment 2. However, the EPITAT was unable to differentiate between the two inpatient groups. The borderline sample scored at approximately the same modal level under both high and low arousal as did the psychotic sample.

DISCUSSION OF EXPERIMENTAL FINDINGS

In Experiment 1, we compared normal subjects under conditions of low and high arousal. The results have important implications for our epigenetic model. From the perspectives of other models, normals may be thought of as possessing stable personality organizations in which dimensions are relatively resilient and resistent to regression. This stability is what facilitates adaptation to the demands of internal and external reality.

We found statistically significant differences in dimensions in response to two levels of arousal. We take this to represent the proclivity for equivalent momentary shifts in their personality organization. Specifically, under low arousal, the mean scores of our normal population was at a Modal level 4. This modal level is defined by us as characterized by conflict over subjectively accessible ideational and Oedipal concerns, such as mature conflicts over sexuality, rivalry, moral anxiety, competence, and guilt. Mode 4 thus represents an epigenetic level of personality generally consistent with normal or neurotic concerns. However, under high-arousal conditions, on the average, the normals' mean dropped to Mode 3. The Oedipal-level capacities of Mode 4 give way to a Mode 3 concern with self-esteem maintenance, the protection of illusions concerning the self in relationship to others, dispelling illusions about one's proper place in the social world, and the preservation of autonomy over thought and action.

An important inferential step is our postulation that moving from a higher to a lower mode due to increased arousal is a demonstration of the phenomenon of regression, and those people who respond to a regressive pull in the testing situation will experience a similar regressive pull in a real life context, or, as we are especially interested in understanding, the psychotherapeutic context. Broadly defined, Mode 4 capabilities are subject to a regressive pull under the high-arousal condition and are superceded by Mode 3 capabilities. On occasion, shifts to lower levels, which we construe as yet deeper regressions, were also observed, and seem to constitute a regular aspect of some normals' experience. These results are understandable from the viewpoint of psychoanalytic theory, and lend support to the construct validity of the modal hierarchy of the EPITAT. The regression is a general group trend, and this generic finding is of course subject to further refinement with the idiographic use of the EPITAT in order to illuminate specific triggers to regression for individuals.

Following this line of reasoning, our results shed light upon a phenomena long observed in the clinical situation, that the quality of a self-other interaction (e.g., between therapist and patient) momentarily shifts regressively when certain threatening (arousing) conditions within the dyad become present, and progressively when the dyad properly modulates arousal (Passik & Wilson, 1987). We are not suggesting that a normal individual will necessarily display a global regression when overaroused; rather, that particular dimensions of thinking, feeling, and acting that are normative at lower epigenetic modes can emerge under some stressful conditions. In other words, we believe that regression is best conceptualized as occurring along particular dimensions.

When seen through the lens of the EPITAT, the regressive characteristics of a normal personality organization appear epigenetically similar to the normal characteristics of a more severely disturbed personality organization. In striving to understand how this is so, in Experiment 2 we examine the differences between normals and a mixed severely disturbed inpatient sample under high- and low-arousal conditions. Although we expected to find differences between the two groups, it was the specific differences in terms of modal organizational shift that were of primary interest.

Our results showed that the inpatients and normals significantly differed in their modal levels of organization. Normals scored at a higher modal level than did the inpatient sample, under both high- and low-arousal conditions. Replicating the findings of Experiment 1, normals shift from Mode 4 to Mode 3 as they move from high to low arousal. Our inpatient sample on average scored, under low arousal, at a modal level of just under 3, which is the modal level that normals regressed to under high arousal. The inpatients, under high arousal, displayed a drop to Modal level 2. The reader is reminded that the typical concerns of Mode 2 pertain to issues of self-regulation, to a psychobiologically dominated representational period that bridges sensorimotor and imagistic representational capacities, polarized experiences of self and other, and acute anxieties over separation phenomena. This regression has as its endpoint dimensions of personality defined as not subjectively accessible to the adult's memorial retrieval. Psychobiologically encoded motives dominate during Modes 1 and 2. The inpatients' regressive shift from Mode 3 to 2 is therefore more problematic than the normals' regressive shift from Mode 4 to 3, because the individual becomes under the sway of motivations less under conscious control, draws objects in to even more primitive enactments and self-regulatory demands that are difficult to understand through introspection, and poses serious challenges to a person's capacity for therapeutic alliance. This makes clinical sense. Inpatients, at their highest organization as reflected by their low arousal stories, retain the ability to self-regulate (see Wilson, Passik, & Faude, in press), albeit using immature defenses. An inchoate autonomy and a fragile (because it is often unrealistic, grandiose, and illusory) system for maintaining self-esteem is in evidence. Under high arousal, though, the inpatients temporarily regress from Mode 3 to Mode 2, or Mode 1 in some cases. We understand this to suggest that they might seek inner regulation of tension and other rudimentary affect states through symbiotic-like strivings. Anaclitic depression, also referred to at times as empty or abandonment depression, becomes the mode-specific depressive reaction (Wilson, 1988). Depending upon character style, other people dimensionally organized at Mode 2 may express primitive rage that sequesters them from a regulating other (Malatesta & Wilson, 1988). The regression to Mode 2 appears to signal a return to a reliance upon preverbal patterns that maintains the fragile stability of the self possible at this level (Wilson 1986). Therefore, the difference between normals and inpatients is not merely one of more or less stability of a personality organization. More to the point is where the regressions begin and end, and whether they end at a level in which self-regulation fails or cannot be autonomously maintained. This phenomenon has been described by several analytic clinicians. For research purposes it is desirable to be able to specify such trends through a model that maps onto a reliable and valid instrument.

The interaction effects for centration/decentration, affect expression, and empathy suggest that these dimensions are the most stable and least susceptible to regression in normals. Our interpretation of this finding is that because inpatients remain vulnerable to regression along these dimensions, it is possible that they are linked to those psychological dilemmas that precipitate hospitalization. Future research is necessary to help us understand the ways in which these dimensions are related to symptoms of major psychiatric diagnoses. For the present, we limit ourselves to the observation that, as compared to normals, inpatients live in worlds in which others are poorly known, perceive themselves at the center of this world, and excursions out of this egocentric world are marked by inappropriate expressions of affectivity, which is the "language" of preverbal states (Wilson & Malatesta, in press).

It is a well-known fact that some borderlines are subject to micropsychotic episodes that can make them temporarily appear schizophreniform, noted from the perspective of both psychoanalysis (Kernberg, 1975) and psychological testing (Singer, 1977). At such times, many such patients are hospitalized until they can recompensate. In Experiment 3, although replicating the results of Experiment 2, we failed to find significant differences between inpatient borderlines and inpatient psychotics. That is, the functioning of the borderline group was impaired enough at the time the measures were applied (shortly after admission) to merit hospitalization. It is possible that if we were to test an outpatient borderline sample, the EPITAT might be able to differentiate between borderlines and psychotics.

The dimension of temporality was not significant in Experiment 1, that utilized normal subjects, but was significant in Experiments 2 and 3, that utilized psychiatric samples. This leads us to suspect that impairments of temporality may be linked to regressions to the lower epigenetic modes, but are relatively resilient to regressive flux in the higher modes. This reminds us of Freud's (1900) repeated admonition that the unconscious as constituted of primary process mentation is timeless, whereas the secondary process as expressed through the lexical abilities of the higher modes is time-bound. This point will require further investigation.

Implications

How information is processed, acquired, coded and stored, the impact of culture, and the functions of affectivity and intersubjective transactions are central concerns of any theory of the ontogenesis of mind. Psychoanalysis is at its most elegant a theory of therapeutic process, and often tends to generalize from the clinical situation into other domains as the basis for its theory of mind. The psychoanalytic theory of therapeutic process, to be sure, receives more attention from most clinical psychoanalysts than its more abstract "general psychology" theory of mind (Klein, 1976). Our conceptualization of the EPITAT dimensions and the results of the experiments in a sense interdigitates with the concepts contained in a broader and more general psychology of mind. In this way, we recognize no unbreachable boundary between the theory of clinical process and a general psychological theory of mind. In attempting this integration, the epigenetic focus of our model leads us to reexamine a certain psychoanalytic view of psychic structure formation.

In psychoanalysis, the concept of psychic structure is often invoked in order to help explain these central processes of mind. Used in this way, it perhaps attempts to explain too much and therefore serves to explain too little. Rapaport and Gill's (1959) definition of psychic structure, as hypothetical entities that are enduring, characterized by a slow rate of change, within which, between which, and by means of which mental processes take place, are hierarchically ordered, and inferred from actions has in many ways dominated the way in which ego psychologists viewed the concept of psychic structure. In studying Rapaport, one is struck by the effort being made to formulate a general psychology within an ego psychological framework (cf. Hartmann, Kris, & Loewenstein, 1946) that explained the stability of structures over time. David Rapaport's intellectual program can be seen to hinge on articulating those elements involved in the transformations from perception and attention cathexes to the establishment of psychic structure. This emphasis upon internalization and the formation of psychic structure has led to more recent views such as equating the absence of structure with pathology (e.g. Kohut, 1971), and early fixation with impaired or pathological structure. By assuming that structure is stable over time, an element of predictability and generalizability is introduced that delimits some of the complexities of human action. The notion of stable structure is carried further by Kernberg (1975, 1976), who speaks of three stable levels of psychic structuralization (neurotic, borderline, psychotic), characterized largely by stage dominant defensive functioning, in which repression predominates on a neurotic level and splitting on a borderline level.

We have empirically questioned, albeit as yet in broad terms, whether personality organization is a relatively stable, enduring configuration of traits and capacities that can be flexibly applied in the service of adaptation. This way of thinking about personality has been empirically referenced by our new instrument. In a general sense our results lead us to assert that stability of a personality organization may be a more fluid phenomenon than was thought to be the case. In the course of our preliminary research we have found that the observed shifts in dimensions of an individual's personality organization determines its relative stability. Our results show that it is not global instability that leads to pathology, rather it appears to be the crossing into the presubjective psychological world of Modes 1 and 2.

These results lead us to offer a refinement of definition of the concept of stability. In our model, stability does not imply relatively static psychic structure but comes to refer to two distinct features: (1) stability of dimension, in which there is a maintenance of relatively mode consistent abilities, between dimensions at any one time and within dimensions over time, despite regressive and progressive flows along particular dimensions, and (2) stability of adaptation, whereby a "lower boundary" posed by Mode 2, regression to loss of autonomous self-regulation, is not too often crossed or overly permeable, despite the range of regressive and progressive fluctuation. Lack of stability refers to the converse of these propositions: (1) an instability of dimension, with broad heterogeneity of dimensions responsive to particular regressive and progressive pulls, in which one cannot find a consistency between dimensions, and (2) instability of adaptation, in which the range of regressive and progressive flow results in a crossing of the boundary imposed by Mode 2. Our research suggests that most normal people, in these senses, are characterized by a normative instability of dimension but a stability of adaptation. Most severely disturbed people, by contrast, are characterized by instability of dimension and adaptation.

There are several limitations in this series of studies that are important to mention. First, our samples for all three experiments tended to be small enough so that replication seems necessary in order to have confidence in internal and external validity. Second, in introducing the EPITAT, we have relied upon a between-groups analysis of the data, to the exclusion of a within-group analysis or even longitudinal repeated measures studies that examine changes in EPITAT scores over time within individuals. A profile analysis using the EPITAT will be of a very different sort than when using this instrument for nomothetic research, in the sense that some important individual differences will be amplified rather than washed out as error variance. To this end, our research team and several dissertation projects are presently examining such possibilities as shifts within individuals over time in psychotherapy, narcissistic and antisocial pathology as viewed through the lens of the EPITAT, the nature of preverbal affective involvement in opiate addiction, the EPITAT profiles of parents with schizophrenic offspring, and the correlation of specific dimensional shifts within diagnostic groups.

REFERENCES

Allison, J., Blatt, S., & Zimet, C. (1968). *The Interpretation of Psychological Tests*. New York: Harper and Row.

Atkinson, J. (1980). Thematic apperceptive measurement of motivation in 1950 and 1980. In G. d'ydewalle & W. Lens (Eds.), *Cognition, human motivation, and learning*. Hillsdale, NJ: Lawrence Erlbaum Associates.

Bergman, A. & Wilson, A. (1984). Thoughts about stages on the way to empathy and the capacity for concern. In J. Lichtenberg, M. Bornstein, & D. Silver. (Eds.), *On empathy* (pp. 81–103). Hillsdale, NJ: Analytic Press.

Bruner, J. (1964). The course of cognitive growth. *American Psychologist, 19*, 1–15.

Bruner, J. (1986). *Actual minds, possible worlds.* Cambridge, MA: Harvard University Press.

Bruner, J. (in press). *Life in text* (tentative title). Cambridge, MA: Harvard University Press.

Ehrenreich, J. (1989). *Psychodynamic aspects of personality and sociocultural identity.* Unpublished dissertation, New School for Social Research, New York City.

Freedman, N. (1985). The concept of transformation in psychoanalysis. *Psychoanalytic Psychology, 2,* 317–339.

Freedman, N., Berzofsky, M., & Passik, S. (in preparation). Levels of associative organization. S.U.N.Y. Downstate Medical Center, Brooklyn, NY.

Freud, S. (1900). The interpretation of dreams. In J. Strachey (Ed. and Trans.), *The standard edition of the complete psychological works of Sigmund Freud* (Vols. 4 & 5). London: Hogarth Press.

Gedo, J. (1979). *Beyond interpretation: Towards a revised theory for psychoanalysis.* New York: International Universities Press.

Gedo, J. (1981). *Advances in clinical psychoanalysis.* New York: International Universities Press.

Gedo, J. (1984). *Psychoanalysis and its discontents.* New York: Guilford Press.

Gedo, J. (1988). *The mind in disorder.* Hillsdale, NJ: Analytic Press.

Gedo, J., & Goldberg, A. (1973). *Models of the mind: A psychoanalytic theory.* Chicago: University of Chicago Press.

Grand, S., Freedman, N., Feiner, K., & Kiersky, S. (in press). Notes on the progressive and regressive shifts in levels of integrative failure: A preliminary report on the classification of severe psychopathology. *Psychoanalysis and Contemporary Thought.*

Greenspan, S. (1979). Intelligence and adaptation: An integration of psychoanalytic and Piagetian developmental psychology. *Psychological Issues, 47/48.* New York: International Universities Press.

Hartley, D., Geller, J., & Behrends, R. (in preparation). *A manual for assessing the developmental level of object representations.* Langley Porter Institute, San Francisco.

Hartmann, H., Kris, E., & Loewenstein, R. (1946). Comments on the formation of psychic structure. In *Papers on psychoanalytic psychology. Psychological issues, #14* (pp. 27–55). New York: International Universities Press.

Horowitz, M. (1972). Modes of representation of thought. In Horowitz, M. *Image formation in psychotherapy.* New York: Aronson. Reprinted (1983).

Kernberg, O. (1975). *Borderline conditions and pathological narcissism.* New York: Aronson.

Kernberg, O. (1976). *Object relations theory and clinical psychoanalysis.* New York: Aronson.

Kitchener, R. (1978). Epigenesis: The role of biological models in developmental psychology. *Human Development, 21,* 141–160.

Klein, G. (1976). *Psychoanalytic theory: An exploration of essentials.* New York: International Universities Press.

Kohut, H. (1971). *The analysis of the self.* New York: International Universities Press.

Krystal, H. (1975). Affect tolerance. *The annual of psychoanalysis, 3,* 179–219.

Malatesta, C., & Wilson, A. (1988). Emotion/cognition interaction in personality development: A discrete emotions, functionalist approach. *British Journal of Social Psychology, 27,* 91–112.

Murstein, B. (1963). *Theory and research in projective techniques, Emphasizing the TAT.* New York: Wiley.

Noy, P. (1969). A Revision of the psychoanalytic theory of the primary process. *International Journal of Psychoanalysis, 50,* 147–154.

Passik, S., & Wilson, A. (1987). Technical considerations on the frontier between supportive and expressive modes in psychotherapy. *Dynamic Psychotherapy, 5,* 51–62.

Rapaport, D., & Gill, M. (1959). The points of view and assumptions of metapsychology. *International Journal of Psychoanalysis, 40,* 153–162.

Rapaport, D., Gill, M., & Schafer, R. (1968). *Diagnostic psychological testing*. New York: International Universities Press.

Ricoeur, P. (1977). The question of proof in Freud's psychoanalytic writings. *Journal of the American Psychoanalytic Association, 25*, 835–872.

Schachtel, E. (1945). Subjective definitions of the Rorschach test situation and their effect on test performance. *Psychiatry, 8*, 419–448.

Schafer, R. (1954). *Psychoanalytic interpretation in Rorschach testing*. New York: Grune & Stratton.

Schafer, R. (1967). How was this story told? In *Projective testing and psychoanalysis*. New York: International Universities Press, pp. 181–210.

Schafer, R. (1983). *The analytic attitude*. New York: Basic Books.

Singer, M. (1977). The borderline diagnosis and psychological tests: Review and research. In P. Hartacollis (Ed.), *Borderline personality disorders* (pp. 193–212). New York: International Universities Press.

Spence, D. (1982). *Narrative and historical truth*. New York: Norton.

Spence, D. (1987). *The Freudian metaphor*. New York: Norton.

Steele, R. (1979). Psychoanalysis and hermeneutics. *International Review of Psychoanalysis, 6*, 389–411.

Stern, D. (1985). *The interpersonal world of the infant: A view from psychoanalysis and develop mental psychology*. New York: Basic Books.

Vaillant, G. (1977). *Adaptation to Life*. Boston: Little, Brown, and Company.

Werner, H. (1948). *The comparative psychology of human development*. New York: International Universities Press.

Werner, H., & Kaplan, B. (1963). *Symbol formation: An organismic-developmental approach to language and expression of thought*. New York: Wiley.

Wilson, A. (1986). Archaic transference and anaclitic depression: Psychoanalytic perspectives on the treatment of severely disturbed patients. *Psychoanalytic Psychology, 3*, 237–256.

Wilson, A. (1988). Levels of depression and clinical assessment. In H. Lerner & P. Lerner (Eds.), *Primitive mental states and the Rorschach* (pp. 441–462). New York: International Universities Press.

Wilson, A., & Malatesta, C. (in press). Affect and the compulsion to repeat: Freud's repetition compulsion revisited. *Psychoanalysis and Contemporary Thought*.

Wilson, A., Passik, S., & Faude, J. (in press). Self regulation and its failures. In J. Masling (Ed.), *Empirical approaches to psychoanalytic theory, Vol. 3*. Hillsdale, NJ: Analytic Press.

5 The Role of Self-Prediction in Psychological Assessment

Timothy M. Osberg
Niagara University

J. Sidney Shrauger
State University of New York at Buffalo

The face of psychological assessment has undergone numerous changes during the past decade, some of which have been more than cosmetic. During the 1980s there has been a proliferation of new psychological measurement devices, assessing dimensions ranging from boredom to bulimia, as well as major revisions of some of the more prominent traditional and contemporary measures such as the WAIS, MMPI, and MCMI. Although the development of new measures and the revision of old ones is nothing new to psychological assessment, some recent developments seem more substantive than superficial. For example, the movement toward increased computerization of the assessment process may bring with it radical changes in how assessment measures are administered, scored, and interpreted.

Another consistent trend among leading assessment theorists has been the call for greater use of self-assessment data (e.g., Burisch, 1984; Dana, 1984; Korchin & Schuldberg, 1981; Lanyon, 1984; Mischel, 1977; Rorer & Widiger, 1983). If this call is heeded, it could significantly influence the assessment process. The present chapter focuses on self-assessment data. Along with the theorists just cited, we believe that greater use of a person's own self-knowledge would contribute significant new data to the field of psychological assessment.

In some ways, the central focus of our chapter may appear to be paradoxical. On the one hand, the notion that self-report or self-assessment should form an integral part of the process of psychological assessment seems obvious. At the same time, how much we really utilize people's self-judgments in the process of gaining a better understanding of them and their situations and in constructing strategies to work with them is unclear.

Although self-assessment data are frequently collected as part of the assessment process, such data are usually accorded only a secondary place behind other sources of information such as historical information, formalized testing data, and often nebulous "clinical judgment." This is unfortunate because, as we have argued elsewhere (Shrauger & Osberg, 1981; 1982), individuals possess a more extensive data base about themselves than even the most ambitious psychological assessor is likely to develop.

The assessment process can be viewed as a means of making predictions or decisions about a person. Therefore, we would like to encourage assessors to develop ways to assist the individual to utilize his or her own self-knowledge to formulate *self*-predictions. Moreover, we believe that such predictions should be given greater weight in the assessment process. In this chapter, our discussion focuses on the evidence supporting such a view. We also describe our recent program of research in which we have attempted to systematically examine (1) the information people use in formulating self-predictions; (2) how accuracy in self-prediction is achieved; and (3) what personal attributes are associated with accurate self-prediction. In addition, we explore the potential clinical advantages of relying more on people's own self-predictions.

THE VALUE OF SELF-ASSESSMENTS

Over the years, theorists have presented varying views on whether self-judgments can form a useful basis for predicting behavior. Indeed, the enterprise of psychological assessment is founded on the implicit assumption that most people are either unable or unwilling to accurately assess their own functioning, and that professionals are, therefore, required to form useful assessments.

Skepticism about the validity of self-reports comes from at least three distinct traditions. From the field of psychological assessment there is concern about the influence of response sets on self-report tests, particularly social desirability (Crowne & Marlowe, 1964; Edwards, 1957). In a similar vein, social psychological research points out that people employ a variety of self-presentational strategies in interacting with others (e.g., Schlenker, 1980), and that self-descriptions are often not reflections of people's actual beliefs, but strategies designed to motivate and protect them (Norem & Cantor, 1986; Showers & Cantor, 1985), or to shape others' reactions to them (Swann, 1983; Swann & Hill, 1982; Swann & Read, 1981a; Swann & Read, 1981b).

Whereas these views question people's *motivation* to describe themselves accurately, psychoanalytic theory questions their *capability* to accurately describe themselves. The psychoanalytic viewpoint assumes that people do not have adequate insight into important processes that influence their behavior, particularly unconscious ones (Freud, 1933). From a different wing of the capability camp, cognitive theorists contend that people manifest biases and shortcomings in their inference processes that impact upon judgments about oneself in the same fashion that they influence judgments of others (e.g., Bradley, 1978; Kahneman & Tversky, 1973; Nisbett & Ross, 1980; Ross, 1977).

Another view, however, is that self-relevant information is particularly abundant and salient to the individual and that people are highly motivated to obtain information about their own skills and personal competence (Trope, 1983). Recent work suggests that, because of the privileged information people have about themselves, they conceptualize the self differently from the way they construe others (McGuire & McGuire, 1986), and that they are motivated to develop *accurate* self-appraisals (e.g., Strube, Lott, Le-Xuan-Hy, Oxenberg, & Deichmann, 1986; Strube & Roemmele, 1985). The abundance of information available about ourselves relative to other people seems self-evident. Certainly, with a lifetime of self-observation people have a vast amount of evidence about their actions and internal states on which to base judgments about future behavior.

Not only is self-relevant information extensive, but it also seems particularly salient to most people. A number of studies have suggested that information about the self is remembered more quickly and accurately than information about others, suggesting that people have better access to relevant data when judging themselves than when judging others (e.g., Bower & Gilligan, 1979; Kuiper, 1981; Markus, 1977; Markus, Crane, Bernstien, & Siladi, 1982; Rogers, Kuiper, & Kirker, 1977).

Awareness of the advantages of self-judgments, as well as the resurgence of interest in the concept of the self in personality and social psychology, may explain the greater acceptance of the potential value and importance of self-assessments that has recently ensued. As noted earlier, several personality assessment theorists, in taking stock of the field's current status, have shown a striking convergence in their recommendations for the future (Burisch, 1984; Dana, 1984; Korchin & Schuldberg, 1981; Lanyon, 1984; Mischel, 1977; Rorer & Widiger, 1983). In varying degrees, all suggest that attention to people's self-assessments would provide greater validity than more traditional means of predicting behavior.

Other recent work suggests the potential value of employing people's self-judgments as *predictions*. For example, there is much evidence that people do spontaneously make self-predictions (Osberg, 1983) and that a significant component of the self-concept is a future or projected "possible" self (Markus & Nurius, 1986; Markus & Wurf, 1987). We believe it is time to tap this aspect of self in the process of psychological assessment.

In summary, both the quantity of information available and people's level of attentiveness suggest the value of employing self-assessments, but the potential for deliberate and unconscious distortion argues for caution. Both views have intuitive appeal, and the relative merit of each position can be best evaluated by examining the validity of self-predictions, particularly as they compare with judgments made from other sources.

THE USE OF SELF-PREDICTION IN PSYCHOLOGICAL ASSESSMENT

There are empirical as well as rhetorical justifications for exploring the utility of self-assessments. A number of sources of evidence suggest that self-judgments are consistent with more objective indices of behavior. Based on an extensive examination of the validity of self-assessments, Mabe and West (1982) concluded that self-assessments of performance in job and school situations typically showed significant positive correlations with other performance criteria. Strong relationships between self-assessments and more objective data have also been shown in a variety of other behavior domains such as alcohol consumption (Sobell & Sobell, 1975; 1978), depression (Billings, Cronkite, & Moos, 1983; Lewinsohn, Mischel, Chaplin, & Barton, 1980), insomnia (Coates et al., 1982), return rates to prison (U.S. Department of Justice, 1985), smoking (Morrell, King, & Martin, 1986), weight control (Stunkard & Albaum, 1981), and dropout from psychotherapy (Beck et al., 1987). Even for groups such as prison inmates, wherein use of self-assessments would appear to be contraindicated, it has been found that such data can be remarkably predictive of important criteria and, therefore, useful in assessment and treatment (Osberg & Nielsen, 1988).

In order to demonstrate that professionals ought to rely more heavily on self-assessments, it must be shown that such data provide a basis for behavior prediction that matches or surpasses the usefulness of the data traditionally used in forming assessments and making predictions, such as test data, historical information, and so forth. In reviewing numerous research studies that have explored the comparative accuracy of self-predictions with predictions formulated through more traditional assessment methods, Shrauger & Osberg (1981) found comparisons between these two prediction methods in several important areas of interest to professional assessors, including reactions to psychotherapy, adjustment following psychiatric hospitalization, job performance, academic achievement, vocational choice, and peer ratings. Although the strength of our conclusion varied depending on the behavior predicted and the type of assessment technique against which self-predictions were pitted (e.g., projective measures, behavioral observation, clinical judgment, etc.), our overall judgment was that self-assessments were at least as accurate as traditional assessment methods, if not more so.

In areas such as the prediction of vocational choice and peer assessments, self-predictions were consistently superior (e.g., Gottfredson & Holland, 1975; Hase & Goldberg, 1967). In the prediction of psychotherapy outcome or academic achievement, self-predictions were slightly favored (e.g., Uhlenhuth & Duncan, 1968; Wallace & Sechrest, 1963). Finally, with respect to the prediction of post-hospital adjustment and job performance, the superiority of one prediction method over the other could not be determined (e.g., Clum, 1978; Mischel, 1965).

Projective measures have generally been poor predictors relative to self-assessments, with the possible exception of TAT indices of achievement. But even psychometrically sophisticated self-report inventories such as vocational interest tests have been outperformed by direct self-predictions. Assessments based on previous behaviors (e.g., grades for predicting academic achievement, previous hospitalization for predicting post-hospital adjustment) are generally comparable to self-assessments. Because no other assessment method has emerged as clearly superior to self-assessments, there is ample evidence to support the increased use of self-prediction in psychological assessment. Numerous questions remain, however, concerning the utility of self-predictions, for example, how people formulate self-predictions and determinants of accuracy of self-prediction both within and across individuals.

DETERMINANTS OF ACCURACY IN SELF-PREDICTION

In a recent series of studies, Osberg and Shrauger (1986) have explored several major issues in the study of self-prediction. First, attention was given to the process of self-prediction and to identifying the strategies best suited to the formulation of accurate self-appraisals of potential future behavior. Second, we attempted to identify individual difference variables that relate to accuracy. Finally, we examined the properties of self-predictions that serve as cues to their accuracy.

In Study 1, 48 subjects made a series of self-predictions about a variety of relevant life events, which are listed in Table 5.1. These subjects were then interviewed concerning the information they used in making their predictions about these 55 situations.

The subjects' open-ended responses were content analyzed. As can be seen in Table 5.2, responses were reliably coded into five basic categories varying in their frequency of usage. The most common basis for self-prediction was attention to frequency of one's own past behavior, which we labeled *personal base rate* information. Assessment of the *circumstances* likely to affect the occurrence of an event and *personal dispositions* relating to the behavior in question formed the next two most commonly used bases for self-predictions. Thus, the information people use as a basis for self-prediction appeared reducible to a small number of discrete categories.

Study 1 set the stage for Studies 2 and 3, which explored the relationship between type of information usage and self-prediction accuracy. In Study 2, 62 subjects made self-predictions. For each prediction, subjects indicated one or two primary types of information used, by checking one or two of the five categories determined in Study 1. Study 3 manipulated information usage by asking subjects to attend to only one category of information in formulating their predictions. Both studies demonstrated that use of personal base rates or personal

TABLE 5.1
Life Events Questionnaire

1. Become very upset with or had an argument with a very close friend.

2. Gone an entire night without sleep.

3. Gone to services at a church or synagogue.

4. Been a patient in a hospital or infirmary because of some physical problem.

5. Gone into finals with a grade of C or below in at least one course.

6. Introduced yourself to someone you are attracted to.

7. Started to play a new sport or physical activity you had not done before.

8. Gone on a diet.

9. Offered advice to a friend concerning his or her romantic relationship.

10. Attended a concert for which an admission was charged.

11. Skipped a class because you simply didn't feel like attending.

12. Met someone new with whom you would like to have a romantic relationship.

13. Agreed with someone or said something you didn't mean or feel so as not to hurt their feelings.

14. Treated someone to a meal in a restaurant or a night out.

15. Will not have enough money to pay an important bill.

16. Will at some point feel generally dissatisfied with the way your life is going.

17. Said something in class which the instructor or another class member criticized or disagreed with.

18. Been to a party or social gathering where you felt badly enough about the way you behaved that you worried about it the next day.

19. Made a joke or humorous comment in a group of at least five people which they laughed at.

20. Will have felt forced to tell someone important to you something negative about themselves which you did not want them to hear.

21. Will have refused to do something that other people wanted you to do even though you thought it might cost you their friendship.

22. Will have written a paper, done a project, or done an exam that you felt was the best you had ever done.

23. Will have changed your plans regarding what you will mainly be doing in the summer (going to school or working, type of work will be doing).

24. Found yourself refereeing an argument between friends or members of your family.

25. Went to a class unprepared for the discussion because you had not done the required reading.

26. Had to have some dental work done.

27. Changed your hairstyle or type of haircut.

28. Will have been unable to sleep for at least an hour after going to bed because you were thinking about some important decision or event.

29. Gotten high on some type of drug besides alcohol.

30. Begun to work particularly hard on some activity in which you currently lack confidence.

31. Will have been in a situation in which your performance was poorer than usual because you were anxious.

(continued...)

(Table 5.1 continued)

32. Go into final exams with a grade of A in at least one course.

33. Will have ended a romantic relationship.

34. Bought a phonograph record.

35. Will have had some type of sexual experience which you have not had previously.

36. Have fallen in love.

37. Will have read at least one book that was not assigned or recommended for a course.

38. Have had period of a day or more when you could get very little done because you feel too down and discouraged.

39. Will have had sexual relations.

40. Become intexicated.

41. Will have gone out and partied when you should have been studying for exams.

42. Eaten your main meal of the day alone.

43. Had an argument with one of your parents that was serious enough for you to be concerned about it the following day.

44. Met someone new whom you expected to be a close friend for years to come.

45. Eaten a type of food you have never had before.

46. Been awakened from your sleep by an unpleasant dream.

47. Gone to a movie.

48. Been rejected by a group of people who were important to you.

49. Participated in a group sports activity.

50. Fretted or worried on and off for at least three days about something someone said that angered or upset you.

51. Had a sexual experience that was frustrating or unsatisfying.

52. Parents or family members will have complained to you about some important aspect of your behavior of which they disapprove.

53. Will have learned that someone whom you thought liked you said something unfavorable about you.

54. You will have become jealous of someone else's good fortune.

55. You will have begun to smoke cigarettes or increased your cigarette smoking.

dispositions was associated with the formulation of more accurate self-predictions. Finally, from a fourth study we determined that more confidently stated self-predictions and predictions that differed from what the person expected for the average individual (which we called *distinctive* predictions) were more accurate than less confident or nondistinctive predictions.

We also explored individual differences in self-prediction accuracy, finding that people high in Fenigstein, Scheier, and Buss's (1975) concept of *private self-consciousness* (or self-attention/introspectiveness) and low in their notion of *public self-consciousness* (or concern with how one is viewed by others) are more accurate self-predictors. Thus, being more self-attentive or introspective, less concerned with public image, and focusing on one's past behavior or rele-

TABLE 5.2

Information Category Titles, Descriptions, and Examples, Along with Percentages of Responses Coded into Each Category

Category	Description	Examples	Percent of Responses Coded into Category
Personal Base Rate	The past frequency with which the event or behavior has occurred.	"Well I predicted that... would occur because I've done that a lot in the past." "I said it wouldn't happen because it never happened before."	41%
Circumstances	Assessment of the likelihood that certain conditions which enhance or reduce the likelihood of the behavior will occur.	"Since I'm already in love and that's not likely to change in the next few months, I predicted it (falling in love) wouldn't occur." "I predicted it wouldn't occur (having an argument with a close friend) because all my close friends are back home and I won't be returning for a while."	29%
Personal Dispositions	Knowledge of one's own personal qualities or dispositions.	"I predicted I wouldn't (tell a joke before a group) in the near future because I'm basically a shy person." "I have this thing (stand) against drugs so I predicted I wouldn't use them."	18%
Intention	The specific intention of whether or not to perform a behavior.	"I've made plans to do that already (go to a movie) so I predicted it would happen."	5%
Population Base Rate	The frequency of the behavior or event in the general population.	"That happens to everybody (having a period where upset or depressed) so I said it would happen."	1%

104

vant personal dispositions as a basis for self-prediction all seem to be factors associated with accuracy in self-prediction. In addition, the personality dimension of *need for cognition* (Cacioppo & Petty, 1982) also appears to demonstrate some potential as a moderator of self-prediction accuracy (Osberg, 1987) as reflected in the recent finding that individuals high in this quality, compared to those low, show a stronger attitude-behavior correspondence (Cacioppo, Petty, Kao, & Rodriguez, 1986).

SELF-PREDICTION: RECENT AREAS OF STUDY

The four studies reported earlier provided answers to a number of questions concerning the process of self-prediction; however, they represent only a beginning in gaining a deeper understanding of this phenomenon. Our more recent research has begun to address a number of basic and applied issues that are of relevance in further clarifying the place of self-prediction within the broader context of psychological assessment.

Although the available data on self-prediction certainly argue for its relative accuracy and its potential relevance in decision-making situations, the best understanding of this process, its merits and its potential, rests on a careful consideration of how self-predictions are arrived at and what factors are likely to influence their accuracy. Much of our most recent research has derived from such a conceptualization. Four factors have been identified that are seen as contributing substantially to the possible accuracy of people's predictions about their behavior. These are (1) previous relevant behavior; (2) knowledge of the context, determinants, and nature of the behavior to be predicted; (3) changes in motivation, competence, or other factors which might modify people's predictions relative to their previous behavior; and (4) biases in self-appraisal. The potential significance of each of these factors is examined along with research relevant to each.

Previous Relevant Behavior.   Perhaps the primary advantage we have as judges of our own behavior is a vast store of personal history from which we can draw. For example, when people are asked to judge their likely response in a social situation, they have their entire previous social history from which to draw. In many contexts we know something about how well we have performed in the past, how likely we've been to engage in certain activities, and how often certain events have occurred to us. Even for events over which we may have little control, such as getting sick, we may have extensive evidence about their frequency of occurrence.

Previous behavior may well be the most frequent and, following conventional wisdom, the best source of information for predicting future behavior. In work we have cited previously, self-prediction accuracy is increased if people focus on their personal base rates (Osberg & Shrauger, 1986). Thus, it seems important at the outset to determine whether self-predictions offer a significant improvement over previous behavior as predictors of future actions. A few observations with regard to the available data may be instructive.

The evidence on the relative accuracy of self-predictions versus previous behavior involves predictions primarily from three areas: academic achievement, sports, and responses to interventions for clinical problems ranging from phobias to addictive behaviors. The work is somewhat scattered and seldom builds on previous investigations, with the notable exception of that stemming from Bandura's concept of self-efficacy (Bandura, 1977), which focuses on changing specific maladaptive behavior.

The overall results of our review suggest self-predictions stack up fairly well when compared to measures of previous behavior in the prediction of future behavior. Research on self-efficacy in particular has shown that self-efficacy measures, which most often are self-predictions of the likelihood of engaging in fear-inducing behavior, by and large outperform measures of previous behavior in similar situations for the prediction of future behavior. Similarly, although not as widely researched, studies of the prediction of competitive sport performance have shown, for the most part, that self-predictions are better predictors of future performance. For example, a prototypical study conducted by Lee (1982) demonstrated that gymnasts' self-predictions were more accurate than previous scores in predicting performance at a gymnastics meet. Thus, there is accumulating evidence to suggest that people's self-predictions are often superior to measures of previous behavior as predictors of future behavior.

Knowledge of the Context, Determinants, and Nature of the Behavior to be Predicted. Although past research has shown that attention to past behavior enhances self-prediction accuracy (Osberg & Shrauger, 1986), determining what previous behavior is "relevant" may not always be easy. Even if people are carefully informed about the outcome to be predicted, they may not know the factors most crucial to achieve that outcome: that is, what behaviors will be required of them, what situations they will be asked to respond to, and what the relative importance of each of these factors will be. In part, this issue parallels Bandura's (1977) differentiation between efficacy and outcome expectations, yet it is more complex because people may not know the conditions under which they will be asked to perform certain behaviors or have a clear sense of how strongly various behaviors will be related to the outcome. For example, if job applicants are asked to predict their work success they should know the job description and the criteria that will be used to evaluate them. The importance of first-hand familiarity in predicting future performance has been demonstrated a number of times in the literature on attitude-behavior correspondence (e.g., Fazio & Zanna, 1978; Regan & Fazio, 1977).

If people know what behavior is being predicted and the context in which it occurs, they may have an advantage over other predictors of that behavior. The individual may know better than anyone what personal attributes will be the strongest determinants of their actions. In a new job, for example, people might have a clear picture that their reaction to their boss or interest in the work will be the most important determinants of their performance, whereas this might not be easily determined from their previous work history. Conceivably, of course, such initial impressions might prove inaccurate. However, it is interesting that in a previously cited study, self-prediction accuracy increased when people were asked, while making their predictions, to focus on the personal attributes that were most important in determining the behavior predicted (Osberg & Shrauger, 1986). With this focus accuracy was as high as when people were asked to focus on their previous behavior. By contrast, in previous studies in which self-prediction has been found to be notably inaccurate, the individuals have often had little knowledge of the behaviors about which self-predictions were made (e.g., Melei & Hilgard, 1964).

In sum, the more one has had the opportunity to behave in situations very similar to those within which behavior is to be predicted, the more accurate the predictions should be. Although this exposure to similar situations may increase the absolute level of self-prediction accuracy, it would also provide a much more representative sample of previous behavior that could also increase the accuracy of that data source as a predictor.

Changes in Motivation, Competence, or Other Factors.   Among the most important predictions that people may make about themselves in many contexts is how they will change. Will they benefit from psychotherapy? Will their athletic performance improve or deteriorate? Will they do as well in college as they did in high school? Can they lick a bad habit?

We explored the issue of the accuracy of self-predicted change in a study examining amateur golfers' self-predictions of their future performance, focusing specifically on people's abilities to predict change, which is often the most meaningful predictor in any athletic or other competence-related activities. Although not of great clinical relevance, the study did allow us to move the examination of self-prediction out of the laboratory and into the real-world domain of athletics, where self-prediction of change is salient and engaged in spontaneously. The subjects were 23 male and 11 female amateur golfers who were members of a university golf league. Midway through a 9-week season, subjects completed a set of personality questionnaires and made self-predictions of their next week's score and their average over the remainder of the season. Subjects' previous week's scores and season averages at the time of prediction were used to calculate indices of predicted change. For predictions of next week's score, an index of predicted improvement was calculated by subtracting subjects' previous week's scores from their predicted next week's scores. A similar procedure was followed in determining a measure of predicted improvement in average score by subtracting subjects' current averages from their predicted averages over the rest of the season.

On the basis of the measures of predicted improvement, subjects who predicted their scores to stay the same or only slightly improve (separately for next week's score and average over the rest of the season) were assigned to the Low Improvement condition, whereas those predicting higher levels of improvement were assigned to the High Improvement condition for the purpose of the analysis. With reference to predicting next week's score, subjects in the Low Improvement condition had a mean predicted improvement of 1.5 strokes and those in the High Improvement condition had a mean predicted improvement of 4.2 strokes. The corresponding figures for predicting average over the rest of the season were -0.1 and 5.0 strokes, respectively.

As expected, subjects in the High Improvement condition, relative to those in the Low Improvement condition, actually improved significantly more in separate analyses for both next week's performance and average over the rest of the season. For the prediction of next week's score, subjects in the High Improvement condition compared to those in the Low Improvement condition improved by more strokes the next week (M s = 2.44 vs. -0.88, respectively), $F(1,32) = 6.23, p <$ .02. A similar pattern was found in the prediction of average score the rest of the season (M s = 2.17 vs. 0.71, respectively), $F(1,32) = 4.46, p = .05$.

Consistent with the previous research cited earlier, scores on Fenigstein et al.,'s (1975) measure of private self-consciousness moderated accuracy in self-prediction of change in golf performance. For the prediction of improvement in next week's scores, among high private self-consciousness subjects, those in the High Improvement condition showed substantially greater actual improvement than those in the Low Improvement condition (M s = 4.00 vs. -2.20, respectively), $t(14) = 3.35, p < .01$. A similar effect for the prediction of improvement in average scores trended toward significance ($p < .09$). These effects did not reach significance for low self-consciousness subjects.

Thus, within the realm of athletics there is some evidence suggesting that self-predictions of change are particularly diagnostic of actual subsequent change, especially for people high in private self-consciousness. Obviously, however, future research into the utility of self-predictions of change should be carried out in more clinically relevant contexts.

Biases in Self-prediction.   Much of the skepticism about self-appraisals described earlier has been based on the recognition that they may be systematically biased, typically by various self-protective strategies. However, many perceptions that have been labeled as reflecting a "bias" have not necessarily been demonstrated to be inaccurate but rather only to reflect different interpretations of positive and negative events (e.g., Miller & Ross, 1975). Furthermore, with only a few exceptions (e.g., Weinstein, 1980; 1982; Weinstein & Lachendro, 1982) studies have focused on the interpretation of previous rather than future events. Our investigations of possible bias in making predictions of future behavior have focused on two areas: (1) predictable individual differences in bias, and (2) accuracy of *self-* judgments versus judgments by people who know the person well. The latter area of investigation may be particularly useful as a means of detecting bias when judging the self.

One source of bias in self-appraisal that has been discussed by a number of theorists (e.g., Greenwald, 1980; Shrauger, 1982; Weinstein, 1980), and that may often erode the accuracy of predictive judgments, is people's tendencies to be *unrealistically optimistic* in their expectations for the future. An initial study in this area conducted by Weinstein (1980) revealed that, compared to ratings of others' chances, people rate their own chances of experiencing positive events as above those of other people while rating their chances of experiencing negative events as below others'. Weinstein's findings also suggested that part of this effect may stem from individuals' "egocentrism," a tendency to focus on factors that improve their likelihood of experiencing desired outcomes while assuming these factors are not present for others as well (Weinstein & Lachendro, 1982). Other writers have interpreted findings such as Weinstein's as reflecting people's tendencies to see the world through "rose-colored glasses," emphasizing that such optimistic biases may be self-protective and even play a role in maintaining mental health (Greenwald, 1980; Shrauger, 1982; Taylor & Brown, 1988).

Interestingly, data from two other studies (Alloy & Abramson, 1979; Lewinsohn et al., 1980) suggest that depressed individuals lack such optimistic biases and in effect may be more realistic in their self-appraisals than normals. Alloy and Abramson (1979) determined that mildly depressed subjects, when compared to normals, were remarkably more accurate in their judgments of control over desirable and undesirable experimental task outcomes. Similarly, Lewinsohn et al., (1980) demonstrated that depressed people's self-appraised social skills showed a remarkable fit to actual ratings made of their social competence by outside observers, whereas normals tended to overestimate themselves on these dimensions. Both studies suggest that depressed people may lack the illusory self-enhancement that seems abundantly present in normal people, and that the depressed may be "sadder but wiser."

Following from this work, two recent studies have examined the relationship between depression and self-predictions about future events. To test traditional cognitive theories of depression (Abramson, Seligman, & Teasdale, 1978; Beck, 1967) that emphasize the role of pessimism or hopelessness about the future, Alloy and Ahrens (1987) compared predictions of the likelihood of future positive and negative academic outcomes of mildly depressed and nondepressed college students. They found that mildly depressed individuals are more pessimistic in their self-predictions of future events than are nondepressed people. When comparing the predictions for self versus others, nondepressed subjects exhibit a self-enhancing pattern wherein, relative to their judgments about others, they overestimate their likelihood of successful outcomes while underestimating their chances for failure. The depressed subjects did not display such a pattern, leading Alloy and Ahrens to infer that the depressed may evidence greater realism in their predictions than normals. These authors have also recently demonstrated similar differences as a function of depression levels in the prediction of a variety of other positive and negative life events, personal attributes, and behaviors (Alloy, Ahrens, & Albright, 1988).

Pyszczynski, Holt, and Greenberg (1987) also reported data suggesting that depressed individuals are more pessimistic in their predictions of hypothetical future life events when compared with the nondepressed. Comparing people's self-predictions with their predictions for others, they concluded that, relative to the nondepressed, depressed people appear more realistic or "evenhanded" in their predictions for the future. They also report that depressed people's tendencies to be overly self-focused may in part explain their pessimistic predictive tendencies.

Although both Alloy and Ahrens (1987) and Pyszczynski et al. (1987) provide strong evidence that depressed people are more pessimistic in their self-predictions of future life events, their results provide no evidence regarding *accuracy* of the self-predictions of depressed and nondepressed people. Employing the same methodology for exploring self-prediction accuracy used in our earlier research (Osberg & Shrauger, 1986), we compared the accuracy of mildly depressed and nondepressed college students' self-predictions of future life events. Several types of accuracy in self-prediction were examined. In addition to overall accuracy in prediction across all of the events predicted, the accuracy of subjects' "optimistic" and "pessimistic" predictions was examined. Optimistic predictions were defined as the prediction of positive events to happen or negative events not to happen. Pessimistic predictions were defined as the prediction of negative events to happen or positive events not to happen. Fifteen events were rated by the authors as positive and 35 were rated as negative.

Consistent with the previously discussed research, the predictive pessimism of the depressed compared to the nondepressed was notable. Depressed subjects made significantly more pessimistic predictions than the nondepressed (M s = 24.9 vs. 20.0, respectively), $F (1,100) = 16.33$, $p < .001$. However, this difference was primarily accounted for by differences in predicting negative events to occur ($p < .001$), as opposed to predicting positive events not to occur ($F < 1$, $p =$ ns).

Turning to the results bearing on accuracy, differences in the accuracy of prediction across all of the events as a function of depression did not emerge. However, accuracy ratios (number of accurate predictions divided by number of predictions of a given type) were also computed separately for optimistic and pessimistic predictions and submitted to arcsine transformations prior to computing ANOVAs. Depressed and nondepressed people did not differ in the accuracy of their optimistic predictions ($F < 1$). However, depressed subjects were significantly more accurate than nondepressed subjects in their pessimistic predictions

(M s $= 76.42\%$ vs. 70.18%, respectively), $F(1,88) = 5.58, p = .02$. This effect was accounted for largely by depressed subjects' greater accuracy in predicting negative events to occur (M s $= 73.67\%$ vs. 63.14%, $p < .01$). There were no differences in the accuracy of predicting positive events not to occur.

These findings suggest, first, that not only do depressed people expect less favorable things to occur to them but that they also report such things as occurring more often. Second, rather than depressed people being generally more accurate than the nondepressed, their realism is confined primarily to the prediction of negative events to occur. Furthermore, the current data suggest that the depressed and nondepressed do not differ in the accuracy of their predictions concerning positive events.

The fact that, for the four types of possible predictions that could be made (occurrence or nonoccurrence of both positive and negative events), the depressed were more accurate than the nondepressed only in predicting the occurrence of negative events suggests a self-fulfilling prophecy interpretation of our findings. That is, depressed subjects' greater accuracy for predicting negative events to happen may owe to the fact that it is much easier to confirm or self-fulfill negative expectations compared to positive ones. In fact, recent data (Showers & Ruben, 1988) suggest that the depressed may actually self-fulfill their negative expectations. The preparatory or coping strategies of depressed people were compared with individuals described as "defensive pessimists." After making relatively pessimistic predictions, these two groups' preparatory strategies directed at an upcoming task were studied over time. Their data suggested that the pessimistic predictions of defensive pessimists energized active and confrontive coping with the upcoming task whereas depressed people's pessimism led to an escapist or avoidant stance as the task drew near. This suggests that the depressed may behave in a way that brings on or self-fulfills their negative predictions.

Certainly the relation of depression to bias in self-prediction needs greater clarification. Some studies have suggested that the depressed are more realistic in their self-appraisals. However, our foregoing discussion suggests that other processes may account for their surface realism, which may be confined to the prediction of negative events and overall may be more apparent than real.

We now turn from individual differences in bias to the question of how important bias is in general. Bias could, for example, undercut the advantages of the extensive data base that people often have when evaluating themselves. To examine the potential hindering effect of self-protective biases, we compared the accuracy of people's self-assessments with assessments made of them by people who knew them well. Close relatives and good friends might have extensive knowledge about a person's previous behavior but not have the same biases in predicting that person's future actions. If so, relatives' or friends' judgments might be as good or better than the person's own self-judgments. In selecting judges it seemed particularly important to choose people whose knowledge of the person was extensive. Previous research on the agreement between self and others' perceptions underscores the importance of attending to others' knowledge of the person (Funder, 1987). When people's knowledge of a target person is modest there is little correlation between their descriptions of the target and the target's self-descriptions (Shrauger & Schoeneman, 1979) but when spouses or close friends are assessed, the agreement is much stronger (Edwards & Klockars, 1981; McCrae, 1982).

In a recently completed study (Ram & Shrauger, 1988), male and female introductory psychology students followed the procedure used by Osberg & Shrauger (1986) in which they predicted the occurrence of a series of events during the next 2 months and then indicated at the end of that time whether or not the events had actually occurred. In addition, predictions for the same events and time period were made for the subject by their mothers and one classmate who knew the subject well. Comparisons of accuracy scores for targets, mothers, and friends indicated that the subjects were more accurate in their self-predictions than were either their mothers or their friends, and that the latter two groups' accuracy did not differ significantly from one another.

It is possible, of course, that subjects distorted their recall of events to appear more accurate, but only a small fraction indicated any awareness that the study had anything to do with self-prediction, and previous research suggests that people are no more accurate in their predictions of events that they recall having predicted than they are for those they do not recall having predicted (Osberg & Shrauger, 1986). However, the available information indicates once again the relative accuracy of self-perceptions, even when judgments are made by others who know the person very well.

SELF-PREDICTION IN CLINICAL CONTEXTS: ISSUES AND APPLICATIONS

Aside from the obvious impact that using people's self-predictions would have in assessment contexts, our focus on the process of self-prediction suggests a number of other potential clinical applications of this phenomenon. In addition, the use of self-prediction in clinical contexts raises some questions or issues for professionals who consider giving greater weight to such data. Some of the issues and applications include (1) using people's self-predictions to foster a sense of collegiality and client responsibility for the work of assessment and treatment; (2) using people's self-predictions as a technique for therapeutic change; (3) viewing unmet self-predicted goals as self-discrepancies that may lead to specific emotional outcomes; and (4) examining the relationship between self-prediction accuracy and psychological adjustment. Each of these issues or applications is considered separately below.

Use of Self-predictions as Fostering Collegiality and Responsibility for Change.   One potential positive side effect of relying more on clients' self-judgments in the assessment process is that it may foster a greater sense of collegiality between assessors and assessees. The benefits of such collegiality may include a more collaborative relationship that will lead clients to be more candid and cooperative, and thus enhance the accuracy of assessments (Mischel, 1977). Others have argued that such collegial or collaborative approaches to assessment, aside from the nonspecific positive effects, produce more useful "individualized" assessments (Fischer, 1985), which involve a give-and-take negotiation between assessor and assessee. Eliciting self-predictions encourages people to talk about themselves more and elaborate more extensively on the potential determinants of their behavior. Finally, a more collegial assessment relationship, which places more emphasis on clients' own self-assessments, may engender greater feelings of responsibility and ownership by clients for therapeutic gains or losses.

The Use of Self-prediction as a Treatment Technique.   Aside from its use as a source of data in assessment, the process of self-prediction may be utilized as an additional tool to meet the goal of therapeutic change. A number of areas of study suggest such a potential use of this process. For example, the use of self-monitoring in behavior therapy programs led to the determination that self-observation or self-recording often produced beneficial effects in and of itself by increasing the frequency of positive behavior and decreasing that of negative behavior (e.g., Kazdin, 1974; Thoresen & Mahoney, 1974). Presumably, the increased attention to problem behaviors and the circumstances in which they occur better prepares and motivates the individual to inhibit these behaviors (Mahoney, Moura, & Wade, 1973; Rimm & Masters, 1979).

More recent data suggest that the act of self-prediction may by itself play a role in engendering more desirable behaviors. In a series of three studies, Sherman (1980) demonstrated that people tend to overpredict the extent to which their future behavior will be socially desirable. The intriguing aspect of his findings was that, compared to individuals who had made no prior predictions, those exhibiting the overprediction of desirable behavior were subsequently more likely to *actually engage* in the behaviors they predicted. Similarly, Greenwald, Carnot, Beach, and Young (1987), in two separate experiments, asked subjects to predict whether they would register to vote and actually vote. Subjects were unanimous in their predictions that they would carry out these behaviors. Furthermore, consistent with Sherman's (1980) findings, those who had made predictions, in comparison with students who had not predicted their voting behavior, were substantially more likely to actually register and vote.

These studies strongly suggest that people are prone to predict that their future behavior will be desirable and that when they make such predictions their subsequent behavior tends to confirm their earlier predictions. Sherman (1980) discussed the potential application of this effect to engendering increased moral behavior. In clinical contexts one might also try to engender predictions of favorable behavioral change in order to build a momentum in the client toward actual change. The procedure would not be unlike efforts to get substance abusers to commit to being abstinent. One potential problem with applying this effect to clinical settings is that clinical samples may not overpredict their participation in socially desirable behaviors to the extent that nonclinical samples do. Therefore, the obvious challenge lies in finding ways to elicit such socially desirable predictions in these people.

Viewing Unmet Self-predicted Goals as Self-discrepancies Leading to Emotional Vulnerabilities. Higgins (1987) recently advanced a theory relating self and affect that he calls *self-discrepancy theory.* It attempts to establish links between various kinds of emotional vulnerabilities and discrepancies between the actual self and either one's ideal or "ought" self. For example, Higgins presents compelling data to suggest that discrepancies between one's actual and ideal self lead to "dejection-related" emotions such as sadness and disappointment, whereas discrepancies between one's actual self and how one feels one ought to be relate more to "agitation-related" emotions such as fear and threat. Higgins' theory and accompanying data suggest that tracking people's self-predicted goals in therapy can be a means of maintaining an ongoing assessment of their vulnerability to various kinds of emotional distress. In line with Higgins' approach, it would be important to identify whether an individual's self-predictions relate to behaviors that they *ideally* would like to engage in or that they feel they *ought* to pursue. Whether or not the ideal or "ought" has been established by oneself or someone else is also important to take into consideration. For a fuller description of self-discrepancy theory see Higgins (1987), Higgins, Bond, Klein, and Strauman (1986), or Higgins, Klein, and Strauman (1985).

The Potential Relationship of Self-prediction Accuracy and Psychological Adjustment. The belief that self-knowledge will relate to psychological adjustment has a long history. A fundamental assumption of psychoanalytic theory, evident in the writings of Freud (1933), was that the acquisition of "insight" or self-knowledge provided the key to overcoming psychological problems. Rogers (1951) emphasized the importance of the individual's gaining full awareness and acceptance of all aspects of the self, a process he labeled *congruence,* as a major step toward attaining psychological health. Gestalt psychology (Perls, 1969; Perls, Hefferline, & Goodman, 1958) has suggested the importance of increasing people's levels of awareness of their own feelings and motives toward the end of improving their functioning. Within the popular literature, best-selling books on self-improvement have trumpeted the virtues of becoming more "self-aware" or "in touch with one's feelings" (Rosen, 1977). Even those who question how knowledgeable people are of the determinants of their behavior (Nisbett & Wilson, 1977) implicitly assume the desirability of such self-knowledge.

Despite the popularity of the view that self-knowledge is an important ingredient in psychological adjustment, it has yet to be subjected to empirical test. Instead, theorists have focused on the more obvious relationship between self-*esteem* and psychological adjustment (e.g., Rogers & Dymond, 1954), which is perhaps more a consequence, rather than a determinant, of adjustment. Our view of the potential value of self-knowledge departs from the traditional. We assume that it is not the acquisition of self-knowledge that is critical to adjustment, but rather the *attainment and use of self-knowledge in a predictive manner* that is crucial. Becoming an accurate self-predictor may allow the person to better appraise potential outcomes of various actions and to select the appropriate behavioral alternative that will maximize gains.

Our ongoing research has begun to examine such an assumption. Viewing our methodology for examining self-prediction accuracy (Osberg & Shrauger, 1986) as a means of assessing the predictive validity of self-knowledge, we have begun to examine differences on global and specific measures of psychological adjustment as a function of the accuracy of people's self-predictions. The development of this methodology alone may represent a contribution to the literature. This stems from the observation that theorists who have emphasized the potential gains to be achieved by increasing self-knowledge have typically not defined the term very precisely or operationalized a means through which such an assumption could be tested. If support for this assumption is found, it would provide an impetus for developing intervention programs to enhance people's effective use of their pool of self-knowledge in the formulation of more predictive self-judgments as a means of furthering their psychological adjustment.

CONCLUSION

From the foregoing discussion it is evident that the use of people's self-predictions has the potential to advance the field of psychological assessment toward the goal of improved behavior prediction. However, we have much to learn about the limits and applications of the self-prediction process. One important issue for future research is to further examine the circumstances under which self-prediction accuracy can be improved. We have begun to explore this issue in our findings that accuracy is greater when people attend to their past behavior or relevant personal dispositions. Nevertheless, a more systematic exploration of the factors that enhance accuracy can lead to the establishment of more detailed guidelines. Such guidelines could be used by professional assessors toward the aim of enhancing people's self-prediction accuracy. Advances in this area not only could have implications for the field of psychological assessment but could potentially be applied toward the broader goal of improving the quality of self-report data used in psychological research in general.

ACKNOWLEDGMENTS

This chapter is an expanded version of a presentation given at the annual mid-winter meeting of the Society for Personality Assessment in San Francisco, March, 1987. Some of the research reported in this article was supported by faculty summer research grants awarded to the first author by the Niagara University Research Council in 1985 and 1987. The authors gratefully acknowledge the comments of Charles Spielberger & Kathleen Nielsen on an earlier draft, and Franceen Rosati who performed admirably in processing the manuscript.

REFERENCES

Abramson, L. Y., Seligman, M. E. P., & Teasdale, J. D. (1978). Learned helplessness in humans: Critique and reformulation. *Journal of Abnormal Psychology, 87,* 49–74.

Alloy, L. B., & Abramson, L. Y. (1979). Judgment of contingency in depressed and nondepressed students: Sadder but wiser? *Journal of Experimental Psychology: General, 108,* 441–485.

Alloy, L. B., & Ahrens, A. H. (1987). Depression and pessimism for the future: Biased use of statistically relevant information in predictions for self versus others. *Journal of Personality and Social Psychology, 52,* 366–378.

Alloy, L. B., Ahrens, A. H., & Albright, J. S. (1988, April). Depression and self-prediction: The role of attributional style and comparison others. In T. M. Osberg (Chair), *Self-prediction: The role of depression, defensive pessimism, and information usage in expectations for the future.* Symposium presented at the annual meeting of the Eastern Psychological Association, Buffalo, NY.

Bandura, A. (1977). Self-efficacy: Toward a unifying theory of behavioral change. *Psychological Review, 84,* 191–215.

Beck, A. T. (1967). *Depression: Clinical, experimental, and theoretical aspects.* New York: Harper & Row.

Beck, N. C., Lamberti, J., Gamache, M., Lake, E. A., Fraps, C. L., McReynolds, W. T., Reaven, N., Heisler, G. H., & Dunn, J. (1987). Situational factors and behavioral self-predictions in the identification of clients at risk to drop out of therapy. *Journal of Clinical Psychology, 43,* 511–520.

Billings, A. G., Cronkite, R. C., & Moos, R. H. (1983). Social-environmental factors in unipolar depression: Comparisons of depressed patients and nondepressed controls. *Journal of Abnormal Psychology, 92,* 119–133.

Bower, G. H. (1981). Mood and memory. *American Psychologist, 36,* 129–148.

Bower, G. H., & Gilligan, S. G. (1979). Remembering information related to one's self. *Journal of Research in Personality, 13,* 420–432.

Bradley, G. W. (1978). Self-serving biases in the attribution process: A reexamination of the fact or fiction question. *Journal of Personality and Social Psychology 36,* 56–71.

Burisch, M. (1984). Approaches to personality inventory construction. *American Psychologist, 39,* 214–227.

Cacioppo, J. T., & Petty, R. E. (1982). The need for cognition. *Journal of Personality and Social Psychology, 42,* 116–131.

Cacioppo, J. T., Petty, R. E., Kao, C. F., & Rodriguez, R. (1986). Central and peripheral routes to persuasion: An individual difference perspective. *Journal of Personality and Social Psychology, 51,* 1032–1043.

Clum, G. A. (1978). Personality traits and environmental variables as independent predictors of posthospitalization outcome. *Journal of Consulting and Clinical Psychology, 46,* 839–843.

Coates, T. J., Killen, J. D., George, J., Marchini, E., Silverman, S., & Thoresen, C. (1982). Estimating sleep parameters: A multitrait-multimethod analysis. *Journal of Consulting and Clinical Psychology, 50,* 345–352.

Crowne, D. P., & Marlowe, D. (1964). *The approval motive.* New York: Wiley.

Dana, R. (1984). Megatrends in personality assessment: Toward a human science professional psychology. *Journal of Personality Assessment, 48,* 563–579.

Edwards, A. L. (1957). *The social desirability variable in personality assessment and research,* New York: Dryden.

Edwards, A. L., & Klockars, A. J. (1981). Significant others and self-evaluation: Relationships between perceived and actual evaluations. *Personality and Social Psychology Bulletin, 7,* 244–251.

Fazio, R. H., & Zanna, M. P. (1978). Attitudinal qualities relating to the strength of the attitude-behavior relationship. *Journal of Experimental Social Psychology, 14,* 398–408.

Fenigstein, A., Scheier, M. F., & Buss, A. H. (1975). Public and private self-consciousness: Assessment and theory. *Journal of Consulting and Clinical Psychology, 43,* 522–527.

Fischer, C. T. (1985). *Individualizing psychological assessment.* Monterey, CA: Brooks/Cole.

Freud, S. (1933). *New introductory lectures on psychoanalysis.* New York: Norton.

Funder, D. C. (1987). Errors and mistakes: Evaluating the accuracy of social judgment. *Psychological Bulletin, 101,* 75–90.

Gottfredson, G. D., & Holland, J. L. (1975). Vocational choices of men and women: A comparison of predictors from the Self-Directed Search. *Journal of Counseling Psychology, 22,* 28–34.

Greenwald, A. G. (1980). The totalitarian ego: Fabrication and revision of personal history. *American Psychologist, 35,* 603–618.

Greenwald, A. G., Carnot, C. G., Beach, R., & Young, B. (1987). Increasing voting behavior by asking people if they expect to vote. *Journal of Applied Psychology, 72,* 315–318.

Hase, H. D., & Goldberg, L. R. (1967). Comparative validity of different strategies of constructing personality inventory scales. *Psychological Bulletin, 67,* 231–248.

Higgins, E. T. (1987). Self-discrepancy: A theory relating self and affect. *Psychological Review, 94,* 319–340.

Higgins, E. T., Bond, R. N., Klein, R., & Strauman, T. (1986). Self-discrepancies and emotional vulnerabilities: How magnitude, accessibility, and type of discrepancy influence affect. *Journal of Personality and Social Psychology, 51,* 5–15.

Higgins, E. T., Klein, R., & Strauman, T. (1985). Self-concept discrepancy theory: A psychological model for distinguishing among different aspects of depression and anxiety. *Social cognition, 3,* 51–76.

Kahneman, D., & Tversky, A. (1973). On the psychology of prediction. *Psychological Review, 80,* 237–251.

Kazdin, A. E. (1974). Self-monitoring and behavior change. In M. J. Mahoney & C. E. Thoresen (Eds.), *Self-control: Power to the person* (pp. 412–418). Monterey, CA: Brooks/Cole.

Korchin, S. J., & Schuldberg, D. (1981). The future of clinical assessment. *American Psychologist, 36,* 1147–1158.

Kuiper, N. A. (1981). Convergent evidence for the self as a prototype: The "Inverted-U RT Effect" for self and other judgments. *Personality and Social Psychology Bulletin, 7,* 438–443.

Lanyon, R. I. (1984). Personality Assessment. *Annual Review of Psychology, 35,* 667–701.

Lee, C. (1982). Self-efficacy as a predictor of performance in competitive gymnastics. *Journal of Sport Psychology, 4,* 405–409.

Lewinsohn, P. M., Mischel, W., Chaplin, W., & Barton, R. (1980). Social competence and depression: The role of illusory self-perceptions. *Journal of Abnormal Psychology, 89,* 203–212.

Mabe, P. A., III, & West, S. G. (1982). Validity of self-evaluation of ability: A review and meta-analysis. *Journal of Applied Psychology, 67,* 280–296.

Mahoney, M. J., Moura, N. G. M., & Wade, T. C. (1973). The relative efficacy of self-reward, self-punishment, and self-monitoring techniques for weight loss. *Journal of Consulting and Clinical Psychology, 40,* 404–407.

Markus, H. (1977). Self-schemata and processing information about the self. *Journal of Personality and Social Psychology, 42,* 38–50.

Markus, H., Crane, M., Bernstein, S., & Siladi, M. (1982). Self-schemas and gender. *Journal of Personality and Social Psychology, 42,* 38–50.

Markus, H., & Nurius, P. (1986). Possible selves. *American Psychologist, 41,* 954–969.

Markus, H., & Wurf, E. (1987). The dynamic self-concept: A social psychological perspective. *Annual Review of Psychology, 38,* 299–337.

McCrae, R. R. (1982). Consensual validation of personality traits: Evidence from self-reports and ratings. *Journal of Personality and Social Psychology, 43,* 293–303.

McGuire, W. J., & McGuire, C. V. (1986). Differences in conceptualizing self versus conceptualizing other people as manifested in contrasting verb types used in natural speech. *Journal of Personality and Social Psychology, 51,* 1135–1143.

Melei, J. P., & Hilgard, E. R. (1964). Attitudes toward hypnosis, self-predictions, and hypnotic susceptibility. *International Journal of Clinical and Experimental Hypnosis, 12,* 99–108.

Miller, D. T., & Ross, M. (1975). Self-serving biases in the attribution of causality: Fact or fiction? *Psychological Bulletin, 82,* 213–225.

Mischel, W. (1965). Predicting the success of Peace Corps volunteers in Nigeria. *Journal of Personality and Social Psychology, 1,* 510–517.

Mischel, W. (1977). On the future of personality measurement. *American Psychologist, 32,* 246–254.

Morrell, E. M., King, A. C., & Martin, J. E. (1986). The validity of cardiac inpatient self-report of smoking. *Behavioral Assessment, 8,* 365–371.

Nisbett, R. E., & Ross, L. (1980). *Human inference: Strategies and shortcomings,* Englewood Cliffs, NJ: Prentice-Hall.

Nisbett, R. E., & Wilson, T. D. (1977). Telling more than we can know: Verbal reports on mental processes. *Psychological Review, 84,* 231–259.

Norem, J. K., & Cantor, N. (1986). Defensive pessimism: Harnessing anxiety as motivation. *Journal of Personality and Social Psychology, 51,* 1208–1217.

Osberg, T. M. (1983). Exploring the process and parameters of self-prediction. (Doctoral dissertation, State University of New York at Buffalo, 1982). *Dissertation Abstracts International, 43,* 3038B.

Osberg, T. M. (1987). The convergent and discriminant validity of the Need for Cognition Scale. *Journal of Personality Assessment, 51,* 441–450.

Osberg, T. M., & Nielsen, K. P. (1988, March). *Prison inmates' self-reports in forensic assessment: Relationship to parole board dispositions.* Paper presented at the annual meeting of the Society for Personality Assessment, New Orleans.

Osberg, T. M., & Shrauger, J. S. (1986). Self-prediction: Exploring the parameters of accuracy. *Journal of Personality and Social Psychology, 51,* 1044–1057.

Perls, F. (1969). *Gestalt therapy verbatim.* Lafayette, CA: Real People Press.

Perls, F., Hefferline, R. F., & Goodman, P. (1958). *Gestalt therapy.* New York: Julian Press.

Pyszczynski, T., Holt, K., & Greenberg, J. (1987). Depression, self-focused attention, and expectancies for positive and negative future life events for self and others. *Journal of Personality and Social Psychology, 52,* 994–1001.

Ram, D., & Shrauger, J. S. (1988). [The accuracy of predictions by self, mothers, and friends]. Unpublished raw data.

Regan, D. T., & Fazio, R. H. (1977). On the consistency between attitudes and behavior: Look at the method of attitude formation. *Journal of Experimental Social Psychology, 13,* 28–45.

Rimm, D. C., & Masters, J. C. (1979). *Behavior therapy.* (2nd. Ed.). New York: Academic Press.

Rogers, C. R. (1951). *Client-centered therapy.* Boston: Houghton-Mifflin.

Rogers, C. R., & Dymond, R. F. (1954). *Psychotherapy and personality change.* Chicago: University of Chicago Press.

Rogers, T. B., Kuiper, N. A., & Kirker, W. S. (1977). Self-reference and the encoding of personal information. *Journal of Personality and Social Psychology, 35,* 677–688.

Rorer, L. G., & Widiger, T. A. (1983). Personality structure and assessment. *Annual Review of Psychology, 34,* 431–463.

Rosen, R. D. (1977). *Psychobabble: Fast talk and quick cure in the era of feeling.* New York: Atheneum.

Ross, L. (1977). The intuitive psychologist and his shortcomings: Distortions in the attribution process. In L. Berkowitz (Ed.), *Advances in experimental social psychology* (Vol. *10,* pp. 173–220). New York: Academic Press

Schlenker, B. R. (1980). *Impression management: The self-concept, social identity, and interpersonal relations.* Belmont, CA: Wadsworth.

Sherman, S. J. (1980). On the self-erasing nature of errors of prediction. *Journal of Personality and Social Psychology, 39,* 211–221.

Showers, C., & Cantor, N. (1985). Social cognition: A look at motivated strategies. *Annual Review of Psychology, 36,* 275–305.

Showers, C., & Ruben, C. (1988, April). Distinguishing pessimism from depression: Negative expectations and positive coping mechanisms. In T. M. Osberg (Chair), *Self-prediction: The role of depression, defensive pessimism, and information usage in expectations for the future.* Symposium presented at the annual meeting of the Eastern Psychological Association, Buffalo, NY.

Shrauger, J. S. (1982). Selection and processing of self-evaluative information: Experimental evidence and clinical implications. In G. Weary & H. Mirels (Eds.), *Integrations of social and clinical psychology* (pp. 128–153). Oxford University Press.

Shrauger, J. S., & Osberg, T. M. (1981). The relative accuracy of self-predictions and judgments by others in psychological assessment. *Psychological Bulletin, 90,* 322–351.

Shrauger, J. S., & Osberg, T. M. (1982). Self-awareness: The ability to predict one's future behavior. In G. Underwood (Ed.), *Aspects of Consciousness* (Vol. *3,* pp. 267–313). London: Academic Press.

Shrauger, J. S., & Schoeneman, T. J. (1979). Symbolic interactionist view of self-concept: Through the looking glass darkly. *Psychological Bulletin, 86,* 549–573.

Sobell, L. C., & Sobell, M. B. (1975). Outpatient alcoholics give valid self-reports. *Journal of Nervous and Mental Disease, 161* 32–42.

Sobell, L. C., & Sobell, M. B. (1978). Validity of self-reports in three populations of alcoholics. *Journal of Consulting and Clinical Psychology, 46,* 901–907.

Strube, M. J., Lott, C. L., Le-Xuan-Hy, G. M., Oxenberg, J., & Deichmann. (1986). Self-evaluation of abilities: Accurate self-assessment versus biased self-enhancement. *Journal of Personality and Social Psychology, 51,* 16–25.

Strube, M. J., & Roemmele, L. A. (1985). Self-enhancement, self-assessment, and self-evaluative task choice. *Journal of Personality and Social Psychology, 49,* 981–993.

Stunkard, A. J., & Albaum, J. M. (1981). The accuracy of self-reported weight. *American Journal of Clinical Nutrition, 34,* 1593–1599.

Swann, W. B., Jr. (1983). Self-verification: Bringing social reality into harmony with the self. In J. Suls & A. G. Greenwald (Eds.), *Psychological perspectives on the self* (Vol. 2, pp. 33–66). Hillsdale, NJ: Lawrence Erlbaum Associates.

Swann, W. B., Jr., & Hill, C. A. (1982). When our identities are mistaken: Reaffirming self-conceptions through social interaction. *Journal of Personality and Social Psychology, 43,* 59–66.

Swann, W. B., Jr., & Read, S. J. (1981a). Acquiring self-knowledge: The search for feedback that fits. *Journal of Personality and Social Psychology, 41,* 1119–1128.

Swann, W. B., Jr., & Read, S. J. (1981b). Self-verification processes: How we sustain our self-conceptions. *Journal of Experimental Social Psychology, 17,* 351–372.

Taylor, S. E., & Brown, J. D. (1988). Illusion and well-being: A social psychological perspective on mental health. *Psychological Bulletin, 103,* 193–210.

Thoresen, C. E., & Mahoney, M. J. (1974). *Behavioral self-control.* New York: Holt.

Trope, Y. (1983). Self-assessment in achievement behavior. In J. Suls & A. G. Greenwald (Eds.), *Psychological perspectives on the self* (Vol. 2, pp. 93–121). Hillsdale, NJ: Lawrence Erlbaum Associates.

Uhlenhuth, E. H., & Duncan, D. B. (1968). Subjective change with medical student therapists: I. Course of relief in psychoneurotic outpatients. *Archives of General Psychiatry, 18,* 428–438.

U.S. Department of Justice, Bureau of Justice Statistics. (1985). *Examining Recidivism* (Publication No. NCJ-96501), Washington, DC: U.S. Government Printing Office.

Wallace, J., & Sechrest, L. (1963). Frequency hypothesis and content analysis of projective techniques. *Journal of Consulting Psychology, 27,* 287–293.

Weinstein, N. D. (1980). Unrealistic optimism about future life events. *Journal of Personality and Social Psychology, 39,* 806–820.

Weinstein, N. D. (1982). Unrealistic optimism about susceptibility to health problems. *Journal of Behavioral Medicine, 5,* 441–460.

Weinstein, N. D., & Lachendro, E. (1982). Egocentrism as a source of unrealistic optimism. *Personality and Social Psychology Bulletin, 8,* 195–200.

6

Rorschach Measures of Psychoanalytic Theories of Defense

Paul Lerner
Toronto Psychoanalytic Society

Howard Lerner
University of Michigan

Beginning with Rapaport, there has been a historically reciprocal and mutually beneficial relationship between psychoanalysis as a theory of personality and psychological test theory and test usage. Although psychological testing within the Rapaport, Gill, and Schafer tradition has served as a pivotal source of generating ideas for theory construction and has provided a method for experimentally evaluating psychoanalytic concepts, psychoanalytic theory has provided a foundation of conceptualization that has given clinical testing a remarkable heuristic sweep never achieved previously. Only recently has psychological testing theory, clinical use, and research begun to keep pace with contemporary developments within psychoanalysis (Kwawer, Lerner, Lerner, & Sugarman, 1980), and as such there is a continued need in psychological assessment to transpose theoretical advances into clinically useful, empirical test-related concepts.

Easer (1974) notes that psychoanalytic theory has never been a static body of knowledge. Historically, psychoanalytic theory has evolved from a concentration on the identification of the instincts and their vicissitudes during psychosexual development, to a focus on defining the characteristics and functions of the ego with specific reference to its defensive organization and role in adaptation, to a more current interest in the early mother–child dyad and its decisive impact on ego development and object relations. This evolution parallels a movement away from an "experience-distant" meta-psychology couched in a mechanistic natural science framework of impersonal structures, forces, and energies to a more "experience-near" clinical theory primarily concerned with the "representational world" as a core focus (Blatt & Lerner, 1982; Stolorow & Atwood, 1979). In terms of test theory, emphasis has shifted away from an exclusive consideration of thought processes toward a consideration of the quality and nature of object relations; that is, from a traditional emphasis on "ego structures," "cognitive styles," and "impulse-defense configurations" framed in an abstract, mechanistic metapsychological language, to a more phenomenological interest in experiential dimensions such as "self" and "object representation" described in a "middle-level language" (Mayman, 1976) geared toward formulating meaningful clinical generalizations about a patient. The comparatively recent elucidation of modern object relations theory, defined as the psychoanalytic approach to the internalization of interpersonal relations (Kernberg, 1976, 1980), coupled with a systematic psychoanalytic theory of the self (Kohut, 1971, 1977) and a broadened psychodynamic developmental theory (Mahler, Pine, & Bergman, 1975) are now providing the conceptual foundation for a less mechanistic, more human and more clinically anchored, experiential psychoanalytic theory. Contemporary psychoanalytic theorists and researchers are progressively appreciating the complex interactions among early formative relationships, the developmental level and quality of intrapsychic structures including thought processes and defensive organization, the internal representational world, and the nature of ongoing interpersonal relationships and the ways they are internalized and become part of the personality.

This broadened conceptual foundation that integrates concepts of drive, defense, and adaptation into a developmental model that focuses primarily on the child's evolving interactions with caregiving agents has extended the scope of psychoanalytic theory, clinical practice, and research. In particular, this broadened psychoanalytic theory has facilitated the diagnosis and systematic study of psychotic, borderline, and narcissistic disorders. It has also sparked a reformulation of psychoanalytic practice and of the mutative forces in psychoanalysis. There is increased focus on directly relevant, experiential dimensions both in theory and in clinical practice (Schafer, 1978) and renewed interest and recognition of the psychoanalytic context (Spence, 1982) and analytic relationship as crucial factors in the therapeutic action of psychoanalysis (Loewald, 1978; Modell, 1976). The expanded conceptualizations of psychoanalytic theory has also led to new approaches to research, including the study of infant–caretaker interactions, the development of language and of self and object representation, as well as the differential impairment of these processes in various forms of psychopathology.

Throughout the wide range of research of psychoanalytic concepts, diagnostic psychological tests, especially projective techniques, have had a central and pivotal role. According to Lerner (1984):

> The past several years have witnessed an enormous broadening of the psychoanalytic base for the study of people by means of projective techniques. From a relatively narrow but solid foundation established by Rapaport and advanced by Schafer and Holt, recent advances in the psychoanalytic understanding of borderline and nar-

cissistic pathology have dramatically expanded this base by providing new formulations for significant and exciting clinical and research efforts. (p. 1)

Representative of these testing efforts, cited by Lerner (1984), include the investigation and systematic assessment of such varied phenomena as object-representations (Blatt, Brenneis, Schmick, & Glick, 1976; Mayman, 1967; Spear, 1980), primitive object relations (Kwawer, 1980), transitional phenomena (Spiro & Spiro, 1980), transference/countertransference paradigms (Gorney & Weinstock, 1980), and primitive defenses (Lerner & Lerner, 1982). These endeavors have sought to operationalize newer concepts in psychoanalytic theory and provide tools for empirically evaluating hypotheses generated by this expanded body of knowledge.

As part of a continued effort to reformulate traditional psychoanalytic concepts in light of recent theoretical advances and to coordinate these conceptualizations with psychological test findings and test usage, the purpose of this chapter is to trace shifts in the psychoanalytic conceptualization of defenses. We first offer a comprehensive review of the various psychoanalytic theories of defense beginning with Freud's drive theory and including ego psychology and object relations theory. Each theoretical review is followed by a discussion of ways in which conceptual formulations have been translated, operationalized, and researched in terms of psychological test concepts. Finally, we extrapolate from these observations inferences directly pertinent to a new and more integrated psychoanalytic theory of defenses. Based on a synthesis of object relations theory with formulations derived from cognitive and developmental theory, a developmental-structural model of defenses conceptualized within an object representational framework is advanced.

FREUD'S CONCEPTIONS OF DEFENSE

Freud's various and changing views of defense have been reviewed and summarized by several authors (Hoffer, 1968; Leeuw, 1971; Madison, 1961; Rapaport, 1958).

In his earliest writings, prior to 1900 and in a period referred to by Rapaport as the stage of "pre-psychoanalytic theory," Freud coined the term defense to describe the ego's struggle against painful ideas and affects. In two papers—"The Neuro-Psychosis of Defense" (1894/1962a) and "Further Remarks on the Neuro-Psychosis of Defense" (1896/1962b)—he outlined the processes of conversion, displacement of affects, withdrawal from reality, repression and projection. Freud's initial concept of defense was presented within the context of his not having yet worked out a complete conceptualization of the ego. Nevertheless, as Rapaport (1958) has noted, the implicit notions within this early view that drives are dammed up and displaced and that defense, by preventing the recall or re-encountering of a reality experience, prevents or delays the experiencing of a painful affect have remained cornerstones of most subsequent psychoanalytic conceptions of defense.

Freud's discovery that his patients' reports of infantile seductions were not reports of actual reality experiences, but rather of fantasies, ushered in a second stage in the evolution of psychoanalytic theory, a period Rapaport (1958) refers to as "the development of psychoanalysis proper." During this stage Freud's interest shifted to the instincts and their vicissitudes throughout development, and as a consequence, his concern with defense diminished and the concept itself changed. His earlier conception of a variety of defenses was replaced by the global concept of repression and only in *Jokes and Their Relation to the Unconscious* (1905/1960) does he use the term defense: "The defense processes are psychical correlates of the flight reflex, having the task to prevent displeasure arising from inner sources" (p. 233). Despite his relative lack of interest in defense, during this stage he identified several important processes including reversal into its opposite and turning around upon the subject's own self. These, together with repression and displacement were conceptualized as ego instincts (Leeuw, 1971). As well, his findings that repression involved the establishment of permanent hypercathexises (Freud, 1915/1959a, 1915/1957), and that the resistances which they bring about are unconscious (Rapaport, 1958), were especially important for they anticipated and laid the groundwork for the next period, the development of the structural theory of the ego.

With the publication of the *Ego and the Id,* Freud (1923/1961a) made explicit his model of the personality and accorded the concept of defense a central role. He replaced the term repression by the earlier term defense (Freud, 1926/1961b), conceived of defense as an ego function, and regarded the defense mechanisms as the executive methods of this ego capacity (Leeuw, 1971). Whereas in his earlier view he conceptualized repression as responsible for the creation of anxiety, with this new model he posited that it was anxiety which created the need for repression: "How do we now picture the process of a repression under the influence of anxiety? . . . The ego notices that the satisfaction of an emerging instinctual demand would conjure up one of the well-remembered situations of danger. This instinctual cathexis must therefore be somewhat suppressed, stopped" (Freud, 1933/1964, p. 89). Freud (1926/1961b) further conceptualized the ego as having a range of defenses at its disposal. He discovered and described isolation, undoing, denial, and splitting of the ego, and reconsidered repression and eventually regarded it as a specific mechanism of defense whose task involved the removal of ideas from consciousness. Finally, Freud also observed an intimate relationship between specific defenses and particular forms of psychopathology. For example, he found the predominance of repression to be associated with hysteria and isolation of affect and intellectualization with the obsessive compulsive.

Based on the structural model, authors immediately subsequent to Freud drew attention to the chronology and genesis of the defense mechanisms as well as to their relation to levels of ego and drive organization. A. Freud (1936), in her publication, *The Ego and the Mechanisms of Defense,* systematized the concepts of the specific defense mechanisms, clarified the relationship between defense and reality relations, and investigated the role of affects (Rapaport, 1958). Reich (1933), in his major work, *Character Analysis,* investigated and outlined the defensive aspects of character formation. He conceived of character as augmenting the primary repression of instincts by way of autoplastic changes. In this regard he built upon Freud's notion that the ego in the process of repressing renounces a portion of its organization. Reich used the term "character armoring" to depict the severe restrictions that are placed on the psychic mobility of the entire personality.

RORSCHACH MEASURES OF DEFENSE

Beginning with Rapaport, several psychoanalytically oriented psychologists saw in Freud's structural model the seeds for a more general ego psychology as well as a conceptual basis for wedding Rorschach usage and theory with psychoanalytic theory. Rapaport, as Mayman (1976) has noted, saw the relationship between testing and psychoanalytic theory as a "two-way street." Whereas psychoanalytic theory could provide the clinical tester with a bedrock of conceptualizations that permitted test inferences with remarkable scope and range, Rapaport also saw, and later demonstrated, how testing provided a means for operationalizing many psychoanalytic concepts that Freud could only describe in the macrocosm of life events. One concept that especially lent itself to operational definition was that of defense.

In the Rorschach literature one finds three major works that have used Freud's structural model as a basis for translating theoretical formulations regarding defense into test-related concepts. Whereas one of the endeavors, that of Schafer (1954), was developed for and has received broad clinical usage, the methods of Holt (1977) and Levine and Spivack (1964) have had limited clinical utility but have been used extensively in research.

SCHAFER'S MEASURES OF DEFENSE

In developing Rorschach measures of defense Schafer (1954) took as his point of departure Freud's (1926/1961b) signal theory of anxiety. Included in this formulation is the notion that the presence of threatening or unacceptable impulses and the possibility of their discharge mobilizes a reaction of anxiety as well as other possible dysphoric affects (i.e., guilt, shame, embarrassment, etc.). This initial anxiety, which tends to be comparatively mild in intensity, is then used by the ego as an indicator or sign of potential danger, and thus, a defensive action is initiated. Because the individual cannot flee from the internal danger posed by the impulse, "intrapsychic maneuvers or operations" are instituted that serve to delay or prevent the discharge of the impulse. Defense, then, is "understood to refer to any psychological operation that is intended to block discharge of threatening, rejected impulses and thereby to avoid the painful emotional consequences of such discharge" (Schafer, 1954, p. 160). Within this context, all aspects of psychological functioning including thoughts, perceptions, feelings, attitudes and actions, so long as they are in the service of blocking the discharge of impulses, may be understood as serving a defensive function.

Using Rapaport's conceptualizations regarding the predictive value of thought process as manifest in Rorschach responses, Schafer extended Freud's theory of signal anxiety and structural model of defense to the Rorschach. Taking into account various aspects of the Rorschach testing situation including the pattern of formal scores, the content of the response, the nature of the relationship the patient establishes with the examiner, and the patient's attitude toward his or her responses, Schafer elaborated 7 general and 36 specific types of expressions of defense and/or the defended against. As well, he also specified six general aspects of test performance from which one could infer the relative success or failure of the defensive operation. The aspects enumerated included the following: the emotional tone of the response, the extent to which the response was specified and articulated clearly, the accuracy of the form (form level), the degree of integration among the score, image, and attitudinal aspects of the response, the extent of thematic moderation and balance, and the presence of thought disorder as indicated by the score, image, or attitude. The categories of expressions of defense together with the indications of success or failure were then applied to the specific mechanisms of repression, projection, denial, and the obsessive-compulsive quaternary of regression, reaction formation, isolation, and undoing. For each of these methods of defense Schafer presented the underlying theoretical base, expected Rorschach indices, and clinical illustrations.

To illustrate the above, Schafer's treatment of the defense of repression is reviewed. Following upon Fenichel (1945), Schafer (1954) defined repression as "unconsciously purposeful forgetting or not becoming aware of internal impulses or external events which, as a rule, represent possible temptations or punishments for, or mere allusions to, objectionable, instinctual demands" (p. 193). Schafer then distilled from this definition the following basic elements: the basic aim of repression is the blocking of objectionable impulses and their derivatives and the repressed continues to exist outside of awareness. Because repression cuts off parts of the personality from growth and development, he further pointed out that a prolonged use of repression produces severe ego restriction and various manifestations of immaturity. Thus, in a repressed individual one typically sees impulsiveness, unreflectiveness, naiveté, diffuse affects, emotional lability, conventional and superficial thoughts, and a tendency to relate oneself to others in a childlike way.

Schafer next devised Rorschach indices designed to assess the above theoretically derived and clinically substantiated behavioral characteristics associated with a reliance on repression. Thus, to indicate the relative paucity of ideas and relative restrictiveness of ideation he suggested that the test record should contain a low number of total responses, few human movement responses, and a limited range of content categories. Formal aspects of the test record related to affectivity and anxiety, according to Schafer, are expected to be prominent. Therefore, one would anticipate a conspicuous number of responses involving color and shading. With regard to the patient's attitude toward the test, the examiner, and the test responses, one would expect egocentricity, vagueness, naiveté, and a lack of reflectiveness. These attitudes coupled with a tendency to think impressionistically could become evident in off-handed comments such as "Isn't that pretty," "What nice colors," "Oh, this is ugly and scary." Finally, Schafer depicts an interpersonal relationship in which the examiner is looked to for permission and direction so that responsibility for the responses lies with the examiner and not the patient.

In summary, Schafer began with the psychoanalytic definition of the defense, inferred from the operation of the defense likely behavioral and attitudinal correlates, and then from the formal scores, specific content, and testing relationship developed Rorschach indices reflective of these correlates.

Although written almost 20 years ago, Schafer's work on Rorschach defense interpretation still remains an integral and indispensable part of the psychodiagnostician's theoretical armamentarium. As well, by casting "defense interpretation within the language and understandings of psychoanalytic ego psychology" (Cooper, 1981, p. 1) he was able to contribute substantially to the broader psychoanalytic theory of defense.

ASSESSMENT OF PRIMARY PROCESS THINKING AND ITS CONTROL

Based on the psychoanalytic theory of thinking, for over 15 years Robert Holt (1977) has been developing and refining a Rorschach scoring manual designed to operationally define the concepts primary and secondary process. In his *Interpretation of Dreams,* Freud (1900/1953) first made the distinction between primary and secondary process. Primary process, a term adopted to indicate a developmentally earlier form of thinking, is organized around drive discharge and involves the formal properties of a disregard for logic and reality. "In primary process, ideas are fluid, they lose their identity through fusion and fragmentation, reflectiveness is abandoned and thoughts are combined in seemingly arbitrary ways. Secondary process, in contrast, is under ego control and operates in accordance with the reality principle; it is goal directed, logical and uses delay of impulse, detours and experimental action until appropriate avenues of gratification have been realized'' (Lerner & Lewandowski, 1975, p. 182).

Holt's scoring system involves the scoring of the following four sets of variables: content indices of primary process, formal indices of primary process, control and defense, and overall ratings. Because ideation is conceived of as an instinctual derivative, that is, only the idea representing the instinct rather than the instinct itself can achieve consciousness, the section of Holt's manual related to control and defense has relevance in this general review of defense and its measurement.

The control and defense scores represent an attempt to assess the manner in which as well as how successful the primary process material is regulated and modulated. There are two aspects to this scoring: an identification of the specific defensive operation being employed and a determination as to whether the operation improves or further disrupts the response. Holt devised the following scores to specify the particular defensive operation being used: remoteness, context, postponing strategies, miscellaneous, and overtness.

Remoteness, which involves several subcategories (remoteness-ethnic, remoteness-animal, remoteness-geographic, etc.), is based on the principle that when an unacceptable impulse is expressed in a response, it may be rendered more acceptable if the subject distances himself/herself from the response by making the percept distant in time, place, person, or level of reality.

Context refers to the setting in which the response is presented and the extent to which this makes the primary process aspects of the response more acceptable. Four levels of context including cultural, esthetic, intellectual, and humorous are distinguished.

Two types of *postponing strategies,* delay and blocking, are scored. As implied in the name, this refers to processes by which the emergence of primary process is delayed or put off.

Miscellaneous defenses is a catch-all category that Holt uses to include an array of defensive maneuvers. He includes under this heading the following: defensive use of reflectiveness, euphemism, and vulgarity; adaptive modulation; rationalization; negation; minimization; counter-phobic imagery; self-depreciation; vagueness; projection; obsessional defenses; isolation; evasiveness and avoidance; impotence and sequence.

Overtness refers to a distinction between potential as contrasted with active types of aggression. Four types of overtness are distinguished: overtness in behavior, verbal overtness, experiential overtness, and potential overtness.

In addition to these specific defense scores, the fourth part of the scoring manual, overall scores, also includes ratings that bear on defense. The *defense demand* rating was devised so as to evaluate the degree to which the nature of the idea underlying a response or the way it emerges demands that some defensive and controlling measure be undertaken in order to make the response a socially acceptable communication. This is scored on a 6-point scale ranging from no apparent need for defense to greatest need for defense. A second rating, *defense effectiveness,* was developed in order to evaluate the relative effectiveness of the defensive operation in reducing or preventing anxiety and in permitting a more successful and adaptive response. This score, too, is related on 6-point scale with positive values indicating good control and negative values indicating more pathological defensive efforts. A final overall rating is *adaptive regression.* This score, which indicates the amount of primary process material and the effectiveness of integration, is obtained by multiplying defense demand and defense effectiveness, response by response, summing the products, and then dividing the summed product by the number of primary process responses.

Studies involving the reliability of the entire Holt scoring system, including the measures of defense, have, in general, investigated the agreement among judges in scoring. Overall, the level of agreement attained with the overall ratings has been satisfactory; however, the findings regarding the individual categories have been discouraging. One should view the latter conclusion with caution, for as Lerner and Lewandowski (1975) noted, "the scoring system has undergone several modifications and revisions, and the degree to which two scorers agree must be considered in light of the edition of the manual used. This becomes especially relevant when one considers that many of the changes were made with the specific intent of enhancing reliability" (p. 192).

McMahon (1964) tested his agreement with another experienced scorer on 20 cases randomly selected from a sample of 40 schizophrenic and 40 medical patients in a V.A. hospital. On the mean defense effectiveness score he reported a product-moment correlation of .56.

In a study involving the Rorschach records of psychotherapists in training, Bachrach (1968) reported reliability coefficients between two well-trained graduate students greater than .89 for the ratings mean defense demand, mean defense effectiveness, and adaptive regression.

Allison (1967) and an independent rater scored the Rorschach protocols of 20 divinity students and obtained the following reliability coefficients: mean defense demand .99, mean defense effectiveness .81, and adaptive regression (DD × DE) .67.

Benfari and Calogeras (1968), in a sample of 40 college students, reported reliability coefficients of .95 for mean defense demand and .90 for mean defense effectiveness.

Rabkin (1967), together with another experienced scorer, scored 25 records randomly selected from a group of 100 Rorschachs obtained from patients participating in the Menninger Foundation Psychotherapy Research Project. The reliabilities reported by Rabkin were mean defense demand .86 and mean defense effectiveness .90.

Russ (1980), in a study involving 20 protocols selected from a group of 51 second graders, obtained inter-rater reliabilities between two experienced scorers of .76 for mean defense demand, .80 for mean defense effectiveness, and .90 for adaptive regression.

As noted previously, findings with respect to the agreement in scoring of the individual categories have been relatively unsatisfactory. Holt (1968), based on raw data from two studies, found that scorer agreement was highly related to the frequency with which a specific category was used. Lerner and Lewandowski (1975), based on their own scoring of protocols obtained in their clinical practice, reported that "if the content and formal variables were scored accurately, then the control and defense scoring was straightforward and afforded little difficulty" (p. 188). In summary, then, although the inter-rater reliability for the overall ratings across several studies is highly adequate, data are inconclusive with respect to the reliability of the individual defense and control scores.

Studies related to the construct validity of the scoring system have involved the following: (1) attempts to link the drive and control measures to behaviors and characteristics theoretically related to primary process thinking; (2) the use of specific scores as criterion measures in studying the effects on thinking and defense of experimentally induced or clinical conditions, and (3) attempts to find differences in the expression of and control of primary process thinking among groups differentiated on the basis of other variables, such as diagnosis and level of conscience development. The studies reviewed here are examined exclusively in terms of the specific and overall indices of defense; for a more detailed and comprehensive review of the findings of these studies as they relate to the entire scoring system refer to Holt (1977) and Lerner and Lewandowski (1975).

Several investigators have attempted to relate aspects of Holt's manual to various cognitive and perceptual variables that are conceptually linked to the expression and control of primary process manifestations. The areas studied include the thought process of individuals who have undergone unusual religious experiences, the capacity to cope with cognitive complexity, creativity, the capacity to tolerate unrealistic experiences, conjunctive empathy, and tolerance for perceptual deprivation.

In a sample of 29 male college students, Maupin (1965) investigated the relationship between responses to a meditation exercise and specific ego capacities, including the capacity to regress adaptively. He reported a correlation (Tau. 49, $p < .001$) between indices of the response to meditation and the measure of adaptive regression. The relative contributions of the various components of the adaptive regression score were explored in a multivariate chi-square analysis. The main contribution to the relationship with response to meditation came from the "defense effectiveness" component ($X^2 = 7.82$, $p < .02$).

Allison (1967) studied the thought processes of individuals who had undergone a religious conversion experience. The sample consisted of 20 male divinity students who were subdivided into three groups on the basis of an autobiographical statement as to whether or not they had undergone an unusual or mystical experience. Allison found that whereas both the defense demand ($p < .05$) and the adaptive regression ($p < .05$) scores were significantly related to the intensity of conversion experience, the defense effectiveness score did not discriminate the subgroups.

The most direct test of the relationship between the amount and control of primary process on the Rorschach and the capacity to deal with cognitive complexity was conducted by Blatt, Allison, & Feirstein, (1969). Fifty male college students were administered the Rorschach and the John-Rimoldi, an apparatus designed to measure the ability to analyze and synthesize abstract and logical relationships. The authors found that although the ability to handle cognitive complexity as defined by the John-Rimoldi was not related to defense demand, it was significantly related to defense effectiveness and adaptive regression.

Similar, but less impressive, results regarding the relationship between adaptive regression and cognitive flexibility were reported by Murray and Russ (1981). In a group of 42 college students, they found a significant relationship between the adaptive regression score and a measure of cognitive flexibility (Mednick's remote association test) for males but not for females.

A third area of investigation that has received considerable attention is that of creativity. Most researchers who have attempted to relate Holt's scores to measures of creativity have tested Kris's (1952) hypothesis that "regression in the service of the ego" is necessary for the artist. In developing this concept, Kris emphasized the relationship between creativity and adaptive regression.

Pine and Holt (1960) attempted to predict from the adaptive regression score, effectiveness of defense measure, and demand for defense index the quality of imaginative productions across a variety of experimental tasks including a TAT literary quality score, Science Test, Brick Use Test, and so forth. In a sample of 27 undergraduate students they found that the adaptive regression score and the effectiveness of defense score were significantly related to a summary imaginative quality measure for the males. For the females the findings were weak and inconclusive. Support for these findings was provided by Cohen (1960), who also studied the relationship between creativity and adaptive regression. In this study, which involved college students as well, sex did not affect the findings.

Pine (1962) attempted to replicate the findings from the earlier study with Holt (Pine & Holt, 1960); however, in this study he used a sample of 56 unemployed actors. He found, in contrast to the previous investigation, that not one of the correlations between the defense measures and creativity was significant. In explaining this discrepant finding Pine noted that the variance in the defense effectiveness scores was too small in this sample to permit a meaningful ranking of subjects.

Finally, Dudek and Chamberland-Bouhadana (1982) compared a group of mature, renowned artists with a group of young art students on the various Holt measures. They found that all three overall scores (defense demand, defense effectiveness, and adaptive regression) significantly differentiated the experienced from the inexperienced artists.

Another cognitive perceptual variable that investigators have studied with respect to its relationship to the amount and successful integration of primary process material is the capacity to "tolerate unrealistic experience." Feirstein (1967) tested the hypothesis that subjects who are able to adaptively integrate (high defense effectiveness) drive-related material into their thinking will also be able to perceive their environment in ways that contradict conventional modes of perception. Twenty male graduate students were administered Rorschachs together with four tests of "tolerance for unrealistic experiences"—Phi phenomena, reversible figures, aniseikonic lenses, and stimulus incongruity. The author reported a significant correlation ($r = .46, p < .05$) between the Rorschach defense effectiveness score and a combined TUE measure. An adaptive regression score, consisting of the defense effectiveness score and an index of the amount of unrealistic thinking, also correlated significantly ($r = .49, p < .025$) with the criterion TUE measure.

Another variable that has been related to the various defense measures is conjunctive empathy. Based on scale ratings derived from tapes of psychotherapy sessions, Bachrach (1968) found that as quality of conjunctive empathy increased, there were significant increases in adaptive regression and defense effectiveness. Defense demand did not significantly relate to the empathy measure; nevertheless, in reviewing the raw data, Bachrach noted a curvilinear relationship with defense demand greater at either extreme of the empathy dimension.

The final factor that investigators have attempted to relate to the expression and control of primary process is the capacity to tolerate perceptual deprivation. Wright and Abbey (1965) found that an index of control score that consisted of the proportion of defense demand to defense effectiveness was significantly related to success in tolerating a deprivation situation ($X^2 = 8.04, df 2, p < .05$) in a sample of 21 subjects. Because in this study the Rorschachs were administered several months after completion of the isolation experiment, and therefore, success or failure in tolerating the deprivation experience might have influenced the Rorschach scores, Wright and Zubek (1969) attempted to replicate the earlier study but used Rorschachs administered prior to the experiment. The obtained results were quite consistent with those reported in the earlier study. That is, the index of control score was again highly related to the capacity to tolerate the perceptual deprivation situation.

Goldberger (1961) employed the manual to predict as well as to study reactions to perceptual isolation. Fourteen college students were isolated for a period of 8 hours and encouraged to openly discuss their thoughts and feelings. From the Rorschach, a series of cognitive tests, clinical ratings, and verbal behavior, Goldberger found the following: (1) defense effectiveness was positively related to controlled primary process thinking during isolation and experience of positive affect during isolation; (2) defense effectiveness was negatively correlated with poorly controlled primary process thinking during isolation, the experience of negative affect during isolation, and cognitive test impairment in the isolation situation; and (3) defense effectiveness did not predict a tendency to prematurely terminate the isolation experience.

In summary, two summary defense scores from the Holt manual have been found to be related to a host of cognitive-perceptual variables that on theoretical grounds are linked to the expression and control of primary process thinking. Across several studies the defense effectiveness score and a measure of adaptive regression have been related to the capacity to tolerate and adaptively cope with situations in which reality contact is temporarily suspended (Zen meditation, religious conversion experiences, perceptual isolation), the ability to tolerate unrealistic experiences, and the capacity to deal with a variety of cognitive tasks. As well, subjects who are able to adaptively regulate drive expressions and integrate logical and illogical thoughts into appropriate Rorschach responses are more empathic in treatment relationships. The findings with respect to creativity were somewhat equivocal. Nevertheless, several investigators were able to demonstrate a relationship between the defense scores and indices of creativity.

A second area of investigation involves studies in which researchers have used defense scores from the Holt manual to assess the impact on thinking of specific clinical conditions.

Saretsky (1966) investigated the effects of chloropromazine on the Rorschach records of a group of schizophrenic patients. Forty male hospitalized patients were divided into an experimental and a control group with subjects in the experimental group receiving chloropromazine and those in the control group a placebo. The pre- and post-drug Rorschach protocols for each subject were scored for mean defense effectiveness. For both groups the author reported significant increases in the defense effectiveness score, thus indicating changes in the patients' attitudes toward disturbing ideation and the manner of controlling it. Furthermore, independent ratings of clinical improvement in both groups correlated significantly with the degree of improvement in the defense effectiveness score.

A second study employed the Holt scoring system to assess changes in thought processes in a patient diagnosed as myxoedema psychosis. Because treatment of this illness with desiccated thyroid results in rapid clinical improvement, Greenberg, Ramsay, Rakoff, and Weiss (1969) administered three Rorschachs over a 7-month period to a 17-year-old female patient having this disease. The patient was tested 3 days after thyroxin treatment was initiated, 2 months later, and during a follow-up period 5 months following the second testing. Between the first and second testing the patient's clinical condition improved dramatically, whereas between the second and third evaluations the improved state was maintained. Ratings on mean defense effectiveness (0.53,

−1.43, −1.38) increased and the increase was in the expected direction and consistent with the improved clinical state.

A final group of studies have investigated differences in the expression and control of primary process manifestations among groups differentiated on the basis of some other variable.

Zimet and Fine (1965) investigated differences in the extent and nature of thought disturbance between subgroups of schizophrenic patients. The Rorschach records of 23 reactive schizophrenics and 36 process schizophrenics were scored using several of the Holt summary ratings. Consistent with clinical expectations, the reactive schizophrenics produced significantly more modulated and controlled primary process responses than did the process group.

Benfari and Calogeras (1968) studied differences in types of thinking between groups distinguished on the basis of conscience development. Forty college students were subdivided into two groups according to their responses to a conscience scale. One subgroup, referred to as "nonintegrated conscience," were characterized by a tendency to hold severe moral principles and strict prohibitions, but with a compelling desire to rebel against these severe standards. Subjects in this group revealed indications of conflict in terms of presenting affects such as guilt, self-reproach, and ambivalence. The other group, designated "integrated conscience," included subjects who held strong ethical beliefs together with a disciplined acceptance of these standards. Conflict regarding values and behavior was not evident in this group. Using scores from the Holt manual, support was found for the proposition that a less well-controlled and defended ego is associated with a more punitive and conflicted conscience.

In conclusion, as part of his attempt to operationalize the concepts primary and second process, Holt devised a number of individual and summary defense scores to evaluate the way in which as well as how effectively primary process manifestations are controlled. Unfortunately, the individual scores have received little currency in the research literature. Data related to agreement in scoring between raters for the individual categories have not been satisfactory; however, Lerner and Lewandowski (1975) found that scoring was relatively easy if the content and formal expressions of primary process were scored accurately. Although the individual scores, in total, have not been used in studies of validity, Lerner and Lerner (1982) found negation and minimization to be effective and useful indices of higher level forms of denial. By contrast, research involving several summary scores has been extensive. Highly satisfactory levels of reliability have been reported for the scores defense demand, defense effectiveness, and adaptive regression. Measures of defense effectiveness and adaptive regression have been related to the following: (1) a number of conceptually related, cognitive, and perceptual factors; (2) changes in thought organization associated with improvement in clinical states; and (3) differences between groups distinguished on the basis of either diagnosis or integration of conscience.

RORSCHACH INDEX OF REPRESSIVE STYLE

Levine and Spivak (1964) devised the Rorschach Index of Repressive Style (RIRS) initially as an attempt to operationalize Freud's concept of repression. In his article, "The Unconscious," Freud (1915/1957) noted that "repression is essentially a process affecting ideas on the border between the systems Ucs and Pcs" (p. 180). The authors inferred from Freud's statement that repression, therefore, works through the cognitive system and has the effect of inhibiting ideational processes. As work on the scale progressed, however, Levine and Spivak modified their conceptual basis. Rather than viewing the scale as a measure of the ideational results of repression, they came to conceive of their scoring system as an indicator of an ideational style that predisposed one to the use of repression. This revised conception, together with the work of earlier Rorschach theorists who began to systematize an additional Rorschach dimension—the manner in which responses are expressed—, led Levine and Spivak (1964) to the following basic principle: "repressive style is a consistent characteristic of an individual and it is manifest in vague, unelaborated language which is lacking in integration and flow" (p. 14). The scoring manual, as such, represents an attempt to operationalize this principle.

The system calls for the scoring of each response along the following seven dimensions: specificity, elaboration, impulse responses, presence of primary process thinking, self-references, presence of movement, and associative flow. Underlying these factors is the thesis that the extent to which the verbalization of a response is impersonal, lacks movement, reflects vague and unelaborated thinking, is unintegrated, and reveals an absence of associative flow, the greater the degree of repression functioning. Conversely, the more specific, detailed, reality bound, and logical is a response, and the more it is offered with a free flow of words, the less the degree of repressive functioning.

The scale has been subjected to several types of tests of reliability. Levine and Spivak (1964) reported on four separate studies in which inter-rater correlations of .95–.98 were obtained. The combined results led the authors to conclude that the scale could be scored with considerable consistency by different scorers across various samples.

Because the scale assumes to measure a more enduring, characterological feature, the authors thought it important to demonstrate the measure's long-term reliability. Data obtained by both Paulsen and Ledwith (Levine & Spivak, 1964) indicated that repressive style is not only an enduring mode of response, but in addition, it is a style that becomes characteristic of a child at about 7 years of age.

Several studies have been conducted to assess the retest reliability of the RIRS. Collectively, these studies found that when the conditions of administration remain constant but different inkblots are used, reliability correlations range from .50 to .67. When the same form of inkblots are administered under the same conditions within a relatively short interval of time, then reliability correlations range between .74 and .82.

Attempts to establish the concurrent validity of the RIRS have involved investigating the relationship between the scale and other Rorschach scores as well as a specific TAT score. In a sample of 68 student nurses Levine and Spivak (1964) found RIRS to be most highly correlated with M, C, and experience balance. Whereas subjects with high RIRS scores tended to offer a dilated experience balance, those with low RIRS scores produced constricted experience balances. The authors took these findings as indicating that subjects who obtain high RIRS scores tend to produce richer and fuller records using as a criteria more traditional Rorschach scores. In a second study, which involved 92 college students and used the Holtzman Inkblots, Levine and Spivak (1964) substantiated the earlier findings and also found a positive and significant correlation between RIRS and the number of pure form responses.

Levine and Spivak also studied the relationship between RIRS and TAT "transcendence scores." This score represents an attempt to assess the extent to which a subject's description of the TAT cards goes beyond the immediate stimulus properties of each card. As predicted, RIRS was found to correlate positively with several indices of transcendence.

From the above studies then, the authors concluded that subjects who produce high RIRS scores (i.e., less repressive functioning) tend, on other measures, to manifest a richness of intellectual and affective responsiveness, reveal a capacity for reflectiveness, and are able to effect delay of impulse gratification.

Further efforts to demonstrate concurrent validity have included investigations of the relationship between RIRS and questionnaire measures of anxiety and repression. In general, the findings have not been impressive. Correlations between the RIRS and various anxiety scales (Taylor Manifest Anxiety Scale, Sarason Test Anxiety Scale, Cattell IPAT) have been at a borderline level of statistical significance and none of the relationships have been strong (Levine & Spivak, 1964). With specific regard to repression, in a sample of 155 college students little relationship was found between the RIRS score and the following MMPI scales: the repression scale, the internalization ratio, Hawley's defensive scale, the K scale, and the repression-sensitization scale.

The construct validity of the scale has been investigated in several studies that have attempted to relate RIRS scores to the ego capacity to tolerate sensory isolation as well as to various cognitive-perceptual dimensions including field dependence–independence and leveling–sharpening.

Using the data obtained by Goldberger (1961) in his study of reactions to sensory isolation, Levine and Spivak (1964) re-scored the Rorschach protocols employing the RIRS scale. RIRS scores were found to correlate positively and significantly with ratings of the capacity to adapt to sensory isolation ($r = .61$, $p < .05$) as well as with a rating of frequency and vividness of imagery ($r = .73$,

$p < .01$). No significant relationship was found between RIRS score and a measure of maladaptive reaction to sensory isolation.

Because Witkin et al.'s (1954) description of the personality characteristics of field dependent and field independent individuals seemed in keeping with their own understanding of repressive style as assessed by the RIRS, Levine and Spivak (1964) investigated the relationship between the RIRS and measures of field dependence. Using a supplied group of Rorschach protocols obtained from 24 ten-year-olds for whom perceptual measures were also available, the authors reported a correlation of $-.25$ between the RIRS score and an index of field dependence. Highly consistent results were obtained on data collected by Young (1959); however, Young's sample consisted of college students. In both studies the results, although not strong, indicate that subjects who manifest repressive functioning on the Rorschach, as measured by the RIRS, tend to be field dependent.

Leveling–sharpening, a cognitive dimension investigated by Holtzman and Gardner (1959), involves determining whether a subject in solving cognitive tasks is guided more by internal cues (sharpeners) or by immediate, external perceptual properties (levelers). Rorschachs, initially obtained by Holtzman and Gardner (1959) on 10 extreme levelers and 10 extreme sharpeners drawn from a sample of 80 female college students, were rescored for RIRS by Levine and Spivak. The authors reported a mean RIRS of 2.25 for levelers and 2.77 for sharpeners, which was significant between the .05 and .10 levels of significance. This, together with the finding that the RIRS correlated especially well with a measure of ranking accuracy, led the authors to conclude that subjects who score higher on the RIRS tend to perceive stimuli more discretely and then use the discrete impression as an internal frame of reference against which new stimuli are judged.

Based on the consistency of findings across these studies of sensory isolation, field independence–field dependence, and leveling–sharpening, Levine and Spivak (1964) interpreted the results as indicating that subjects who differ on the RIRS dimension also differ with respect to the degree to which they have available and use their own thoughts and fantasies in interpreting experience, the extent to which they rely upon the external properties of the situation, and in the tendency to respond to their surroundings in terms of an internal frame of reference. More specifically, whereas low RIRS subjects (those more repressive) tend to be more reliant on immediate perceptual aspects of a situation, look outside of themselves for guiding cues, and have little inner frame of reference, high RIRS subjects (those less repressive), by contrast, respond to given situations by interpreting them in terms of their own and readily available ideas and memories.

Another group of studies have sought to compare RIRS scores between clinical groups who on theoretical grounds are assumed to differ with respect to their reliance on repression. Clinical theory would hold that the typical patient who would rely on repression as a defense is the hysteric, whereas, by contrast, intellectualization and isolation of affect are more typical defenses one expects to find in the obsessive compulsive. Based on this clinical proposition, Levine and Spivak reviewed several well-established textbooks, gleaned 16 Rorschach records, 8 of each syndrome, and scored the protocols using the RIRS scale. Whereas the mean score for the eight hysterics was 1.97, that for the obsessive compulsives was 3.55. Using the U test this difference was found to be significant at the .001 level of significance. An investigation of the individual records indicated that the two hysterical cases with the highest RIRS scores were also described as individuals who were tested at a point in which their repressive defenses were failing.

In keeping with this latter finding, in a second study RIRS scores were compared among four patients each of whom represented a different level of severity of breakdown of repressive defenses. The scores for the respective patients were as follows: well-defended hysteric with repressive trends 1.47, hysteric with phobic and depressive features presenting precarious defenses 1.59, hysteric with badly faltering defenses 2.66, and a borderline psychotic with multiple phobias but with a heavy reliance of repressive defenses 1.92. In this study of individual cases, then, lower RIRS scores were associated with well-functioning repressive defenses, whereas higher scores seemed to be associated with failing defenses.

Based on the thesis that psychosomatic involvement is associated with a reliance on repression, in a third study Rorschach records of a group of neurotic patients with somatic complaints were compared with the records of a group of neurotic patients who presented with other psychological complaints. As predicted, the patients with psychosomatic disorders, in general, produced more repressed Rorschach protocols as judged by RIRS scores.

In summary, based on Rapaport's pioneering effects to systematize the ways in which Rorschach responses are delivered, Levine and Spivak creatively quantified this dimension in attempting to devise a scale for measuring a specific mode of cognition. Although the scale has considerable face validity and has generated much research, its conceptual base is somewhat ambiguous and many of the supporting studies suffer from methodological weaknesses.

As noted previously, the scale was initially developed to assess the specific defense of repression; however, in time the authors modified this conceptualization and began to conceive of the scale as measuring a more general cognitive style that predisposed one to the use of repression. As a consequence of this shift, it appears that several studies were designed and based on the initial conceptualization (i.e., studies involving a comparison of different diagnostic groups), whereas other studies (i.e., studies involving the relationship between the scale and specific cognitive controls) were based on the latter conceptualization. Thus, it is not always clear which construct the studies are meant to validate.

In addition, apart from suggesting that the ideational style predisposes one to the use of repression, the authors did not develop as fully as possible the more general relationship between cognition and defense nor did they fully explore and detail the specific cognitive style under discussion. Shapiro (1965), for example, has comprehensively described a cognitive style, which he refers to as the hysterical style, strikingly similar to the one described by Levine and Spivak, carefully delineated the relationship between this style and repression, but also cautioned "that this mode of functioning or, specifically, of cognition decidedly *favors* the phenomenon we describe as 'repression' " (p. 117). In other words, and consistent with clinical experience, Shapiro is suggesting that there is not a one-to-one relationship between cognitive style and defense, and that cognition is only one aspect of the matrix that determines the specific defense.

Because of the conceptual ambiguities and the authors' contention that the scale assesses a unitary dimension, there is much confusion regarding the meaning of higher scale scores. Although higher scores are conceived of as indicating less repressive functioning, in certain studies high scores seem to indicate the use of defenses other than repression and in other studies the higher scores are taken to indicate a breakdown in the defense of repression. Clearly, a preference for other defenses and the faltering of repression are quite different matters.

With respect to methodology, most of the results reported by Levine and Spivak were taken from studies in which the original data were collected by others and typically for other purposes. The authors, characteristically, secured Rorschachs obtained in other projects and then scored these records for RIRS. Thus, the Rorschachs were not only obtained under varying circumstances, but in addition, examiners differing in experience, training, and method of administration initially obtained the records. The authors (Levine & Spivak, 1964) themselves found that although the correlation between RIRS scores is high when the conditions of reexamination are constant, changes in certain conditions of administration affect the mean level of RIRS.

Despite the noted conceptual difficulties and methodological weaknesses, the scale does represent an attempt to systematize an important component of Rorschach testing (the delivery of the response) and within an overall theoretical framework. Several of the component dimensions identified by Levine and Spivak (1964) (specificity, elaboration, impulsivity, and associative flow) are similar to indices Schafer (1954) used as indicators of a reliance on repression. This, together with the consideration that studies involving the scale have yielded positive findings, suggests that if the conceptual ambiguities can be clarified, especially in light of later works on repression (Horowitz, 1972; Krohn, 1978; Shapiro, 1965), then the scoring system could serve as a basis for constructing a Rorschach measure of repression. With the more recent growing interest in primitive defenses (Lerner & Lerner, 1982), especially as they contrast with repression, the need for a valid measure of repression is particularly pressing at this time.

MEASURES OF ADAPTATION

With the elaboration of the structural model, Freud began to systematically take into account the role of external reality as well as elevate defense and reality relations to the same level of importance as the drives. Although the concept of adaptation was implied in this theory, it was Hartmann (1939), and later Rapaport (1959), who extended and refined his incipient theory of adaptation into a core aspect of psychoanalytic theory. Hartmann, in particular, drew attention to psychological structures independent of the drives and conceived of these structures as guarantees of a state of adaptiveness with external reality.

Although intimately related to defense, the concept of adaptation has appeared sparingly in the Rorschach literature. A notable exception is found in the work of Schafer and, in particular, in a paper (Schafer, 1978) in which he attempted to detail differences in the nature of defensive/adaptive efforts amongst patients engaged in varying types of struggles—manic efforts against depressive decompensation, non-manic attempts to stave off further depression, and struggles against decompensation into acute psychosis. In keeping with his earlier discussion of defense, Schafer (1978) outlined differences in formal aspects, content, and attitude toward responses and the examiner that differentiate patients involved in these varying struggles. For example, whereas the patient using manic efforts to ward off depressive feelings will offer benign content (peace, harmony, vitality, plenty) in which themes of gloom, destruction, and emptiness are denied, the patient attempting to ward off psychosis, by contrast, will make strenuous efforts to reduce the amount of stimulation and challenge. Thus, records of these patients will contain few responses and those responses offered will adhere closely to the stimulus properties of the cards.

Although the concept of adaptation has found further, but indirect, expression in Holt's concept of defense effectiveness and Schafer's attention to the relative success or failure of the defensive operation, his attunement in this paper to the nature of the more regressive experience being warded off has much therapeutic importance, as well as pinpoints a relatively neglected area of Rorschach inquiry.

BRITISH OBJECT RELATIONS THEORISTS

Paralleling, but also originating in several of Freud's specific formulations, are those notions of defense that have evolved from the British School of Object Relations, stimulated largely by the contributions of Melanie Klein. Historically, the Kleinian approach and its influence on Fairbairn, Balint, Winniccott, and Guntrip was distinguished from and seen in opposition to the ego psychological approaches of Anna Freud, Hartmann, Loewenstein, and Rapaport. In recent years as part of the widening scope of psychoanalysis, Klein's seminal theoretical and clinical contributions have increasingly been integrated into the mainstream of psychoanalytic thinking, even including ego psychology (Kernberg, 1975).

With the Kleinian point of view has come a major reconceptualization of defenses in that such mechanisms are not only used to manage affects and instincts but are also related to the effects on intimacy and cognition of the experience, organization, and internalization of object relations. While taking Freud's (1920/1955) dual instinct theory—life and death instinct—as a point of departure, Klein increasingly came to regard them as manifested in the interplay of love and hate in relation to objects. As such, her formulations veered away from Freud's economic and topographical model to a consideration of object relations as the fundamental determinant of personality. According to Klein (1975):

> The analysis of very young children has taught me that there is no individual urge, no anxiety situation, no mental process which does not include objects, external or internal, in other words, object relations are at the center of emotional life. Furthermore, love and hatred, fantasies, anxieties, and defenses are also operative from the beginning and are *ab initio* indivisibly linked with object relations. (pp. 51–52)

Klein accepted Freud's structural theory and concept of libidinal stages, but in modified form. She formulated her clinical findings along phenomenological–experiential–interpersonal lines highlighting "positions"—a developmental concept including cognitive, affective, and relational elements. Klein used the term position to emphasize the fact that the phenomenon she was describing was not a passing "stage" or "phase"—her term position implies a specific configuration of object relations, anxieties, and defenses that persist through life (Segal, 1964). Of major significance for Klein was the notion that defenses not only protect the ego from overwhelming sensations, but are also nondefensive organizing principles of infantile mental life.

Based on the assumption that there is sufficient ego in earliest infancy to experience anxiety, use defenses, and form primitive object relations, Klein outlined the first position, the "paranoid-schizoid" position, in which, against the anxiety of annihilation, the ego evolves a series of defenses including splitting, projection, introjection, projective and introjective identification, idealization, and denial. The paranoid-schizoid position is characterized by an unawareness of "persons," relationships being with part objects, and by the prevalence of splitting processes and paranoid anxiety.

Klein's view of splitting comes from Freud's use of the concept in *Instincts and Their Vicissitudes* in which he suggests the notion of an early developmental distinction between a purified pleasure ego and a collection of excessively negative object impressions (Grala, 1980). Whereas the pleasure ego represents an internalization of gratifying self-object relations, the latter results from a projection of feelings associated with nongratifying, frustrating object relations. Thus, in situations of heightened anxiety or aggression, there may be an exaggeration of the division of all good and all bad representations (Grotstein, 1981) as a way of preserving the pleasure ego from annihilation by projected sadistic components.

A special form of projection elaborated by Klein is projective identification. Here, unwanted parts of the self and internal objects are split off and projected into an external object, primarily the mother and her breast. Because the object is not felt to be separate, but rather is identified with the projected parts, it affords possession and control of the object. The complex process is thought to be equivalent to the fantasy of omnipotent expulsion of bodily substances as a means of controlling the object (Meissner, 1979). A complementary process is identification by introjection. In this process, good parts of the self are projected into the object and then the entire good self-object unit is reintrojected. Bion (1967) amplified the concept of projective identification in terms of the metaphor of the container and the contained. He suggested that projective identification not only allows the disowning and projection of unwanted parts of the self, but also permits the containment of such parts within the object.

When the above defenses occur in Klein's second position, the "depressive" position, they are thought of as "manic defenses." Although the organization of manic defenses in the depressive position includes the same processes evidenced in the paranoid-schizoid position, these processes are more highly organized owing to the more integrated state of the ego (Segal, 1964). Further, as contrasted with the paranoid-schizoid position in which the major anxiety prompting defensive operations is the threat of annihilation of the good self by the projected sadistic aspects of the bad self, in the depressive position the child's main anxiety is that his/her own sadistic impulses have or will destroy the object that is both loved and depended on. Klein also specifies in the depressive position the defensive use of reparation as well as a triad of affects. Specifically, control, triumph, and contempt are regarded as defenses against the depressive feelings of valuing the object, depending on it, and fearing its impending loss.

Based on several of Klein's pioneering contributions, Fairbairn attempted to replace what he regarded as Freud's drive psychology with a dynamic psychology rooted in internal object relations (Rinsley, 1979). Fairbairn argued convincingly that the foundation of personality development rests not in the satisfaction of instincts but in imparting to the infant that he or she is a person, valued and enjoyed ". . . for his own sake, as a person in his own right." According to Fairbairn (1954): "The clinical material from which the whole of my special views are derived may be formulated from the general proposition that *libido is not primarily pleasure-seeking but object seeking* (p. 137)." Fairbairn rejected the term defense "mechanism" regarding it as mechanistic and impersonal and spoke, rather, of defensive activities of the ego in relation to bad objects. Of major importance for Fairbairn was the defensive aspect of introjection. In that experience is inherently a mixture of good and bad, gratification and frustration, the infant must cope with an unpredictable outer world through a series of what Fairbairn characterized as spontaneous psychic maneuvers that culminate in external objects becoming represented by internal psychological counterparts. These internal psychological objects or representations are what Klein referred to as ''internal objects'' and what are currently termed object representations. In his earlier writings Fairbairn (1944) regarded introjection as a defensive reaction in relation to bad objects that are internalized with a view toward mastery, control, or management of negative experiences that cannot be tolerated on the outside. As a consequence of primal introjection, there is a creation of an inner world of bad objects that in turn calls for the creation of internal good objects as protection (Guntrip, 1961). Internal objects become enduring features of psychological life and develop as the structural pattern of the personality. Fairbairn demonstrated how Klein's notion of object splitting is paralleled by ego splitting, and he systematically formulated a calculus of internal object relations expressed in dreams, symptoms, and disordered interpersonal relationships. thus, as with Klein, one finds an implied view that representational capacities and defensive functions are inextricably related (Rinsley, 1979). That is, that symbolic representation can only arise from defensive operations.

The intimate relationship between aspects of the actual mother–infant relationship, as opposed to fantasy-laden inner representations of that relationship, and the development of a specific defensive structure is graphically represented in Winnicott's (1960) concept of the ''false self.'' Winnicott conceives of the false self as a defense serving to hide and protect the ''true self'' through compliance with external demands. The origins of the false self are found in the infant's seduction into a compliant relationship with a nonempathic mother. Unable to sustain the infant's sense of self through failures in empathy, such mothers substitute their own needs impingingly for those of the infant and then prompt the infant into a position of complying with those needs. A continuum of varying levels of false self organization is advanced ranging from one extreme in which the false self substitutes for the real person, through a level at which the false self seeks out conditions that would permit the emergence of the true self, to an opposite extreme in which the false self finds expression in an adaptive ''politeness and mannered social attitude.'' According to Meissner (1982), true and false self organizations are intimately related to splitting:

> In this case . . . there is a split within the organization of the personality that allows the true self to retreat to an inner withdrawal colored with narcissistic isolation and self-sufficiency, while another self organization is constructed based on compliance and the need to protectively buffer the true self from the impingements of the outside world. The false-self organization may thus carry on at a high level of adjustment and involvement with reality, but the true self remains hidden and withdrawn. Consequently, the pathology takes the form of the internal organization of the self that is motivated by underlying narcissistic and object-related conflicts. (p. 36)

An important example of the increasingly productive integration of self psychology, object relations theory, and the ego psychological theory of affects is represented in the work of Modell (1975, 1976, 1980). Weaving Winnicott's conceptual use of the self in the service of defense and a slight reformulation of Fairbairn's maxim that "libido is not pleasure seeking but object seeking," in a series of papers he has described a group of narcissistic patients in which the defensive noncommunication of affects is the most outstanding clinical feature. Rooted in the notion that a defense against affects is equivalent to a defense against objects, that is, a way of nonrelating, he suggests that the noncommunication is defensive and serves to support an illusion of omnipotent self-sufficiency as well as avoiding the risk of exposing a precocious and precariously established self to the assumed dangers of control, exploitation, and domination.

An attempt to integrate the two streams of psychoanalytic formulations of defense, the ego psychological and that evolving from the British school of object relations, is found in the work of Kernberg (1975) and, in particular, his structural concept of levels of defensive operation. Kernberg proposes a hierarchical organization of levels of character pathology linked to type of defensive functioning and developmental level of internalized object relations. According to Kernberg, internalized object relations are organized on the basis of specific defensive structures. As part of this model he systematically defines and coordinates the primitive defenses previously reported by Klein and clarifies the relationship between splitting and repression. He suggests that although splitting serves developmentally as a defensive precursor of repression, it continues to function pathologically in those patients who are pre-oedipally fixated, that is, in those individuals incapable of whole object relations or evocative object constancy.

In keeping with this position Kernberg has systematically identified two overall levels of defensive organization of the ego associated with pre-oedipal and oedipal pathology. At the lower level primitive dissociation or splitting is the crucial defensive operation with a concomitant impairment of the ego's synthetic function. In addition, splitting is bolstered through the related defenses of denial, primitive idealization, primitive devaluation, and projective identification. At a more advanced developmental level associated with oedipal pathology repression supplants splitting as a major defense and is accompanied by the related defensive operations of intellectualization, rationalization, undoing, and higher forms of projection.

RORSCHACH ASSESSMENT OF PRIMITIVE DEFENSES

Based upon these theoretical conceptualizations of defense advanced by Kernberg and the clinical test work of Mayman (1967), Pruitt and Spilka (1964), Holt (1977), Peebles (1975), and Lerner and Lerner (1980) devised a Rorschach scoring manual designed to evaluate the specific defensive operations presumed to characterize the developmentally lower level of defensive functioning.

The scoring manual is divided into sections on the basis of the specific defenses of splitting, devaluation, idealization, projective identification, and denial. Within each section the defense is defined, Rorschach indices of the defense are presented, and clinical illustrations are offered. The sections on devaluation, idealization, and denial call for an identification of these defenses as well as a ranking of the defense on a continuum of high versus low order. In keeping with both Kernberg's notion that these defenses organize as well as reflect the internalized object world and with the empirical relationship found between human responses on the Rorschach and quality of object relating (Blatt & Lerner, 1982), the system involves a systematic appraisal of the human figure response. In assessing the human percept attention is paid to the precise figures seen, the way in which the figure is described, and the action ascribed to the figure.

To evaluate Kernberg's assertion that this constellation of lower level, more primitive defenses distinguishes borderline and psychotic patients from neurotic patients as well as to assess the reliability and construct validity of the scoring system, two separate studies were conducted. In one study Rorschach records of nonhospitalized borderline patients were compared with those of neurotic patients (Lerner & Lerner, 1980), whereas in the second study the protocols of hospitalized borderline and schizophrenic patients were compared with respect to manifestations of primitive defenses (Lerner, Sugarman, & Gaughran, 1981).

In Study I, 30 Rorschach protocols (15 from borderline patients and 15 from patients falling within the neurotic range) were selected from private files and scored using the system. Because the testing was initially conducted for research purposes, the test protocols were not used in formulating a final diagnosis. In this way the selection procedures were guaranteed to be unconfounded by psychological test data. The assessment also included independently obtained mental status examinations and social-developmental histories. As each of the patients subsequently entered either psychotherapy or psychoanalysis, the initial diagnosis was confirmed in discussions with the patient's therapist or analyst. The patients were matched as groups on the variables of age, sex, and socioeconomic status. The Rorschach records obtained from the two groups did not differ significantly with regard to the number of total responses.

In Study II, Rorschach protocols were obtained from the files of a population of psychiatric inpatients hospitalized at a university teaching hospital. All patients at this facility receive psychological testing as part of standard procedure within the first several weeks of admission. Patients selected for this study met the following initial screening criteria: (1) age between 16 and 26 years; (2) no evidence of organic impairment and/or mental subnormality; and (3) availability of complete Rorschach protocols.

The schizophrenic sample, consisting of 19 patients was selected using the

Research Diagnostic Criteria (RDC) (Spitzer, Endicott, & Robbins, 1975). The RDC was applied to information gleaned from a preadmission report that included history of the present illness, past history, a mental status exam, and a tentative diagnostic formulation. As such, the RDC selection procedure was entirely independent of the psychological test data.

The borderline sample, consisting of 21 patients, was selected according to criteria as set out in DSM-III. The borderline diagnosis is conceptualized in DSM-III as consisting of two major groups—Borderline Personality Disorder and Schizotypal Personality Disorder. Based on the findings and recommendations of Rosenthal (1979) and Spitzer, Endicott, and Gibbon (1979), the two categories were collapsed for this study. According to Spitzer et al. (1979), a combined item set presents a high degree of sensitivity and specificity in contrasting borderline and nonborderline patients. The DSM-III criteria were then applied to information gleaned from the preadmission summaries in the same manner as for the schizophrenic sample. As in Study I, the Rorschach records for the schizophrenic and borderline groups did not differ significantly with regard to the number of total responses.

For purposes of determining reliability, that is, inter-rater agreement in scoring, in both studies all Rorschachs were coded and scored independently by two raters, and then the ratings were correlated.

Results of Study I: Comparison of Defenses in Borderline and Neurotic Outpatients

The data were analyzed by multiple t-test comparisons and in some cases, by chi-square analysis. A review of the comparisons indicated the following: satisfactory inter-rater reliabilities, assessed by Spearman product moment correlations, were obtained for all categories (.42–1.00 for the continuum variables and .76 for splitting); borderline patients were found to use Rorschach test indices of low-level devaluation ($t = -3.64$, $df = 28$, $p < .05$) significantly more often than did the neurotic patients; and indices of high-level devaluation and high-level denial, by contrast, were found more frequently among the neurotic group. While the idealization scale did not yield statistically significant differences between groups, in general and irrespective of level of severity, measure of idealization occurred more frequently in the Rorschach records of the neurotic group. With respect to devaluation the reverse was found. That is, the borderline patients tended to use test indices of depreciation more often than did the neurotic patients.

Strikingly, indices of splitting and projective identification appeared exclusively in the borderline group. Thus, of the various defense scores, splitting ($X^2 = 9.00$, $p < .01$) and projective identification ($X^2 = 10.0$, $p < .01$) proved especially significant in discriminating groups.

In addition to comparing measures of defense, the groups were also compared with respect to the developmental level of their human responses using a measure devised by Blatt et al. (1976). The results indicate that the neurotic patients offered significantly more human responses of the developmentally advanced full human ($t = 3.10$, $df = 28$, $p < .01$) variety than did the borderline patients. Conversely, borderline patients produced significantly more developmentally less differentiated quasi-human ($t = -2.12$, $df = 28$, $p < .05$) responses than did their neurotic counterparts. The differences between groups in quality of response productivity in terms of maintaining a "humanness" dimension temporally and spatially (Pruitt & Spilka, 1964) can be determined through a comparison between human sum (H + Hd) and quasi-human sum ([H] + [Hd]) scores. Whereas neurotic patients offered significantly more sum human and human detail responses ($t = 3.09$, $df = 28$, $p < .01$), the borderline group produced significantly more temporally and spatially distanced sum quasi-human and quasi-human detail responses ($t = 2.11$, $df = 28$, $p < .05$).

In summary, the results from Study I indicate that the defense scale is a reliable instrument and that the specific test measures of low-level devaluation, low-level denial, splitting, and projective identification distinguished samples of borderline and neurotic patients in the expected direction. Further, the study also revealed that borderline patients produced human responses at a lower developmental level that were distanced in time and space than did neurotics.

Results of Study II: Comparison of Defenses in Borderline and Schizophrenic Inpatients

As in Study I, high levels of inter-rater reliability were obtained (.47–.95 for the continuum variables and .97 for splitting). Collapsing the continuum variables into composite scores yielded reliability correlation coefficients ranging from .94–.96. These coefficients may be considered as particularly impressive for ink blot measures.

Several significant findings emerged when the defense scores of the borderline and schizophrenic patients were compared. Splitting significantly distinguished the two groups in the predicted direction ($t = -2.50$, $df = 38$, $p < .05$) and four of the five continuum measures of devaluation also separated the two groups ($p < .05$) with borderline patients offering significantly more depreciated human responses (composite devaluation). As for idealization, by contrast, only the low-level score provided significantly discriminatory ($t = -2.56$, $df = 38$, $p < .05$). Although schizophrenic patients, in general, produced fewer human responses, those they did offer tended to be skewed in a comparatively positive and/or benign direction. With regard to denial, the borderline group gave significantly more responses at the middle ($t = 2.91$, $df = 38$, $p < .01$) and lower ($t = .3.33$, $df = 38$, $p < .01$) levels than did the schizophrenics. Denial, when treated as a composite score, especially distinguished the two groups ($t = 4.46$, $df = 38$, $p < .001$).

As in Study I, the scale measures of projective identification occurred exclusively in the borderline group (9 to 21 cases). The data for this score were subjected to a chi-square analysis and the findings reveal that this defense was especially significant in distinguishing the two groups in the predicted direction ($X^2 = 8.19$, $p < .01$).

These groups were also compared on the Blatt et al. (1976) measure of developmental level of human responses, and the results indicated that the borderline patients as compared with their schizophrenic counterparts offered more human responses at all levels. The borderlines produced more full human responses ($t = 2.61$, $df = 38$, $p < .05$), quasi-human responses ($t = .266$, $df = 38$, $p < .05$), human sum responses ($t = 2.63$, $df = 38$, $p < .05$), and quasi-human sum responses ($t = 2.87$, $df = 38$, $p < .01$).

In summary, the results of Study II reveal that the borderline patients achieved statistically significant higher scores on all of the defense measures, especially denial and projective identification, as compared with the schizophrenic patients. Further, although the groups offered a near equal number of total Rorschach responses (R), the borderlines produced significantly more human responses at each developmental level of differentiation.

The combined findings of both studies lend convincing support to the contention that borderline patients exhibit a specific and discernible defensive constellation different from that of both neurotic and schizophrenic patients, and that the scoring manual is a reliable and valid indicator of these defenses. The results further demonstrate the heuristic value of Kernberg's (1975, 1977) emphasis on internal psychostructural organization as the nidus around which the differential diagnosis of borderline personality disorders from neurotic and schizophrenic conditions may be made. Empirically, the Rorschach Defense Scale proved effective in distinguishing among diagnostic groups on the basis of an assessment of defensive organization. Conceptually, implicit in the construction of the scale was the notion that representational capacities and each of the defensive functions are inextricably related. Thus, findings from the studies have implications pertinent to the growing realization of the complex interactions among early object relations; the level and quality of psychological structures including thought processes, defensive functioning, and the internal representational world; and ongoing object relations and the ways in which these units of structure and experience are internalized and become part of the personality.

There have been two major attempts to cross-validate Lerner and Lerner's Rorschach scale by applying expanded versions of defense measures to samples of neurotic, borderline, and schizophrenic patients. Collins (1982) and Cooper (1981, 1982) have independently broadened Lerner and Lerner's Rorschach defense scale to include animate and inanimate responses as well as human percepts with a view toward improving the discriminatory power of Rorschach indices of defense. In addition, Collins (1982) developed a rating of defense effectiveness, similar to Holt's score of defense effectiveness, whereas Cooper

(1982), based on Stolorow and Lachmann's (1980) formulations of developmental arrest, distinguished between "prestages" of defense involving a developmental inability to register events or integrate objects and defenses proper based on intense ambivalence conflicts within a more fully structuralized ego and secondary to intrapsychic conflict. Both research endeavors are aimed at further refining Rorschach indices of defense by including additional criteria and are informed by recent developments and critical issues within psychoanalytic theory.

Collins, taking Kernberg's concept of borderline personality organization as point of departure, advances a continuum or spectrum notion of borderline phenomena from "successful" to "unsuccessful" based on social, vocational, and interpersonal functioning. The case illustrations he cites as exemplary of the "successful" and "unsuccessful" borderline suggests that this distinction may be along outpatient-inpatient lines. By extension, Collins regards defensive structures within borderline patients as effective or ineffective along a 3-point continuum. According to this author "fully effective defenses" structure impulse, affect, and fantasy elaboration into socially acceptable behavior. Freud's concept of sublimation illustrates an effective defense. "Partially effective defenses" while modulating affective expression and anxiety result in symptom formation detrimental to optimal adaptive functioning. "Ineffective defenses" fail to bind affect and anxiety and result in a serious incapacitation of human functioning. Collins proposes an expansion of the traditional ego psychological schema of impulse-defense configurations to what he terms "defenses of the self" and with this in mind, he examines the two central defenses of borderline personality organization—splitting and projective identification—and offers Rorschach examples of relatively "successful" and "unsuccessful" manifestations.

Cooper (1981, 1982) offers a comprehensive and sophisticated conceptual rationale for a Rorschach defense scale based on a careful examination of a broad range of content, including the patient-examiner relationship and geared toward drawing important distinctions between levels of defense reflective of developmental arrest (Stolorow & Lachmann, 1980) and structural conflict. Cooper (1981) offers definitions of borderline defenses and advances specific criteria and examples for the Rorschach assessment of splitting, devaluation, primitive idealization, omnipotence, and projective identification. Regarding the Rorschach protocol as a sample of the patient's representational world, Cooper (1981) systematically examines various levels of defensive operations in patients diagnosed as borderline personality organization. According to Cooper (1982):

> It is proposed that defensive operations among borderline patients are richly varied and that some borderline patients demonstrate prestage defensive operations while others show defense process per se. The Rorschach assessment of such differences in level of defense may provide implications for whether psychotherapy is better

focused on the interpretation of frightening ambivalence conflicts ensconsed within protective defense/fantasy structures versus the interpretation of difficulties with the differentiation between self and object. (p. 1)

Although there is considerable conceptual and operational consensus between the Rorschach defense scales of Lerner and Lerner and of Cooper, the following highlights some of those areas where Cooper offers broader operational criteria and finer distinctions between "prestage" and more fully structuralized defensive operations. Cooper conceptualizes early or prestages of splitting as a "passive" stage of defensive activity in which the ego is unable either to perceive objects as a totality or to register whole object images in the context of diverse affective experiences. In contrast, defensive splitting, reflecting greater ego structuralization and a consolidated representational world, is aimed at resolving intense ambivalence conflicts by polarizing one set of emotions toward one object with an opposite set attached to another object. Prestages of splitting are manifested and scored on the Rorschach when a single image is fragmented into disparate parts of opposite affective valence or in percepts containing alternating, fluid, chaotic, and contradictory descriptions about animate or inanimate objects. Later stages of splitting as a defense are directed at the "splitting of representations" (Lichtenberg & Slap, 1973) and are scored in Rorschach percepts containing "all good" and "all bad" object images linked to two or more separately perceived objects.

Cooper also advances operationalized Rorschach indices of idealization and devaluation, which extends Lerner and Lerner's criteria in an attempt to distinguish between prestage and defensive manifestations of these processes. Accounting for the fragmented and fluid perceptual processes characteristic of seriously disturbed patients, Cooper scores all percepts and associative elaborations for possible manifestations of idealization and devaluation, even including an analysis of the patient-examiner relationship. Idealization and devaluation based on oedipal-level conflicts is embellished in Rorschach responses that are more clearly demarcated, less fabulized, and more ambivalent. A defense considered by Cooper, closely allied to idealization, and not scored on the Lerner and Lerner scale is omnipotence defined as an idealization of the self. Several categories of omnipotence are scored including self-aggrandizing statements, use of the "editorial we" (Schafer, 1954), "lecturing" the examiner in a condescending manner, and demonstrations of haughtiness in the patient-examiner relationship.

A valuable aspect of Cooper's scale involves his attempt to operationalize the complex defensive process of projective identification. Guided by the work of Ogden (1979), Cooper (1981) defines projective identification as "a psychological process that is simultaneously a type of defense, a mode of communication, a primitive form of object relationship and a pathway for psychological change" (p. 362; p. 20). In keeping with Lerner and Lerner, Cooper assesses the presence of projective identification by identifying constituent elements of the process. Salient elements include fantasies of literally putting dangerous or endangered aspects of the self into another object, "fearfully empathizing" with objects containing aggressive projections, and hyperalertness to external threat or attack linked with expressions of primitive rage. Operationalized indices of projective identification, according to Cooper, include the translocation of substances in feelings from one object to another; the placement of a vulnerable or valued object into another object for projection, and signs of "fearful empathy" often observed in the subject's reactions to responses such as an identification with aggressive figures, texture responses with a clear indication of external threat, and hyperalertness as indicated by the F(c) determinant (Lerner & Lerner, 1980) associated with aggressive content.

Utilizing this comprehensive and sophisticated defense scale to discriminate borderline, character-disordered, manic depressive, and schizophrenic patients, Cooper's (1982) preliminary data suggest two distinct groups of borderline patients. The first group consists of those borderline patients unable to fully differentiate from objects as well as exhibiting problems integrating opposite representations; that is, patients who may be considered as developmentally arrested at a prestage of defense (Stolorow & Lachmann, 1980). The second group consists of borderline patients unable to resolve intense feelings of ambivalence toward whole objects; that is, patients who exhibit borderline defense proper. According to Cooper (1982):

> It is possible that a group of borderline patients are constrained by developmental inabilities to achieve integration/differentiation. This view is more compatible with Modell's (1963, 1968) perspective on the borderline as developmentally arrested at the stage of the transitional object prior to genuine differentiation between self and object; in this view the borderline is construed as having a capacity for recognition of an object, existing outside the self, but which owes its existence to processes arising within the individual in contrast to Kernberg's regression/re-fusion hypothesis. (p. 12)

From the purview of diagnostic-clinician, Grala (1980) offers a thorough review of the psychoanalytic literature on one defense central to borderline personality organization—splitting—and then advances several, well-formulated and example-anchored illustrations of splitting phenomena on the Rorschach. Taking Schafer's (1954) treatment of adaptive and defensive operations manifested on the Rorschach as a point of departure, Grala regards splitting as a wide-ranging regulative and defensive process. Grala suggests a developmental continuum of splitting ". . . ranging from the fragmentation of experience at the lower end to a simplified mode of organizing perceptions, memories, and fantasies into uniform representational systems at the higher end" (p. 269). Consistent with this position and in keeping with the formulations of Stolorow and

Lachmann (1980) as well as Cooper (1981), splitting is not regarded as pathognomonic of a particular nosological entity, that is, borderline, but rather as an index of prevailing levels of ego organization and adaptation. Similar to Stolorow and Lachmann's (1980) distinction between prestages of splitting and defensive splitting, Grala demarcates splitting along pre-rapprochement and rapprochement lines. A representational capacity is the nidus around which rapprochement splitting is organized. Pre-rapprochement splitting reflects a fragmented organization of the ego, cognitive immaturity, and extremely primitive part object representations lacking sufficient structuralization or organization to express a predominant affective valence or cohesive representational capacity. Rapprochement splitting indicates a more advanced level of development, ego structuralization, and a more complex representational system that is defensively split into opposite affective aggregates in order to prevent the simultaneous awareness of divergent, contradictory, and conflicting impulses toward the same object.

Based on a comprehensive review of the theoretical literature on splitting and his own formulations of a developmental continuum of splitting phenomena, Grala systematically identifies a number of varying manifestations of splitting on the Rorschach. According to this author ". . . the fundamental process [of splitting] should be discernible in the mode of organization and in the mental contents the individual brings to bear on the test stimuli" (p. 261). Grala considers Rorschach manifestations of splitting in terms of formal scores: location, determinants, and content. Although various forms of splitting can be expressed through all areas of the stimulus, the organization of experience according to polarized affective qualities favor the formation of global, vague, and impressionistic whole percepts. A predominance of dissociative mechanisms and inconsistent ego states is reflected in no synchronous pattern or sequence of location components. Because splitting defies a modification of experience based on objective or abstract criteria, color outweighs form as a determinant and a predominance of CF and arbitrary FC responses may be expected. The human movement response represents the most important determinant of splitting phenomena according to Grala. A close examination of this response along a number of dichotomous dimensions provides an important index of splitting; that is, a proclivity to fragment of dissociate significant object representations. "Inspection of the action tendencies represented in M responses," according to Grala, "should provide a window to the patient's prevailing modes of organizing and defending his representational system" (p. 265). Thematic analysis of Rorschach responses is particularly useful for unearthing splitting phenomena. Oscillating positive and negative percepts, parallel positive and negative images, and fragmented percepts all reflect various manifestations of splitting processes. Grala notes that the tendency to strictly segregate representations of opposite affective valence impairs integrative capacities and the ability to screen out incompatible percepts. This tendency leads to a juxtaposition of incongruent details and the formation of fabulized combination responses. Thus, Grala posits a relationship between splitting and the fabulized combination response.

TOWARD A DEVELOPMENTAL-STRUCTURAL MODEL
OF DEFENSE

Until relatively recently the concept of defense within traditional psychoanalytic theory remained comparatively immune to the impact of object relations theory in general and formulations concerning the development of object representations in particular. As Stolorow and Lachmann (1980) noted: "An examination of the history of the concept of defense indicates that while ideas about what a defense wards off have evolved, the concept of defense itself has remained static" (p. 89). Although several writers have attempted to introduce developmental schemes in terms of ranking defenses from "archaic" or "primitive" to "higher order" or "advanced" (e.g., A. Freud, 1936; Gedo & Goldberg, 1973; Jacobson, 1971; Kernberg, 1975; Kohut, 1977), most of these conceptualizations have remained exclusively wedded to the notion of vicissitudes of psychosexual development and have failed to give sufficient attention to defenses within the context of an evolving representational world. Correspondingly, advances in understanding the complex psychological processes involved in representational development and the pathology of self and object representations (Kernberg, 1975, 1976; Kohut, 1971, 1977) have not contributed to an understanding of defensive processes within a representational framework. A noteworthy exception is found in the work of Stolorow and Lachmann (1980) who propose a developmental line for each defensive process. Although their distinction between psychopathology stemming from defense against structural conflict (neurosis) and psychopathology rooted in an "arrest" in representational development at a *prestage* of defense has much clinical utility, it leaves the notion of arrest and prestage poorly defined and tends to confuse levels of conceptualization. That is, the authors tend to mix formulations rooted in the structural theory of psychoanalysis on a metapsychological level with formulations more closely tied to the clinical theory of psychoanalysis on a phenomenological level.

Nonetheless, in keeping with the thrust of Stolorow and Lachmann's (1980) work our findings regarding the differential utilization of defenses among neurotic, borderline, and schizophrenic patients are consistent with and suggestive of a developmental-structural model of defense conceptualized within an object representational framework. Self-representations and object representations, as the product of internalized relationship paradigms, have been studied according to the degree to which they are, in Kernberg's (1975) terms, introjective, primitive, and unintegrated at one end of a continuum as contrasted with the degree to which they are metabolized, organized, differentiated, and stably integrated at the other end of the continuum. In a similar way, defenses, their function and developmental vicissitudes, also may be outlined along the same dimension of internalization and progressive structuralization. From this perspective, at the least differentiated, most primitive end of the developmental spectrum where the self-other boundary is most precarious, defenses function in a relatively simple, automatic and global manner to alter drive-affective dispositions or valences in a biologically triggered, somatically based, vacant, fluid pre-object representational world that reflects a fundamental failure in introjection. With increased structuralization and formation of a self-other boundary, the inner world becomes populated by introjects that retain an undifferentiated affective-cognitive quality characterized solely by the valence of the object—the earliest affective response to an actual object. With the evolving consolidation of the self-other boundary external objects become internalized and for the first time are represented psychologically; however, owing to the permeability of the boundary, these more primitive object representations are inconsistent and unstable and are internalized as crude and global positive and/or negative images based on fantasy drenched part properties of the object. As a consequence of the polarization along drive-affective lines of the self-representations and object representations, object relations have a ''transitional object'' quality in that they are characterized by confusion amongst the external object, the inner representation of the object, and the affect response to the object. Unlike the previous stage, defenses at this level are intimately related to the developing representational capacity. That is, such processes as splitting, projective identification, denial, primitive devaluation, and primitive idealization are represented object relationally, serve an organizing function, yet at the same time reflect the relatively undifferentiated, incompletely metabolized quality of the representations. As cognitive-affective structures become increasingly differentiated, articulated, and integrated and as the internalization process progressively bears the stamp of early identifications (Kernberg, 1975) object representations become increasingly more stable, integrated, and complex, as, for example, their including such aspects as an anticipatory sense of objects, a greater awareness of roles and functions of objects, and an increasingly modulated affective coloring to the tie between self and other. In concert with these developmental advancements, defensive operations at this level do not alter the fundamental affective disposition or basic integrity of self-representations and object representations but, rather, function in a more circumscribed and subtle fashion to protect a more flexible and integrated ego from drive-affective derivatives. Such derivatives, experienced in the form of anxiety, arise from conflict between well-developed, more fully structuralized self-representations and object representations. Defenses at this higher level revolve around repression and include higher level forms of projection, idealization, depreciation and denial (intellectualization, minimization, etc.). These achievements reflect advances in levels of internalization (identification, ego identity) and concomitant cognitive and affective development, all within the matrix of a progressive differentiation, articulation, and integration of the representational world.

In essence, defenses at the lowest developmental level involve the alteration of primitive, somatically based drive-affect dispositions. As development proceeds and a representational capacity is achieved (i.e., the psychological birth of the infant), defenses take on an increasingly organizing function and protect the cohesion and integrity of poorly differentiated self-representations and object representations. At higher developmental levels featured by enhanced affective-cognitive differentiation and corresponding representational capacity, more encapsulated defenses, limited in scope and related to specific drive-affective derivatives, function to protect a well-structuralized ego from anxiety stemming from conflict between intrapsychic structures composed of more fully metabolized and specific self-representations and object representations.

Although we have attempted to formulate these developmental and structural conceptions, which account for and integrate the role of defenses within an evolving representational framework, in a middle-level clinical language (Mayman, 1976), they may also be coordinated with formulations posited on a more abstract, metapsychological level. The empirical findings of Lerner and Lerner (1982) and Cooper (1982), for example, are also consistent with Hartmann's (1939) concepts of neutralization of drive energy and Rapaport's (1959) notion of the ego as a hierarchically organized system of detours.

An object relational model of defenses, formulated in a middle-level clinical language of empirically derived constructs rooted in developmental and structural terms and coordinated systematically with metapsychological formulations, extends beyond the more traditional ego psychological conceptions of defense while still allowing for continuity with the adaptive point of view as espoused by Hartmann and articulated by Rapaport. These formulations regarding defense are forwarded as part of an increasing effort (Kernberg, 1975, 1976) to integrate object relations theory with ego psychology and thus provide a broader theoretical and clinical foundation for examining issues at the interface of these approaches, such as the relationship of object relations to thinking, drive to affect, affect to object relations, and the intrapsychic to the interpersonal realms of experience.

SUMMARY

Psychoanalytic theory and Rorschach test theory have enjoyed a mutually beneficial relationship that continues to evolve. As outlined in this chapter, psychoanalytic theory has grown from an early concern with an identification of the instincts and their vicissitudes to an emphasis on examining the ego, its processes and functions, to a more contemporary focus on object relations including the systematic exploration of the early mother–child relationship, and its impact on the development of the self and the internal representational world. Each shift in theory has, in turn, provided new and stimulating conceptualizations that have served to broaden and enrich the theoretical basis for the clinical and research application of the Rorschach. In this chapter we have attempted to systematically review and enlarge upon the psychoanalytic conceptual base for the study of defense by means of the Rorschach. We began with a review of the psychoanalytic literature on defense beginning with Freud's earliest formulations and attempted to correlate subsequent advances in theory with Rorschach endeavors to assess defensive processes. Originating in the pioneering efforts of Rapaport and Schafer, we touched upon the contributions of Holt and other ego psychologists and, finally, discussed several more recent contributions to an evolving and expanding literature.

REFERENCES

Allison, J. (1967). Adaptive regression and intense religious experiences. *Journal of Nervous and Mental Disorders, 145,* 452–463.

Bachrach, H. (1968). Adaptive regression, empathy and psychotherapy: Theory and research study. *Psychotherapy, 5,* 203–209.

Benfari, R., & Calogeras, R. (1968). Levels of cognition and conscience typologics. *Journal of Projective Techniques and Personality Assessment, 32,* 466–474.

Bion, W. (1967). *Second thoughts.* New York: Jason Aronson.

Blatt, S. J., Allison, J., & Feirstein, A. (1969). The capacity to cope with cognitive complexity. *Journal of Personality, 37,* 269–288.

Blatt, S. J., Brenneis, B., Schimek, J. G., & Glick, M. (1976). Normal development and psychopathological impairment of the concept of the object on the Rorschach. *Journal of Abnormal Psychology, 85,* 364–373.

Blatt, S. J., & Lerner, H. (1983). The psychological assessment of object representations. *Journal of Personality Assessment, 47,* 7–28.

Collins, R. (1983). *Rorschach correlates of borderline personality.* Unpublished doctoral dissertation, University of Toronto.

Cooper, S. (1981). *An object relations view of the borderline defenses: A Rorschach analysis.* Unpublished manuscript.

Cooper, S. (1982, March). *Restage versus defense process and the borderline personality: A Rorschach analysis.* Paper presented to the Mid-winter Meeting of the Division of Psychoanalysis of the APA. Puerto Rico.

Dudek, S., & Chamberland-Bouhadana, G. (1982). Primary process in creative persons. *Journal of Personality Assessment, 46,* 239–247.

Easer, R. (1974). Empathic inhibition and psychoanalytic technique. *Psychoanalytic Quarterly, 43,* 557–580.

Fairbairn, W. (1954). *An object relations theory of personality.* New York: Basic Books.

Fairbairn, W. (1952). Endopsychic structure considered in terms of object relationships. In W. Fairbairn (Ed.), *Psychoanalytic studies of the personality* (pp. 82–136). London: Tauistock. (Original work published 1944)

Feirstein, A. (1967). Personality correlates for unrealistic experiences. *Journal of Consulting Psychology, 31,* 387–395.

Fenichel, D. (1945). *Psychoanalytic theory of neurosis.* New York: Norton.

Freud, A. (1936). *The ego and the mechanisms of defense.* New York: International Universities Press.

Freud, S. (1953). The interpretation of dreams. In J. Strachey (Ed. and Trans.), The standard edition of the complete psychological works of Sigmund Freud (Vols. 4 & 5, pp. 1–630). London: Hogarth. (Original work published 1900)

Freud, S. (1955). Beyond the pleasure principle. In J. Strachey (Ed. and Trans.), The standard edition of the complete psychological works of Sigmund Freud (Vol. 17, pp. 7–66). London: Hogarth. (Original work published in 1920)

Freud, S. (1957). The unconscious. In J. Strachey (Ed. and Trans.), The standard edition of the complete psychological works of Sigmund Freud (Vol. 14, pp. 166–215). London: Hogarth. (Original work published in 1915)

Freud, S. (1959). Repression. In J. Strachey (Ed. and Trans.), The standard edition of the complete psychological works of Sigmund Freud (Vol. 14, pp. 146–158). London: Hogarth. (Original work published in 1915)

Freud, S. (1960). Jokes and their relation to the unconscious. In J. Strachey (Ed. and Trans.), The standard edition of the complete psychological works of Sigmund Freud (Vol. 8, pp. 9–256). London: Hogarth. (Original work published in 1905)

Freud, S. (1961a). The ego and the id. In J. Strachey (Ed. and Trans.), The standard edition of the complete psychological works of Sigmund Freud (Vol. 19, pp. 13–68). London: Hogarth. (Original work published in 1923)

Freud, S. (1961b). Inhibitions, symptoms and anxiety. In J. Strachey (Ed. and Trans.), The standard edition of the complete psychological works of Sigmund Freud (Vol. 20, pp. 87–172). London: Hogarth. (Original work published in 1926)

Freud, S. (1962a). The neuro-psychosis of defense. In J. Strachey (Ed. and Trans.), The standard edition of the complete psychological works of Sigmund Freud (Vol. 3, pp. 45–70). London: Hogarth. (Original work published 1894)

Freud, S. (1962b). Further remarks on the neuro-psychosis of defense. In J. Strachey (Ed. and Trans.), The standard edition of the complete psychological works of Sigmund Freud (Vol. 3, pp. 162–188). London: Hogarth. (Original work published 1896)

Freud, S. (1964). New introductory lectures on psychoanalysis. *Standard Edition, 22*:7–182. London: Hogarth. (Original work published in 1933)

Gedo, J., & Goldberg, A. (1973). *Models of the mind: A psychoanalytic theory.* Chicago: University of Chicago Press.

Goldberger, L. (1961). Reactions to perceptual isolation and Rorschach manifestations of the primary process. *Journal of Projective Techniques, 25,* 287–302.

Grala, C. (1980). The concept of splitting and its manifestations on the Rorschach test. *Bulletin of the Menninger Clinic, 44,* 253–271.

Greenberg, N., Ramsay, M., Rakoff, V., & Weiss, A. (1969). Primary process thinking in myxoedema psychosis: A case study. *Canada Journal of Behavioral Science, 1,* 60–67.

Greenspan, S. (1979). Intelligence and adaptation. [monograph] *Psychological Issues, 47/48.* New York: International Universities Press.

Grotstein, J. (1981). *Splitting and projective identification.* New York: Jason Aronson.

Guntrip, H. (1961). *Personality structure and human interaction.* New York: International Universities Press.

Hartmann, H. (1939). *Ego psychology and the problem of adaptation.* New York: International Universities Press.

Hoffer, W. (1968). Notes on the theory of defense. *Psychoanalytic Study of the Child, 23,* 178–188.

Holt, R. (1968). *Manual for scoring primary process manifestations in Rorschach responses.* Unpublished manuscript, New York University Research Center for Mental Health.

Holt, R. (1977). A method for assessing primary process manifestations and their control in Rorschach responses. In M. Rickers-Orsiankina (Ed.), *Rorschach psychology* (pp. 375–420). Huntington, NY: Krieger.

Holtzman, P., & Gardner, R. (1959). Leveling and repression. *Journal of Abnormal and Social Psychology, 59,* 151–155.

Horowitz, M. (1972). Modes of representation of thought. *Journal of the American Psychoanalytic Association, 20,* 793–819.

Jacobson, E. (1971). *Depression: Comparative studies of normal, neurotic, and psychotic conditions.* New York: International Universities Press.

Kernberg, O. (1975). *Borderline conditions and pathological narcissism.* New York: Jason Aronson.

Kernberg, O. (1976). *Object relations theory and clinical psychoanalysis.* New York: Jason Aronson.

Kernberg, O. (1977). The structural diagnosis of borderline personality organization. In P. Hartocollis (Ed.), *Borderline personality disorders.* New York: International Universities Press.

Kernberg, O. (1980). *Internal world and external reality.* New York: Jason Aronson.

Klein, M. (1975). *The collected works of Melanie Klein: Volume III.* London: Hogarth.

Kohut, H. (1971). *The analysis of the self.* New York: International Universities Press.

Kohut, H. (1977). *The restoration of the self.* New York: International Universities Press.

Kris, E. (1952). *Psychoanalytic explorations in art.* New York: International Universities Press.

Krohn, A. (1978). *Hysteria: The exclusive neurosis.* New York: International Universities Press.

Kwawer, J. (1980). Primitive interpersonal modes, borderline phenomena, and the Rorschach test. In J. Kwawer, H. Lerner, P. Lerner, & A. Sugarman (Eds.), *Borderline phenomena and the Rorschach Test* (89–106). New York: International Universities Press.

Kwawer, J., Lerner, H., Lerner, P., & Sugarman, A. (Eds.). (1980). *Borderline phenomena and the Rorschach Test.* New York: International Universities Press.

Leeuw, P. (1971). On the development of the concept of defense. *International Journal of Psycho-Analysis, 52,* 51–58.

Lerner, H., & Lerner, P. (1982). A comparative study of defensive structure in neurotic, borderline, and schizophrenic patients. *Psychoanalysis and Contemporary Thought, 1,* 77–115.

Lerner, H., Sugarman, A., & Gaughran, J. (1981). *Borderline and schizophrenic patients: A comparative study of defensive structure. Journal of Nervous & Mental Disease, 168,* 705–711.

Lerner, P. (1984). Projective techniques and personality assessment: The current perspective. In N. Endler & J. McVicker Hunt (Eds.), *Personality and the behavioral disorders* (pp. 283–312). New York: Wiley.

Lerner, P., & Lerner, H. (1980). Rorschach assessment of primitive defenses in borderline personality structure. In J. Kwawer, H. Lerner, P. Lerner, & A. Sugarman (Eds.), *Borderline phenomena and the Rorschach Test* (pp. 257–274). New York: International Universities Press.

Lerner, P., & Lewandowski, A. (1975). The measurement of primary process manifestations: A review. In P. Lerner (Ed.), *Handbook of Rorschach scales* (pp. 181–214). New York: International Universities Press.

Levine, M., & Spivack, G. (1964). *The Rorschach index of repressive style.* Springfield: Charles C. Thomas.

Lichtenberg, J., & Slap, J. (1973). Notes on the concept of splitting and the defense mechanism of splitting of representations. *Journal of the American Psychoanalytic Association, 21,* 772–787.

Loewald, H. (1978). Instinct theory, object relations, and psychic structure formation. *Journal of the American Psychoanalytic Association, 26,* 493–506.

Madison, P. (1961). *Freud's concept of repression and defense, its theoretical and observational language.* Minneapolis: University of Minneapolis Press.

Mahler, M., Pine, F., & Bergman, A. (1975). *The psychological birth of the human infant: Symbiosis and individuation.* New York: Basic Books.

Maupin, E. (1965). Individual differences in response to a Zen meditation exercise. *Journal of Consulting Psychology, 29,* 139–145.

Mayman, M. (1967). Object representations and object relationships in Rorschach responses. *Journal of Projective Techniques and Personality Assessment, 31,* 17–24.

Mayman, M. (1976). Psychoanalytic theory in retrospect and prospect. *Bulletin of the Menninger Clinic, 40,* 199–210.

Mayman, M. (1977). A multi-dimensional view of the Rorschach movement response. In M. Rickers-Ovusiankina (Ed.), *Rorschach psychology* (pp. 229–250). New York: Krieger.

McMahon, J. (1964). *The relationship between "overinclusive" and primary process thought in a normal and a schizophrenic population.* Unpublished doctoral dissertation, New York University.

Meissner, W. (1979). Methodological critique of the action language in psychoanalysis. *Journal of the American Psychoanalytic Association, 27,* 79–105.

Meissner, W. (1982). Notes on the potential differentiation of borderline conditions. *International Journal of Psychoanalytic Psychotherapy, 9,* 3–50.

Modell, A. (1963). Primitive object relationships and the predisposition to schizophrenia. *International Journal of Psycho-Analysis, 44,* 282–292.

Modell, A. (1968). *Object love and reality.* New York: International Universities Press.

Modell, A. (1975). A narcissistic defense against affects and the illusion of self sufficiency. *International Journal of Psycho-Analysis, 56,* 275–282.

Modell, A. (1976). The holding environment and the therapeutic action of psychoanalysis. *International Journal of Psycho-Analysis, 24,* 285–307.

Modell, A. (1980). Affects and their non-communication. *International Journal of Psycho-Analysis, 61,* 259–268.

Murray, J., & Russ, S. (1981). Adaptive regression and type of cognitive flexibility. *Journal of Personality Assessment, 45,* 59–65.

Ogden, T. (1979). On projective identification. *International Journal of Psycho-Analysis, 60,* 357–373.

Peebles, R. (1975). Rorschach as self-system in the telophasic theory of personality development. In P. Lerner (Ed.), *Handbook of Rorschach Scales* (pp. 71–136). New York: International Universities Press.

Pine, F. (1962). Creativity and primary process: Sample variations. *Journal of Nervous and Mental Disorder, 134,* 506–511.

Pine, F., & Holt, R. (1960). Creativity and primary process: A study of adaptive regression. *Journal of Abnormal and Social Psychology, 61,* 370–379.

Pruitt, W., & Spilka, B. (1964). Rorschach empathy—object relationship scale. *Journal of Projective Techniques and Personality Assessment, 8,* 331–336.

Rabkin, J. (1967). *Psychoanalytic assessment of change in organization of thought after psychotherapy.* Unpublished doctoral dissertation, New York University.

Rapaport, D. (1958). An historical survey of psychoanalytic ego psychology. In M. Gill (Ed.), *The collected papers of David Rapaport* (pp. 745–757). New York: Basic Books.

Rapaport, D. (1959). The structure of psychoanalytic theory: A systematizing attempt. *Psychological Issues, 6.* New York: International Universities Press.

Reich, W. (1933). *Character analysis.* NY: Farrar, Straus, & Giroux.

Rinsley, D. (1979). The developmental etiology of borderline and narcissistic disorders. *Bulletin of the Menninger Clinic, 44,* 147–170.

Rosenthal, O. (1979). Was Thomas Wolfe a borderline? *Schizophrenia Bulletin, 34,* 87–94.

Russ, S. (1980). Primary process integration on the Rorschach and achievement in children. *Journal of Personality Assessment, 44,* 338–344. Saretsky, T. (1966). Effects of chlorpromazine on primary process thought manifestations. *Journal of Abnormal Psychology, 71,* 247–252.

Schafer, R. (1954). *Psychoanalytic Interpretation in Rorschach Testing.* Boston: Grune & Stratton.

Schafer, R. (1978). Psychological test responses and decompensation. *Journal of Personality Assessment, 42,* 562–571.

Segal, H. (1964). *Introduction to the Work of Melanie Klein.* New York: Basic Books.

Shapiro, D. (1965). *Neurotic styles.* New York: Basic Books.

Spear, W. (1980). The psychological assessment of structural and thematic object representations in borderline and schizophrenic patients. In J. Kwawer, H. Lerner, P. Lerner, A. Sugarman (Eds.), *Borderline phenomena and the Rorschach Test* (pp. 321–342). New York: International Universities Press.

Spence, D. (1982). *Narrative truth and historical truth*. New York: Norton.

Spiro, R., & Spiro, T. (1980). Transitional phenomena and developmental issues in borderline Rorschachs. In J. Kwawer, H. Lerner, P. Lerner, A. Sugarman (Eds.), *Borderline Phenomena and the Rorschach Test* (pp. 189–202). New York: International Universities Press.

Spitzer, R., Endicott, J., & Robbins, E. (1975). Research diagnostic criteria. *Psychopharamalogical Bulletin, 11*, 22–24.

Spitzer, R., Endicott, J., & Gibbon, M. (1979). Crossing the border into borderline personality and borderline schizophrenia. *Archives of General Psychiatry, 36*, 17–24.

Stolorow, R., & Atwood, G. (1979). *Faces in a cloud*. New York: Jason Aronson.

Stolorow, R., & Lachmann, F. (1980). *Psychoanalysis of developmental arrest*. New York: International Universities Press.

Winnicott, D. (1960). Ego distortion in terms of true and false self. In D. Oinnicott (Ed.), *The maturational processes and the facilitating environment*. London: Hogarth Press, reprinted 1965.

Witkin, H., Lewis, H., Hertzman, M., Machover, K., Neissner, P., & Wapner, S. (1954). *Personality through perception*. New York: Harper.

Wright, N., & Abbey, D. (1965). Perceptual deprivation tolerance and adequacy of defense. *Perceptual and Motor Skills, 20*, 35–38.

Wright, N., & Zubek, J. (1969). Relationship between perceptual deprivation tolerance and adequacy of defenses as measured by the Rorschach. *Journal of Abnormal Social Psychology, 74*, 615–617.

Young, H. (1959). A test of the Witkin's field-dependence hypothesis. *Journal of Abnormal Social Psychology, 59*, 188–192.

Zimet, C., & Fine, H. (1965). Primary and secondary process thinking in two types of schizophrenia. *Journal of Projective Techniques and Personality Assessment, 29*, 93–99.

Conducting Psychological Evaluations with AA-Oriented Alcoholism Treatment Programs: Implications for Practical Treatment Planning

Steven Walfish
University of South Florida

Renelle Massey
University of South Florida

Anton Krone
Koala Treatment Center

Butcher (1988) suggests that alcoholism is one of the most prevalent and destructive social problems facing Western Civilization. Although the etiology of this problem continues to be debated in the literature, its path of destruction may be seen in the physical, familial, social, occupational, and legal difficulties of the alcoholic.

Miller and Hester (1980) point out that Alcoholics Anonymous (AA) represents the most widespread and long-standing approaches to the treatment of alcoholism. A self-help organization that started over 50 years ago, AA now claims millions of individuals to be members and is clearly the best known approach to the lay public for the treatment of this problem. Indeed, most of the residential treatment programs in this country are based on AA principles. Initially developed at the Hazelden Foundation, this approach has become known as the "Minnesota Model" in which clients are introduced to the AA program and AA philosophy of life. As opposed to a behavioral problem, moral weakness, or major character defect, alcoholism in this approach is viewed as a "disease process" very similar to diabetes or high blood pressure. In this regard the client is not viewed as responsible for obtaining the disease but is responsible for placing it in arrest and remission. This model has been adopted by most of the major corporations that provide residential treatment for alcoholism including Koala Centers, Care Units, Recovery Centers of America, and Glenbeigh Centers.

Traditionally professional psychologists have been left out of these treatment programs and most of the time have been unwelcome. The reasons for this are many and there has been a "mutual antagonism" between those in the AA community and professional psychologists. The reasons for this antagonism are discussed by both Miller (1978) and Marlatt and Gordon (1985). Miller views the ideological differences to include (1) source of help (a recovering alcoholic vs. nonrecovering alcoholic); (2) etiology of alcoholism (disease vs. social learning models); and (3) goal of treatment (abstinence vs. reduction of problem drinking). In addition to these issues Marlatt and Gordon view the major difference to lie in the area of locus of control. That is, in the behavioral model the alcoholic is seen as a person who is capable of self-control. In the disease model the person is viewed as a victim of the disease's force, which is beyond one's control.

Unfortunately, this antagonism has precluded much meaningful dialogue on how traditional psychology and AA approaches can coexist in peaceful harmony, and in some cases complement each other. As recently as 1978, Miller presented an example of achieving this goal in a case study of how a behavioral psychologist could help an AA member achieve a vital goal in their Twelve-Step program. In this seminal example the individual alcoholic client was taught, from a consulting psychologist via behavioral methods, communication skills, coping skills, relaxation training, and assertion skills so that he could complete the Fifth and Sixth Steps of the AA program. Although no evaluation of the effectiveness of the intervention was offered due to a geographical move by the psychologist, the importance of this case study lies in the cooperative arrangement developed by the AA treatment program and the behavioral psychologist. Miller credits the positive response of the staff of the halfway house in which the client resided being due to neither side trying to convert the other to their respective approach. To the contrary, each "faction" was acutely aware of the basic difference in philosophy. Anecdotally, Miller offered that both the consulting behavior therapist and the AA-oriented treatment providers gained a more complete respect for each other's position, which led to a more thorough analysis of common ground.

Similarly, in a very important advance into the integration of psychological and AA approaches, Brown (1985) presents a developmental model of recovery. In this book she discusses how psychotherapy can be integrated into the AA approach, especially at different phases of the recovery process. Further, she presents a "psychological view" of the Twelve Steps.

Levy (1978) suggests that the most obvious way in which psychologists can be of help to self-help organizations is through a consultation process. Altrocchi (1972) suggests that factual preparation and establishing an effective relationship is essential if a consultation experience is to be successful. Preparation, or laying the groundwork, involves getting to know the clients, the nature of their work, and their treatment philosophy. Establishing a relationship involves the development of a mutual learning atmosphere, respect for the consultees' competence, sensitivity to the consultees' anxieties, and acceptance of them as people. Sarason's (1974) concept of "professional preciousness," in which the psychologist is viewed as the expert and the recovering counselor viewed as the student; would clearly be counter-productive in a consultative role. At times, the counselors feel threatened by psychologists and/or believe that psychologists lack experience (of personal addiction and recovery) or knowledge needed in alcoholism treatment.

In this regard it is imperative that the psychologist come to understand the nature of the treatment process and the dynamics of membership in the self-help model. We believe that it is essential that the psychologist become thoroughly familiar with the AA treatment process and the "culture" of this self-help organization if the treatment staff are to be empowered to use the tools that psychologists have to offer toward a recovery process. In addition, if the psychologist is to act in the role of a consultant it is important to follow the adage, "When in Rome do as the Romans do." This will be seen more clearly when the concept of controlled drinking is discussed further. For example, there may be some scientific basis for the use of controlled drinking strategies in some limited populations and in some limited circumstances. However, the adoption of such a treatment stance for clients in an AA-oriented treatment program would demonstrate a lack of respect for this particular self-help model, as well as the competence and personal integrity of the consultee, who is most often a recovering alcoholic and has chosen abstinence as the only appropriate treatment goal.

In order for psychologists to effectively act as consultants with an AA-oriented treatment approach it is imperative that they become cognizant of the treatment approach, philosophy, and basic principles of this self-help group. Although Brown (1985) discusses this in great depth from a professional's point of view and Robertson (1988) discusses the AA experience from a member/journalist's point of view, a few of the key concepts are outlined in the following sections.

The Twelve Steps

The Twelve Steps represents the basis for treatment and the philosophy of life for AA members. It is a treatment approach that first allows the alcoholics to obtain their sobriety and once obtained, to maintain it. These are presented in Table 7.1. Traditionally the alcoholic will progress through these steps one at a time, in sequential order. The time frame for completing them is not typically given and remains on an individual basis. In addition, once sobriety is obtained certain steps are often repeated, when the need arises. For example, it is not unusual for

TABLE 7.1
The Twelve Steps of Alcoholics Anonymous

1. We admitted we were powerless over alcohol and that our lives had become unmanageable.

2. We came to believe that a power greater than ourselves could restore us to sanity.

3. We made a decision to turn over our will and our lives to the care of God as we understood Him.

4. We made a searching and fearless moral inventory of ourselves.

5. We admitted to God, to ourselves, and to another human being the exact nature of our wrongs.

6. We were entirely ready to have God remove all these defects of character.

7. We humbly asked Him to remove our shortcomings.

8. We made a list of all persons we had harmed and became willing to make amends to them all.

9. We made direct amends to such people whenever possible, except where to do so would injure them or others.

10. We continued to take personal inventory and, when we were wrong, promptly admitted it.

11. We sought through prayer and meditation to improve our conscious contact with God as we understood Him, praying only for knowledge of His will for us and the power to carry that out.

12. Having had a spiritual awakening as the result of these steps, we tried to carry the message to alcoholics and to practice these principles in all our affairs.

the recovering alcoholic to "take inventory" on a regular basis or to take another Fifth Step when a great deal of guilt or shame has built up due to past wrong-doings.

Powerlessness

The First Step refers to the need for the alcoholic to discover and accept powerlessness over alcohol. Springborn (1983) refers to this as the laying of the foundation in which a recovery program may be based. Powerlessness of one's drinking represents what Brown (1985) refers to as the "Paradox of Control." That is, in order to gain control to end one's drinking one has to admit that there is indeed no control over one's drinking. Tiebout (1953) suggests that two important characteristics of the alcoholic hinder this process: defiance and grandiosity.

Failure to accept one's powerlessness is viewed as a form of denial. Anderson (1981) argues that denial is a "short-hand term" for a wide repertoire of psychological defenses and maneuvers that alcoholic persons unwittingly set up to protect themselves from the realization that they do in fact have a drinking problem. He elaborates on several forms of denial including minimization, rationalization, blaming or projecting, intellectualization, and overt hostility. Essentially alcoholics will do whatever is possible to make sure that they do not have to change.

Furthermore, it is believed that for most alcoholics there is a need to "hit bottom" before this high level of denial can be broken. That is, there has to be a significant path of destruction left behind (either vocationally, legally, psychologically, or psychosocially) that can no longer, even through the most rigid defenses, be denied. For other individuals who have only begun to experience consequences related to their drinking it may be necessary to "raise their bottom" in order to facilitate the acceptance of their powerlessness. This is typically done by extensive confrontation by others who have "walked the same path before them" and were not able to avoid the destruction that then ensued due to the denial of their alcoholism.

Surrender

Essential in this accepting of one's powerlessness is the concept of *surrender*. This is distinguished from compliance in that the latter suggests an agreement or "going along with" process, whereas the former implies "enthusiasm, wholehearted assent and approval." (Tiebout, 1953). With surrender there is an emotional sense of well-being, and an end to inner struggles of whether or not one is actually an alcoholic. Labeling oneself as an alcoholic and accepting the need to do something constructive about this is the sign of emotionally accepting the First Step.

Surrender has the emotional connotation of defeat. Brown (1985) points out that individuals who value control (and this more than anything describes the personality of the alcoholic) will have a difficult time with this process. But, once again, this is the paradox, in that the alcoholic has to admit defeat in order to win. When this occurs defiance of the disease ceases and the alcoholic behaviorally begins to demonstrate positive steps in the direction of recovery.

Spirituality and Higher Power

One of the common misconceptions of both the professional and the lay public is that AA is a religiously oriented organization. A literal reading of the Twelve Steps without a conceptual understanding can clearly give this impression, as six of the steps make reference to God, or a "Higher Power."

Although most individuals rely on God as their higher power, this is not essential. The essential task is to believe that there is a power greater than oneself to rely on. This does not have to be God in the traditional sense of an organized religion, but rather, "God as we understand him." Those with nontraditional religious beliefs or those who are atheists are asked to place their faith either in the AA group as a whole or in those individuals who are "making it" (Stewart, 1955). Brown (1985) suggests that acceptance of a higher power allows AA members to remove themselves from an ego-centered position in the world and consider other ways of thinking, feeling, and behaving.

Brown further points out that "turning things over" to one's higher power is most difficult to the newly recovering and often causes great furor and anxiety. One can easily see how this would be true for individuals who are as stubborn and rebellious as the alcoholic and who insist on doing things "their way," even though this route has been, to say the least, nonproductive and problematic. Placing "blind faith" in a higher power to let things occur "exactly as they are supposed to" has the potential to greatly reduce anxiety in the alcoholic who is constantly struggling for control and order and achieving none; still, "letting go" is a very difficult process.

Abstinence

A great deal of the rift between the psychological community and the AA community relates to the concept of controlled drinking. We would like to point out that this is not a scientific issue but rather a clearly emotional one, and this is elaborated upon by Marlatt (1983). Behavioral psychologists clearly believe that controlled drinking is not only a possibility but also a reasonable treatment goal for many alcoholics (Miller & Hester, 1980). On the other hand the AA members clearly believe that abstinence is the only appropriate treatment goal. Their belief is that if one can accomplish controlled drinking then one was probably not alcoholic in the first place, but rather, merely a problem drinker.

Brown (1985) points out that the possibility of controlled drinking is very threatening to the AA member. She suggests that the belief in the possibility of controlled drinking represents a regression to an earlier phase in the recovery process. Acceptance of the lack of control over one's drinking is viewed in the AA model as a solid foundation for ongoing recovery. To introduce the viewpoint that "having just a few" may be acceptable for the alcoholic, will clearly be, to say the least, counter-productive.

Group Healing

In a careful reading of the Twelve Steps one will notice that the word "I" never appears at all, but the word "We" is included in each step. The rationale behind this is related to the concept of powerlessness in which the alcoholic finds that controlling one's drinking on one's own is a fruitless endeavor. The obtaining and maintaining of one's sobriety is viewed as an interpersonal rather than an intrapsychic phenomenon. As it is put more simply in the context of the AA program, "I can't, but we can."

The elements of this group healing process can be seen in a number of different ways. First, *attendance at AA meetings* is necessary so that new concepts can be learned and old concepts are constantly reinforced. In this way, through listening to others who have been through similar life experiences, the alcoholic becomes reminded of his/her own powerlessness and unmanageability over alcohol. Second, *identification with a larger group* helps reduce the typical alienation and isolation of the alcoholic. In addition, by identifying with others the guilt and shame of being an alcoholic can often times be turned around to be a positive emotional experience of joy and pride that one has come into a recovery process. Third, *self-disclosure to others* of one's experiences, problems, fears, and doubts helps to reduce the burden of facing life alone. The social support that is provided to the alcoholic helps to buffer the effects of negative life events. Along these same lines the alcoholic chooses *a sponsor,* one more advanced in recovery, who will help guide him/her through the trials and tribulations of the recovery process. The alcoholic develops a special relationship with this individual, who acts as a guide, mentor, and confidant to help the alcoholic work the Twelve Steps of the program and to deal with major life crises that may precipitate a relapse to drinking. Finally, once a solid basis of recovery has been reached the alcoholic then *reaches out to others* by helping to spread the word of the AA program and seeks to bring other active alcoholics into a recovery process. This "helper therapy principle" has long been documented in the literature in that the process of giving help to others is not only beneficial to the recipient of the help but to the helper as well (Riessman, 1965). This serves to reinforce the recovery process of the alcoholic.

Education and Continuing Education

While in a treatment process the alcoholic is educated in terms of learning new facts and concepts related to alcoholism. This includes presentation of information that alcoholism is a disease and not a moral weakness or failure of character. The format for this educational process lies in lectures, formal reading, and participation in group discussions.

The important issue here is that the alcoholic must make a commitment to learning and continuing to learn about alcoholism. There are two basic "textbooks" that the alcoholic is asked to consult on a regular basis. These are the *Big Book* of AA, and the *Twelve Steps and Twelve Traditions of AA.* These materials present, if searched correctly, advice for approaching any or all of life's problems, as well as ways to reinforce one's sobriety. If the alcoholic is not able to read then these materials are available for use on audiotape. In addition, readings related to recovery that are published by the Hazelden Foundation are often recommended as a way to view recovery and to deal with life's problems through a Twelve-Step model.

Lifestyle Change and Continuing Care

Alcoholics must first and foremost make a *commitment to recovery.* Put more simply, everything else in life must come after recovery in terms of priorities, including job, family, money, vacations, and so forth. For alcoholics this includes making changes in the lifestyle that brought about their downfall and eliminating those factors that may lead back down that path in the future. *Time* must be set aside for attendance at AA meetings, reading the educational materials, and discussions with a sponsor. Extremely negative influences that may lead back to drinking must be eliminated. More simply put, *people, places, and things* must be changed if they may lead to relapse. New forms of recreation will most likely have to be developed as most leisure time has been spent drinking. Friends who will not be supportive of a recovery process (most likely due to the realization that they may be drinking too much) must be eliminated and replaced with positive ones.

A very difficult concept for most alcoholics to accept early in recovery is the need for continued support for their sobriety by participation in AA for the rest of their lives. Although a lifetime of recovery is only reached by recovering "one day at a time" the danger of discontinuing active participation is seen by us everyday. In discussing the sequence of events that lead to relapse for our clients who have had a period of sobriety the most frequently mentioned fact is that they stopped going to AA meetings. They report thinking that their sobriety was solidified and that they could handle things on their own. Unfortunately, many individuals take on their sobriety as a project and do not see the need for continuing care and the reinforcement that they obtain for their ongoing participation in the group healing process.

CONTRIBUTIONS FROM PSYCHOLOGY: RELAPSE PREVENTION

Although many treatment programs make claim to the effectiveness of their methods, the relapse rates for the treatment of alcoholism and other drug addictions are quite high. Marlatt and his colleagues (Cummings, Gordon, & Marlatt, 1980; Marlatt & Gordon, 1985) are cognitive/behavioral psychologists in the area of relapse prevention, which is clearly most important for understanding the treatment of alcoholism. Thus, in addition to the concepts outlined earlier we have integrated this work into our consultation/assessment work.

Using a data-based approach these researchers have identified "high-risk" situations that precipitate relapse in alcoholics. These relapse situations have been broadly defined as intrapersonal and interpersonal determinants. Specific situations include inability to cope with negative emotional states such as depression, anger, boredom, anxiety, and social pressure. By identifying these high-risk situations for the individual alcoholic through an assessment process specific treatment plans can be developed to teach coping skills for dealing with these difficult areas. This, in turn, may reduce the likelihood of a relapse for the alcoholic.

THE SETTING AND THE ROLE
OF THE PSYCHOLOGIST

Conducting psychological assessments within the context of an AA-oriented treatment program is an excellent medium for integrating psychological concepts with AA-oriented treatment. As not all alcoholics are alike the measure of individual differences may act as an aid in helping to devise individual treatment planning for the client in treatment. If the psychologist can understand the nature of the AA-oriented treatment philosophy and treatment process and respect this as a viable approach to the treatment of alcoholism, then, as Miller (1978) has discussed, the two groups can effectively collaborate to provide improved treatment of alcoholism.

The setting in which our work takes place is a for-profit intensive residential treatment center that addresses problems of alcoholism, as well as other drug dependencies. Knowles (1983) points out that although outpatient treatment of alcohol problems is gaining popularity, the major proportion of the total dollars spent on clinical services to alcoholics occurs on an inpatient basis. The treatment model is based on the Principles of Alcoholics Anonymous, which is also the predominant model used in this country in inpatient treatment programs. During the course of this 28-day treatment program clients are expected to complete the first five steps of the AA program. This includes accepting one's alcoholism, the development of the basis of a spiritual program, and accepting the need for ongoing (lifetime) participation in "the program" as a means of maintaining sobriety. The treatment modalities typically utilized are group therapy, individual therapy, educational lectures, recreational therapy and leisure planning, relaxation training and stress management, and family therapy, if possible. Almost all of the counselors providing this treatment are themselves recovering alcoholics, as is the Medical Director.

Initially clients enter the treatment program and are placed in the Medical Evaluation and Detoxification Unit. This process usually takes 3 days in which the client becomes detoxified and medically stable, a mental status examination is performed, a psychosocial history is taken, and an initial treatment plan is developed.

Five to 7 days after being transferred to the Rehabilitation Unit the client then undergoes, in a group testing format, a psychological testing battery. After the testing is completed a psychological report is written and feedback is provided to the Medical Director, the counselor, and the client.

The remainder of this chapter discusses how psychological assessment tools and principles have been implemented in this particular AA-oriented treatment program with respect to treatment planning. The client population, whose assessment data are described in this chapter, is 300 individuals who entered this intensive program for the treatment of their alcoholism. Although this is a for-profit treatment setting, with the majority of the reimbursement being provided by third-party payors, approximately 15% of the clients are treated at no cost to the client. The sample is predominantly male (74%), and Caucasian (94%). The average age of the client population is 36.54, with a range of 18–72.

PSYCHOLOGICAL CHARACTERISTICS OF THE TREATMENT POPULATIONS AND IMPLICATIONS FOR TREATMENT PLANNING

The tests chosen are based on trying to (1) predict how the client will emotionally and behaviorally respond to being in the treatment program; (2) identify potential blocks to the client accepting the philosophy and principles of the AA program; (3) identify potential "high-risk" relapse issues, and (4) evaluate general level of psychopathology.

Intellectual Functioning

As a measure of general intellectual capabilities the Shipley Institute of Living Scale is administered. This is a time-efficient measure of IQ and its limitations are recognized. That is, one cannot make any clinical reference about patterns of subtest scores or relative strengths and weaknesses using this instrument, as one could utilizing the WAIS-R. However, in 20 minutes (or less) one can get a general estimate of the client's abilities. The main reason for administering a measure of intelligence is to determine if the client has the cognitive capabilities to profit from an intensive treatment program. Identifying if the client can read the *Big Book* and other related materials is essential early in treatment. If severe deficits can be recognized then alternative methods for presenting treatment concepts (audio-cassette, a tutor) can then be implemented.

In the revised manual for this instrument, Zachary (1986) presents data on estimated Full Scale WAIS IQ scores from the combined vocabulary and abstraction scores based on the age of the client. The correlation between Shipley Total Scores and WAIS Full Scale IQ scores ranges between .74 and .85. It should be pointed out that the Shipley best predicts WAIS scores between one standard deviation above and below the mean, and does not predict well at the upper and lower ends.

The mean IQ estimate in our sample is slightly above average (107). Table 7.2 presents the distribution of IQ scores based on the estimated WAIS scores and what is to be expected from the general population (Wechsler, 1981). As can be seen in Table 7.2 there is a larger concentration of clients in the high average range of functioning and a smaller concentration of clients in the low average range of functioning compared to the general population. Perhaps this is due to the fact that most of the clients are gainfully employed and must be so in order to

TABLE 7.2
Ranges of Estimated IQ Scores for Our Alcoholic Sample
Versus the General Population

Category	General Population	Alcoholic Sample
Very Superior (130 and above)	2.6%	1.7%
Superior (120-129)	6.9%	9.7%
High Average (110-119)	16.6%	28.1%
Average (90-109)	49.1%	54.3%
Low Average (80-89)	16.1%	5.6%
Borderline (70-79)	6.4%	0.6%
Mentally Retarded (69 and below)	2.3%	0.0%

afford (mostly through third-party insurance payments) treatment at a for-profit center. Perhaps these differences would not have occurred in a not-for-profit public setting. The results presented in Table 7.2 suggest that almost all of the clients would not have a problem with the written materials utilized in the program. A small percentage (6% or less) require the aid of audio-cassettes or a reading tutor.

Goldman (1983), in reviewing the research on cognitive impairment in alcoholics, suggests that when the solution to a task is not readily available from prior experience, but requires a new synthesis of information, alcoholics seem to have difficulty. Chelune and Parker (1981) similarly conclude that alcoholics show deficits in abstract thinking and problem-solving integration of novel material. This being the case, a portion of alcoholics may have difficulty with abstract reasoning abilities. This is important in terms of learning "new concepts." Because much of the treatment approach is educational in nature this ability to readily learn is important to measure. The Shipley yields such a measure by comparing the Vocabulary-age scores with the Abstraction-age scores achieved. Vocabulary represents "old learning," whereas abstractions represent "new learning." If the vocabulary scores are much higher than the abstraction scores then information needs to be presented in an alternative manner.

By way of determining if there is a discrepancy between the two scores we utilize a measure of proportional difference of 25% of the questions answered correctly. That is, if the vocabulary raw score exceeds the abstraction raw score by more than 25% then we consider some level of cognitive impairment in abstract reasoning to be present. This could be due to either the aging process in older alcoholics and/or the effects of alcohol. In our sample there was a significant discrepancy between vocabulary and abstraction scores for 20% of the population. For those individuals who evidence such a "split" it is suggested that new concepts be presented in a concrete and repetitive manner in order to assure that they will learn what is being taught in the program. In addition, they should often be asked to "feed back" the new concepts in their own words to demonstrate that they actually understand these teachings. Although Goldman (1983) has suggested that much of the cognitive impairment in alcoholics is recoverable with long-term sobriety, in a short-term program only minimal levels of these functions can be expected to be repaired.

Interpersonal Relationships

The Fundamental Interpersonal Relations Orientation-Behavior Scale (FIRO-B) was originally developed by Schutz (1978) to examine one's interpersonal relationships with other people. The three domains tapped in this instrument are (1) Inclusion (how much one likes to be by oneself versus with other people); (2) Control (how much charge one likes to take in a situation or how much one allows others to take the lead), and (3) Affection (how close or how distant one likes to be in emotional relationships.)

Although Schutz (1978) developed the initial manual describing psychometric aspects of the scales, which has since been supplemented by Gluck (1983), an excellent clinical manual for the interpretation of profiles within each of the three domain areas has been developed by Ryan (1977). Because the primary focus of the recovery process is interpersonal in nature (e.g., group therapy, attendance at meetings of Alcoholics Anonymous) and control is a very major issue in the process of "Admitting one's powerlessness" and "Turning things over to a higher power," the FIRO-B lends itself to be a very valuable tool in practical treatment planning.

Table 7.3 presents the FIRO-B classifications within the three domains for our sample of alcoholics as compared to the normative data set for the general population provided by Ryan (unpublished). In the Inclusion area it can be seen that the largest percentage are "Loners" (almost half). Indeed, most of the other categories within this domain are not largely different between the two populations, with this exception. As with all psychological test data it cannot be determined if this is a precursor or consequence of alcoholism. However, it is clear that most of these clients will have trouble becoming comfortable with new people. "Loners," according to Ryan (1977), are individuals who prefer to be by themselves or with a few select people, are very concerned about rejection, and will try to avoid situations that might involve rejection whenever possible. For those individuals who appear to be "Loners" the following recommendations and warnings are offered:

TABLE 7.3
FIRO-B Classifications for Our Alcoholic Sample
Versus the General Population

Category	General Population	Alcoholic Sample
Inclusion		
Cautious Association	4%	4%
Hidden Inhibitions	5%	5%
Inhibited Individual	5%	9%
Loner	34%	48%
Now You See Him, Now You Don't	24%	15%
People Gatherer	17%	10%
Social Flexibility	7%	5%
The Conversationalist	4%	3%
Control		
Checker	14%	15%
Dependent or Super-Tolerant Female	6%	13%
Independence-Dependence Conflict	3%	4%
Let's Take a Break	2%	2%
Loyal Lieutenant	3%	2%
Matcher	14%	11%
Mission Impossible	10%	9%
Rebel	38%	34%
Self-Confident	10%	10%
Affection		
Careful Moderation	12%	15%
Cautious Lover	26%	25%
Image of Intimacy	6%	5%
Living Up To Expectations	3%	1%
Optimist	16%	12%
Pessimist	23%	33%
Warm Individual	14%	9%

Because they are uncomfortable around most people it will take them a while to "warm up" to being at the treatment center.

They may find it difficult to attend meetings of either Alcoholics Anonymous upon their own. Therefore, upon discharge they should be instructed to attend meetings "with someone" so they will know at least one other person in the room. The linking up for the client with a "temporary sponsor" is essential to increase the likelihood that they will attend these support group meetings.

They are the type of people who need to establish a "home base" for themselves rather than going from "meeting to meeting."

In the Control area we find that our alcoholic sample is not different from the general population at large. As with the general population the largest concentration of our alcoholics are "Rebels." According to Ryan (1977) these individuals resist being controlled by others, need to present to others with an "image of adequacy'' (whether or not real adequacy actually exists), and although capable of leadership do not like being pushed faster than they want to go. In terms of practical treatment issues we recommend the following for individuals whose profile is labeled ''Rebel'':

They are the type of people that need to go at their ''own pace.'' If they are ''pushed'' faster than they want to go they will get into many ''avoidance'' responses (e.g., procrastination, tantrums, threatening to leave against medical advice). Not that they should not be pushed nor confronted but this behavior should be closely monitored at these times.

It may be difficult for them to ''self-disclose'' a great deal about themselves in the context of group therapy. To talk about their own fears, worries, and inadequacies would be risking losing the ''image of adequacy'' which they hold so important. They should be encouraged to ''open-up'' a ''little bit at a time'' and to experience what it is like to do so. They should then be encouraged to talk about this process and what it is like to reveal themselves to others in a group situation.

In the Affection area we find that our alcoholic clients are not that different from the general population. The main exception is in the category labeled ''Pessimist.'' These individuals, according to Ryan (1977), can get emotionally close to others but it is extremely difficult for them to do so. Therefore, such close relationships will be ''few and far between'' and only after a great deal of trust has been established in the relationship. Typically this results from being ''deeply hurt'' in past relationships. For these individuals we suggest the following:

They are uncomfortable with emotional ''closeness.'' Their reactions to much of the ''affectively oriented'' activities in treatment (e.g., hugging, sharing of feelings) should be monitored closely.

Past relationships that are painful for these clients in which a great deal of hurt and/or rejection have taken place may need to be discussed/addressed either in primary treatment or aftercare.

In addition to the recommendations that we make for the most commonly occurring profiles for our alcoholic sample, other recommendations can be made for other types of profiles within each of these three domains. For example, in the Affection area 40% of the sample have difficulty initiating close personal relationships (e.g., ''Cautious Lover'' and ''Careful Moderation''). For these individuals we suggest social skills training with an emphasis on approaching others rather than waiting for others to approach them. In the Control area 30% of the sample have trouble with decision making and being susceptible to peer pressure (''Checker,'' ''Loyal Lieutenant,'' and ''Dependent Individual'' or

"Super-Tolerant Female"). For these individuals we encourage the practice of making decisions and living with the responsibility of one's "successes" and "mistakes," as well as assertiveness training in "how to say no" to a drink when "coerced" by peers.

Depression

Nathan (1988) points out that the most frequently mentioned characteristic of alcohol dependence is depression. He suggests that rather than an antecedent to alcoholism, depression is a consequence of this disorder. This may especially be seen when a client reaches the point when a residential treatment center is necessary. Losses are typically seen in the areas of money, job, family, and physical health, and involvement with the criminal justice system is not uncommon (e.g., arrest for DWI).

Although there has been controversy in the literature (Hagan & Schauer, 1985; Hesselbrock, Tennen, Hesselbrock, Workman-Daniels, & Meyer, 1985) as to the best way to measure levels of depression, in our assessment battery we utilize two separate instruments. These are the Beck Depression Inventory (BDI) and the Depression (D) Scale of the MMPI.

Beck, Steer, and Garbin (1988) present a review of the literature on the psychometric properties of the BDI. In this review they present classifications on level of depression based on the score obtained on the BDI. Table 7.4 presents the percentages for levels of depression for our alcoholic sample. As can be seen more than half of the sample are not depressed, and the clear majority (84%) are less than moderately depressed. A small minority (3%) are severely depressed.

One advantage of the BDI over the Depression Scale on the MMPI is that there is a direct question regarding suicidal ideation and intent (on the MMPI the question reads "Sometimes I feel as if I must hurt myself or others," which may confuse the issue between violence toward self and violence toward others). In our sample a clear majority (75%) indicated no thoughts about wanting to kill themselves. A significant proportion (24%) indicted that they thought about killing themselves but would not act on these feelings. Only a small minority (less than 1%) indicted that they would like to kill themselves. None of the respondents indicted that they would kill themselves if they had the chance.

The lack of significant levels of depression found on the BDI in our sample

TABLE 7.4
Distribution of Beck Depression Scores

Level of Depression	Percentage
None or Minimal (less than 10)	54%
Mild to Moderate (10-18)	30%
Moderate to Severe (19-29)	13%
Severe (30-63)	3%

may be a result of the instructions given for completing this instrument. Clients are asked to respond as to how they have been feeling during the past week. By the time that they were tested clients were detoxified and had begun the rehabilitation process. Feelings of guilt, shame, and remorse may have begun to dissipate as they became involved in the treatment process.

On the other hand, as opposed to a recency measure of depression found on the BDI, the scores on the D Scale on the MMPI yields a more generalized level of depression. As can be seen in Table 7.9 in the section to come discussing the results of the MMPI the average client's D-Scale was almost two standard deviations above the mean.

Anxiety

In reviewing the research on the "alcoholic personality" Cox (1979) suggests that a prominent personality characteristic of this population is a high level of anxiety. In identifying seven MMPI "subtypes" of alcoholic personalities using multivariate analysis, anxiety emerged as a factor in three of these subtypes (Ensbaugh, Tosi, & Hoyt, 1978). Some have suggested a tension-reduction hypothesis due to the possibility that the expected effects of alcohol are to reduce anxiety. However, Marlatt and Donovan (1981), in reviewing the research in this area, cite evidence to refute this line of "theorizing." Rather, they suggest that contrary to expectation drinking may indeed increase an alcoholic's anxiety level.

As can be seen from Table 7.5 the alcoholics in our sample are clearly very anxious individuals. Approximately two thirds scored above the 75th percentile on the Trait Anxiety portion of the State-Trait Personality Inventory (Spielberger, 1979). Indeed, just slightly below half of the sample scored above the 90th percentile when compared with the general population.

In terms of practical treatment planning the role of anxiety and anxiety management is important with this population. Marlatt and Gordon (1985) have identified anxiety to be among the "high-risk" situations that precipitate relapse in alcoholics. For those clients achieving anxiety levels above the 85th percentile we recommend:

A relaxation training program that is to be practiced on a daily basis;

A vigorous exercise program as a means of reducing tension;

The focusing on the development of a spiritual program. It would be quite helpful for clients to learn to turn over worries and allow a Higher Power to do their worrying.

In addition, stress management procedures as suggested by Meichenbaum and Novaco (1978), including cognitive restructuring, are behavior procedures often

TABLE 7.5
Distribution of Trait Anxiety Percentiles

Percentile	Percentage
1 - 25	7%
26 - 50	13%
51 - 75	15%
76 - 90	23%
90 - 99	42%

recommended to clients. The important issue is for these individuals to develop nonchemical means of controlling their anxiety levels.

Anger and Anger Expression

Marlatt and Gordon (1985) found their category of "Frustration and Anger" to be the leading precipitant of a relapse to drinking. They suggest that rather than expressing anger in a direct and constructive manner, alcoholics will drink instead.

As can be seen from Table 7.6 the alcoholics in our sample are clearly very angry individuals. More than half scored above the 75th percentile on the Trait Anger portion of the State-Trait Personality Inventory (Spielberger, 1979). Indeed, just slightly more than one quarter of the sample scored above the 90th percentile when compared with the general population. As such these individuals will have a propensity to respond to the world with anger and resentment when faced with a frustrating situation. Given the "high-risk" relationship between anger and relapse we tell clients who are extremely angry that "resentments must be let go of, as they are a luxury that substance abusers cannot afford."

As an outgrowth of his measures on anxiety and anger Spielberger (in press) has developed a new instrument examining the expression of anger. Spielberger, Krasner, and Solomon (1988) discuss the development of this scale and review the research related to the consequences of retaining anger or being anger expressive. Feshbach (1986) has suggested that the appropriate expression of anger, rather than suppressing anger or exploding with it, is related to both physical and emotional health.

TABLE 7.6
Distribution of Trait Anger Percentiles

Percentile	Percentage
1 - 25%	11%
26 - 50%	17%
51 - 75%	17%
76 - 90%	30%
91 - 99%	25%

As already mentioned Marlatt and Gordon have discussed the role of the appropriate expression of anger as it relates to relapse in the alcoholic. The new measure, the Anger Expression Scale, which allows an individual assessment of how the client deals with anger. Marlatt and Gordon have suggested that holding in anger when frustrated is a "high-risk" situation that may lead an alcoholic to relapse. The data on our alcoholic sample support the idea that these clients do hold their anger within themselves, more so than they express their anger. On the Anger Expression Scale the mean Anger-In score was 18.01 and the mean Anger-Out score was 15.77.

In terms of practical treatment planning we recommend to those individuals with difficulties in the area of anger (either by scoring above the 85th percentile on the Trait Anger Scale or holding in anger as measured by the Anger Expression Scale):

To learn to "let go" of many of the resentments from their past that are harbored toward people and life in general by making Resentment Lists and turning them over to one's Higher Power. These resentments typically will lead to unmanageable behavior.

The need in current and future situations to express anger in a direct and appropriate manner. The client could benefit from learning to do this rather then expressing these feelings in the indirect and "passive-aggressive" ways that he does.

What is interesting to note is the combination of high Trait Anger Scores with the typical alcoholic client holding their anger within themselves. This clearly is a dangerous combination, for once the anger does become vented for these clients, without appropriate therapeutic direction, these individuals can become violent. In this regard it is possible to utilize the Anger Expression Scale as an instrument for identifying individual expectancies as they relate to drinking and the expression of anger in an alcoholic population. We are currently in the midst of a study suggested to us by Charles Spielberger comparing the alcoholic's expression of anger while sober and, alternatively, while drinking. Clients were first requested to complete the Anger Expression Scale with how they typically respond in general. They were then asked to complete this instrument once again with the instructions of responding to the questions as they would "while they were drinking." Preliminary data with 58 subjects, presented in Table 7.7, suggest that the relationship between Anger-In and Anger-Out changes while drinking. It appears that while sober the alcoholic tends to "stuff" anger. However, while drinking these controls are discarded and anger is more easily expressed. Utilizing the Anger Expression Scale in the manner just mentioned as an instrument to identify this behavior may help lead to reducing potential violence by making treatment recommendations on the appropriate expression of anger for these clients.

TABLE 7.7
Mean Anger-In and Anger-Out Scores
Under Conditions of Sobriety and While Drinking

	While Sober	While Drinking
Anger-In	18.24	17.40
Anger-Out	15.40	19.91

Level of Alcohol Dependence

At the Addiction Research Foundation Skinner and Allen (1982) have developed a scale to examine the alcohol dependence syndrome. This was done to distinguish between alcohol-related problems and disabilities and alcohol dependence. They developed a 29-item scale that focused on four basic areas: (1) loss of behavior control; (2) obsessive drinking style; (3) psychoperceptual withdrawal, and (4) psychophysical withdrawal.

In their work, Skinner and Allen, based on quartile scores, were able to categorize their subjects into four levels of alcohol dependence: low, moderate, substantial, and severe. A low level of dependence suggested psychological dependence with very little indication of physical symptoms. A moderate level suggested psychological dependence plus the possible beginnings of physical dependence and withdrawal symptoms. A substantial level of dependence suggests that physical dependence is likely and that physical disorders and psychosocial problems related to alcohol abuse are probable. A severe level of dependence suggests that physical dependence is highly likely, that serious physical problems (e.g., liver disease) are probably present, as well as serious psychosocial problems (e.g., job loss, marital disruption, legal difficulties).

As can be seen in Table 7.8, in our sample of 300 alcoholics the majority of clients fall into the low and moderate levels of dependence. The mean score (18.7) was slightly lower than the mean score (23.1) presented by Skinner and Allen in their validation sample. However, they also reported a similar skewness of their distribution toward lower scores.

The significant contributions in the development of this instrument by Skinner and Allen for abstinence-oriented treatment programs lie in the client's attitude toward the acceptance of abstinence-oriented treatment goals as opposed to controlled drinking. Essentially, given a choice would the client rather "cut out" or

TABLE 7.8
Distribution of Clients Across the Four
Levels of Alcohol Dependence

Low (1 - 37)	104	34%
Moderate (14 - 21)	99	33%
Substantial (22 - 30)	59	20%
Severe (31 - 47)	38	13%

"cut down." They suggest that clients in the low and moderate levels of alcohol dependence are likely to reject abstinence-oriented treatment strategies. Clinically this may be seen in statements such as "I'd just like to have wine with dinner," or "a few beers while mowing the lawn couldn't hurt." In the substantial and severe level of dependence clients are more likely to recognize and accept that abstinence is the only reasonable treatment goal for them. In discussing this issue with clients their usual response is "I've tried to cut down before and now I know that this doesn't work."

This skewness suggests potential difficulties with clients in accepting the basic philosophy of an AA-oriented treatment approach. That is, in the AA model abstinence is the only acceptable treatment goal. Although the possibility of controlled drinking being a potential outcome still continues to be debated by researchers (Marlatt, 1983), on a practical treatment level those in an AA-oriented model currently view controlled drinking as (1) a denial of alcoholism as a disease and (2) the quickest way to an early grave. As such a substantial part of treatment may focus on working through a client's denial through educational techniques, confrontation by peers who have accepted the disease model, and by having the client complete a "First Step" in which all alcohol-related consequences are reviewed and brought to the surface.

General Level of Psychological Functioning: The MMPI

Butcher (1988) points out that the MMPI is the most widely used of all personality instruments. Graham and Streiger (1988) in their review of MMPI characteristics of alcoholics point out that hundreds of studies have been conducted examining the personality characteristics of alcoholics utilizing this instrument. In an earlier chapter in this book series Megargee (1985) has reviewed the utility of the MMPI as a method for screening for alcohol and drug problems, with a special emphasis on employment issues.

The inclusion of a measure of psychopathology in the testing battery is very important because, in addition to alcohol-related problems, other personality/psychiatric problems are not uncommon in this population. As with depression, whether other psychological disturbances are precursors of alcoholism or consequences of alcoholism is difficult to determine. However, knowing that emotional/behavioral extremes are present in certain clients is important for participation in an intensive program, practical treatment planning, and aftercare planning. On a rare occasion a client is acutely psychotic and may need to be stabilized before benefit can be achieved from the residential program. With clients who present extremely aberrant MMPI profiles it is important to realize the limits of what emotional/behavioral changes can be achieved in 30 days. As such, for these individuals either long-term treatment or placement in a halfway house upon completion of primary treatment may be indicated. The MMPI is an extremely useful tool in this regard.

TABLE 7.9
Mean Score and Percentage of Clients Scoring Above a
T-Score of 70 and 80 on the Clinical Scales on the MMPI

Clinical Scales	Mean T-Score	Percentage 70 - 80	Percentage Above 80
Hs	57.58	14.3%	6.1%
D	68.67	20.3%	21.0%
Hy	60.98	16.3%	7.0%
Pd	70.38	28.3%	22.3%
Pa	62.72	20.7%	6.0%
Pt	65.81	22.1%	15.0%
Sc	66.18	17.5%	16.7%
Ma	64.98	28.0%	9.7%
Si	56.70	15.6%	1.6%

Graham and Streiger (1988), as well as Butcher and Owen (1979), have pointed out that the most consistent finding in comparing alcoholic to non-alcoholic population is a relatively high score on Scale 4 (Pd) on the MMPI. Graham and Streiger also suggest that this finding holds true across several moderator variables including setting of treatment (inpatient vs. outpatient), race, age, and sex. The most consistent 2-point code type has been the 24/42 (Pd and D-scales). Several cluster analytic studies have attempted to identify several types of "alcoholic personalities." Graham and Streiger point out that at least six rather distinct alcoholic profiles have emerged from this work.

Table 7.9 presents the mean scores on the clinical scales in our alcoholic sample. Consistent with the previous literature, the highest scores were on scales 4 (Pd) and 2 (D). However, beyond just presenting mean scores we also present in Table 7.9 the percentage of clients scoring between 70 and 80 on the clinical scales, as well as 80 and above. This helps put the heterogeneity of the profiles of the sample into perspective. For example, although the mean 3-scale (Hy) was not very high, 20% of the sample scored in the clinically significant range. Similarly, the 6-scale (Pa) mean score was relatively low, but more than 25% of the sample scored in the clinically significant range.

For research striving to understand the personality dynamics of alcoholics as well as the development of typologies of alcoholics, code-type research is a very fruitful endeavor. However, due to the heterogeneity of MMPI profiles in this population (e.g., Ensbaugh et al., 1978 found that seven types of profiles only accounted for 48% of their alcoholic sample) treatment planning by MMPI code-type is not practical.

On a practical clinical basis, in terms of special treatment planning, we are typically not "alarmed" when T-score elevations are between 70 and 80. However, when scores reach T-scores of 80 and above special attention is placed on these findings. This did occur at least 10% of the time for this sample on 5 of the 9 clinical scales.

In terms of treatment planning, elevations (70 and above) on the clinical scales have meaning for both personality styles and difficulties that the client will have while trying to obtain sobriety while in treatment, as well as on longer-term issues to maintain sobriety upon completion of the program.

Graham (1987) presents personality and behavioral descriptions for high and low T-scores for each of the MMPI clinical scales. Based upon the descriptors provided by Graham and our own clinical experience we view high scorers on the 4-scale (Pd) as being rebellious and non-conforming individuals. They have trouble with authority figures and do not like being "told what to do." Others view them as stubborn, hard-headed, and tough to teach because they think that they are experts about what is right and what is wrong. From these descriptions it can easily be seen how these individuals will be resistant to treatment. As such the following recommendations are made:

The client needs to keep an "open mind" and indeed question as to who is indeed the "expert" when it comes to achieving and maintaining sobriety. Remind the client that it is their "expertise" that led them to an inpatient treatment program in the first place.

The client will find it difficult to accept the concept of "surrender." They need to be *in control* of all facets of their lives. They will find it extremely difficult to be "vulnerable" at all in relationships, and indeed usually attempt to stay "one-up" in the relationships in which they becomes involved.

As discussed earlier a large portion of our clients achieve significant elevations on the 2-scale (D) on the MMPI. Nathan (1988) hypothesizes this to be a consequence of one's alcoholism. According to Graham (1987) and our clinical experience high scorers on the 2-scale are depressed, unhappy, and often times hopeless. They are listless, apathetic, and difficult to motivate. They are pessimistic about themselves and their future and see little hope in ever overcoming their alcoholism. Scores this high (40% above a T-score of 70 and 20% above a T-score of 80) typically represent a depressive style that is chronic and characterological in nature, rather than one that is situational and transitory in nature. In their research on relapse prevention Marlatt and Gordon (1985) have identified depression as a high-risk situation leading to relapse. For individuals with elevations on these scales we recommend:

Participation in an active and rigorous exercise program;

The learning of depression management skills;

Work on building self-esteem and assertiveness to reduce self-depreciating thoughts and self-efficacy.

As can be seen in Table 7.9 a large part of the sample scored in the clinically significant range on the 7-scale (Pt). Graham (1987) suggests that this represents as index of psychological turmoil and discomfort. The recommendations presented on the section on trait anxiety hold true regarding the need for relaxation training and the development of a spiritual program, in which worries and anxieties may be turned over to one's Higher Power.

Graham (1987) views high scorers on the 9-scale (Ma) as active and energetic, to be involved in many activities but do not see projects through to completion, preferring action to thought, are easily bored and have a low frustration tolerance. Further, we view these individuals as ''sensation seekers'' who crave excitement. For these individuals many of the pitfalls to obtaining and maintaining sobriety can be seen. As such we note of these clients that:

They need to have a great many short-term goals to work on. It is difficult for them to work on long-term strategies as they will often become bored with these.

They get ''bored'' very easily and need to learn how to deal with boredom in a way that does not include drugs or alcohol as a way of overcoming the boredom.

They need to be warned not to take on their sobriety as a ''project.'' If they treat it as such they will become ''bored'' with the project as they have with every other one in their lives. They need to consider their program as part of an entire ''lifestyle change.'' If not, most likely in the near future they will begin to think that they have the program ''down pat'' and stop ''working'' the program that earned them their sobriety in the first place. If this occurs drinking behavior will resume in the not too distant future after that stance is adopted.

Further recommendations based on scale elevations and specific profile configurations (e.g., 4/9, high 3 and high 4 combined with a low 5 in women) have been developed. The presentation of each recommendation based on scale elevations and combinations is clearly beyond the scope of this chapter. However, in this section we have attempted to illustrate the potential for utilizing the MMPI within the Twelve-Step framework.

CONCLUSIONS

Opportunities for collaborative work between self-help groups and psychologists are readily available. Rappaport et al. (1985) have clearly demonstrated this in their work with Project Grow in developing alternatives to psychiatric hospitalization.

Conducting psychological evaluations with AA-oriented treatment programs is an area fruitful for collaborative work between recovering individuals and professional psychologists. However, this requires that the psychologist meet the AA-based treatment staff on ''their turf.'' This requires learning and working with their basic premises and goals. By demonstrating this basic respect the abilities of the psychologist may in turn be respected and sought after by these treatment providers. We suggest that it is worth the time and effort of the psychologist to nurture a positive relationship demonstrated in this chapter and by Miller (1978). This may turn the traditional level of "mutual antagonism" toward "mutual collaboration."

REFERENCES

Altrocchi, J. (1972). Mental health consultation. In S. Golann & C. Eisdorfer (Eds.), *Handbook of community mental health* (pp. 477–508). New York: Appleton-Century-Crofts.

Anderson, D. (1981). *The psychopathology of denial.* Center City, MN: Hazelden.

Beck, A., Steer, R., & Garbin, M. (1988). Psychometric properties of the Beck Depression Inventory: Twenty-five years of evaluation. *Clinical Psychology Review, 8,* 77–100.

Brown, S. (1985). *Treating the alcoholic: A developmental model of recovery.* New York: Wiley.

Butcher, J. (1988). Introduction to the special series on personality factors in addiction: Issues and empirical research. *Journal of Consulting and Clinical Psychology, 56,* 171.

Butcher, J., & Owen, P. (1978). Objective personality inventories: Recent research and some contemporary issues. In B. Wolman (Ed.), *Clinical diagnosis of mental disorders: A Handbook* (pp. 475–546). New York: Plenum Press.

Chelune, G., & Parker, J. (1981). Neuropsychological deficits associated with chronic alcohol abuse. *Clinical Psychology Review, 1,* 181–195.

Cox, W. M. (1979). The alcoholic personality: A review of the evidence. In B. Maher (Ed.), *Progress in experimental personality research: Volume 9* (pp. 89–148). New York: Academic Press.

Cummings, C., Gordon, J., & Marlatt, G. A. (1980). Relapse prevention and prediction. In W. Miller (Ed.), *The addictive behaviors: Treatment of alcoholism, drug abuse, smoking and obesity* (pp. 291–322). Great Britain: Pergamon Press.

Ensbaugh, D., Tosi, D., & Hoyt, C. (1978). Some personality patterns and dimensions of male alcoholics: A multivariate description. *Journal of Personality Assessment, 42,* 409–417.

Feshbach, S. (1986). Reconceptualization of anger: Some research perspectives. *Journal of Social and Clinical Psychology, 4,* 123–132.

Gluck, G. (1983). *Psychometric properties of the FIRO-B: A guide to research.* Palo Alto: Consulting Psychologists Press.

Goldman, M. (1983). Cognitive impairment in chronic alcoholics: Some cause for optimism. *American Psychologist, 38,* 1045–1054.

Graham, J. (1987). *The MMPI: A practical guide.* New York: Oxford.

Graham, J., & Streiger, V. (1988). MMPI characteristics of alcoholics: A review. *Journal of Consulting and Clinical Psychology, 56,* 197–205.

Hagan, L., & Schauer, A. (1985). Assessment of depression in alcoholics: Comment on Hesselbrock et al. *Journal of Consulting and Clinical Psychology, 53,* 64–66.

Hesselbrock, M., Tennen, H., Hesselbrock, V., Workman-Daniels, K., & Meyer, R. (1985). Assessment of depression in alcoholics: Further considerations—Reply to Hagan and Schauer. *Journal of Consulting and Clinical Psychology, 53,* 67–69.

Knowles, P. (1983). Inpatient versus outpatient treatment of substance misuse in hospitals, 1975–1980. *Journal of Studies on Alcohol, 44,* 384–387.

Levy, L. (1978). Self-help groups viewed by mental health professionals: A survey and comments. *American Journal of Community Psychology, 6,* 305–313.

Marlatt, G. A. (1983). The controlled drinking controversy: A commentary. *American Psychologist, 38,* 1097–1110.

Marlatt, G. A., & Donovan, D. (1981). Alcoholism and drug dependence: Cognitive social learning factors in addictive behaviors. In W. Craighead, A. Kazdin, & M. Mahoney (Eds.), *Behavior modification: Principles, issues and applications* (pp. 264–285). Boston: Houghton Mifflin.

Marlatt, G. A. & Gordon, J. (1985). *Relapse prevention.* New York: Guilford.

Megargee, E. (1985). Assessing alcoholism and drug abuse with the MMPI: Implications for employment screening. In C. D. Spielberger & J. N. Butcher (Eds.), *Advances in personality assessment: Volume 5* (pp. 1–34). Hillsdale, NJ: Lawrence Erlbaum Associates.

Meichenbaum, D., & Novaco, R. (1978). Stress innoculation: A preventative approach. In C. D. Spielberger & I. Sarason (Eds.), *Stress and anxiety: A sourcebook of theory and research* (Vol. 5) (pp. 317–330). Washington: Hemisphere.

Miller, P. (1978). Behavior modification and Alcoholics Anonymous: An unlikely combination. *Behavior Therapy, 9,* 300–301.

Miller, W., & Hester, R. (1980). Treating the problem drinker: Modern approaches. In W. Miller (Ed.), *The addictive behaviors: Treatment of alcoholism, drug abuse, smoking and obesity* (pp. 11–142). Great Britain: Pergamon Press.

Nathan, P. (1988). The addictive personality is the behavior of the addict. *Journal of Consulting and Clinical Psychology, 56,* 183–188.

Rappaport, J., Seidman, E., Toro, P., McFadden, L., Reischl, T., Roberts, L., Salem, D., Stein, C., & Zimmerman, M. (1985). Collaborative research with a mutual help organization. *Social Policy, 15,* 12–24.

Riessman, F. (1965). The "helper" therapy principle. *Social Work, 10,* 27–32.

Robertson, N. (1988). *Getting better: Inside Alcoholics Anonymous.* New York: Morrow.

Ryan, L. (1977). *Clinical interpretation of the FIRO-B.* Palo Alto: Consulting Psychologists Press.

Ryan, L. Unpublished normative data tables on the FIRO-B. Available from the author from the Psychology Service, Bay Pines Veterans Administration Medical Center, Bay Pines, Florida.

Sarason, S. (1974). *The psychological sense of community: Prospects for the community psychology.* San Francisco: Jossey-Bass.

Schutz, W. (1978). *The FIRO scales manual.* Palo Alto: Consulting Psychologists Press.

Skinner, H., & Allen, B. (1982). Alcohol dependence syndrome: Measurement and validation. *Journal of Abnormal Psychology, 91,* 199–209.

Spielberger, C. D. (1979). *Preliminary manual for the State-Trait Personality Inventory.* Tampa: University of South Florida, Human Resources Institute.

Spielberger, C. D. (in press). *Manual for the State-Trait Anger-Expression Scale.* Odessa, FL: Psychological Assessment Resources.

Spielberger, C. D., Krasner, S. S., & Solomon, E. P. (1988). The experience, expression and control of anger. In M. Janisse (Ed.), *Health psychology: Individual differences and stress* (pp. 89–108). New York: Springer-Verlag.

Springborn, W. (1983). *Step 1: The foundation of recovery.* Center City, MN: Hazelden.

Stewart, D. (1955). The dynamics of fellowship as illustrated in Alcoholics Anonymous. *Quarterly Journal of the Studies on Alcohol, 16,* 251–262.

Tiebout, H. (1953). Surrender vs. compliance in therapy with special reference to alcoholism. *Quarterly Journal of Studies on Alcohol, 14,* 58–68.

Wechsler, D. (1981). *Manual for the Wechsler Adult Intelligence Scale-Revised.* New York: Psychological Corporation.

Zachary, R. (1986). *Shipley Institute of Living Scale-Revised Manual.* Los Angeles: Western Psychological Services.

8

Strelau Temperament Inventory (STI): General Review and Studies Based on German Samples

Jan Strelau
University of Warsaw and University of Bielefeld

Alois Angleitner
University of Bielefeld

Willibald Ruch
University of Duesseldorf

Fifteen years have passed since the time the Strelau Temperament Inventory (STI) was first published in English (Strelau, 1972a). This questionnaire, aimed at diagnosing the Pavlovian nervous system properties, gained increasing popularity in the West after being published once again (Strelau, 1983) with more information comprising its psychometric characteristics—its construct validity in particular. The aim of this chapter is to present the accumulated results obtained with the STI and to introduce new results based on a broad study conducted on six German samples. In order to show how the STI is related to the Pavlovian theory of nervous system properties, a short introduction into this theory is given.

THE PAVLOVIAN NERVOUS SYSTEM PROPERTIES

It was in the first decades of this century when Pavlov, studying conditioned reflexes (CRs) in dogs, arrived at the conclusion that individual differences in the speed and efficiency of conditioning as well as in the dogs' behavior in laboratory surroundings can be explained by certain properties of the central nervous system (CNS). These properties include strength of excitation, strength of inhibition, the equilibrium of nervous processes (between strength of excitation and strength of inhibition), and their mobility. Depending on the configuration of those properties, different types of CNS may be distinguished. Pavlov, being under the influence of the ancient Greek temperament typology, limited the number of CNS types to four. He conceived of the types of the CNS as the physiological basis of temperament. However, these terms (i.e., types of the CNS and types of temperament) were used by him interchangeably, especially when referring to nervous system types in humans. "The mentioned types are what we call in man temperaments. The temperament constitutes the most general characteristic of every man, the most general and most essential characteristic of his nervous system" (Pavlov, 1952, p. 339).

In spite of the term "processes," which refers to excitation and inhibition through which strength, mobility and balance are characterized, the CNS properties should be regarded according to Pavlov as traits and not as states.

When defining the basic CNS properties Pavlov did not refer to the physiological mechanisms or processes underlying those properties, as may be expected from a physiologist. He described them from a functional point of view. Being under the influence of Darwin (see Windholz, 1987), Pavlov characterized the types of nervous system, as well as the CNS traits, taking into account the ability of the individual to adapt. This characteristic has been presented thoroughly elsewhere (Strelau, 1983), thus we will limit ourselves to a short description of the four Pavlovian basic CNS properties.

Strength of excitation refers to the functional capacity of the nervous system, thus to the ability of the cortical cells to work. It is manifested in the withstanding of either exceedingly strong, or prolonged excitation without slipping into protective (transmarginal) inhibition. The appearance of protective inhibition under strong, prolonged or recurrent stimulation, manifested in the decrease or in the disappearance of reactions to those stimuli, has been used by Pavlov as the main index of strength of excitation. Individuals in whom transmarginal inhibition occurs in reaction to stimuli of low intensity or duration are characterized as having a weak CNS, whereas individuals with a strong CNS are able to react adequately (i.e., without slipping into protective inhibition) to stimuli of high intensity and long duration. The strong type has a higher endurance (working capacity) of the CNS as compared with the weak CNS type. Because individuals are confronted in their every day lives with stimuli of great intensity, Pavlov considered the strength of excitation as the most important property of the nervous system (Pavlov, 1951–52).

The understanding by Pavlov of the concept of strength of inhibition was rather confused, owing to the fact that during his 30 years of research in the field of CNS types he often changed his view regarding this CNS property. In his last publications, especially in his paper *General Types of Higher Nervous Activity in Animals and Man* published in 1935, it became clear that strength of inhibition referred to conditioned (acquired) inhibition, that is, to those types of inhibition that are known as extinction, delay, differentiation, and conditioned inhibition (in its narrow sense). The strength of inhibition reveals itself in the ability to maintain a state of conditioned inhibition. The persistence of inhibition, that is, the amount of time a neuron can remain in an uninterrupted state of conditioned inhibition, is one of the basic indicators of that property. Individuals with weak inhibitory processes are unable to sustain conditioned inhibition for a long time, which results in disturbances in CR activity, including neurotic behavior. In individuals with a strong inhibitory process, prolonged conditioned inhibition does not cause disturbances. The ease of evoking inhibitory CRs and their stability are, according to Pavlov, the main indicators of the strength of inhibition. It has to be added that strength of inhibition has been measured almost exclusively only when equilibrium of the nervous processes was to be diagnosed. This statement holds true not only for Pavlov and his associates but also for his followers (Nebylitsyn, 1972a; Strelau, 1983; Teplov, 1964).

According to Pavlov the equilibrium of nervous processes should be regarded as the ratio of the strength of excitation to the strength of inhibition. As stressed by him, the functional meaning of this property consists of the ability to inhibit certain excitations, when required, in order to evoke other reactions in concert with the environmental demands. The followers of Pavlov have extended the equilibrium concept to other CNS properties. For example, Kupalov (1952) regarded equilibrium as a secondary trait that appears not only as a result of the ratio between strength of excitation and strength of inhibition, but also as the ratio of mobility of excitation to mobility of inhibition. Nebylitsyn (1972a) attributes to equilibrium the role of a general principle of organization of the CNS properties. According to him, this trait comprises strength, mobility, lability, and dynamism when the ratio between excitation and inhibition within those properties is characterized (see also Golubeva, 1980). The concept "equilibrium" or "balance" of CNS processes was and still is a source of many misunderstandings (Strelau, 1983).

Mobility of the nervous system was the last property to be discovered by Pavlov. It manifests itself in the ability to react quickly and adequately to changes in the surroundings. The essence of mobility is "the ability to give way—according to external conditions—to give priority to one impulse before the other, excitation before inhibition and conversely" (Pavlov, 1952, p. 540). The ability to respond adequately as soon as possible to continuous changes in the environment has to be distinguished from the speed with which nervous processes are initiated and terminated. For the latter characteristics the property labeled as lability has been proposed by Teplov (1963) and Nebylitsyn (1972a).

The basic properties of the CNS have to be regarded as explanatory concepts, which Pavlov related to the functions of the CNS in trying to explain the relatively stable individual differences in animals' CR activity and behavior (Strelau, 1983). Pavlov was interested above all in the objective examination (the salivary reflex conditioning paradigm) of the activity of the cerebral hemispheres in animals. His "physiological" approach to the CNS properties consists of interpreting certain forms of behavior, assumed to express temperamental traits, by using hypothetical neurophysiological constructs referring to the central nervous system. The research underlying his theory of higher nervous activity is centered primarily on the behavior (CR reactions) that he tried to explain by means of hypothesized mechanisms of the CNS. These mechanisms, however, have not been subject in Pavlov's laboratory to physiological or neurophysiological studies. Pavlov's research on behavior gives persuasive reason for recognizing him as a psychologist (Strelau, 1969, 1983; Watson, 1978; Windholz, 1987); his investigations on CNS properties may be regarded as the first laboratory studies in the field of temperament.

Since Pavlov was mainly interested in studying CRs, the conditioned reflex paradigm gained also the highest popularity when diagnosing the NSP in animals (e.g., Kolesnikov & Troshikhin, 1951). Also in the first studies conducted in humans, more exactly in children, the diagnosis of NS properties, and hence of types of CNS, was limited to CR activity (Ivanov-Smolensky, 1935; Krasnogorsky, 1953). The situation changed radically when Teplov and his followers started to investigate CNS properties in adults. Although still using the CR paradigm, mostly constrained to the so-called photochemical reflex (e.g., Rozhdestvenskaya, 1963) and to conditioned EEG alpha-blocking (Nebylitsyn, 1972a), they enlarged the number of phenomena on the basis of which CNS properties might be diagnosed. The sensitivity threshold, sensitivity restoration, adequate optical chronaxie, photic driving reaction, critical frequencies of flicker-fusion, click-fusion and flashing phosphene, and background alpha rhythm characteristics can be mentioned here as examples (see Nebylitsyn, 1972a; Strelau, 1983). Most of these phenomena refer to involuntary reactions. This is the consequence of one of the theses of the methodological "credo" formulated by the Moscow group (Teplov & Nebylitsyn, 1963). It says that it is essential to investigate the CNS properties by reference to involuntary movements in which these properties are clearly manifested, undisguised by the individual experience.

Soon thereafter the motor and/or verbal RT paradigm in diagnosing CNS properties became popular among the neo-Pavlovian typologists (Nebylitsyn, 1960, 1972a), though being in contradiction with the credo just mentioned. The RT paradigm has also been broadly used in other laboratories centered on studies of CNS properties (Kopytova, 1963; Peysakhov, 1974; Saprykin & Mileryan, 1954; Strelau, 1969, 1983; Troshikhin, Moldavskaya, & Kolchenko, 1978).

Parallel to the laboratory studies aimed at diagnosing CNS properties, the Pavlovian typologists have developed methods that allow the study of those properties in children and adolescents in natural settings. Most of these studies have been based on observations (e.g., Davydova, 1954; Leites, 1956) or on field experiments—different types of games, such as block building (Samarin, 1954), or "signalman" (Umansky, 1958) and "driver" (Chudnovsky, 1963), were arranged.

Physicians working in clinics and hospitals have undertaken attempts to diagnose the patients' nervous system properties on the basis of anamnesis and interviews. The contribution of Birman (1951), Cytawa (1959) and Pervomaysky (1964) should be mentioned here. All of these methods did not allow, however, for a quantitative measure of the nervous system properties.

As can be learned from the studies conducted by Pavlov and his students, the four CNS properties described earlier are not orthogonal to each other as some personality/temperament researchers would like them to be (Carlier, 1985; Eysenck, 1987; Stelmack, Kruidenier, & Anthony, 1985), and no such an assumption was made by the Pavlovian typologists. Let us consider the relationship between strength of excitation and mobility. In experiments conducted by Fedorov (1961) in mice, by Krasusky (1971) in dogs, and in studies aimed at diagnosing the CNS properties in man (Nebylitsyn, 1972a; Turovskaya, 1963) it became evident that strength of excitation is positively correlated with mobility of the nervous processes. To give one example, Troshikhin et al. (1978), in a study conducted on 225 subjects (aged from 5 to 24 years), stated that mobility correlates positively with strength of excitation from .51 to .83, depending on the developmental stage of the subjects (7 groups differing in age have been separated). In this study mobility was measured by the so-called alteration method and strength of excitation by means of the change of simple reaction time (RT) under repeatedly applied stimuli.[1]

NERVOUS SYSTEM PROPERTIES AND THE STRELAU TEMPERAMENT INVENTORY

On the basis of several experiments conducted during a period of over 15 years, Strelau (1972b) concluded that there exists a strongly limited generality in the diagnosis of CNS properties. The results show that the estimation of these properties depends on the modality of stimuli used (Nebylitsyn, 1972b; Strelau 1965a), on the type of reinforcements applied in CR experiments (Ivanov-Smolensky, 1935; Strelau, 1969), on the kind of reaction to be measured (Strelau, 1969, 1983), as well as on the criteria (indicators) on the basis of which the diagnosis is made (Strelau, 1983). These modality- and reaction-specific phenomena are also well known in studies on stress (Lacey, 1950, 1967) and currently in personality research based on the arousal concept (Fahrenberg, 1987; Fahrenberg, Walschburger, Foerster, Myrtek, & Mueller, 1983; Kohn, Cowles, & Lafreniere, 1987).

This rather pessimistic outcome in the diagnostic research on CNS properties

---

[1]These methods as well as most of the methods aimed at diagnosing the CNS properties distinguished by Pavlov and his followers are described in details by Strelau (1983, see also Mangan, 1982; Nebylitsyn, 1972a).

has led Strelau (1965b, 1969) to construct an observation chart, further developed into the Strelau Temperament Inventory (STI). The observation chart, based on a 4-point rating scale, is a kind of standard observation program, comprising 75 items that refer to various kinds of behavior and different situations. For each property, that is, for strength of excitation, strength of inhibition, and for mobility of nervous processes, 25 items were generated. The balance of nervous processes was estimated as the ratio between strength of excitation to strength of inhibition.

Situations and behaviors (supposed to indicate particular CNS properties) were selected upon an analysis of other methods for diagnosing the CNS properties in humans and, after examining Pavlov's theory of higher nervous activity, with special reference to the typology of the nervous system. It was the intention of the author to follow Pavlov's conceptualizations regarding the basic properties of the CNS as faithfully as possible. The properties have been defined in a way that Pavlov has understood them, without taking into account the modifications introduced by Teplov (1964) and Nebylitsyn (1972a). The main reason for not including the CNS properties as proposed by the neo-Pavlovian typologists into the research program was the lack of orthogonality of these traits against the original (Pavlovian) ones and their low consistency, as has been shown by Strelau (1983). This means, among other things, that the observation chart (and this holds true for the STI also) was aimed at measuring the strength of excitation, understood as the endurance of the nervous system. It does not comprise the sensitivity pole of the strength of excitation dimension, as it has been proposed by Teplov (1964) and Nebylitsyn (1972a). Mobility refers first of all to the ability to react adequately and quickly to changes in the surroundings, and not to the speed component present in the initiation and termination of nervous processes, the latter being comprised by lability, a property of the CNS introduced by the neo-Pavlovian typologists (see Nebylitsyn, 1972a; Teplov, 1972). Equilibrium of nervous processes does not take into account the ratio between excitation and inhibition in mobility (Kupalov, 1952) or in dynamism (Golubeva, 1980; Nebylitsyn, 1972a) but only in the strength of nervous processes, that is, as Pavlov has understood this trait.

We shall not go into the details of the observation chart here (see Strelau, 1965b, 1969). The first version of the STI was constructed in such a way as to be a duplicate of the observation chart, the difference consisting in the fact that, for each of the 75 items from this chart, one parallel item was generated. The answering format consisted in a 3-point rating scale. Thus the STI comprised 150 items, 50 for each of the three basic CNS properties. The first stage of research with the STI, with information regarding its reliability and validity, has been presented elsewhere (Strelau, 1972a). The item analysis of the first version of STI resulted in reformulating several items and in reducing their number to 134.

Finally, the second version of the STI, used since 1972 until now, comprises 134 items, 44 for strength of excitation (SE), 44 for strength of inhibition (SI), and 46 for mobility of nervous processes (M). Because the number of items for the SE scale and SI scale is equal, the balance of nervous processes may be indicated by the quotient of SE index divided by the SI index. Because the STI is based on a 3-point rating scale ("yes," "no," and "don't know") the maximum value of points to be received is 88 for both strength of excitation and strength of inhibition, and 92 for mobility of CNPs. A quotient higher than unity indicates the predominance of strength of excitation over strength of inhibition, whereas a quotient smaller than unity is an indicator of the reverse dominance.

Because a further parallel item was generated for each existing item in the observation chart, it was possible to construct two equivalent versions of the STI (A & B), both containing 67 items (22 for SE, 22 for SI, and 26 for M). These parallel versions were used mainly for measuring the internal consistency of the STI. In most of the studies the full version of the STI was applied.

It has to be remembered that in spite of the physiological terms used for labeling the properties to be measured by means of this inventory, the STI does not allow any insight into the physiological mechanisms to which these properties pertain. The STI refers to overt behavior, like most of the inventories do. The CNS properties have the status of explanatory concepts belonging to Pavlov's theory of higher nervous activity. This means that the STI is intended to measure temperamental traits, to be interpreted within the Pavlovian theory of types of the nervous system.

Because strength of the nervous system is expressed—according to Pavlov— by the ability to endure intense or long-lasting stimulation without passing into protective inhibition, the items comprising the SE scale refer to the following domains of behavior: (a) readiness for an action (activity) in highly stimulating situations; (b) carrying on activity in highly stimulating situations; (c) lack of emotional disturbances in stress situations (high load of stimulation); and (d) lack of evident changes in efficiency during conditions of intensive or long-lasting stimulation.

Regarding strength of inhibition as the functional capacity of the CNS for conditioned (learned) inhibition, especially as the ability to endure long-lasting conditioned inhibition, the items of the SI scale include such domains of behavior as (a) restraining from reactions; (b) delay of action; and (c) ability to interrupt an action.

All of the items included in the M scale refer to the ability to react quickly and adequately to changing conditions, which is the essence of mobility of the CNS according to Pavlov. A detailed ex post analysis of the items has shown, however, that some of the M scale items are rather bound with a more general temporal characteristic of behavior, including lability of the CNS.

It does not follow from Pavlov's theorizing whether or not the different CNS properties are related to each other. However, from the configurations of these properties in Pavlov's four types of the nervous system one may assume that they are conceptualized as rather being independent from each other.

NERVOUS SYSTEM PROPERTIES AS REPRESENTED IN THE STI AND OTHER PERSONALITY/TEMPERAMENT DIMENSIONS

The CNS properties to be represented by the STI scales (strength of excitation, strength of inhibition, mobility and balance between strength of excitation and inhibition) were partly subject to investigation by several authors. The aim of these studies was to explore the relationships between these properties and temperamental traits or biologically determined personality dimensions introduced by psychologists from the West. This section gives a short review of this research. As regards the empirical evidence for the relationships mentioned earlier, only those studies are included in which the Pavlovian CNS properties were measured on the basis of experimental methods, mainly developed by Teplov, Nebylitsyn, and their students. The data collected by means of the STI are presented in the following section.

The first attempts to relate CNS properties to other personality concepts stem from Pavlov (1951–52). In his studies on types of nervous systems he discovered that dogs with weak nervous processes are characterized by high anxiety, the latter being diagnosed on the basis of behavioral indicators. This hypothesis has been verified in several studies conducted in dogs (Kolesnikov, 1953; Krushinsky, 1947). In humans this relationship has been suggested by Nebylitsyn (1959) and Marton and Urban (1966). Taking into account the fact that in highly anxious individuals CRs to negative reinforcements are elaborated with higher speed than in nonanxious individuals (Spence, 1956), the authors hypothesized that high anxiety goes together with weak nervous processes. This is due to the weaks' high sensitivity of the nervous system which, in turn, determines the speed of conditioning. This idea has been further developed by Strelau (1969, 1983).

A significant step in searching for links between the CNS properties and personality dimensions has been done by Gray (1964). His reinterpretation of the concept of strength of the nervous system within the theory of arousal has stimulated personality researchers to study the relationships between this property of the CNS and personality dimensions based on the arousal concept. According to Gray, "the weak nervous system is more easily or more highly 'aroused'; and the personality dimension known as 'strength of the nervous system' could be described as a dimension of 'levels of arousal' or of 'arousability' " (1964, p. 289). This hypothesis has been used by Eysenck (1966; Eysenck & Levey, 1972) as well as by Gray (1967) in order to explain the relationship between strength of excitation and extraversion. Taking into account his reticulo-cortical arousal loop theory, Eysenck assumed that introverts and individuals with the weak CNS should be regarded as having generally higher levels of arousal as compared with the extravert and the strong type of the CNS. Some studies in which experimental measures of the strength of the nervous system have been used give evidence supporting this hypothesis. For example, Frigon (1976), using the EEG variant of the extinction with reinforcement method for diagnosing the strength of the nervous system and the EPI questionnaire for measuring extraversion, has found a positive correlation between extraversion and strength of the CNS. Similar results by using the same indicators of both dimensions were obtained by Gilliland (1985). Karpova (1974), using the slope of RT curve and the change of RT under repeatedly exposed stimuli for measuring strength of excitation and an undescribed method for diagnosing extraversion, reports a positive correlation between the two traits under discussion. There are, however, also data that do not support Eysenck's and Gray's "extraversion-strength of excitation" hypothesis. Loo (1979), using the slope of RT curve for measuring strength of excitation and the EPQ for diagnosing extraversion, stated that extraversion comprises one factor together with the weak CNS. Keuss and Orlebeke (1977), taking also the slope of RT curve as an indicator of strength and the MPI for measuring extraversion, obtained a negative correlation between both variables. A negative correlation between both dimensions under discussion was also obtained by Zhorov and Yermolayeva-Tomina (1972), who used the slope of RT curve and the MPI for diagnosing both strength and extraversion. Also, studies can be found that show that strength of excitation, as measured by laboratory techniques, and extraversion are not related to each other (Gupta & Nicholson, 1985; Kohn, 1987; Kohn et al., 1987). As can be easily stated, experimental studies of strength of the CNS as related to extraversion, the latter diagnosed by means of Eysenck's inventories, do not allow for unequivocal conclusion regarding the relationship between those two dimensions. One of the reasons for the lack of agreement may be the fact that extraversion is a very broad concept, comprising such diverse factors as sociability and impulsivity.

As described in detail elsewhere (Strelau, 1983) studies have also been conducted with the aim of establishing the relationship between experimentally measured mobility of the CNS and extraversion, with results not allowing a definite conclusion (see Loo, 1979; Mangan, 1967, 1978; Troshikhin et al., 1978). Research conducted in the last years suggests that extraversion and mobility, the latter measured in experimental settings, do not correlate with each other (see Dall & White, 1985; Rawlings, 1987).

The existence of a relationship between strength of the CNS and neuroticism has been suggested by Eysenck (1947) in the 1940s and almost 20 years later by Gray (1964). However, the latter author rejected this position. The reason for doing so was the fact that the sensory threshold has been regarded by the neo-Pavlovian typologists (see Nebylitsyn, 1972a; Teplov, 1964) as one of the main indicators of the strength of the nervous system, whereas neuroticism seems not to be related to sensory sensitivity. The hypothesized relationship between these two traits was subject to study in several experiments. Mangan and Farmer (1967) stated that strength of excitation, measured by means of the slope of RT curve, does not correlate with neuroticism as diagnosed with the MPI. This lack of correlation has been supported in other studies based on experimental indicators of the strength of the nervous system (Frigon, 1976; Karpova, 1974; Kovac & Halmiova, 1973; Orlebeke, 1972). An experiment conducted by Gupta and Nicholson (1985), where, among other things, the slope of RT curve was used for diagnosing strength of excitation, shows that neuroticism, as measured by the EPI, goes together with weak nervous processes. Keuss and Orlebeke (1977), also using the RT method for diagnosing strength, reported similar results.

Few studies have been conducted in which experimentally diagnosed mobility was related to neuroticism. The results are negative, that is, no relationship was found between the dimensions under discussion (Dall & White, 1985; Rawlings, 1987).

Aside from extraversion, neuroticism, and anxiety, further personality/temperament[2] dimensions have been confronted with the CNS properties under discussion. For example, Zuckerman (1979) has hypothesized that the basic nervous system properties, especially the strength of excitation, are related to sensation seeking. Using the absolute auditory threshold as a measure of strength of excitation, Goldman, Kohn, and Hunt (1983) have shown that this CNS property correlates positively with sensation seeking as measured by Zuckerman's SSS-IV (General scale). Rawlings (1987), applying the "alteration" method for diagnosing mobility of the CNS, and the EPQ for estimating psychoticism, has shown that there exists a strongly expressed negative correlation between the two traits, but only for males. Sales and Throop (1972) have hypothesized a positive correlation between Petrie's reducing-augmenting dimension and strength of the nervous system. Measuring the former dimension by means of the kinesthetic figural aftereffect (KFA) and the latter one on the basis of the slope of RT curve they were able to state that reducers have a stronger CNS as compared with augmenters. This regularity was not found in a study presented by Kohn (1987), where strength of excitation was measured with the slope of RT curves (visual and auditory) and the reducing-augmenting dimension with Vando's RAS inventory (see also Kohn et al., 1987). Also, the relationship between strength of the nervous system and dimensions occurring in Cattell's theory of personality was the subject of interests. Cattell (1972) hypothesized that such traits as assertive ego, general inhibition, hypomanic temperament, exuberance, cortertia, capacity to mobilize versus regression, and exvia versus invia should be linked to strength of the nervous system. Studies conducted by Orlebeke (1972) show, however, that the only dimension among those to be measured by the 16PF that correlates with strength is surgency. In this experiment this CNS property was measured on the basis of the RT max/RT min index. (for explanation see Nebylitsyn, 1972a or Strelau, 1983).

There are no studies in which experimentally measured strength of inhibition

---

[2]The interchangeable use of the terms personality/temperament is used here because several authors label the same dimensions, depending on the context in which they occur, once as belonging to temperament and once as personality traits. If the latter label is used it has to be assumed that we are dealing with personality characteristics that are first of all biologically determined (see Strelau, 1982, 1987a).

and/or balance between strength of excitation and inhibition (i.e., the remaining CNS properties as measured by the STI) were related to the personality/temperament dimensions presented earlier.

In most of the investigations in which personality/temperament dimensions, conceptualized by psychologists from the West, were compared with the Pavlovian CNS properties, the STI was used for diagnosing these properties.

THE CURRENT STATE OF RESEARCH USING THE STI

In order to present the reader with a full range of data regarding the STI research, this inventory is presented, taking into account the results found in the literature that refer to the item analysis, to the psychometric characteristics of the separate scales, including reliability measures, and to a broad range of validity studies.

Item Analysis

The item analysis of the STI is one of the weakest points of this questionnaire. In its original Polish version the items have been analyzed only for endorsement, and this procedure led to a reduction of items from 150 (first version of STI) to 134 (the actual version). In one of the two studies (Paisey & Mangan, 1980) with the English version of the STI, 33 items were deleted from the 134-item inventory, and in the second study (Stelmack et al., 1985), 23 items. In both studies the criterion for deleting was less than 25% or more than 75% endorsement. There is no information, however, on which of the items did not fulfill the endorsement criterion.

There is probably only one study in which the item-scale correlation of the STI has been analyzed; this is a German version of this questionnaire (Daum & Schugens, 1986). Taking as the lowest value acceptable for future work with the STI a correlation coefficient of .20, the authors stated that 6.8% of the SE items, 9.1% of the SI items, and 34% of the M items have item-scale correlations of less than .20. The high percentage of mobility items not fulfilling the .20 value may be related to the fact that the M scale also comprises items that refer to lability (see p. 189).

Distribution Characteristics

Table 8.1 presents the means and standard deviations of the separate scales obtained in 14 studies, these comprising four mixed groups (males and females), six male samples and four female ones. Among these 14 studies 10 refer to the Polish population, 2 to the West German, and 2 to English-speaking populations.

With respect to strength of excitation, the values vary from 47.11 to 64.41 (median = 54.91) when all of the results (males and females) are taken into

TABLE 8.1

Means and Standard Deviations of the STI Scales

No.	References	No. of SS	Sex	Age	Properties of the Nervous System							
					SE		SI		M		B	
					M	SD	M	SD	M	SD	M	SD
1.	Nosal (1974)	100	M,F	19-22 (Ugr)	47.11	12.56	55.48	13.2	55.13	11.70	0.89	0.29
2.	Terelak (1974)	115	M	20-45 (LA)	62.23	12.34	67.65	13.59	60.69	10.07	0.94	0.22
3.	Terelak (1974)	95	M	20-45 (HA)	64.41	13.02	70.67	11.58	61.22	11.04	0.93	0.21
4.	Koscielak (1979)	100	M	25-45 (I)	56.89	12.12	62.50	11.79	57.12	9.42	0.94	0.26
5.	Koscielak (1979)	100	F	25-45 (NI)	55.53	11.17	58.66	12.57	53.35	10.33	0.97	0.21
6.	Klonowicz (1979) (SP)	78	F	Ugr (Moscow)	54.3	13.8			55.5	12.5		
7.	Klonowicz (1979) (SP)	78	F	Ugr (Warsaw)	51.0	13.1			59.1	10.5		
8.	Strelau (1983)	235	M,F	18-24	49.8	11.8						
		241	M,F	18-24			60.6	11.3				
		242	M,F	18-24					56.0	10.7		
		234	M,F	18-24								
9.	Strelau (1983)	130	M	18-34	57.7	15.92	60.9	15.85	59.4	13.13	0.85	0.30
10.	Strelau (1983)	116	F	18-30	48.0	12.94	55.7	15.91	57.1	12.43	0.99	0.39
11.	Daum and Schugens (1986)	108	M	23,1 (2,9)	53.9	11.6	59.6	11.9	56.0	8.6	0.94	0.40
12.	Daum and Schugens (1986)	73	F	23,2 (3,9)	47.3	11.4	56.9	10.4	56.4	9.9		
13.	Haase (1986)	22	M,F	18-26 (Ugr)	59.1	9.3	55.3	12.3	54.8	8.6		
14.	Kohn (1987)	212	M,F	Ugr	104.09 (?)	11.19						

M = males
F = females
Ugr = undergraduate students
ST = students
I = inventors
NI = noninventors
LA = low alpha index
HA = high alpha index

account. For males the median is 57.30 (53.9–64.41) and for females Me = 49.50 (47.3–54.30), implying sex differences.

In spite of the equal number of items in both scales, SE and SI, the medians are higher for strength of inhibition as compared with strength of excitation for all three groups of samples. The median for all samples is 59.60 (55.3–70.67), for males Me = 61.70 (55.3–70.67) and in the two female samples the mean values vary from 55.7 to 56.9. As can also be seen, the men in this case score higher than females, but it is not clear whether this difference is significant.

The Mobility scale seems to be less sex specific, relative to the SE and SI scales. The median for all samples is 56.4 (53.35–61.22), whereas for males it is 58.26 (53.35–61.22) and for females, M = 56.4 (55.5–59.1).

As mentioned earlier (see p. 193) the balance of nervous processes is estimated by means of the quotient of SE index divided by the SI index. This quotient was calculated only in 8 studies among the 14 quoted in Table 8.1. The median for all studies is .94 (.85–.99), and exactly the same value for men (with distribution varying from .93–.99) was obtained. In the only female sample the mean (.94) is equal to the median. Thus no sex differences exist in scores of the B scale. All of the values are below 1.00, which suggests that in general strength of inhibition dominates to some degree over strength of excitation.

There are not many studies informing about the distribution of scores of the STI scales, and probably only two of them took place outside Poland (Daum & Schugens, 1986; Vyatkina, 1976). Stawowska (1973, 1977) conducted in Poland a study on 2520 subjects (1255 females and 1265 males) aged 17–60, which yielded normal distributions for all four CNS properties. Similar results were obtained in two other projects (Klonowicz, 1979; Vyatkina, 1976). Also Daum and Schugens (1986), in a study carried out on a German sample comprising 181 subjects (108 men and 74 women) with mean ages 21.1 and 23.2, have shown a similar regularity for the SE and M scales. For the SI scores, a weak negatively skewed tendency occurred. The B scale scores were not taken into account. The results of two independent studies conducted by Strelau (1983) show, however, that the distributions of scores for the SI and B scales do not resemble the normal curve. This was especially evident in females.

Reliability Measures

Reliability of the STI scales was subject to investigation in a number of studies (see Table 8.2). There exists information about the following types of reliability: internal consistency based on the estimation of reliabilities from item parameters, split-half reliability where scores from version A were correlated with scores from version B (see p. 193), and stability measures. The latter are based on retest studies conducted over rather long time intervals.

The only studies that are informative about internal consistency of the STI scales stem from German and English samples. Daum and Schugens (1986) have

TABLE 8.2
Reliability Measures of the STI

No.	References	No. of SS	Sex	Age	SE	SI	M	B	Type of Reliability
1.	Daum and Schugens (1986)	181	M,F	Ugr	.84	.82	.68		IC
2.	Kohn (1987)	212	M,F	Ugr	.81				IC
3.	Kohn et al.(1987)	53	M,F	Ugr	.75				IC
4.	Corulla (1989)*	312	M	17-55	.80	.83	.73		IC
5.	Corulla (1989)*	288	F	16-53	.73	.77	.61		IC
6.	Strelau (1983)	234-242	M,F	18-24	.70	.68	.63		SHR
7.	Carlier (1985)	202	M,F	Ugr	.73	.75	.66		SHR
8.	Daum and Schugens (1986)	181	M,F	Ugr	.89	.83	.76	.73	SHR
9.	Strelau (1983) (6 months interval)	195-241	M,F	18-24	.677	.692	.594	.660	STA
10.	Strelau (1983) (13-15 months interval)	126-136	M,F	18-24	.632	.700	.586	.660	STA

* a yes/no response format was applied

M = males
F = females
Ugr = undergraduate students

IC = internal consistency measured by Cronbach's alpha
SHR = split-half reliability
STA = stability

reported adequate Cronbach's alpha coefficients for the SE and SI scales, whereas the value for the M scale is below .70. Also in Corulla's (1987) study the alpha coefficient is the lowest in case of mobility; this is especially evident among females (.61). For the SE scale, for which internal consistency was measured in five studies, the values vary from .73 to .84, which should be considered satisfactory. The same can be said about the SI scale where the lowest value is .77 and the highest is .84. Probably due to the fact that there do not exist separate items for the B scale, the latter being based on secondary scores (see p. 193), internal consistency of this scale has not yet been estimated.

The split-half reliability measures are generally consistent with the Cronbach's alpha scores. Here again it turns out that mobility shows the lowest values. Among the three coefficients, two are rather unacceptable (.63 & .66). One of those stems from a Polish sample (Strelau, 1983) and the other from a French one (Carlier, 1985). Also not acceptable is one of the three coefficients drawn from the SI scale (an alpha score of .68), obtained in Strelau's study (1983). All of the other scores vary from .70 to .89 and may be regarded as satisfactory or sufficiently high. The only score for the B scale (.73) follows from the fact that, in general, balance of the nervous system was not often the subject for research and this holds true also for all other results presented later.

There exists only scanty information about the stability of the STI scores. The only studies have been conducted by Strelau (1983), one with a 6-month interval and the other one with an interval varying from 13 to 15 months. The results of these two studies are homogeneous. As can be seen from Table 8.2, the coefficients of correlation obtained in these studies for all four scales vary from .59 to .70. Taking into account the rather long time interval, these scores should be regarded as satisfactory. However, they are lower than the split-half and internal consistency measures. Interestingly enough, here again the lowest scores were obtained for the M scale (.59 and .59).

Internal Validity

There exist many data that refer to different aspects of internal as well as external validity of the STI. As regards internal validity, the correlations between the STI scales and factor analytic studies based on the STI items are presented.

Correlations between the STI Scales. The data that are informative about the intercorrelations between the STI scales are presented in Table 8.3, which includes 17 studies. At first glance it is obvious that many significant correlations between the scales are being compared. Most important for us are the comparisons between strength of excitation, strength of inhibition, and mobility.

The SE and SI scales have been correlated in 16 studies. The results are consistent in that they show positive correlations only, varying from .26 to .61 (Me = .42). Taking into account the seven male samples, the median value of

TABLE 8.3

Coefficients of Correlation Between the Properties of the Nervous System

No.	References	No. of Ss	Sex	Age	Properties of the Nervous System					
					SE & SI	SE & M	SE & B	SI & M	SI & B	M & M
1.	Terelak (1974)	115	M	25–45 (LA)	.589a	.595a	.282b	.283b	-.555a	-.266b
2.	Terelak (1974)	95	M	20–45 (HA)	.448a	.713a	.535a	.305b	-.465a	-.385a
3.	Koscielak (1979)	100	M	25–45 (I)	.439	.399	.524	.653	-.483	-.288
4.	Koscielak (1979)	100	M	25–45 (NI)	.568	.536	.250		-.624	-.288
5.	Zarzycka (1980)	59	M	27–49 (NA)	.522a	-.522b	-.579b	.198b	.180c	-.388b
6.	Zarzycka (1980)	59	M	27–49 (A)	.614a	.711b	-.506b	.405b	-.249	-.398b
7.	Strelau (1983)	159	M,F	Ugr	.390b	.597a		.088		
8.	Carlier (1985)	202	M,F	Ugr	.27c	.45c		-.01		
9.	Gilliland (1985)*	63	M,F	Ugr	.41c	.51c	.53c	.20	-.53c	.28
10.	Stelmach et al. (1985)*	258	M,F	Ugr 23,7	.44b	.61b		.26		
11.	Daum and Schugens (1986)	181	M,F	23,1 & 23,2	.40a	.51a		.10		
12.	Haase (1986)	22	M,F	18–26 (Ugr)	.33	.60		.01		
13.	Schoenpflug and Muendelein (1976)	72	?	OW	.40b	.52b		.26b		
14.	Przymusinski and Strelau (1986)	211	M,F	17–21		.614				
15.	Barclay (1987)	85	M,F	19–24 (Ugr)	.26c	.539a	.527a	.053	-.616a	.339a
16.	Corulla (1987)	312	M	17–55	.53	.63	.35	.36	-.57	.19
	Corulla (1987)	288	F	16–53	.35	.54	.55	.24	-.55	.27

* a yes/no response format
  was applied

M = males
F = females
Ugr = undergraduate students
I = inventors
NI = noninventors
OW = office workers
LA = low alpha index
HA = high alpha index
NA = nonaccident engine-drivers
A = accident engine-drivers

$a = p < .001$
$b = p < .01$
$c = p < .05$

the coefficients of correlation increases to Me = .53. There is only one study in which females have been investigated, thus not allowing any conclusions about regularities regarding the interrelations between these CNS properties in females. The same holds true for all of the STI scales to be presented in Table 8.3. It is not easy to answer the question, "In what manner do the positive correlations refer to Pavlov's idea regarding the relationships between the properties under discussion?" If one takes his statement seriously, that excitation (connected with the process of dissimilation) and inhibition (referring to the process of assimilation) are inseparable (Pavlov, 1951–52), then the links between those two properties should not be regarded as unexpected. This relationship is also consistent with Pavlov's assumption, according to which strength of excitation and strength of inhibition should be high in the strong types and low in the weak type.

The positive correlations between strength of excitation and mobility of the nervous processes stated by several Pavlovian typologists (see p. 191) are also evident in the research conducted by means of the STI. In all of the 17 studies, positive correlations were obtained (with the median correlation being .54). The median for the seven male samples is .59. If we consider that searching for novelty and variations in the surroundings has a high stimulating value (see Fiske & Maddi, 1961; Zuckerman, 1979), the lack of orthogonality between these two properties should not be surprising.

The interrelationships between strength of inhibition and mobility of nervous processes based on 15 studies presented in Table 8.3 are considerably consistent also. The, on the average, weak positive relationships between the SI and M scales stated in the studies compared do not seem to be explainable in Pavlov's theory.

Because the balance score is the result of the ratio between the SE and SI values, the correlations between balance of the CNS and strength of excitation, and balance and strength of inhibition, are confounded and thus difficult to interpret. However, we report these correlations because they are presented in the literature.

The results of studies in which the values representing the balance of nervous processes have been compared with all of the three STI scales are rather inconsistent, except for strength of inhibition and balance of the CNS, where 9 of the 10 studies show negative correlations varying from −.25 to −.62 (median = −.54). The median for the male samples decreases to Me = −.48. This regularity can hardly be explained in the light of Pavlov's typology. There do not exist any other empirical data that allow for a reasonable comparison. The correlation coefficients for SE and B scores vary from −.58 to .55 and for M and B scores, from −.40 to .38, thus contradicting any regularities regarding these comparisons.

Factor Analysis of the STI Items. According to our knowledge, there exist four studies in which the items of the STI scales have been factor analyzed. The first was conducted by Paisey and Mangan (1980) on a sample of 277 subjects

(M and F). Taking as the starting point 101 items (33 have been excluded because of the endorsement criterion), the authors obtained 16 oblique factors from which 6 second-order factors emerged. "The first second-order factor combines strength of excitation and mobility; the second obviously reflects a component of strength of inhibition; the third, equally obviously, represents the negative pole of strength of inhibition" (Paisey & Mangan, 1980, p. 127). The three remaining factors did not allow for any reasonable interpretation. It can be stated that the first second-order factor remains the regularity to be found in correlative studies.

Similar results, especially regarding the first two factors, were obtained by Carlier (1985). In her study with 202 subjects (M and F), four orthogonally rotated factors emerged form the analysis of the 134 STI items. F1 is saturated by SE and M items, F2 by SI items, F3 comprises SE items in working situations[3] and F4, ability to adapt to others, that is, mainly mobility items.

Stelmack et al. (1985), using the method of principal components, extracted from 111 STI items 26 factors (23 items were eliminated because they did not fulfill the endorsement criterion). A second-order factor analysis based on results obtained from 258 undergraduate students of both sexes yielded seven factors: F1—Restrain (mainly SI items), F2—Work effort (SE and M items), F3—Flexibility (SE and M items), F4—Emotional control (SI, SE, and M items), F5—Social adaptability. Factors 6 and 7 are regarded by the authors as not interpretable. Factor 1 from this study is the second factor in both former studies and factors F2 and F3 are comparable to the first factors found in Paisey and Mangan's and Carlier's studies. There exist in all of the three scales (SE, SI, M) items that refer to emotional behavior (reactions). It is therefore not surprising that also an emotional factor (F4) showed up.

Six factors were obtained not only by Paisey and Mangan but also in Van Heck's (1987) research, by means of the factor analysis based on principal components. One hundred and sixty-five persons (both sexes almost equally represented) were subjects for the studies. However, and not explicitly stated by the author, the SE items primarily load on the Disturbance (in stress situations) factor. The second factor, Strength of inhibition, is composed of SI items. Strength of excitation in work situations, being a combination of SE and M items, is the third factor. In the fourth factor, Mobility, M items are the most salient ones. The last two factors, Perseverance and Flexibility, are also composed mainly of M items.

No matter what labels are used by the authors of the factor analytic studies in order to identify the extracted factors, it can be concluded that in all of them a separate factor, which comprises SI items, was found. The same holds true for a

---

[3]In the English as well as in the German translation of the STI the items related to activity, or to human action in general, have been mostly translated as referring to occupational activity, which explains to a given degree the fact that a working-specific SE factor emerged in Carlier's study. The same explanation holds true for the next two studies to be presented in this section.

factor being composed of SE and M items. In the remaining factors, being different in the consecutive studies, no configurations of items have been found that are in contradiction to the regularities presented in correlative studies.

External Validity: STI and other Personality/Temperament Scales

The interrelationships between the CNS properties as measured by the STI and such personality/temperament dimensions as extraversion, neuroticism, psychoticism, anxiety, sensation seeking, and augmenting/reducing are presented, taking into account the correlative studies to be found in the literature as well as factor analytic research comprising those and certain other dimensions. Since there exists only one female sample in which these comparisons have been subject to investigation, the analysis of data does not take into account sex-specific relationships.

STI and Extraversion/Introversion.   Since the time Eysenck (1966, 1972) and Gray (1967) put forward the hypothesis that strength of excitation correlates positively with extraversion, there has been a growing interest in studying the relationship between these dimensions. As has been shown in the previous section, the results in which psychometrically diagnosed extraversion was compared with laboratory measures of strength of excitation are contradictory. This cannot be said when both dimensions under discussion are compared on the same level of behavior organization, that is, by means of psychometric tools. The 20 studies presented in Table 8.4 show unequivocally, with only one exception (Stelmack et al., 1985), that extraversion correlates positively with strength of excitation as measured by the STI. The median of the correlation coefficients is Me = .40, with a range from .07 to .60.

Among the 20 studies, comprising 21 samples, 8 were conducted on Polish groups, where extraversion was measured with the MPI. This is the only Eysenckian inventory adapted to the Polish population. The median for these samples is Me = .46, with coefficients varying from .35 to .60. In four studies, where the EPI was used, the median decreases to Me = 34 (.22–.46) and a similar result (Me = .37; .07–.49) was obtained for eight samples in which extraversion was diagnosed by means of the EPQ (including the revised form). On the basis of these results it can be concluded that the fact that, in the Extraversion scale, impulsivity items are included (EPI) or excluded (EPQ) does not essentially influence the relationship between strength of excitation and extraversion. The lack of correlation stated in the study conducted by Stelmack et al. (1985) can be explained partially be the fact that instead of a 3-point rating scale, the authors used a yes/no scale. Further, they deleted 23 items from the correlative analysis because of the endorsement criterion. The endorsement criterion problem also holds true for Paisey and Mangan's (1982) study, which

TABLE 8.4

Coefficients of Correlation Between Extraversion and Properties of the Nervous System

No.	References	No. of Ss	Sex	Age	Properties of the Nervous System				Inventory
					SE	SI	M	B	
1.	Strelau (1969)	78	M,F	Ugr	.449a	.007	.667a		MPI
2.	Strelau (1970)	159	M,F	Ugr	.476a	.028	.652a		MPI
3.	Strelau (1971)*	171	M,F	Ugr	.444a				MPI
		183	M,F	Ugr		.08			MPI
		178	M,F	Ugr			.694a		MPI
		199	M,F	Ugr				.350a	MPI
4.	Terelak (1974)	115	M	20-45 (LA)	.381a	.052	.563a	.356a	MPI
5.	Terelak (1974)	95	M	20-45 (HA)	.597a	.266	.730a	.313a	MPI
6.	Ciosek and Oszmianczuk (1974)	70	M	?	.349b	.165	.517a		MPI
7.	Zarzycka (1980)*	59	M	27-49 (NA)	.504a	.160	.536a	-.413c	MPI
8.	Zarzycka (1980)*	59	M	27-49 (A)	.548a	.156	.448a	-.504a	MPI
9.	Carlier (1985)	202	M,F	Ugr	.38c	-.21c	.54c		EPI
10.	Gilliland (1985)	63	M,F	Ugr	.22	-.16	.35c	.36c	EPI
11.	Kohn (1987)	212	M,F	Ugr	.30b				EPI
12.	Kohn et al. (1987)	53	M,F	Ugr	.46b				EPI
13.	Paisey and Mangan (1982)	174	?	?	.37	-.07			EPQ
14.	Gilliland (1985)	63	M,F	Ugr	.42c	.32c	.19	.12	EPQ
15.	Stelmack et al. (1985)**	258	M,F	Ugr 23, 7	.07	-.09	.15		EPQ
16.	Daum and Schugens (1986)	108	M,F	Ugr	.42a	-.14	.63a		EPQ
17.	Larsen and Baggs (1986)	40	M,F	Ugr	.20	-.14	.44b	.23	EPQ
18.	Richards (1986)*	79	M,F	17-39	.49a	.03	.59a		EPQ
19.	Daum et al. (1988)	59	M	Ugr (20-32)	.40b	-.22	.59a		EPQ
20.	Corulla (1989)**	312	M	17-55	.18	-.05	.27	.19	EPQ-R
		288	F	16-53	.31	.02	.30	.23	EPQ-R

*data published in Strelau (1983)
**a yes/no response format was applied

M = males
F = females
Ugr = undergraduate students

LA = low alpha index
HA = high alpha index
NA = nonaccident engine drivers
A = accident engine-drivers

a = p <.001
b = p <.01
c = p <.05

deleted 33 items for the same reason. In spite of that, the correlation between extraversion and strength of excitation was still positive (.37).

The second CNS property to which considerable attention has been paid in studies of extraversion is mobility. As can be seen from Table 8.4, the results reflecting the relationship between the two traits under discussion are unequivocal and they confirm the hypothesis that there is a positive correlation between extraversion and mobility of the CNS. The median of the coefficients of correlation obtained from 18 studies is rather high (Me = .54; .15–.73) and extends the median for strength of excitation to .46. These data, again, are not in accordance with the experimental studies that suggest a lack of correlation between these two variables. If we consider the results separately for the eight Polish samples (with MPI applied) and for those obtained by means of EPI and EPQ, then we can see that the coefficients of correlation are the highest for MPI (Me = .67; .45–.73) and the lowest for EPQ (Me = .37; .15–.63) where also eight samples were investigated. There are only two results for the EPI (.35 and .54), and they are situated within the range of the EPQ-M coefficients.

The two remaining CNS properties, strength of inhibition and balance of nervous processes, have not been related in the non-STI studies to extraversion, and this holds true also for studies where other personality/temperament dimensions were related to the CNS properties. Not going into the details, one has to state that strength of inhibition as diagnosed by means of the STI does not correlate, in general, with extraversion (Me = .02, with distributions from −.22 to .32). Among the 19 studies, the coefficients attained a value >.17 in four samples. In case of balance of the CNS there are only 8 studies in which this property of the CNS was compared with extraversion. The results are not univocal. In two samples (Zarzycka, 1980) the coefficients of correlation are negative and significant, whereas in 6 studies they are positive, but not extending the value of .36. The main trend (Me = .27) suggests a low positive correlation between extraversion and balance of the CNS.

STI and Neuroticism.   The relationship between strength of excitation and neuroticism predicted by Eysenck (1947) some decades ago has been proven in psychometric research. Table 8.5 displays 20 studies that show a negative correlation between those dimensions (Me = −.46, with distribution from −.13 to −.56).

Among the 20 samples there are 8 where the MPI was applied, that is, the Polish studies (Me = −.46; −.38 to −.56). In three samples the EPI (Me = −.49; −39 to −.54) was used, and in nine the EPQ (Me = −.48; −.13 to −.56). The coefficients of correlation do not essentially differ as a function of the kind of inventory used to diagnose neuroticism. The unanimous relationship between strength of excitation and neuroticism, observed in psychometric studies, does not correspond with the experimental data, where contradictory results exist.

As shown in the previous section, neuroticism and mobility do not seem to be

TABLE 8.5
Coefficients of Correlation Between Neuroticism and Properties of the Nervous System

No.	References	No. of Ss	Sex	Age	Properties of the Nervous System				Inventory
					SE	SI	M	B	
1.	Strelau (1969)	78	M,F	Ugr	-.478a	-.450a	-.300c		MPI
2.	Strelau (1970)	159	M,F	Ugr	-.557a	-.526a	-.215c		MPI
3.	Strelau (1971)*	169	M,F	Ugr	-.378a				MPI
		178	M,F	Ugr		-.246b			MPI
		177	M,F	Ugr			-.174		MPI
		197	M,F	Ugr				-.08a	MPI
4.	Terelak (1974)	115	M	20-45 (LA)	-.538a	-.588a	-.209c	-.108	MPI
5.	Terelak (1974)	95	M	20-45 (HA)	-.444a	-.331b	-.349a	-.152a	MPI
6.	Ciosek & Oszmianczuk (1974)	70	M	?	-.504a	-.396b	-.296c		MPI
7.	Zarzycka (1980)*	59	M	27-49 (NA)	-.442a	-.496a	-.141	-.112	MPI
8.	Zarzycka (1980)*	59	M	27-49 (A)	-.426b	-.545b	-.173	-.020	MPI
9.	Carlier (1985)	202	M,F	Ugr	-.49c	-.48c	-.21c		EPI
10.	Gilliland (1985)	63	M,F	Ugr	-.39c	-.02	-.23	-.33c	EPI
11.	Kohn (1987)	212	M,F	Ugr	-.54b				EPI
12.	Paisey & Mangan (1982)	174	?	?	-.53	-.14			EPQ
13.	Gilliland (1985)	63	M,F	Ugr	-.36c	-.29	-.24	-.08	EPQ
14.	Stelmack et al. (1985)**	258	M,F	Ugr 23, 7	-.13	-.12	-.07		EPQ
15.	Daum & Schugens (1986)	108	M,F	Ugr	-.51b	-.25b	-.24c		EPQ
16.	Larsen & Baggs (1986)	40	M,F	Ugr	-.56b	-.41b	-.33c	-.02	EPQ
17.	Richards (1986)**	79	M,F	17-39	-.50a	-.40a	-.33b		EPQ
18.	Daum et al. (1988)	59	M	Ugr(20-32)	-.48a	-.38b	-.34b		EPQ
19.	Corulla (1989)**	312	M	17-55	-.24	-.26	-.10	.07	EPQ-R
		288	F	16-53	-.16	-.15	-.01	.00	EPQ-R

* data published in Strelau (1983)
**a yes/no response format was applied

M = males
F = females
Ugr = undergraduate students
LA = low alpha index
HA = high alpha index
NA = nonaccident engine-drivers
A = accident engine-drivers

a = $p < .001$
b = $p < .01$
c = $p < .05$

correlated with each other when mobility was diagnosed in experimental settings. The data presented in Table 8.5 contradict this statement partially in that they show a clear-cut tendency for a negative, though not high, correlation between both dimensions under discussion. The median for the 18 studies in which these dimensions were related to each other is Me = −.22 (with a range from −.01 to −.35). When the different measures of neuroticism (MPI, EPI, and EPQ) are taken into account, the mean value in fact does not change. For the MPI samples the median is −.21 (−.14 to −.35), for EPQ, Me = −.24 (varies from −.01 to −.34), and the two coefficients of correlation for EPI are −.21 and −.23.

As regards the two remaining CNS properties, strength of inhibition is negatively correlated with neuroticism (Me = −.38; with a range from −.02 to −.59), whereas balance of the nervous processes does not correlate with this temperament dimension (Me = −.08; −.33 to −.7). Among the 10 scores representing the "balance-neuroticism" relationship, there is only one coefficient of correlation (−.33) which extends the value of −.15.

STI and Anxiety.   Links between anxiety and the type of nervous system have been suggested by Pavlov and some of his followers. The weak type is supposed to have a higher level of anxiety as compared with the strong type of CNS. As mentioned in the previous section, this regularity came out in animal research (Kolesnikov, 1953; Krushinsky, 1947), and theoretical arguments for this relationship may be found in several publications (Marton & Urban, 1966; Nebylitsyn, 1959; Strelau, 1969, 1983).

Nine of the psychometric studies aimed at examining the relationships between the CNS properties and anxiety have been conducted on Polish samples, where the MAS and the STAI inventories were used as measures of anxiety. Only four studies have been found by the authors that present results obtained outside of Poland, mainly on German samples. In these studies the STAI was used to diagnose anxiety. The only exception is Carlier's (1985) French project in which the Cattell Anxiety Scale was applied. As may be shown from Table 8.6, the kind of inventory by means of which anxiety was measured does not have much influence on the value and sign of the coefficients of correlation. This allows us to present the regularities expressed in Table 8.6 without taking into account the specific anxiety measures.

The results for the SE scale correspond fully with the regularity found in animal research. In all 13 studies anxiety correlates negatively with strength of excitation. The median (Me = −.58) suggests that the correlation is rather high. In all of the studies in which the coefficients vary from −.39 to −.72, the above stated relationship is statistically significant.

Also, negative correlations, however of lower value, were obtained when anxiety scores were compared with scores from the M scale. Among the 11 studies, 10 negative coefficients came out, varying from −.18 to −.60. The

TABLE 8.6

Coefficients of Correlation Between Anxiety and Properties of the Nervous System

No.	References	No. of Ss	Sex	Age	SE	SI	M	B	Inventory
1.	Strelau (1969)	75	M,F	Ugr	-.595a	-.412a			MAS
2.	Strelau (1971)**	148	M,F	Ugr	-.481a				MAS
		159	M,F	Ugr		-.202c			MAS
		157	M,F	Ugr			-.177		MAS
		200	M,F	Ugr				-.190c	MAS
3.	Strelau (1973)**	159	M,F	Ugr	-.554a	.359a	.289b		MAS
4.	Terelak (1974)	115	M	20-45 (LA)	-.617a	-.581a	-.282b	.002	MAS
5.	Terelak (1974)	95	M	20-45 (HA)	-.505a	-.477a	-.345a	-.063	MAS
6.	Sosnowski and Wrzesniewski (1986)	48	M	19-24	-.63a	-.45b	-.41b		MAS
7.	Sosnowski and Wrzesniewski (1986)	48	M	19-24	-.72a	-.52a	-.60a		STAI
8.	Zarzycka (1980)	59	M	27-49 (NA)	-.467a	-.489a	-.226c	-.226c	STAI
9.	Zarzycka (1980)	59	M	27-49 (A)	-.394a	-.332c	-.224	.140	STAI
10.	Muendelein (1982)	126	M,F	18-55	-.57a				STAI
11.	Schoenpflug & Muendelein (1986)	72	M,F	OW	-.64b	-.34b	-.22c	.36c	STAI
12.	Daum et al. (1988)	59	M	Ugr(20-32)	-.62a	-.29c	-.42b		STAI
13.	Carlier (1985)	202	M,F	Ugr	-.58c	-.59c	-.25c		CAS*

* Catell Anxiety Scale
** data published in Strelau (1983)

M	= males
F	= females
Ugr	= undergraduate students
OW	= office workers
LA	= low alpha index
HA	= high alpha index
NA	= nonaccident engine-drivers
A	= accident engine-drivers

a = $p < .001$
b = $p < .01$
c = $p < .05$

median for all 11 studies is Me $= -.25$. The only positive coefficient of correlation (.29) occurs, for unexplained reasons, in Strelau's (1983) study. The fact that strength of excitation correlates positively with mobility of the CNS elucidates, to some degree, the negative correlation between mobility and anxiety.

With one exception (Strelau, 1983) all of the 12 studies give support for a moderate negative correlation between anxiety and strength of inhibition (Me $= -.43$). As regards the relationship between balance of the nervous system and anxiety, the results obtained from 6 studies are contradictory (Me $= -.03$, with distribution of correlations varying from $-.23$ to $.36$), thus not allowing any reasonable conclusion.

STI and Psychoticism. The fact that Eysenck and Eysenck (1975) have developed an inventory that includes not only extraversion-introversion and neuroticism (as was the case with the former Eysenckian inventories) but also psychoticism, has given us an opportunity to search for links between this personality/temperament trait and the CNS properties. Some general hypotheses that psychoticism should be related to nervous system types as understood by Pavlov have been put forward by Claridge (1985, 1987). However, the kind of relationship between these two concepts has not been specified by him. It has to be stated that psychoticism was seldom compared with the Pavlovian concepts.

If we consider that psychoticism as measured by the EPQ has much in common with impulsivity and with "impulse control" (Eysenck, 1970; Eysenck & Eysenck, 1985), then one may predict that this dimension should be related to strength of inhibition and to balance of the CNS as defined by Pavlov and operationalized in the STI. High level of psychoticism (i.e., high impulsivity and low "impulse control") should correlate negatively with strength of inhibition and positively with balance of nervous processes. The positive correlation of the latter property is explained by the fact that the higher the scores indicating the balance of nervous processes, the larger the dominance of excitation over inhibition.

We were able to locate 8 studies in which the EPQ psychoticism scale was related to CNS properties measured by means of the STI. They are presented in Table 8.7. The table does not include Polish data, given that the EPQ is not used in Poland. This is caused by difficulties in adapting the psychoticism scale to the Polish population.

If we take into account the SE scale, it is easy to observe that strength of excitation does not correlate with psychoticism (Me $= -.02$; with coefficients varying from $-.26$ to $.16$). The same holds true for the mobility scores, where the median of the correlations between psychoticism and mobility, derived from eight samples, is Me $= -.04$ (from $-.18$ to $.11$). Because Rawlings (1987) has stated in his study a high negative correlation between psychoticism and experimentally measured mobility (but only for men), let us have a look at the two male samples. Daum, Hehl, and Schugens (1988) obtained a zero correlation (.06)

TABLE 8.7

Coefficients of Correlation Between Psychoticism and Properties of the Nervous System

No.	References	No. of Ss	Sex	Age	Properties of the Nervous System				
					SE	SI	M	B	Inventory
1.	Paisey and Mangan (1982)	174	?	?	-.14	-.54			EPQ
2.	Gilliland (1985)	63	M,F	Ugr	.12	-.03	.13	.16	EPQ
3.	Stelmach et al. (1985)*	258	M,F	Ugr 23,7	-.02	-.12	-.03		EPQ
4.	Daum and Schugens (1986)	108	M,F	Ugr	.04	-.40a	-.03		EPQ
5.	Larsen and Baggs (1986)	40	M,F	Ugr	.16	-.27c	.11	.53b	EPQ
6.	Richards(1986)*	79	M,F	17-39	-.09	-.43a	-.02		EPQ
7.	Daum et al. (1988)	59	M	Ugr(20-32)	.00	-.24	-.06		EPQ
8.	Corulla (1989)*	312	M	17-55	-.26	-.37	-.18	.11	EPQ-R
		288	F	16-53	-.15	-.25	-.10	.06	EPQ-R

* a yes/no response format
  was applied

M = males
F = females
Ugr = undergraduate students
LA = low alpha index
HA = high alpha index

a = $p < .001$
b = $p < .01$
c = $p < .05$

between these two dimensions, whereas in Corulla's large sample (312 men) a low negative, but statistically significant correlation ($-.18$) was obtained, thus partially supporting Rawlings data.

As hypothesized, the correlation between strength of inhibition and psychoticism is negative (Me $= -.27$). All coefficients of correlation have a minus sign ($-.03$ to $-.54$). However, in two studies (Gilliland, 1985; Stelmack et al., 1985) the scores should be interpreted as a lack of correlation ($-.03$ and $-.12$). There exist only four projects in which balance of the CNS was compared with psychoticism. The results are not very consistent. Whereas the coefficient of correlation derived from Larsen and Baggs' (1986) data confirms the previously presented hypothesis (.53), this cannot be said in the case of the three remaining samples where the positive correlation varies from .06 to .16 and is statistically not significant.

STI and Sensation Seeking.   As known to the authors, the hypothesis put forward by Zuckerman (1979) that there exist links between the Pavlovian types of the CNS and sensation seeking has been subject to investigation in five psychometric studies with respect to strength of excitation. The number of studies decreases to four when strength of inhibition and mobility are related to this personality/temperament trait, and to three, when balance of the CNS is compared with sensation seeking. In the studies mentioned above and presented in Table 8.8, the SSS-IV or the SSS-V forms were used as measures of this trait.

The SE scores, when related to sensation seeking, seem to be positively correlated with the TO (Me $= .21$) and TAS (Me $= .27$) scales. The medians of the three remaining scales indicate a zero correlation between strength of excitation and sensation seeking. Thus the experimentally stated positive correlation between the two dimensions under discussion (Goldman et al., 1983) has been proved in psychometric studies only partially.

When the remaining CNS properties are considered, only some results are mentioned here. Strength of inhibition seems to correlate negatively, however low, with four of the SSS scales. In three from the four studies the TO, ES, Dis and BS scales correlate with the SI scores in the range from $-.17$ to $-.34$. In the case of mobility of the CNS, if significant correlations between this property and sensation seeking occur, all of them have a positive sign, and this is true for all SSS scales. Except for one coefficient of correlation with a minus sign and indicating a zero correlation ($-.03$ for ES), all of the 20 coefficients related to mobility are positive and vary from .04 to .63. The highest single scores were obtained for TO (.63), TAS (.51), Dis (.48) and for BS (.47). The SSS scores, when compared in three studies with balance of the CNS, show a tendency to correlate positively and this holds true for all five SSS scales. Among the 15 coefficients of correlation in which balance was related to sensation seeking, there are eight scores, varying from .20 to .31, which support the earlier mentioned tendency.

TABLE 8.8
Coefficients of Correlation Between Sensation Seeking and Properties of the Nervous System

No.	SE					SI					M					B				
	TO	TAS	ES	DIS	BS	TO	TAS	ES	DIS	BS	TO	TAS	ES	DIS	BS	TO	TAS	ES	DIS	BS
1.	.25b	.36a	.08	.01	.25b	.11	.30c	.18	-.09	.00	.26	.34c	.31c	.06	.16	.11	.06	.11	.10	-.03
2.	.21	.33c	.28c	.00	-.01	-.26	-.12	-.29c	-.33c	-.25	.63a	.51a	.32c	.48a	.47a					
3.	.28c	.27c	.12	.17	.31c	-.29	-.01	-.17	-.34	-.27	.12	.18	-.03	.04	.11	.23	.11	.02	.26	.25
4.	-.07	.12	-.17	-.12	-.03	-.21	-.01	-.19	-.18	-.22	.23	.18	.15	.16	.14	.31	.20	.23	.20	.23
5.	.15	.24	.05	.04	.07															

1. Oleszkiewicz-Zsurzs, 1984; SSS-IV; 171 males (16-20 years)
2. Gilliland, 1985; SSS-V; 58 males and females (undergraduates)
3. Daum et al., 1988; SSS-IV; 59 males (20-32 years)
4. Corulla, 1989; SSS-V; 312 males (17-55 years)
5. Corulla, 1989; SSS-V; 288 females (16-53 years)

STI and Reducing/Augmenting and Reactivity.   To finish the review of research in which the STI has been compared with other personality/temperament dimensions, two studies have to be mentioned in which Kohn (1987) and co-workers (Kohn et al., 1987) have searched for links between strength of excitation as measured by the STI and the augmenting/reducing dimension, diagnosed by means of the Vando's Reducer-Augmenter Scale (RAS). As predicted, the coefficients of correlation were positive in both studies (Kohn, 1987—.29, *p* < .01; Kohn et al. 1987—.48, *p* < .01). This means that individuals with a strong nervous system are reducers, whereas augmenters tend to have a weak nervous system. The theoretical considerations justifying this relationship have been presented in several studies (see Kohn, 1987; Kohn et al., 1987; Strelau, 1982, 1987b).

In the two studies just mentioned, the SE scale was also related to psychometrically measured reactivity. The latter was estimated by means of the Reactivity Scale developed by Kohn and aimed at measuring reactivity as understood in Strelau's (1983) regulative theory of temperament. In two studies (212 subjects in one study and 53 in the other one) the same coefficient of correlation was obtained (−.45, <.01) (Kohn, 1987; Kohn et al., 1987). A negative correlation stated in these projects is in accordance with the theory, which says that high scores on the strength of excitation dimension are indicators of low level of reactivity (see Strelau, 1983).

External Validity: Studies Based on Factor Analyses

There exist at least eight studies in which the STI scales were factor analyzed together with other temperament/personality scales. The first one was conducted by Terelak (1974; Strelau & Terelak, 1974) on two pilot samples (95 and 115 men aged from 20 to 45) differing in scores of the EEG alpha index. The STI scales have been factor analyzed together with the MAS, MPI, Guilford-Zimmerman Temperament Survey (GZTS), and the Thurstone Temperament Schedule (TTS) scales. The study comprised 24 traits altogether. By means of the principal components method, in one of the groups six and in the other one seven factors have been extracted. The structure of factors is similar, thus we are limiting the description to the six factors to be separated in the high alpha index pilot group: F1 (Vigorousness or Energeticness) comprises such traits as extraversion, strength of excitation, mobility, ascendance, sociability, impulsive, dominant, and sociable[4]; F2 (Emotionality) includes such traits as manifest anxiety, neuroticism, strength of excitation, strength of inhibition, emotional stability and emotional stable, the latter four dimensions with negative signs; F3 (Thoughtfulness) has the highest loadings in the restraint, thoughtfulness, and

---

[4]The denominations of traits for the separate factors have been given in accordance with the names used by the respective authors themselves.

reflective scales; F4 (Sociability) comprises personal relations, objectivity, and friendliness; F5 (Equilibrium of nervous processes) has the highest loading in the B scale; F6 (Masculinity) includes the masculinity trait only.

The structure of the first two factors corresponds to the correlational data presented in the former section. Factor 1 loads, among other things, on extraversion, strength of excitation, and mobility, and these traits correlate positively with each other, as shown in Table 8.4. In Factor 2 neuroticism and anxiety go together with weak excitatory and weak inhibitory processes. A negative correlation between anxiety and neuroticism, on the one hand, and strength of excitation and strength of inhibition, on the other hand, has been found in correlational studies (see Tables 8.5 and 8.6).

Van Heck (1987) has factor analyzed the scores representing 31 traits as measured by several inventories. Among them were the STI and the GZTS scales. The STI items have been subject to factor analysis prior to the analysis comprising all the temperament/personality dimensions being researched. On the basis of this analysis, six first-order STI factors were separated and those were taken as a starting point for further factorial procedures, thus making impossible any comparison with other studies, where the STI scales were factor analyzed with other temperament scales.

The number of factors as well as their specific structure in which the STI scales occur together with other temperament scales changes from study to study. Curiously enough, in five studies, in which the Eysenckian extraversion and neuroticism dimensions were factor analyzed together with the STI scales, three of the studies (Daum et al., 1988; Paisey & Mangan, 1980; Richards, 1986) show consistently that extraversion composes one factor, together with strength of excitation and mobility of nervous processes, as has been shown in Terelak's project. These data, again, are consistent with correlational studies. There are, however, two studies conducted by Stelmack et al. (1985) and Corulla (1989) that show that strength of excitation, mobility, and strength of inhibition make up one factor that is not saturated with extraversion.

Contradictory results were obtained in studies where, among other scales, the sensation seeking traits were factor analyzed together with the CNS properties. In two investigations (Corulla, 1989; Paisey & Mangan, 1980) nervous system properties and the sensation seeking scales constitute separate factors, whereas two other studies show that sensation seeking constitutes one factor together with strength and excitation (Van Heck, 1987) or with strength of excitation and mobility of the CNS (Daum et al., 1988).

In two of the four studies (Daum et al., 1988; Richards, 1986) psychoticism, diagnosed by means of the EPQ, composes one factor together with strength of inhibition. This regularity does not occur in Paisey and Mangan's (1980) and in Corulla's (1989) studies, where both dimensions under discussion fall into separate factors.

In one of the factorial projects (Barclay, 1987) the STI scales were the subject of the research together with the 16PF scales.[5] However, the Cattellian personality factors are not in the core of our interests, but it is worthwhile to note that some interesting regularities came out of this study. Results obtained from 85 males aged 19 to 24 years allowed the author to separate the following four factors: F1 (Emotional stability): Strength of excitation and the C, Q3, L, Q4, and O scales from the 16PF inventory; F2 (Tough mindedness): Mobility and A, F, H, E, and Q2; F3 (Activity): Strength of excitation, Mobility, Balance, and H, F, Q1, E, and N; F4 (Driven compulsion): Balance, Strength of inhibition, Q4, and E.

Barclay's study suggests that the range of interrelationships between the Pavlovian CNS properties and the personality factors as separated by Cattell is much broader than suggested by Orlebeke (1972). On the basis of his experimental data Orlebeke was able to show that the only factor to be related to strength of excitation is surgency (see p. 196). However, before any reasonable conclusion can be made, research based on factor analytic studies comprising the STI and the 16PF scales calls for replication.

In general, one has to state that the factor analytic studies comprising scores from the STI and the inventory scales under discussion are much less unequivocal regarding the relationships between the Pavlovian CNS properties and other temperament/personality dimensions, as was the case in correlational studies presented in the previous section.

External Validity: Laboratory and Field Studies

Among the four Pavlovian CNS properties as measured by the STI, it was strength of excitation to which almost exclusively attention was paid when examining the construct validity of the STI scales. This holds true for studies in which experimental settings were used or for which the correspondence of STI data with laboratory indices of the CNS properties was analyzed. There is no place to refer to the dozens of studies in which the Strength of Excitation scale was used for this purpose,[6] thus we will limit our description to some general statements having support in experimental data.

In most of the studies where the scores of the SE scale were compared with laboratory indices of this CNS property, such as the Slope of RT Curve (Beauvale & Placzynta, 1986; Carlier, 1985; Daum et al., 1988; Kohn, 1987) or Extinction with Reinforcement (Gilliland, 1985), a lack of correlation between

---

[5]Also, four scales of adjective ratings from the Barclay Classroom Assessment System were factor analyzed. For clarity they are omitted in our discussion.

[6]For a detailed description see Eliasz (1985a, 1985b, 1987), Friedensberg (1985), Klonowicz (1974, 1985, 1987), Muendelein (1982), and Strelau (1983, 1984).

the relevant variables was found. This negative result between inventory data and experimental indices of strength of the CNS cannot, however, be regarded as evidence for lack of validity of the SE scale. The reason for this conclusion consists in the fact that laboratory studies aimed at diagnosing the Pavlovian CNS properties show that the estimation of these traits is highly dependent on the type of stimuli, kind of reaction, and sort of CNS trait indicator used in experimental settings (see Kohn et al., 1987; Nebylitsyn, 1972b; Strelau, 1965a, 1972b, 1983).

Field studies as well as experimental settings in which individuals, varying in strength of excitation (as measured by the SE scale), were confronted with behaviors and situations differing first of all in their stimulative value show some regularities.

In situations under stress consisting of performing activities of high stimulative value or of situations that are regarded as highly stimulating, the performance of individuals differs depending on the strength of the nervous system. Individuals with a weak nervous system perform usually lower as compared with individuals characterized by a strong nervous system (see e.g., Halmiova & Sebova, 1986; Klonowicz, 1985; Schulz, 1986; Strelau, 1983).

In the solution of operational tasks or in decision-making situations, "strong" individuals prefer risk taking over risk avoiding, whereas in "weak" individuals a reverse relationship dominates, that is, risk avoidance is preferred over risk taking (see Kozlowski, 1977; Przymusinski & Strelau, 1986; Strykowska, 1978).

Individuals who perform professional activity of high stimulating value (e.g., pilots, steel-workers, locomotive engineers) have, on the average, higher scores on the SE scale as compared with the sample representing the Polish population (Strelau, 1983).

In order to avoid the state of stress, individuals differing in strength of excitation use different styles of action to cope with stressors. The "weak" individuals perform, as compared with the "strong" ones, significantly more auxiliary activities, which consist in orienting, preparatory, corrective, controlling and protective activities (see e.g., Friedensberg, 1985; Muendelein, 1982; Schoenpflug & Muendelein, 1986; Strelau, 1983). The auxiliary actions, by safeguarding, facilitating, and/or simplifying the performance, lower the stimulative value of activity or situation in which the activity is performed.

When the psychophysiological costs of performance under stress are considered, it has been stated in several experiments (Klonowicz, 1974, 1985, 1986) that the "weaks" pay more costs in situations of high stimulative value, as compared with normal situations. In situations of deprivation such a relationship occurs in individuals with the strong nervous system, that is, in such situations they pay more psychophysiological costs as compared with normal situations.

The results, which support the earlier stated regularities, are relatively consistent in that they show from study to study similar regularities. This suggests that the STI, at least when the SE scale is considered, seems to have some predictive value as regards the relationship between behaviors and strength of excitation when behavior and/or situations are considered from the point of view of their stimulative value.

STUDIES ON THE STI CONDUCTED ON GERMAN SAMPLES

In this section, we report empirical studies conducted with the STI on German samples. These empirical studies differ to some degree from those reviewed until now. First, the analysis of data has been done separately for males and females; second, the age distribution of our samples is much broader as compared to the published studies; and third, much attention has been paid to the item statistics as well as to the validity characteristics of the scales. The STI scales have been correlated with the Eysenckian and with the sensation seeking scales, and also with the Personality Research Form (PRF). The PRF has not yet been used in studies dealing with the STI.

Method and Procedure

Subjects.   Four samples, including altogether 883 subjects, were used in our studies. For gender distribution and details regarding age characteristics for all samples see Table 8.12. The largest sample, Bielefeld 1 (B1), was recruited by means of announcements in local newspapers. Test materials were sent and received by mail. This sample, consisting of 428 males and females, covers an age range from 15 to 80 years. Sixty percent of the females and 71% of the males were at least high-school graduates.

The recruiting of the remaining three samples was done in a homogeneous manner, but different from sample B1. For course requirements, psychology students had to test two to five acquaintances with different inventories and tests, including the STI. The Bielefeld 2 (B2) sample consisted of 189 subjects of both sexes. Their age range, varying from 17 to 47, was somewhat more restricted as compared with the other samples. This sample was recruited by students taking a 1987 summer course in personality testing at the University of Bielefeld. The same recruitment method was used for the Bielefeld 3 (B3) sample by students taking a similar course in the 1987 winter semester. This sample included 173 males and females, aged from 16 to 66.

For replicational purposes, a fourth sample, consisting of 131 subjects of both sexes in the age range from 17 to 65 years, was studied in Duesseldorf (D). The recruitment procedure was comparable with samples B2 and B3.

For studying the external validity of the STI scales, different inventories in the separate samples were used. Subjects who answered the PRF were given feedback regarding their PRF personality profile.

Measures.   Seven different inventories were used in our studies. Their description follows.

The STI was used in the German version translated by K. H. Meyer (Institute of Psychology, Leipzig).

For measures within the framework of the personality theory as developed by Eysenck, the following instruments were used: (1) the Eysenck Personality Questionnaire (EPQ) in the German adaptation by Ruch (1988), used in samples B1 and D; (2) the Eysenck Personality Inventory (EPI)-Form A, used in samples D and B3, and Form B (sample D), in the German version prepared by Eggert (1974); (3) corresponding scales from the revised version of the Freiburger Persoenlichkeitsinventar (FPI-R) developed by Fahrenberg, Hampel, and Selg (1984), applied in sample B2.

For measuring the sensation seeking dimensions, the SSS Form 4 in the German adaptation by Unterweger (1980) was used in the D sample. The SSS Form 5, as adapted by Andresen (1986), was applied in sample B2.

The Personality Research Form (PRF), as constructed by Jackson (1967), and based on the concept of needs developed by Murray (1938), was used in sample B1. Stumpf, Angleitner, Wieck, Jackson, and Beloch-Till (1985) are the authors of the German version of the PRF.

Results and Comments

Characteristics of the Scales.   The means and the standard deviations of the STI scales are given in Table 8.9. As regards the SE scale, the means for males vary from 48.7 to 56.7, whereas for women, from 49.0 to 52.4. The SI scale shows variations for males in the realm of 60.6 to 62.9, and for females in the range of 56.1 to 57.6. The means for the M scale oscillate for males between 51.6 and 58.1, and for females between 56.1 and 59.8. The fluctuation of the means of the B scale is .83 to .99 for males, and .88 to .99 for females.

The means are comparable with those presented in the literature (see Table 8.1). We would also like to draw attention to the gender differences. For the three Bielefeld samples, a multivariate analysis of variance of the scales by the factors sample and sex showed significant sex differences in all scales except the B scale.[7] Considering the SE and SI scales, men scored higher than women. In the case of the M scale, the pattern was reversed.

---

[7]The tables for the analysis of variance may be obtained by writing to the authors.

TABLE 8.9

Means and Standard Deviations of the STI-Scales

Studies	N	Sex	Age	SE		SI		M		B	
				M	SD	M	SD	M	SD	M	SD
Bielefeld 1 (Announcement)	184	M	15-18 x=33, SD=13.5	56.71	11.96	60.57	13.17	56.25	11.22	.99	.37
	244	F	16-18 x=33, SD=13.2	51.73	11.14	57.62	11.80	56.88	10.69	.95	.35
Bielefeld 2 (Student-course SS 87)	95	M	17-42 x=27, SD=5.7	48.70	10.44	60.35	9.41	51.55	11.89	.83	.20
	94	F	19-47 x=27, SD=6.2	50.74	9.50	56.97	10.64	59.14	12.91	.92	.23
Duesseldorf (Student-course SS 87)	63	M	18-63 x=32, SD=12	55.19	11.03	62.89	12.44	53.64	10.26	.91	.29
	75	F	17-65 x=31, SD=11.4	52.40	11.42	56.44	13.20	59.80	8.98	.99	.33
Bielefeld 3 (Student-course WS 87)	37	M	16-58 x=27, SD=8	52.60	13.36	56.57	12.14	58.91	11.06	.96	.28
	100	F	18-66 x=26, SD=8	49.03	11.05	56.10	11.53	56.17	10.59	.88	.27

x = mean age
SD = standard deviation

221

Reliability.   The reliability score of the B scale was calculated by means of the correlations of the balance measures between Form A and Form B of the STI items (see p. 193), that is, the split-half reliability was measured. Except for the B scores, the Cronbach-Alpha coefficient was used. The results are presented in Table 8.10.

The medians of the Cronbach-Alpha coefficients are .81 for the SE scale, .83 for the SI scale, and .76 for the mobility scale. The balance measure shows a median of .78. These values are also comparable to those reported in earlier studies (see Table 8.2). In general, the reliability estimates may be regarded as satisfactory. However, it has to be kept in mind that the scales sample quite a large number of items (44 to 46), somewhat unusual for advanced personality scales.

Item Statistics.   In spite of the rather high reliability values, a more detailed consideration of the items, as presented in Table 8.11, shows some disadvantages of the STI scales. Considering the item means, it can be said that more than one third of the items have extreme endorsement frequencies (below 25% or above 75%). On the average, the SI scale has the most extreme item endorsement (41.8%), followed by the SE scale (36.4%), and the M scale, having an average

TABLE 8.10
Reliability (Cronbach-Alpha) of the STI-Scales in the German Sample

Studies	N	Sex	Age	SE	SI	M	B
Bielefeld 1 (Anouncement)	173	M	15–80 x=33, SD=13	.85	.87	.78	.87
	218	F	16–80 x=33, SD=13	.81	.83	.75	.78
Bielefeld 2 (Student-course SS 87)	85	M	19–42 x=27, SD=5.6	.78	.72	.80	.65
	75	F	19–47 x=27, SD=6.2	.64	.79	.85	.71
Duesseldorf (Student-course SS 87)	63	M	18–63 x=32, SD=12	.80	.85	.71	
	75	F	17–65 x=31, SD=11.4	.83	.87	.68	
Bielefeld 3 (Student-course WS 87)	37	M	16–58 x=27, SD=8	.87	.84	.77	.83
	100	F	18–66 x=26, SD=8	.81	.82	.76	.79

x = mean age
SD = standard deviation

Note. The reliability score of the B scale was calculated by means of the correlations of the B scores between Form A and Form B of the STI items (split-half reliability).

TABLE 8.11

Item-Statistics of the STI-Scales in the German Studies

Study	N	Sex	Extreme Item Means (a)			Unsatisfactory Item-Scale Correlations (Corrected) (b)		
			SE (44 Items)	SI (44 Items)	M (46 Items)	SE (44 Items)	SI (44 Items)	M (46 Items)
Bielefeld 1 (Announcement)	173	M	19 (43.2%)	19 (43.2%)	14 (30.4%)	3 (6.8%)	5 (11.4%)	16 (34.8%)
	218	F	18 (40.9%)	18 (40.9%)	14 (30.4%)	8 (18.2%)	9 (20.5%)	22 (47.8%)
Bielefeld 2 (Student-course SS 87)	85	M	15 (34.1%)	21 (47.7%)	7 (15.9%)	17 (38.6%)	19 (43.2%)	18 (39.1%)
	75	F	12 (27.3%)	18 (40.9%)	17 (38.6%)	26 (59.1%)	16 (36.4%)	12 (26.1%)
Duesseldorf (Student-course SS 87)	63	M	19 (43.2%)	24 (54.5%)	11 (23.9%)	13 (29.5%)	9 (20.5%)	26 (56.5%)
	75	F	16 (36.4%)	17 (38.6%)	20 (43.5%)	12 (27.3%)	5 (11.4%)	22 (47.8%)
Bielefeld 3 (Student-course WS 87)	37	M	13 (29.5%)	16 (36.4%)	14 (30.4%)	9 (20.5%)	8 (18.2%)	17 (37.0%)
	100	F	16 (36.4%)	14 (31.8%)	12 (26.1%)	13 (29.5%)	12 (27.3%)	22 (47.8%)
Means			16 (36.4%)	18.4 (41.8%)	12.6 (31%)	12.6 (28.6%)	10.4 (23.6%)	19.4 (42.1%)

Note. (a) Number and percentages of item means revealing extreme endorsements
(below 0.50 and above 1.50)
(b) Number and percentages of items with not acceptable corrected
item-scale correlations (below 0.20)

Percentages are given in brackets. The age distribution of the samples are given in Table 8.10.

of 31%. The results of our research point to a higher number of extreme item responding as revealed by Paisey and Mangan (1980), and Stelmack et al. (1985) in studies conducted with the English version of the STI.

For considering the item-scale relationships of the STI we have used the Daum and Schugens' (1986) proposal, counting item-scale correlations below .20 as unsatisfactory. As Table 8.11 indicates, the percentage of nonacceptable item-scale correlations varies considerably from sample to sample, especially for the SE and SI scales. The highest mean percentage is found for the M scale (42.1%), followed by SE scale (28.6%), and the SI scale (23.6%). From this rather unsatisfactory result, it may be concluded that the probability that items correlate with scales for which they are not constructed is rather high. Negative item-scale correlations are found, especially in the case of the M scale. Our pattern of results is similar to Daum and Schugens', in that the M scale comprises the highest number of unsatisfactory item-scale relationships.

Correlations between the STI Scales.   Inspection of the internal validity of the STI may be carried out by looking at the correlations between the scales. As shown in Table 8.12, the medians of the inter-scale correlations are as follows: SE × SI = .28, SE × M = .48, SI × M = .0, M × B = .39.

There is strong evidence that strength of excitation and mobility, as well as mobility and balance, correlate with each other. The SI scale also shows a

TABLE 8.12
Pearson Correlations of the STI-Scales

Study	N	Sex	Age	SE x SI	SE x M	SI x M	M x B
Bielefeld 1 (Anouncement)	184	M	15-80 x=33, SD=13.5	.38a	.59a	.07	.29a
	244	F	16-80 x=33, SD=13.2	.23a	.48a	-.10	.39a
Bielefeld 2 (Student-course SS 87)	85	M	19-42 x=27, SD=5.6	.08	.46a	-.20c	.49a
	75	F	19-47 x=27, SD=6.2	.38a	.46a	.23c	.15
Duesseldorf (Student-course SS 87)	63	M	18-63 x=32, SD=12	.28c	.53a	.02	.39a
	75	F	17-65 x=31, SD=11.4	.30c	.43a	-.11	.42a
Bielefeld 3 (Student-course WS 87)	37	M	16-58 x=27, SD=8	.37c	.55a	.09	.46b
	100	F	18-66 x=26, SD=8	.28b	.49a	-.05	.44a

a = $p < .001$ x = mean age
b = $p < .01$ SD = standard deviation
c = $p < .05$

considerable positive correlation with the SE scale. Practically no correlation exists between the SI and M scales. This pattern of results is somewhat different from those summarized in Table 8.3. The main differences refer to the degree of the size of the correlations and to the relations between the M and B scales. In our studies, the median correlations, except for the balance scale, are lower, as compared with the median values reported in the literature (Table 8.3). For the correlation between M and B, contradictory results are reported in Table 8.3, whereas our data show rather high positive correlations. Theoretically, the correlations between strength of excitation and mobility seem to be acceptable (see Strelau, 1983), but they are too high for using these scales as measures for separate theoretically distinguished concepts. For the relationship between strength of excitation and strength of inhibition, no clear predictions are deducible from Pavlov's theorizing. However, it is our assumption that these concepts should also be viewed as rather independent from each other, in contrast to our findings (median correlation = .28).

External Validity: STI and the Eysenckian Personality Scales.   The personality dimension most often compared with the Pavlovian properties of the nervous system is extraversion, which correlates—in reports to be found in the literature—positively with strength of excitation as well as with mobility (see Table 8.4). As mentioned before, in our studies different instruments were used for measuring extraversion.

Inspection of Table 8.13 reveals that this postulated relationship between extraversion and strength of excitation depends on the extraversion scale used. No significant correlation is found in the case of the EPI-A Form. Coefficients of correlation referring to other extraversion scales indicate a positive and statistically significant correlation, with one exception only (.19). The medians of the coefficients of correlation of all of the extraversion scales with the STI measures are as follows: SE = .34, SI = −.27, M = .48, and B = .45. Also in the literature, the highest coefficients of correlation were recorded in the case of mobility. In all of our samples a negative (usually statistically significant) correlation between extraversion and strength of inhibition occurs, which is in disagreement with studies reported in the literature, where positive as well as negative results were registered, with a median showing zero correlation. The rather high correlation between balance and extraversion may be explained by the circumstance that a high B score implies predominance of strength of excitation over strength of inhibition. By definition (see p. 193), the latter concept refers to control of behavior.

We now turn to the neuroticism dimension as related to the STI scales, the results of which are summarized in Table 8.14. The medians of the coefficients of correlation are: SE × N = −.37, SI × N = −.28, M × N = −.15, and a near-zero correlation (−.01) is found for B with N. This finding replicates the results of former studies presented in Table 8.5.

TABLE 8.13

Pearson Correlation Coefficients Between Extraversion-Scales and the STI-Scales

Study	N	Sex	Age	SE	SI	M	B	Inventory
Bielefeld 1	78	M	20-79 x=38.9, SD=13.9	.19c	-.36a	.46a	.44a	EPQ
	103	F	17-80 x=37.4, SD=14.6	.35a	-.20c	.58a	.33a	EPQ
Bielefeld 2	34	M	19-42 x=25, SD=4	.53a	-.30c	.72a	.60a	FPI-R(E)
	41	F	20-47 x=25, SD=6	.50a	-.19	.62a	.63a	FPI-R(E)
Duesseldorf	62	M	18-63 x=32, SD=12	.17	-.38b	.46a	.48a	EPI-A
	72	F	17-65 x=31, SD=11.4	.10	-.47a	.42a	.47a	EPI-A
	62	M	18-63 x=32, SD=12	.35b	-.15	.45a	.41b	EPI-B
	72	F	17-65 x=31, SD=11.4	.34b	-.27c	.54a	.50a	EPI-B
	62	M	18-63 x=32, SD=12	.19	-.21	.48a	.36b	EPQ
	72	F	17-65 x=31, SD=11.4	.37b	-.25c	.52a	.45a	EPQ
Bielefeld 3	47	F	19-48 x=24, SD=5.6	.01	-.45a	.40b	.33b	EPI-A

a = $p < .001$
b = $p < .01$
c = $p < .05$

x = mean age
SD = standard deviation

TABLE 8.14

Pearson Correlation Coefficients Between Neuroticism-Scales and the STI-Scales

Study	N	Sex	Age	SE	SI	M	B	Inventory
Bielefeld 1	78	M	20-79 x=38.9, SD=13.9	-.37a	-.55a	-.06	.26c	EPQ
	103	F	17-80 x=37.4, SD=14.6	-.35a	-.28b	-.07	-.01	EPQ
Bielefeld 2	34	M	19-42 x=25, SD=4	-.34c	.07	-.32c	-.29c	FPI-R(N)
	41	F	20-47 x=25, SD=6	-.43b	-.23	-.31c	-.17	FPI-R(N)
Duesseldorf	62	M	18-63 x=32, SD=12	-.44a	-.27c	-.26c	-.13	EPI-A
	72	F	17-65 x=31, SD=11.4	-.43a	-.52a	-.13	.11	EPI-A
	62	M	18-63 x=32, SD=12	-.46a	-.19	-.30c	-.19	EPI-B
	72	F	17-65 x=31, SD=11.4	-.37b	-.41a	-.12	.08	EPI-B
	62	M	18-63 x=32, SD=12	-.33b	-.24	-.15	-.06	EPQ
	72	F	17-65 x=31, SD=11.4	-.34b	-.50a	-.12	.16	EPQ
Bielefeld 3	47	F	19-48 x=24, SD=5.6	-.47a	-.46a	-.18	.10	EPI-A

a = $p < .001$
b = $p < .01$
c = $p < .05$

x = mean age
SD = standard deviation

TABLE 8.15
Pearson Correlation Coefficients Between Psychoticism-Scales and the STI-Scales

Study	N	Sex	Age	SE	SI	M	B	Inventory
Bielefeld 1	78	M	20-79 x=38,9, SD=13.9	-.21c	-.60a	.17	.40a	EPQ
	103	F	17-80 x=37,4,SD=14.6	.06	-.39a	.13	.36a	EPQ
Duesseldorf	62	M	18-63 x=32, SD=12	.00	-.20	.03	.22	EPQ
	72	F	17-65 x=31, SD=11.4	.21	-.34b	.25c	.47a	EPQ

a = $p < .001$ x = mean age
b = $p < .01$ SD = standard deviation
c = $p < .05$

The negative correlation between strength of excitation and neuroticism is expected if one considers the conceptualization of this CNS property. The relatively high negative correlations between strength of inhibition and the neuroticism scales may be viewed as indicating a lack of discriminant validity in the STI scales.

Psychoticism as measured by the EPQ shows inconsistent data for the SE scale and consistent patterns of results for the remaining STI measures (see Table 8.15).

The coefficients of correlation for psychoticism and strength of excitation vary from $-.21$ to $.21$, a finding that may be expected when looking at Table 8.7. Highly significant correlations came up in the negative direction for strength of inhibition and in a positive one for balance. These results are in agreement with our hypothesis (see p. 211).

External Validity: STI and the Sensation Seeking Scales.   When following Zuckerman's (1979) theorizing, a positive correlation between sensation seeking and strength of excitation may be expected. This has been partially proven by our results, as revealed in Table 8.16. The significant correlations between the sensation seeking scales—Total (TO), Thrill and Adventure Seeking (TAS), Experience Seeking (ES) and Boredom Susceptibility (BS)—are positive, indicating some relationships between these concepts under discussion. The Disinhibition scale (Dis) shows no correlation with the SE measure, a finding that replicates the results of earlier studies (see Table 8.8). The SI scale, in general, correlates negatively with the SS scales. However, among the 20 coefficients comprising the four samples, only half of them reach the level of statistical significance.

Also the mobility scale points to high positive correlations with the sensation seeking scales. The only exception is one significant negative correlation to be found for the Dis scale ($-.47$). This configuration of the correlation coefficients replicates the findings obtained in former studies (see Table 8.8). However, one may speculate as to why our correlations are considerably higher than those reported in the literature. It might be due to the German speaking versions of our tests. This reasoning has some support in the data published by Daum et al. (1988)

TABLE 8.16

Pearson Correlation Coefficients Between Sensation-Seeking-Scales and the STI-Scales

No.	SE					SI					M					B				
	TO	TAS	ES	Dis	BS	TO	TAS	ES	Dis	BS	TO	TAS	ES	Dis	BS	TO	TAS	ES	Dis	BS
1.	.24	.24	.27c	.07	.12	-.12	-.10	-.11	-.15	-.02	.27c	.25c	.29c	.19	.06	.33b	.29c	.33b	.26c	.13
2.	.31b	.33b	.32b	.12	.23c	-.32	-.03	-.31b	-.47a	-.25c	.42a	.31b	.39b	.33b	.34b	.49a	.27c	.48a	.49a	.37b
3.	.29c	.66a	.01	-.20	.26c	-.57a	-.23	-.55a	-.45a	-.27c	.10	.40b	.00	-.47a	.52a	.62a	.73a	.37b	.07	.43a
4.	-.03	-.05	-.04	-.06	-.05	-.63a	-.45a	-.21	-.17	-.72a	.48b	.70a	.01	-.14	.35c	.51a	.37c	.21	.09	.58a

1. Duesseldorf; SSS-IV; 62 males (18-63); mean age = 32; SD = 12
2. Duesseldorf; SSS-IV; 72 females (17-65); mean age = 31; SD = 11.4
3. Bielefeld 2; SSS-V; 51 males (20-36); mean age = 29; SD = 6
4. Bielefeld 2; SSS-V; 34 females (19-45); mean age = 29; SD = 6

$a = p < .001$
$b = p < .01$
$c = p < .05$

showing also higher correlations between the STI scales and the sensation seeking scales, as compared with studies using other language versions.

The largest number of significant correlations occurred for the balance measure. Here almost all coefficients indicate highly significant positive correlations. This profile of results is not expected from former studies, where, in general, no relationships were found. It is, however, consistent with conclusions to be drawn from other findings. For example, positive correlations between balance and psychoticism were found in our studies, and as known from the literature, correlations of the same direction are reported between sensation seeking and psychoticism (see e.g., Zuckerman, 1979, Table 6.7).

External Validity: STI and the Content Scales of the Personality Research Form (PRF). The correlational patterns for the STI and the PRF scales are highly similar for men and women. The data are given in Table 8.17.

In general, it has to be stated that many statistically significant correlations have been found between the STI and the PRF scales. Fifty-five percent of the correlations for the male sample and 52% for the female sample are statistically significant. The large number of significant correlations does not allow us to discuss them in detail. Therefore, only some general trends are presented.

The SE scale correlates positively with achievement (Ac), dominance (Do), endurance (En), and exhibition (Ex), and negatively with harmavoidance (Ha) and succorance (Su). Because strength of excitation is regarded as an activity-oriented temperament dimension (Mangan, 1982; Strelau, 1983) and characterized by Pavlov (1951–52) as endurance in the face of strong stimuli, our results are in agreement with this hypothesizing.

The profile of correlations for the SI scale clearly reveals the impulse control mechanism underlying the concept of inhibition. The PRF aggression (Ag), Ex, impulsivity (Im), play (Pl), social recognition (Sr), and Su scales show consistently, and in both samples, a significant negative correlation, whereas the En and the Order (Or) scales exhibit a positive correlation with the SI scale.

An inspection of the correlation of the mobility scale with the PRF scales seems to suggest that interpersonal relation characteristics are significantly correlated with this Pavlovian property. The PRF Af, Do, Ex, Im, nurturance (Nu), and Pl scales are positively correlated with mobility and the Ha scale is negatively correlated with mobility.

The correlations between the balance measure and the PRF scales are also similar for both sexes. Significant positive correlations are found for Ac, Ag, Do, Ex, and Im scales, whereas negative correlations are found between the Ha scale and the B measure. One may speculate that the balance property is related to ascendance striving.

The STI Scales and Response Distortions. First, we consider the correlations between the different lie (L) scales used in the Eysenckian inventories and the STI scales. These correlations are presented in Table 8.18.

TABLE 8.17

Pearson Correlation Coefficients Between the STI-Scales and the Scales of the PRF for the Bielefeld 1 (Announcment) Sample

	Men (N = 130, Mean Age = 34.4, SD = 13.4) Range = 18–80 years				Women (N = 165, Mean Age = 34.4, SD = 14.3) Range = 16–80 years			
Scales	SE	SI	M	B	SE	SI	M	B
PRF-Content-Scales								
Ac	.46a		.15c	.24a	.41a	.17c		.21b
Af	.26b		.34a	.26b		-.16c	.41a	.43a
Ag	-.21b	-.59a		.40a		-.50a	.30a	.42a
Do	.53a		.33a	.43a	.51a			
En	.51a	.27b	.39a	.44a	.56a	.33a	.47a	.46a
Ex	.24b	-.27b	-.38a	-.27b	-.37a	-.25b	-.21b	-.26a
Ha	-.24b		.29a	.38a	-.17c	-.46a	.25a	.23b
Im		-.51a	.17c	.15c			.17c	
Nu	.27b					.14c		
Od	.21b	.24b				-.19b		
Pl		-.23b	.22b			-.20b	.41a	
Sr		-.24b			-.28a	-.19b		
Su	-.24b	-.23b			-.35a	.14c		-.14c
Un	.17c				.15c			
PRF-Control-Scales								
In	.43a				-.17c			-.17c
Sd		.43a			.27b	.44a		-.18c

Note. Only significant correlations are given.

a = $p < .001$
b = $p < .01$
c = $p < .05$

231

The SE scale shows only one significant correlation (for men). All other correlations are about zero. However, a different picture emerges considering the SI scale. Especially the female samples point to a significant positive relationship between the L scales and strength of inhibition scales. This may suggest that, especially for women, SI values may be regarded as indicators of response distortions. Also the M scale shows again that the female samples generally exhibit significant negative correlations to a higher degree than do the males, and therefore, the mobility scale may also suffer from response distortions. Furthermore, the female samples again are the only ones that show significant correlations of negative value with the L scales.

Second, we turn to the results of the PRF control scales, infrequency (In) and desirability (Sd), related to the STI scales (see Table 8.17). Jackson (1967) defines infrequency in terms of careless responding, whereas desirability is characterized by describing oneself in a favorable, socially desirable manner.

The infrequency control scale shows a negative correlation with the SE and B scales for the women sample only, a pattern that corresponds to the previously mentioned results.

Taking in account the correlations of the STI scales with the Sd measure, it may be stated that the SE and SI scales are highly positively correlated with this control scale for both sexes. This consistent finding suggests that, for the future, more attention should be paid to the desirability aspect of the STI item content.

CONCLUSIONS AND RECOMMENDATIONS

Research conducted until now shows that it is a scientifically fruitful approach to assess temperament traits according to Pavlov's conceptualization of nervous system properties, and for comparing them with personality/temperament dimensions as developed in the West. It may be noted, that the STI is until now the only inventory that allows such comparisons on a psychometric level. Behavioral and laboratory studies in which the STI was used point to the promising predictive validity of this inventory, especially of the SE scale.

The construction of the Strelau Temperament Inventory, primarily developed for use in the Warsaw Laboratory for Individual Differences, was originally not guided by advanced psychometric personality scale construction strategies, as suggested by Angleitner, John, and Loehr (1986). After the presentation of the STI in English by Strelau (1972a, 1983), this inventory became increasingly popular in Eastern Europe as well as in Western countries. However, in reviewing the evidence on the STI, it became clear that this inventory has the following disadvantages:

1. On the item level, too many items show extreme endorsements.
2. The item-content, at least of the German and English versions, is too much

TABLE 8.18
Pearson Correlation Coefficients Between Lie-Scales and the STI Scales

Study	N	Sex	Age	SE	SI	M	B	Inventory
Bielefeld 1	78	M	20-79 x=38.9,SD=13.9	.33a	.44a	-.03	-.15	EPQ
	103	F	17-80 x=37.4,SD=14.6	-.00	.31a	-.22c	-.27b	EPQ
Bielefeld 2	34	M	19-42 x=25,SD=4	-.08	-.28c	.17	.13	FPI-R(10) reversed keying
	41	F	20-47 x=25,SD=6	-.08	-.29c	-.00	.20	FPI-R(10) reversed keying
Duesseldorf	62	M	18-63 x=32,SD=12	.03	.21	-.18	-.20	EPI-A
	72	F	17-65 x=31,SD=11.4	.21	.51a	-.31b	-.29c	EPI-A
	62	M	18-63 x=32,SD=12	-.05	.04	-.26c	-.10	EPI-B
	72	F	17-65 x=31,SD=11.4	.15	.39a	-.37b	-.24c	EPI-B
	62	M	18-63 x=32,SD=12	-.02	.10	-.31c	-.13	EPQ
	72	F	17-65 x=31,SD=11.4	.18	.39a	-.30c	-.17	EPQ
Bielefeld 3	47	F	19-48 x=24,SD=5.6	.24	.29c	.08	-.04	EPI-A

a = $p<.001$
b = $p<.01$
c = $p<.05$

x = mean age
SD = standard deviation

restricted to behavior in work and occupational situations in order to constitute a representative sample of the universe of human conduct.

3. Many items have rather low, unsatisfactory item-scale correlations, and a high number of items correlate higher with other STI scales than with the one they are constructed for.

4. The scales contain too many items as compared with contemporary personality/temperament scales.

5. The STI scales correlate with each other to a higher degree than theoretically expected—this is especially true for the SE and M scales.

6. The scales show high correlations with social desirability responding.

7. The scales are not balanced in the keying, showing extreme predominance of "yes."

8. The use of the question mark in the answering format for counting one point is ambiguous from an interpretational viewpoint, and is not empirically valid.

Taking into account that the Pavlovian concepts are probably scientifically fruitful, gaining more and more attractiveness, and having in mind the disadvantages of the current STI, the authors conclude: (1) the current STI may be considered as unsatisfactory, and (2) a new STI should be constructed, based on current theorizing about personality scale development and on advanced psychometric strategies (Angleitner & Wiggins, 1986).

Further studies that lead to the construction of the new, revised version of the Strelau Temperament Inventory (STI-R) as well as a detailed description of the steps in developing this new instrument will be reported in the near future. The program of developing the STI-R[8] is based on a cross-cultural approach, by studying simultaneously different language versions in different cultures.

ACKNOWLEDGMENTS

We would like to thank Robert A. Wicklund for helpful comments on an earlier version of this manuscript.

Correspondence concerning this chapter should be sent to Jan Strelau, University of Warsaw, Faculty of Psychology, Stawki 5-7, 00-183 Warsaw, Poland.

REFERENCES

Andresen, B. (1986). Reizsuche- und Erlebnismotive I: Eine psychometrische Reanalyse der SSS V Zuckermans im Kontext der MISAP-Entwicklung. *Zeitschrift fuer Differentielle und Diagnostische Psychologie, 7,* 177–203.

Angleitner, A., John, O. P., & Loehr, F. J. (1986). It's *what* you ask and *how* you ask it: An

---

[8]The experimental version of the STI-R may be obtained by writing to the authors.

itemmetric analysis of personality questionnaires. In A. Angleitner, & J. S. Wiggins (Eds.), *Personality assessment via questionnaires: Current issues in theory and measurement (pp. 61–107)*. New York: Springer Verlag.

Angleitner, A., & Wiggins, J. S. (Eds.). (1986). *Personality assessment via questionnaires: Current issues in theory and measurement*. New York: Springer Verlag.

Barclay, J. R. (1987). The Strelau Temperament Inventory as a broad classification system. *Archives of Clinical Neuropsychology, 2,* 307–327.

Beauvale, A., & Placzynta, M. (1986). Relation between stimulus intensity and simple reaction time contingent upon basic nervous system properties. *Polish Psychological Bulletin, 17,* 55–61.

Birman, B. N. (1951). An attempt to make a clinico-physiological determination of types of higher nervous activity. *Zhurnal Vysshei Nervnoi Deyatelnosti, 1,* 879–888 (in Russian).

Carlier, M. (1985). Factor analysis of Strelau's Questionnaire and an attempt to validate some of the factors. In J. Strelau, F. H. Farley, & A. Gale (Eds.), *The biological bases of personality and behavior: Theories, measurement techniques, and development* (Vol. 1, pp. 145–160). Washington: Hemisphere.

Cattell, R. B. (1972). The interpretation of Pavlov's typology and the arousal concept, in replicated trait and state factors. In V. D. Nebylitsyn, & J. A. Gray (Eds.), *Biological bases of individual behavior* (pp. 141–164). New York: Academic Press.

Chudnovsky, V. E. (1963). The study of nervous system type's properties in children *Voprosy Psikhologii, 3,* 5–20 (in Russian).

Ciosek, M., & Oszmianczuk, J. (1974). Wlasciwosci procesow nerwowych a ekstrawersja i neurotyzm [Nervous system properties and extraversion and neuroticism]. *Przeglad Psychologiczny, 17,* 235–246.

Claridge, G. (1985). *Origins of mental illness: Temperament, deviance and disorder*. New York: Basil Blackwell.

Claridge, G. (1987). Psychoticism and arousal. In J. Strelau, & H. J. Eysenck (Eds.), *Personality dimensions and arousal* (pp. 133–150). New York: Plenum Press.

Corulla, W. J. (1989). The relationships between the Strelau Temperament Inventory, sensation seeking and Eysenck's dimensional system of personality. *Personality and Individual Differences, 10,* 161–173.

Cytawa, J. (1959). Badanie typu ukladu nerwowego czlowieka na podstawie wywiadu [The study of the nervous system type in man based on an interview]. *Annales Universitatis Mariae Curie-Sklodowska, 14,* 137–156.

Dall, P. J., & White, K. D. (1985). Mobility, extraversion, and neuroticism. *The Pavlovian Journal of Biological Science, 20,* 171–176.

Davydova, A. N. (1954). Monographic study of children with features of various types of nervous system. *Izvestiya Academii Pedagogicheskikh Nauk RSFSR, 52,* 141–183 (in Russian).

Daum, I., Hehl, F. J., & Schugens, M. M. (1988). Construct validity and personality correlates of the Strelau Temperament Inventory. *European Journal of Personality, 2,* 205–216.

Daum, I., & Schugens, M. M. (1986). The Strelau Temperament Inventory (STI): Preliminary results in a West German sample. *Personality and Individual Differences, 7,* 509–517.

Eggert, D. (1974). *Eysenck-Persoenlichkeits-Inventar (E-P-I): Handanweisung fuer die Durchfuehrung und Auswertung*. Goettingen: C. J. Hogrefe.

Eliasz, A. (1985a) Mechanisms of temperament: Basic functions. In J. Strelau, F. Farley, & A. Gale (Eds.), *The biological bases of personality and behavior: Theories, measurement techniques, and development* (Vol. 1, pp. 45–59). Washington: Hemisphere.

Eliasz, A. (1985b). Transactional model of temperament. In J. Strelau (Ed.), *Temperamental bases of behavior: Warsaw studies on individual differences* (pp. 41–78). Lisse: Swets & Zeitlinger.

Eliasz, A. (1987). Temperament-contingent cognitive orientation toward various aspects of reality. In J. Strelau, & H. J. Eysenck (Eds.), *Personality dimensions and arousal* (pp. 197–213). New York: Plenum Press.

Eysenck, H. J. (1947). *Dimensions of personality*. London: Kegan Paul, Trench, Trubner and Co.

Eysenck, H. J. (1966). *Conditioning, introversion-extraversion and the strength of the nervous system*. Paper presented at the meeting of the International Congress of Psychology, Moscow, SU.

Eysenck, H. J. (1970). *The structure of human personality*. London: Methuen.

Eysenck, H. J. (1972). Human typology, higher nervous activity, and factor analysis. In V. D. Nebylitsyn, & J. A. Gray (Eds.), *Biological bases of individual behavior* (pp. 165–181). New York: Academic Press.

Eysenck, H. J. (1987). [Special review of *Temperamental bases of behavior: Warsaw studies on individual differences & The biological bases of personality and behavior* (Vol. 1 & 2)]. *Personality and Individual Differences, 8,* 289–290.

Eysenck, H. J., & Eysenck, M. W. (1985). *Personality and individual differences: A natural science approach*. New York: Plenum Press.

Eysenck, H. J., & Levey, A. (1972). Conditioning, introversion-extraversion and the strength of the nervous system. In V. D. Nebylitsyn, & J. A. Gray (Eds.), *Biological bases of individual behavior* (pp. 206–220). New York: Academic Press.

Fahrenberg, J. (1987). Concepts of activation and arousal in the theory of emotionality (neuroticism): A multivariate conceptualization. In J. Strelau, & H. J. Eysenck (Eds.), *Personality dimensions and arousal* (pp. 99–120). New York: Plenum Press.

Fahrenberg, J., Hampel, R., & Selg, H. (1984). *Das Freibuerger Persoenlichkeitsinventar FPI. Revidierte Fassung FPI-R und teilweise geaenderte Fassung FPI—A1: Handanweisung*. Goettingen: C. J. Hogrefe.

Fahrenberg, J., Walschburger, P., Foerster, F., Myrtek, M., & Mueller, W. (1983). An evaluation of trait, state, and reaction aspects of activation processes. *Psychophysiology, 20,* 188–195.

Fedorov, V. K. (1961). Comparison of results of different studies of basic properties of higher nervous activity in mice. *Zhurnal Vysshei Nervnoi Deyatelnosti, 11,* 746–752 (in Russian).

Fiske, D. W., & Maddi, S. R. (Eds.). (1961). *Functions of varied experience*. Homewood: Dorsey Press.

Friedensberg, E. (1985). Reactivity and individual style of work exemplified by constructional-type task performance: A developmental study. In J. Strelau, F. H. Farley, & A. Gale (Eds.), *The biological bases of personality and behavior: Theories, measurement techniques, and development* (Vol. 1, pp. 241–253). Washington: Hemisphere.

Frigon, J. Y. (1976). Extraversion, neuroticism and strength of the nervous system. *British Journal of Psychology, 67,* 467–474.

Gilliland, K. (1985). The Temperament Inventory: Relationship to theoretically similar Western personality dimensions and construct validity. In J. Strelau, F. H. Farley, & A. Gale (Eds.), *The biological bases of personality and behavior: Theories, measurement techniques, and development* (Vol. 1, pp. 161–170). Washington: Hemisphere.

Goldman, D., Kohn, P. M., & Hunt, R. W. (1983). Sensation seeking, augmenting-reducing, and absolute auditory threshold: A strength-of-the-nervous-system perspective. *Journal of Personality and Social Psychology, 45,* 405–411.

Golubeva, E. A. (1980). Some problems of the experimental study of the inborn prerequisites of general capacities. *Voprosy Psikhologii, 26,* 23–37 (in Russian).

Gray, J. A. (Ed.). (1964). *Pavlov's typology*. Oxford: Pergamon Press.

Gray, J. A. (1967). Strength of the nervous system, introversion-extraversion, conditionability and arousal. *Behavior Research and Therapy, 5,* 151–169.

Gupta, S., & Nicholson, J. (1985). Simple visual reaction time, personality and strength of the nervous system: A signal-detection theory approach. *Personality and Individual Differences, 6,* 461–469.

Haase, R. F. (1986). Polychronicity and strength of the nervous system as predictors of information overload. In J. Strelau, F. H. Farley, & A. Gale (Eds.), *The biological bases of personality and behavior: Psychophysiology, performance, and application* (Vol. 2, pp. 135–142). Washington: Hemisphere.

Halmiova, O., & Sebova, E. (1986). Nervous system properties and coding processes. In J. Strelau, F. H. Farley, & A. Gale (Eds.), *The biological bases of personality and behavior: Psychophysiology, performance, and application* (Vol. 2, 127–134). Washington: Hemisphere.

Ivanov-Smolensky, A. G. (1935). The experimental investigation of higher nervous activity in children. *Fiziologicheskii Zhurnal SSSR, 19,* 133–140 (in Russian).

Jackson, D. N. (1967). *Manual for the Personality Research Form.* Goshen: Research Psychologists Press.

Karpova, A. K. (1974). Generality and specificity in mathematical interrelations of orthogonal indices of temperament features in different social-developmental samples. In V. S. Merlin (Ed.), *The problems of temperament theory* (pp. 42–86). Perm: MP RSFSR & PGPI (in Russian).

Keuss, P. J. G., & Orlebeke, J. F. (1977). Transmarginal inhibition in a reaction time task as a function of extraversion and neuroticism. *Acta Psychologica, 41,* 139–150.

Klonowicz, T. (1974). Reactivity and fitness for the occupation of operator. *Polish Psychological Bulletin, 5,* 129–136.

Klonowicz, T. (1979). "Kwestionariusz do badania temperamentu" J. Strelaua—proba badan miedzykulturowych [Strelau Temperament Inventory: An attempt at cross-cultural studies]. *Studia Psychologiczne, 18,* 83–92.

Klonowicz, T. (1985). Temperament and performance. In J. Strelau (Ed.), *Temperamental bases of behavior: Warsaw studies on individual differences* (pp. 79–115). Lisse: Swets & Zeitlinger.

Klonowicz, T. (1986). Reactivity and performance: The third side of the coin. In J. Strelau, F. H. Farley, & A. Gale (Eds.), *The biological bases of personality and behavior: Psychophysiology, performance, and application* (Vol. 2, pp. 119–126). Washington: Hemisphere.

Klonowicz, T. (1987). Reactivity and the control of arousal. In J. Strelau, & H. J. Eysenck (Eds.), *Personality dimensions and arousal* (pp. 183–196). New York: Plenum Press.

Kohn, P. M. (1987). Issues in the measurement of arousability. In J. Strelau, & H. J. Eysenck (Eds.), *Personality dimensions and arousal* (pp. 233–250). New York: Plenum Press.

Kohn, P. M., Cowles, M. P., & Lafreniere, K. (1987). Relationships between psychometric and experimental measures of arousability. *Personality and Individual Differences, 8,* 225–231.

Kolesnikov, M. S. Material on the description of the weak type of nervous system. *Trudy Instituta Fiziologii im. I. P. Pavlova, 2,* 120–135 (in Russian).

Kolesnikov, M. S., & Troshikhin, V. A. (1951). The small standard battery of tests for determining type of higher nervous activity in the dogs. *Zhurnal Vysshei Nervnoi Deyatelnosti, 1,* 739–743 (in Russian).

Kopytova, L. A. (1963). Expression of typological properties of the nervous system in the activity of machine operators when machines are idle. *Voprosy Psikhologii, 9,* 59–72 (in Russian).

Koscielak, R. (1979). The role of nervous system traits in inventive creativity. *Polish Psychological Bulletin, 10,* 225–232.

Kovac, D., & Halmiova, O. (1973). Is there a direct correlation between emotional stability and strength of nervous processes? *Studia Psychologica, 15,* 1–7.

Kozlowski, C. (1977). Demand for stimulation and probability preferences in gambling decisions. *Polish Psychological Bulletin, 8,* 67–73.

Krasnogorsky, N. I. (1953). Typological properties of higher nervous activity in children. *Zhurnal Vysshei Nervnoi Deyatelnosti, 3,* 169–183 (in Russian).

Krasusky, V. K. (1971). On some additional criteria of assessment of higher nervous activity properties. In V. K. Krasusky, & V. K. Fedorov (Eds.), *Methods of assessment of higher nervous activity properties* (pp. 64–72). Leningrad: Nauka (in Russian).

Krushinsky, L. V. (1947). Inheritance of passive-defensive behavior (cowardice) as connected with types of nervous system in the dog. *Trudy Instituta Evolutsionnoi Fiziologii i Patologii im. I. P. Pavlova, 1,* 39–62 (in Russian).

Kupalov, P. S. (1952). Experimental neuroses in animals. *Zhurnal Vysshei Nervnoi Deyatelnosti, 2,* 457–473 (in Russian).

Lacey, J. I. (1950). Individual differences in somatic response patterns. *Journal of Comparative and Physiological Psychology, 43*, 338–350.

Lacey, J. I. (1967). Somatic response patterning and stress: Some revisions of activation theory. In M. H. Appley, & R. Trumbull (Eds.), *Psychological stress: Issues in research* (pp. 14–37). New York: Appleton-Century-Crofts.

Larsen, R. J., & Baggs, D. W. (1986). Some psychophysical and personality correlates of the Strelau Temperament Inventory. *Personality and Individual Differences, 7,* 561–565.

Leites, N. S. (1956). An attempt to give a psychological description of temperaments. In B. M. Teplov (Ed.), *Typological features of higher nervous activity in man* (Vol. 1, pp. 267–303). Moscow: RSFSR Academy of Pedagogical Sciences (in Russian).

Loo, R. (1979). Neo-Pavlovian properties of higher nervous activity and Eysenck's personality dimensions. *International Journal of Psychology, 14,* 265–274.

Mangan, G. L. (1967). Studies of the relationship between neo-Pavlovian properties of higher nervous activity and Western personality dimensions: IV. A factor analytic study of extraversion and flexibility, and the sensitivity and mobility of the nervous system. *Journal of Experimental Research in Personality, 2,* 124–127.

Mangan, G. L. (1978). The relationship of mobility of inhibition to rate of inhibitory growth and measures of flexibility, extraversion, and neuroticism. *Journal of General Psychology, 99,* 271–279.

Mangan, G. L. (1982). *The biology of human conduct: East-West models of temperament and personality.* Oxford: Pergamon Press.

Mangan, G. L., & Farmer, R. G. (1967). Studies of the relationship between neo-Pavlovian properties of higher nervous activity and Western personality dimensions: I. The relationship of nervous strength and sensitivity to extraversion. *Journal of Experimental Research in Personality, 2,* 101–106.

Marton, L., & Urban, J. (1966). The relationship between typological personality traits and characteristics of the process of elaboration and extinction of conditioned links. *Voprosy Psikhologii, 12,* 92–100 (in Russian).

Muendelein, H. (1982). *Simulierte Arbeitssituation an Bildschirmterminals: Ein Beitrag zu einer okologisch orientierten Psychologie.* Frankfurt/Main: Fischer Verlag.

Murray, H. A. (1938). *Explorations in personality.* New York: Oxford University Press.

Nebylitsyn, V. D. (1959). Relationship between strength and sensitivity of the nervous system. In B. M. Teplov (Ed.), *Typological features of higher nervous activity in man.* (Vol. 2, pp. 48–82). Moscow: RSFSR Academy of Pedagogical Sciences (in Russian).

Nebylitsyn, V. D. (1960). Reaction time and strength of nervous system. *Doklady Akademii Pedagogicheskikh Nauk RSFSR, 4,* 93–100; *5,* 71–74 (in Russian).

Nebylitsyn, V. D. (1972a). *Fundamental properties of the human nervous system.* New York: Plenum Press.

Nebylitsyn, V. D. (1972b). The problem of general and partial properties of the nervous system. In V. D. Nebylitsyn, & J. A. Gray (Eds.), *Biological bases of individual behavior* (pp. 400–417). New York: Academic Press.

Nosal, C. S. (1974). Interrelation of features of controlled movements and overt properties of the central nervous system (CNS). *Polish Psychological Bulletin, 5,* 137–141.

Oleszkiewicz-Zsurzs, Z. (1984). *Zapotrzebowanie na stymulacje a preferencje do wyboru zawodu* [Need for stimulation and preferences in choice of profession]. Unpublished doctoral dissertation. University of Warsaw, Warsaw.

Orlebeke, J. F. (1972). *Aktivering, extraversie en sterke van het zenuwstelsel* [Arousal, extraversion and strength of the nervous system]. Assen: Van Gorcum and Comp.

Paisey, T. J. H., & Mangan, G. L. (1980). The relationship of extraversion, neuroticism, and sensation seeking to questionnaire-derived measures of nervous system properties. *Pavlovian Journal of Biological Science, 15,* 123–130.

Paisey, T. J. H., & Mangan, G. L. (1982). Neo-Pavlovian temperament theory and the biological bases of personality. *Personality and Individual Differences, 3,* 189–203.

Pavlov, I. P. (1951–1952). *Complete works* (2nd ed.). Moscow & Leningrad: SSSR Academy of Sciences (in Russian).

Pawlow, I. P. (1952). *Dwadziescia lat badan wyzszej czynnosci nerwowej (zachowania sie) zwierzat* [Twenty-five years of objective study of the higher activity (behavior) in animals]. Warszawa: Panstwowy Zaklad Wydawnictw Lekarskich.

Pervomaysky, B. Ya. (1964). Methods of assessment of the type of nervous system in man. In (no editor) *Clinic problems, pathophysiology and treatment of psychological diseases.* Lugansk: Lugansk Medical College Press.

Peysakhov, N. N. (1974). The diagnosis of strength of the excitatory process by means of motor-reaction methods. In N. N. Peysakhov, V. M. Shardin, & A. P. Kashin (Eds.), *Problems of psychology of individual differences.* Kazan: Kazan University Press (in Russian).

Przymusinski, R., & Strelau, J. (1986). Temperamental traits and strategies of decision-making in gambling. In A. Angleitner, A. Furnham, & G. VanHeck (Eds.), *Personality psychology in Europe: Current trends and controversies* (Vol. 2, pp. 225–236). Lisse: Swets & Zeitlinger.

Rawlings, D. (1987). Four experiments on the relation between Eysenck's psychoticism dimension and the Pavlovian concept of nervous system mobility. *Journal of Research in Personality, 21,* 114–126.

Richards, M. (1986). Relationships between the Eysenck Personality Questionnaire, Strelau Temperament Inventory and Freiburger Beschwerdenliste Gesamtform. *Personality and Individual Differences, 7,* 587–589.

Rozhdestvenskaya, V. I. (1963). Typological features in the nervous system of man during the development of delayed photochemical reflexes. In B. M. Teplov (Ed.), *Typological features of higher nervous activity in man* (Vol. 3, pp. 117–132). Moscow: RSFSR Academy of Pedagogical Sciences (in Russian).

Ruch, W. (1988). *Deutsche Erprobungsfassung des EPQ von Eysenck.* Unpublished manuscript, University of Duesseldorf, Department of Psychology, Duesseldorf.

Sales, S. M., & Throop, W. F. (1972). The relationship between kinesthetic aftereffects and strength of the nervous system. *Psychophysiology, 9,* 492–497.

Samarin, Yu. A. (1954). An attempt at the experimental psychological study of typological features of the nervous system in children. *Izvestiya Akademii Pedagogicheskikh Nauk RSFSR, 52,* 81–140 (in Russian).

Saprykin, P. G., & Mileryan, E. A. (1954). *An attempt to develop a method for the experimental investigation of individual features of higher nervous activity in man.* Proceedings of a conference on psychology held on 3-8 July, 1953. Moscow: RSFSR Academy of Pedagogical Sciences (in Russian).

Schoenpflug, W., & Muendelein, H. (1986). Activity and reactivity: Theoretical comments and an experimental approach. In J. Strelau, F. H. Farley, & A. Gale (Eds.), *The biological bases of personality and behavior: Psychophysiology, performance, and application* (Vol. 2, pp. 213–218). Washington: Hemisphere.

Schulz, P. (1986). Activity structures as related to individual differences in temperament. In J. Strelau, F. H. Farley, & A. Gale (Eds.), *The biological bases of personality and behavior: Psychophysiology, performance, and application* (Vol. 2, pp. 219–226). Washington: Hemisphere.

Sosnowski, T., & Wrzesniewski, K. (1986). Research with the Polish form of the State Trait Anxiety Inventory. In C. D. Spielberger, & R. Diaz-Guerrero (Eds.) *Cross-cultural anxiety* (Vol. 3, pp. 21–35). Washington: Hemisphere.

Spence, K. W. (1956). *Behavior theory and conditioning.* New Haven: Yale University Press.

Stawowska, L. (1973). *Diagnoza typow osobowosci* [The diagnosis of personality types]. Kielce: Wydawnictwo Uniwersytetu Slaskiego.

Stawowska, L. (1977). *Rola zroznicowania typologicznego w funkcjonowaniu jednostki* [The role of typological differentiation in the individual's functioning]. Opole: Wydawnictwo WSP.

Stelmack, R. M., Kruidenier, B. G., & Anthony, S. B. (1985). A factor analysis of the Eysenck Personality Questionnaire and the Strelau Temperament Inventory. *Personality and Individual Differences, 6,* 657–659.

Strelau, J. (1965a). *Problemy i metody badan typow ukladu nerwowego czlowieka* [Problems and methods of research into types of nervous system in man]. Wroclaw: Ossolineum.

Strelau, J. (1965b). *O temperamencie i jego poznawaniu* [On temperament and its diagnosis]. Warszawa: Nasza Ksiegarnia.

Strelau, J. (1969). *Temperament i typ ukladu nerwowego* [Temperament and type of nervous system]. Warszawa: Panstwowe Wydawnictwo Naukowe.

Strelau, J. (1970). Nervous system type and extraversion-introversion: A comparison of Eysenck's theory with Pavlov's typology. *Polish Psychological Bulletin, 1,* 17–24.

Strelau, J. (1972a). A diagnosis of temperament by nonexperimental techniques. *Polish Psychological Bulletin, 3,* 97–105.

Strelau, J. (1972b). The general and partial nervous system types—Data and theory. In V. D. Nebylitsyn, & J. A. Gray (Eds.), *Biological bases of individual behavior* (pp. 62–73). New York: Academic Press.

Strelau, J. (1982). Biologically determined dimensions of personality or temperament? Personality and Individual Differences, 3, 355–360.

Strelau, J. (1983). *Temperament—personality—activity*. London: Academic Press.

Strelau, J. (1984). *Das Temperament in der psychischen Entwicklung*. Berlin: Volk und Wissen Volkseigener Verlag.

Strelau, J. (1987a). The concept of temperament in personality research. *European Journal of Personality, 1,* 107–117.

Strelau, J. (1987b). Personality dimensions based on arousal theories: Search for integration. In J. Strelau, & H. J. Eysenck (Eds.), *Personality dimensions and arousal*. New York: Plenum Press.

Strelau, J., & Terelak, J. (1974). The alpha-index in relation to temperamental traits. *Studia Psychologica, 16,* 40–50.

Strykowska, M. (1978). Effect of reactivity on choice of strategy in solving typical operators' tasks. *Polish Psychological Bulletin, 9,* 139–145.

Stumpf, H., Angleitner, A., Wieck, T., Jackson, D. N., & Beloch-Till, H. (1985). *Deutsche Personality Research Form (PRF): Handanweisung*. Goettingen: C. J. Hogrefe.

Teplov, B. M. (1963). New data for the study of nervous system properties in man. In B. M. Teplov (Ed.), *Typological features of higher nervous activity in man* (Vol. 3, pp. 3–46). Moscow: RSFSR Academy of Pedagogical Sciences (in Russian).

Teplov, B. M. (1964). Problems in the study of general types of higher nervous activity in man and animals. In J. A. Gray (Ed.), *Pavlov's typology* (pp. 3–153). Oxford: Pergamon Press.

Teplov, B. M. (1972). The problems of types of human higher nervous activity and methods of determining them. In V. D. Nebylitsyn, & J. A. Gray (Eds.), *Biological bases of individual behavior* (pp. 1–10). New York: Academic Press.

Teplov, B. M., & Nebylitsyn, V. D. (1963). The study of basic properties of the nervous system and their significance in psychology of individual differences. *Voprosy Psikhologii, 9,* 38–47 (in Russian).

Terelak, J. (1974). Reaktywnosc mierzona indeksem alfa a cechy temperamentalne [Alpha index as a measure of reactivity and temperament features]. In J. Strelau (Ed.), *Rola cech temperamentalnych w dzialaniu* (pp. 45–70). Wroclaw: Ossolineum.

Troshikhin, V. A., Moldavskaya, S. I., & Kolchenko, N. V. (1978). *Functional mobility of nervous processes and professional selection*. Kiev: Naukova Dumka (in Russian).

Turovskaya, Z. G. (1963). The relation between some indices of strength and mobility of the nervous system in man. In B. M. Teplov (Ed.), *Typological features of higher nervous activity in man* (Vol. 3, pp. 248–261). Moscow: RSFSR Academy of Pedagogical Sciences (in Russian).

Umansky, L. I. (1958). Experimental study of typological features of children, nervous systems (using play material). *Voprosy Psikhologii, 4,* 184–190 (in Russian).

Unterweger, E. (1980). *Regiditaet und Reizsuche.* Unpublished doctoral dissertation, University of Graz, Graz.

Van Heck, G. L. (1987). *Temperament and coping strategies.* Unpublished manuscript.

Vyatkina, Z. N. (1976). Nervous system properties and the teacher's individual style of activity during lecture. In B. A. Vyatkin (Ed.), *Temperament and sport* (Vol. 3, pp. 99–118). Perm: MP RSFSR, PGPI & UOOP.

Watson, R. I. (1978). *The great psychologists* (4th ed.). Philadelphia: J. B. Lippincott.

Windholz, G. (1987). Pavlov as a psychologist: A reappraisal. *The Pavlovian Journal of Biological Science, 22,* 103–112.

Zarzycka, M. (1980). *Rola cech temperamentu i osobowosci w powodowaniu wypadkow przez maszynistow PKP* [The role of temperament and personality in causing accidents by engine-drivers]. Unpublished doctoral dissertation, University of Warsaw, Warsaw.

Zhorov, P. A., & Yermolayeva-Tomina, L. B. (1972). Concerning the relation between extraversion and the strength of the nervous system. In V. D. Nebylitsyn, & J. A. Gray (Eds.), *Biological bases of individual behavior* (pp. 262–268). New York: Academic Press.

Zuckerman, M. (1979). *Sensation seeking: Beyond the optimal level of arousal.* Hillsdale, NJ: Erlbaum.

9
Toward a Consensual Set of Symptom Clusters for Assessment of Personality Disorder

Lee Anna Clark
Southern Methodist University

With the publication of DSM-III (APA, 1980), the American Psychiatric Association introduced a multiaxial system for psychiatric diagnosis. In doing so it officially recognized the Personality Disorders (PDs) as a significant and independent area of psychopathology, distinguishing them from the major clinical syndromes in a separate "Axis II." The APA Task Force proposed 11 categories of PDs, generally described as sets of "inflexible and maladaptive" traits that are "characteristic of an individual's current and long-term functioning, are not limited to discrete episodes of illness, and cause either significant impairment in social or occupational functioning or subjective distress" (APA, 1980, p. 305). This definition of chronic maladaptive traits is congruent with the prevailing view of normal range personality dispositions and will facilitate much needed integration of the two realms (Gunderson, 1983).

While this new axis has been widely hailed as a significant advance in psychiatric diagnosis, and a great deal of research has been published supporting its addition, many conceptual and empirical problems remain. One concern that has been voiced is whether the domain of personality disorders may be better understood dimensionally than categorically (Eysenck, Wakefield, & Friedman, 1983; Frances, 1980, 1982; Gunderson, 1983; Kass, Skodol, Charles, Spitzer, & Williams, 1985; Penna, 1981; Widiger & Frances, 1985; Widiger & Kelso, 1983). To classify disorders into separate types, one ideally requires that they be distinct and largely mutually exclusive, and that the number of cases falling at the boundary between disorders (and, more generally, between disorder and normality) be *relatively* few (Kendell, 1975). This is, of course, more true of the classical than the prototypic model of categorization, but it applies to the prototypic model as well. Briefly, in the classical model, a category is defined by a set of necessary and sufficient defining features, whereas in the prototypic model, the defining features need only to be correlated with category membership—they need not be necessary and sufficient. Extensive discussion of classification models, however, is beyond the scope of this chapter. (For in-depth discussions see Cantor, Smith, French, & Mezzich, 1980; Clarkin, Widiger, Frances, Hurt, & Gilmore, 1983; Horowitz, Post, French, Wallis, & Siegelman, 1981; Horowitz, Wright, Lowenstein, & Parad, 1981; Widiger, 1982; Widiger & Frances, 1985).

Few natural categories fit the classical model, and the prototypic model is certainly more applicable to psychiatric disorders. With the advent of DSM-III-R (APA, 1987), all 11 of the PDs follow this model of categorization, yet it is not clear whether even the prototypic model is appropriate for the personality disorders. For example, the categories proposed for the PDs are not clearly distinct, either from normal range functioning or from each other.[1] Terms such as "maladaptive" and "inflexible" are neither defined nor quantified; accordingly, it is left to the individual clinician to determine the cutting point between normal and disordered functioning, and there are little data to suggest where this cutting point should be (Frances, 1982; Shepard & Sartorius, 1974). Furthermore, despite specification of explicit inclusion and exclusion criteria for diagnosis and steps taken in DSM-III-R to reduce the diagnostic overlap between the disorders, a number of related problems remain. These include: (1) the large percentage of patients receiving "mixed," "atypical," or multiple diagnoses, (2) the loss of information occurring when patients just fail to meet criterion for a category, and (3) the high degree of heterogeneity found within diagnostic groups (see Frances & Widiger, 1986; Widiger & Kelso, 1983 for more extensive discussions).

The logical alternative that has been suggested to circumvent these problems is the use of a dimensional or trait system (Eysenck et al., 1983; Frances, 1982; Penna, 1981; Widiger & Frances, 1985; Widiger & Kelso, 1983),[2] the advantages of which were recognized some time ago, even before DSM-III (e.g., Hine & Williams, 1975; Kendell, 1975; Presley & Walton, 1973; Tyrer & Alexander, 1979; Tyrer, Alexander, Cicchetti, Cohen, & Remington, 1979). A number of recent investigators have moved in the direction of using a dimensional system for assessing personality disorder (e.g. Kass et al., 1985; Mann, Jenkins, Cutting, &

---

[1] Major steps have been taken in DSM-III-R towards eliminating this problem. However, while conceptually more satisfying, it is not yet clear whether the new, more distinct categories are empirically well-founded. The overlap may lie in nature, not just in our diagnostic schemes.

[2] Two other approaches to personality assessment and diagnosis have also been proposed: the interpersonal circumplex model (Benjamin, 1974; Conte & Plutchik, 1981; Kiesler, 1983; Wiggins, 1979, 1982), and the act-frequency approach (Borkenau, 1986; Buss & Craik, 1983, 1984, 1987). These are both, however, fundamentally variants of the basic dimensional approach, and detailing similarities and differences among them is beyond the scope this chapter.

Cowen, 1981; Tyrer, Strauss, & Cicchetti, 1983; Tyrer et al., 1984), and have taken one of two approaches. Some researchers (e.g., Kass et al., 1985; Mann et al., 1981) have preserved the use of categories but have converted dichotomous present–absent judgments to scaled ratings (e.g., 1 = no or very few traits, 2 = some traits, 3 = almost meets criteria, 4 = meets full criteria for diagnosis). This approach does circumvent some of the problems inherent in a categorical system; for example, it preserves information about patients who fall short of criterion. It does not, however, address other problems, such as overlapping symptoms among categories, heterogeneity within a category, and so on. Nor does it address the more basic question of what are the fundamental maladaptive traits that comprise the personality disorders.

In contrast, Tyrer and his colleagues have followed more closely in the tradition of normal personality assessment, selecting 24 attributes that they felt would be maladaptive if present in an extreme degree, and that appeared relatively indepen-dent of one another (Tyrer et al., 1979). They have reported some success with this method (Tyrer et al., 1983; Tyrer et al., 1984), but admit that the traits were not chosen systematically, nor were they explicitly related to a defined domain of personality disorder (Tyrer, 1986).

What is necessary, therefore, is a systematic investigation of the boundaries and content of the PD domain. This will provide the basis for development of a comprehensive trait system for personality disorder, which can then be used to compare the categorical and dimensional approaches to assessment. This is parallel to a major structural approach in the domain of normal personality, which began with cataloguing all trait names in the English language (Allport & Odbert, 1936; Norman, 1967). These were then systematically reduced first through rational judgments of semantic meaning (Cattell, 1946), and then empirical studies of covariation among individuals (Cattell, 1945; Norman, 1963). This approach has ultimately clarified a number of issues regarding the nature of personality, the basic personality traits, and the structure of personality (e.g., Cattell, 1965; Eysenck, 1970; Hogan, 1985, 1986; McCrae & Costa, 1985; Norman, 1967; Tellegen, 1985, 1986). The domain of personality disorders, in contrast, has not been systematically defined nor its content explored. This chapter presents one approach to the investigation of this domain.

It is important to stress that whether the domain of personality disorders is best described dimensionally or categorically is not a fundamental issue at this stage. In either case, it is first necessary to identify, as Cattell (1946) did for normal personality, the basic synonym groupings of the domain. Only then can empirical research proceed to address the question of how these clusters are ordered in individuals. Furthermore, the question of the existence of categories or types is not foreclosed even if a dimensional approach proves useful. For example, in normal personality, Eysenck (1970) has proposed a hierarchical structure, in which several dimensions, such as Dominance and Affiliation, are combined into a higher order "type," such as Extraversion. An explication of the fundamental traits that underlie the domain is thus an important first step in examining these questions empirically.

I present and discuss the results of two studies, one in which the basic groupings of symptoms potentially relevant to personality disorder are investigated using the symptom criteria of DSM-III and other alternative conceptualizations, and a second that extends these findings to incorporate the new criteria included in DSM-III-R. I then discuss the implications of these two studies together.

STUDY I

Method

To identify the important symptom groups that characterize the entire domain of personality disorders, a complete set of relevant symptom criteria was assembled. Qualified raters then grouped these criteria into synonym categories. Finally, a consensual set of symptom clusters was determined through factor analysis of these groupings.

Symptom List.   In an initial exploration of a domain, it is important for the content to be over- rather than underinclusive, because content identified as irrelevant may easily be discarded, whereas addition of content into the structure at a later point is more problematic (Loevinger, 1957; Norman, 1963; Wiggins, 1973). The symptoms included, however, need not be *exhaustive,* provided they sample sufficiently widely from the domain so that the resulting structure represents a comprehensive *framework* for further investigation. Needless to say, it would be inefficient to include symptoms clearly outside the realm of personality disorders (e.g., frank delusions or hallucinations), or to return to Allport and Odbert's list of over 4500 trait terms and examine each of them for possible relevance to personality disorder. Every attempt should be made, however, to include all symptoms that have been explicitly proposed as potentially relevant, whether or not they are currently recognized in the official nomenclature.

If specific sets of proposed symptoms do not overlap with those of the currently defined domain, this indicates either that they fall outside the realm of personality disorder, or that the current domain is defined too narrowly. Which alternative is correct cannot, of course, be decided on conceptual grounds alone. Rather, further empirical research must determine whether or not any additional categories are important or useful. If, on the other hand, symptoms from alternative conceptualizations or diagnoses show some overlap with the DSM-III PD criteria, this may suggest that the scope of personality disorder may be somewhat broader than that currently specified. Again, only further empirical research can determine the utility of any revision.

I, therefore, began with the complete set of personality disorder criteria in DSM-III, but did not limit myself to those symptoms. Rather, symptoms from related diagnoses and from alternative conceptualizations were used as well. Specifically, symptoms from DSM-III's Axis I Dysthymic Disorder, Cyclothymic Disorder, and Generalized Anxiety Disorder were included on the basis of their historical derivation (e.g., Cyclothymic and Asthenic personality appeared in DSM-II) and/or because several writers have noted that maladaptive personality traits are centrally important to them (Akiskal, Hirschfeld, & Yerevanian, 1983; Clark, 1989; Frances, 1980; Tellegen, 1985; Watson & Clark, 1984). Symptoms from Cleckley's (1964) psychopathic personality, Klein's hysteroid dysphoric PD (Liebowitz & Klein, 1981), four alternative sets of criteria for Borderline PD (Perry & Klerman, 1978), and ICD and DSM-II PDs not covered in DSM-III (e.g., Explosive PD, Masochistic PD) were also examined for possible inclusion. With the exception of Cleckley's set, however, the majority of the symptoms found among these criteria were already included in the set of symptoms derived from DSM-III, and those that were not were either inappropriate to the task or overly broad or vague (e.g., history of transference, displays primitive fantasy). Therefore, only criteria from Cleckley were added. Multiple symptoms or examples that comprised a single criterion were divided into their component parts. For example, criterion (1) for Compulsive Personality Disorder is "restricted ability to express warm and tender emotions, e.g., the individual is unduly conventional, serious and formal, and stingy"; this was broken down into five component parts. Examples of criteria were included as symptoms if they were sufficiently broad (e.g., "exaggerated expression of emotions"), but were omitted if they referred to quite specific behaviors (e.g., "failure to obtain medical care for a seriously ill child").

The final set comprised 167 symptoms: 68 from DSM-II or -III Axis II alone, 41 from DSM-III Axis I alone, 17 from Cleckley (1964) alone, and 41 that were included in two or more sources. Each of the criteria was typed on a separate 3 × 5 index card.

Procedures.   Raters were presented with the set of cards in random order, and were given the following instructions: "The task is to sort the cards into groups of items with similar meaning, or synonym groups. This is not a test, and we are not interested in how these items might combine in patients; rather, we are interested in how people in general see the meanings of these items.

The number of groups is up to you, but you will probably end up with somewhere between 10 and 25 groups. Some groups will have a lot of items, some may have only a few, and that is fine. You may find a few cards that do not seem to fit anywhere. If you do, you may put them aside in a miscellaneous group, but it would be best not to have more than 4 cards in that group, and it is certainly all right not to have any miscellaneous cards if you feel you can group them all. If you have any questions, feel free to ask them at any time."

The task required 45–60 minutes. The mean number of groups used by the raters was 15 (range = 6–28), and the mean number of symptoms not grouped was 2.3 (range = 0–15, with the modal number 0). These data indicate that the groupings fell largely within the broad guidelines suggested, but also suggest that the raters felt free to ignore them as they saw fit.

Raters.   Raters were 15 professional (7 M.A. and 8 Ph.D.) psychologists and 14 second-year graduate students in clinical or counseling psychology in the Dallas area. All were familiar with DSM-III and the criteria for personality disorders. The psychologists had an average of 6.67 years of post-degree experience (STD = 7.4, range = 0–27 years).

One reason for using students in addition to professionals was to provide a check against the clinicians' potential bias toward grouping the symptoms on the basis of their knowledge of the diagnostic categories. This might lead to inappropriate lumping of diagnostically linked but semantically unrelated symptoms. Because of their limited experience, students would be less likely to commit this error. Clinicians did, in fact, provide slightly fewer symptom clusters (14.5 vs. 15.6); this difference is not, however, statistically significant. Lay raters, of course, would provide the least biased sample, but might not understand the meaning of many of the psychological terms (e.g., ideas of reference, affective instability).

Data Analysis.   The judges' sortings were converted to a square (167 × 167) co–occurrence matrix and divided by the number of raters, so that each cell x_{ij} contained the percentage of judges who placed items i and j in the same category. This matrix was then subjected to a Varimax–rotated principal components analysis, and examined for the appropriate number of dimensions to be extracted. (See Watson, Clark, & Tellegen, 1984, for a more detailed explanation of this procedure.)

Such a matrix differs from the normal correlation matrix in two major ways: (1) All numbers in such a matrix are positive, ranging from 0 to 1.0. As a result, the obtained factors are almost exclusively unipolar, and bipolar factors are uninterpretable. (2) The data on which the matrix is based are inherently hierarchical (assuming they are orderly): Some raters (lumpers) create larger, more general groupings, while others (splitters) create numerous smaller categories. If the smaller categories of the splitters are, for the most part, subdivisions of the lumpers' larger groups, then the first factors to emerge will correspond to those created by the lumpers, while later factors will represent the finer differentiations of the splitters. The decision regarding the number of factors to be extracted, therefore, must include consideration of whether lumping or splitting is more appropriate for the specific purposes of the investigation. In this particular case, a more finely differentiated set of symptom groups is desirable, because more general, higher order groups can always be developed later on the basis of other types of data, such as actual symptom ratings of patients, and so on. Just as it is easier to eliminate irrelevant categories than to add new ones to an existing structure, combining over-differentiated clusters at a later stage is much easier than recovering information lost through lumping.

Results and Discussion

Because the views of practicing clinicians and graduate students regarding the symptoms might differ, the sortings of each group were first analyzed separately. Although some differences were observed, visual inspection suggested that the solutions of the two groups of raters were remarkably similar. In many cases, there appeared to be a clear one-to-one match between related factors of the two solutions, and in the remaining cases, a single large factor in one solution seemed to correspond to two smaller factors in the other. Therefore, combining the data appeared justified and, moreover, increases the reliability of the final structure. Accordingly, I initially present analyses of the entire data set; however, because it is interesting to examine differences in the structures of experienced clinicians versus relatively untutored students, I analyze the data of these subgroups more rigorously in a later section.

The Overall Structure of Symptoms Relevant to Personality Disorder.   The slope of the eigenvalues indicated a wide range of possible solutions. Specifically, there were sizable drops in the eigenvalues down to 13 factors; the values then decreased gradually until 29 factors, at which point the decrements became exceedingly small. Therefore, a number of Varimax–rotated solutions were examined, beginning with a minimum of 13 up to a maximum of 28 factors. A plot of the eigenvalues is shown in Figure 9.1. In order to view the critical area in sufficient detail, only the factors from 13 to 32 are presented.

Initial inspection of a number of solutions indicated that the structure did not stabilize until the 15th factor, after which the extraction of successive factors resulted primarily in a larger factor breaking into two components; therefore, the factor solutions from 15 to 28 were examined in more detail. The 15 factor solution contained a large factor that combined symptoms of low self-esteem, dependency, and passive–aggressive behavior. This is not an illogical grouping, but it may reflect, in part, the clinical bias toward grouping according to diagnosis mentioned earlier (e.g., low self-esteem and dependency are both criteria for DSM-III Dependent PD). In later solutions (starting at 17 or more factors), however, this cluster split into its three constituent parts. In this case, the more differentiated structure seems to capture the basic semantic categories more accurately. The 15-factor solution also contained an overly general antisocial factor, composed of three aspects: disregard for social convention; inconsideration of others' feelings; and superficiality. Again, this appears to be a diagnostic rather than a truly semantic clustering. These three components first appeared separately in the 23-factor

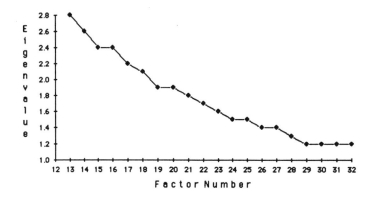

FIG. 9.1.   Eigenvalues of the 13th to 32nd principal components.

solution, after which further extraction resulted in singlets (factors with only one marker variable), or factors with no markers at all (a symptom was considered a marker variable if it had a factor loading of .40 or higher on that factor). Generally speaking, for a factor to be retained it should be defined by at least three variables (Guilford, 1952); therefore, the 23-factor solution was the most differentiated solution in which all factors could be retained.

TABLE 9.1
Percent of Extracted Variance Accounted for
by 23 Rotated Factors

Factor	Percent of Variance
Suspiciousness	10.6
Grandiose Egocentrism	7.6
Emotional Coldness	7.1
Antisocial	6.4
Self-Derogation	6.4
Anger/Aggression	6.0
Negative Affect	5.9
Anhedonia	5.6
Dependency	5.5
Social Isolation	4.7
Eccentric Thought	4.5
Rigidity	4.2
High Energy	3.9
Impulsivity	3.8
Hypersexuality	3.7
Exhibitionism	3.6
Self-centered Exploitation	3.4
Hypersensitivity	2.9
Pessimism	2.9
Passive-Aggressiveness	2.8
Suicide Proneness	2.4
Instability	2.3
Insincerity	2.0

Accordingly, this solution (which accounted for 65% of the total variance) was adopted as the final structure. All but 6 of the 167 symptoms loaded on at least one of the 23 factors, and only 17 items split across 2 factors. The percentage of extracted variance accounted for by each factor is shown in Table 9.1, and representative symptom markers and their diagnoses of origin are presented in Table 9.2.[3] Cleckley's (1964) symptoms are classified under the diagnosis Antisocial, while seven DSM-III symptoms shared with Hysteroid Dysphoria (Liebowitz & Klein, 1981) are marked wherever they appear. However, for simplicity's sake, 28 symptoms shared by DSM-III and one of the alternative conceptualizations of Borderline PD (Perry & Klerman, 1978) are classified only by their DSM-III diagnoses.

The factor names used in the tables are based on the responses of eight clinicians and seven second-year graduate students who were presented with lists of the symptoms comprising the factors and asked to provide labels that captured the underlying category. In most cases, the responses were synonyms or variations of each other (e.g., Self-defacing vs. Self-derogation; Hostile vs. Aggressive). The author surveyed the responses and selected a name that most accurately reflected the various labels for a given factor. Obviously, these labels should be considered descriptive rather than definitive.

Within each factor the symptoms are arranged by diagnosis of origin, listing the predominant diagnosis first, the next most important diagnosis second, and so on. Where the constituent parts of multi-faceted symptoms loaded on different dimensions, the portions are presented separately.

Several important points may be made about the resulting categories:

1. Every grouping contains symptoms from more than one disorder or conceptualization, indicating that the symptom categories underlying the domain are not currently limited to a single diagnosis, but are relevant to a range of personality disorders.

2. Conversely, every diagnostic category is multi-factorial; that is, in no case do all the criteria for one diagnosis fall entirely in one symptom group. These two points together provide evidence for the importance of clarifying the basic symptom clusters of the domain of personality disorders.

3. In most cases, the component parts of complex criteria reconverged onto a single factor. For example, of the eight symptoms provided to diagnose "pervasive, unwarranted suspicion and mistrust of people" (DSM-III Paranoid PD), seven appeared together on the Suspiciousness factor. Thus, these data provide support for the current structure or wording of most symptom descriptions.

4. In specific cases, the component parts of symptoms did not reconverge. Continuing the above example, "avoidance of accepting blame when war-

---

[3]A complete list of symtoms for each factor is available from the author.

TABLE 9.2

Primary Symptoms Categories in the Personality Disorder Domain

Factor	Diagnostic Category	Criterion Examples
Suspiciousness	Paranoid	expectation of trickery or harm
		overconcern with hidden motives and special meanings
		ready to counterattack any perceived threat
		is preoccupied with unsubstantiated conspiratorial theories[b]
	Schizotypal	suspiciousness or paranoid ideation
	Avoidant	apprehensively alert to signs of social derogarion[a]
	Narcissistic	is preoccupied with feelings of envy[b]
Grandoise Egocentrism	Narcissistic	grandiose sense of self-importance or uniqueness
		entitlement: expectation of special favors...
	Passive-Aggressive	believes s/he is doing a better job than others think s/he is doing
		protests that others make unreasonable demands on him/her
	Cyclothymia	exaggerates past achievements[a]; inflated level of self-esteem
	Histrionic	egocentric, self-indulgent, vain and demanding
	Compulsive	insistence that other submit to his/her way of doing things
Emotional Coldness	Paranoid	appearance of being "cold" and "unemotional"[a]
	Compulsive	restricted ability to express warm and tender emotions
	Schizoid	rarely, if ever, experiences strong emotions[b]
	Schizoid/Schizotypal	emotional coldness and aloofness
		rarely makes reciprocal gestures or facial expressions[b]
	Antisocial	generally lacks depth in emotional reactions[d]
	Narcissistic	generally unresponsive in interpersonal relations[d]
		lack of empathy; inability to recognize how others feel[a]
Antisocial	Antisocial	failure to honor financial obligations or to accept social norms
		deceitful, unreliable, irresponsible, insincere[d]
		totally lacking in remorse or shame[b,d]
	ASP/Sadistic	disregard for the truth; lies for the purpose of harming others[b]
	Paranoid	avoids accepting blame when warranted[a]
	Histrionic	(perceived by others as) shallow and lacking genuineness[a]
Self-Derogation	Avoidant[c]	low self-esteem, e.g., devalues self-achievements[a]
		desire for affection and acceptance[a]
	Dysthymia	low self-esteem; self-deprecation[a], feels inadequate[a]
	Dependent	lacks self-confidence[a]; sees self as helpless, stupid[a]
	Borderline	unstable self-identity

(table 9.2 continued)

Dimension	Diagnostic Category	Criterion Examples
Anger/ Aggression	Borderline	inappropriate intense anger or lack of control of anger
	Dysthymia	prone to excessive anger [a]
	Cyclothymia	irritable mood
	Histrionic	irrational, angry outburst or tantrums
	Antisocial	irritability and aggressiveness; repeated physical fights
	Sadistic	fascinated by violence; uses physical cruelty for dominance
	GAD	irritable; impatient [a]
Negative Affect	GAD[e]	easily startled, restless, anxious, worried, feels "on edge"
	Avoidant	fears being embarrassed or showing signs of anxiety[b]
	Schizotypal	excessive social anxiety
	Cyclothymia	restlessness
	Paranoid	unable to relax [a]
Anhedonia	Dysthymia	low energy level; chronic tiredness or fatigue little interest in or enjoyment of pleasureable activities depressed mood; sad; blue
	Dysthymia/Schizoid	lacks interest in sex[a]; little desire to have sexual experiences[b] unable to respond with apparent pleasure to praise or rewards
	Borderline	emptiness; boredom
	Self-defeating	turns down opportunities for pleasure
Dependency	Dependent	allows others to make most of his or her important decisions subordinates own needs...[a]; agrees with people for fear of rejection[b]
	Borderline/Dependent	intolerance of being alone[a], frantic efforts to avoid abandonment
	Histrionic	dependent[a], helpless[a], constantly seeking reassurance
	Avoidant	desires affection and acceptance[a]
Social Isolation	Schizoid	chooses solitary activities[b]
	Szd/Stp/Avd	no close friends or confidants
	Dysthymia	socially withdrawn
	Avoidant	social reticence[b]; peripheral social/vocational roles
Eccentric Thought	Schizotypal	recurrent illusions; depersonalization or derealization[a] magical thinking, e.g., superstitions; clairvoyance; odd speech; odd behaviors or mannerisms[b] ideas of reference
	Dysthymia	inability to think clearly[b]
	Histrionic	speech that is excessively impressionistic[b]

(continued...)

(Table 9.2 continued)

Dimension	Diagnostic Category	Criterion Examples
Rigidity	Compulsive	conventional, serious, and formal [a], excessive devotion to work perfectionism [b]; preoccupation with detail [b] overconscientious, scrupulous, and inflexible [b] lacks true sense of humor [a]; pride taken in being objective [a]
	Paranoid	
High Energy	Cyclothymiac	elevated or expansive mood; has high amounts of energy extremely talkative, gregarious, overoptimistic unusually productive (keeps odd, self-imposed working hours)
	Histrionic	craving for activity and excitement [a]
Impulsivity	Antisocial	failure to plan ahead; impulsivity; recklessness lacks life plan [d]; poor judgment [d] fails to learn from experience [d], lacks insight into motivation [d] inability to sustain consistent work behavior
	Borderline	impulsive or unpredictable in potentially self-damaging ways
Hypersexuality	Antisocial	repeated sexual intercourse in a casual relationship [a] inability to maintain enduring attachment to a sexual partner impersonal, trivial, and poorly integrated sex life [d]
	Cyclothymia Histrionic	hypersexuality without concern for the consequences inappropriately sexually seductive
Exhibitionism	Histrionic [c]	exaggerated expression of emotions uncomfortable if not the center of attention [b]
	Narcissistic	exhibitionistic [a], requires constant attention and admiration
Self-centered Exploitation	Narcissistic Histrionic Borderline Schizoid Compulsive Sadistic	interpersonal exploitativeness; takes advantage of others inconsiderate of others [a] manipulation (consistently using others for one's own ends) [a] indifference to feelings of others [a] lack of generosity when no personal gain is likely to result [b] humiliates or demeans people in front of others [b]
Hypersensitivity	Avoidant [c]	hypersensitive to rejection [a], fears negative evaluation [b] easily hurt by criticism or disapproval [b]
	Paranoid Histrionic	holds grudges or is unforgiving of insults [b]; easily slighted overreacts to minor events [a]

(continued...)

Dimension	Diagnostic Category	Criterion Examples
Pessimism	Dysthymia	broods over past events[a], feels guilty concerning past activities[a]; pessimism
	Par[a]/Avd[b]	exaggeration of difficulties
	GAD[f]	anticipates misfortune to self or others
Passive-Aggressiveness	Passive-Aggressive	procrastination[a]; intentional inefficiency[a] social and occupational ineffectiveness obstructs the efforts of others[b]
	Compulsive	indecisiveness; decision-making is avoided or postponed
	Dysthymia	ineffective or underproductive at school, work, or home[a]
	Self-defeating	fails to accomplish tasks crucial to personal objectives[b]
Suicide Proneness	Histrionic[c]	prone to manipulative suicide threats, gestures, or attempts[a]
	Borderline[c]	physically self-damaging acts, e.g., suicidal gestures
	Dysthymia	recurrently thinks of death or suicide[a]
Instability	Narcissistic[c]	reacts to criticism with feeling of rage or humiliation
	Borderline	a pattern of unstable and intense interpersonal relationships
	Histrionic	displays rapidly shifting and shallow expressions of emotions[b]
Insincerity	Histrionic	lacks genuineness[a] shallow[a] insincered
	Antisocial	

Note. All symptoms are from both DSM-III and DSM-III-R except as noted. Cyclothymia corresponds to DSM-III Cyclothymic Disorder-Hypomanic, and Dysthymia corresponds to either Dysthymic Disorder or Cyclothymic-Depressed. GAD is Generalized Anxiety Disorder.

[a] From DSM-III
[b] From DSM-III-R
[c] Also from Hysteriod Dysphoria (Leibowitz & Klein, 1981)
[d] From Cleckley's (1984) 16 primary symptoms of psychopathy
[e] Symptoms that are primarily physical (e.g., shaky, muscle aches, eyelid twitch, etc.) were not included.

255

ranted'' was viewed by the raters as more relevant to Antisocial Behavior than to Suspiciousness. Careful inspection of these data, therefore, may illuminate symptom criteria that are not optimally placed or worded. It is interesting to note that this criterion has been eliminated in DSM-III-R.

5. Some of the symptoms from Cleckley's alternative conceptualization of antisocial personality disorder are grouped together with symptoms from DSM-III's Antisocial PD, indicating that the extreme behavioral criteria of the latter may be complemented by a more psychological view of the disorder.

6. No factor contained only symptoms from non-PD diagnoses (as currently defined), although two were dominated by such symptoms. The Pessimism factor contains only one PD symptom, and is otherwise dominated by Dysthymia. Similarly, High Energy is primarily characterized by symptoms of Cyclothymia, although Histrionic PD and Hysteroid Dysphoria are also represented. This may initially suggest that these factors are, therefore, not relevant to personality disorder; however, as mentioned earlier, no empirical claim one way or the other can be made solely from the emergence of these conceptual factors. Further data must answer the question of whether these factors are important in personality disorder. If they are not, they can simply be eliminated from the structure without affecting the remainder. What the present data do contribute is information regarding the various aspects of these symptom categories that need to be considered by those interested in this area. This can indicate directions for future research.

For example, ''pessimism'' is a central characteristic of Winokur's (1972, 1973) depression spectrum disorder and Akiskal's character spectrum disorder (Akiskal, 1984; Akiskal et al., 1980, 1983; Yerevanian & Akiskal, 1979), both of which are conceptualized as chronic personality disturbances associated with affective disorder. At the same time, ''brooding'' and ''anticipation of misfortune'' are key elements in the pervasive personality trait of Neuroticism/Negative Affectivity (Watson & Clark, 1984). The grouping of these symptoms in the present data informs us that there may be some commonality between these conceptualizations. Furthermore, I have suggested the possibility of a ''generalized affective (personality) disorder'' (Clark, 1989) which characterizes patients whose chronic personality difficulties fall in an area of overlap currently defined by generalized anxiety disorder, dysthymia, atypical depression, and several Axis II disorders (e.g., Avoidant PD). Taken together, these writings suggest that it is premature to close the door on assignments to Axis I versus Axis II.

The Structures of Professional versus Student Raters. While the overall structure presented is more reliable than that of either contributing group alone, it is also interesting to investigate similarities and differences in the structures generated by each set of raters. There are several ways to do this, but the method used here is that described by Watson and Tellegen (1985), to whom the reader is referred for a more complete explanation. In this method, both sets of data are subjected to separate principal components analyses and are rotated to a predetermined solution. The solutions are inspected visually, and a preliminary assessment of factor convergence is made on the basis of the marker variables. This correspondence is then tested more objectively with an index of factor similarity, which is computed by correlating the values of the Varimax loadings of the matched factors. Factors hypothesized to be similar may be taken to be convergent if the correlation between their loadings is high, both in absolute terms and relative to their correlations with other factors.

These procedures were carried out for the professional and graduate student raters' data sets. The co-occurrence matrix of each group was subjected to a separate principal components analysis, and on the basis of the overall analysis, 23 factors were extracted in each case. These solutions accounted for virtually the same percentage of the total variance in the two data sets (70% and 68%, respectively). As shown in Table 9.3, the sizes of corresponding factors were also quite similar, although the clinicians' first factor was slightly larger than that of the student raters (19.1% vs. 16.9% of the variance). As can be seen in the table, beginning with the 13th factor the differences became very small (0.1 or less), so the eigenvalues beyond the 15th factor are not shown. These data suggest a strong convergence in the two structures, at least with regard to their dimensionality. Further analysis of convergence of content is, therefore, appropriate.

Applying the three-marker criterion noted earlier for defining a factor, the

TABLE 9.3
Percent of Total Variance Accounted for by the First Nine
Unrotated Factors in the Clinicians and Student Data Sets

Factor	Percent of Variance	
	Clinicians	Students
1	19.4	16.9
2	11.6	11.3
3	10.6	10.2
4	8.5	9.4
5	7.2	6.7
6	6.4	5.9
7	5.7	5.6
8	5.0	5.5
9	4.9	4.7
10	4.2	3.9
11	3.8	3.8
12	3.4	3.2
13	3.0	3.1
14	2.9	3.0
15	2.8	2.8

professional structure contained 22 factors, while the graduate student data produced only 21 retainable factors. This difference resulted from the clinicians producing two smaller factors that were combined into a single larger factor in the student data; this is described later. The 23rd factor in each solution failed to show any convergent relation between the two groups. For this reason only the first 22 factors (in the overall structure) will be retained for future analyses.

All of the remaining factors in each solution could be matched impressionistically, on the basis of marker variables, with at least one factor in the other solution. In several cases a match could be made with two or more factors, but 16 pairs showed a simple one-to-one correspondence; therefore, I first investigated the relationship of these 16 pairs more objectively, using the method described earlier. The hypothesized correspondence between a pair was considered confirmed if the two factors were correlated .65 or higher, and if their correlations with other factors were all lower by a difference of at least .15. Thirteen of the 16 factors met these criteria, and their correlations as shown in Table 9.4. The other three sets of matched factors (also shown in Table 9.4) had significant correlations only with each other, but the level of relationship was unacceptably low. Although these factors are by no means identical, there is some semantic overlap between them that is not shared by any other factors. It is important to note that each of these 16 sets of factors—including the 3 with low correlations—clearly corresponds to one of the factors that emerged in the overall analysis, and they are listed accordingly in the table.

Six pairs of factors remain to be accounted for. These factors comprise three distinct subgroups. The first subgroup contained items pertaining to interpersonal relations: suspiciousness, hypersensitivity, and instability. The disagreement be-

TABLE 9.4
Convergent Correlations Between the Factors of
Professionals and Graduate Student Raters

Factor	Correlation
Grandiose Egocentrism	.90
Emotional Coldness	.86
Self-Derogation	.80
Anger/Aggression	.85
Negative Affect	.84
Anhedonia	.90
Dependency	.83
Social Isolation	.79
Eccentric Thought	.87
High Energy	.78
Impulsivity	.77
Hypersexuality	.68
Exhibitionism	.74
Pessimism	.46
Suicide Proneness	.36
Passive-Aggressiveness	.33

Note. Correlations are based on $n = 167$ items.

tween clinicians and students regarded the hypersensitivity items: The clinicians grouped these items with suspiciousness, whereas the students grouped them with instability. In the overall analysis these symptoms emerged on three separate factors, which seems most appropriate given their content.

The second subgroup of items reflected irresponsible and unsocialized behavior, and showed a similar pattern. Each group of raters produced a relatively large core factor and each also identified a smaller, idiosyncratic set of items from the same general domain. In the overall structure, two factors emerged (labeled Antisocial and Self-centered Exploitation in Tables 9.1 and 9.2), and thus the consensus structure was related to each of the separate organizations but not identical to either.

Finally, the third set of items reflected rigid conventionality and a strong work orientation. These two sets of items formed a single 10-item factor in the student data that split into 6-item and 4-item factors in the clinicians' structure. In the overall structure, the students' conception prevailed, and a separate work-orientation factor did not appear.

In sum, the broad outlines of the two structures were quite similar, although subtle differences in organization between the sets of raters were evident at certain points. It may be useful to investigate these differences further in order to understand the development of students' conceptions of psychiatric symptoms in this domain. For example, one could examine student structures at various points in their professional training. The primary object of this investigation, however, is to identify semantically similar sets of symptoms on which to base further empirical studies of their relations. For these purposes, the analyses indicate a sufficiently high degree of empirical convergence that we may be confident that the overall structure adequately captures the basic conceptions of both sets of raters. This is particularly important because it informs us that the derived categories do not simply reflect clinicians' opinions or knowledge about symptom relations, but are more generally applicable. That is, because the students were at an early stage in their training and their acquaintance with DSM-III was quite limited compared to the clinicians', their sortings could not have been biased by experience with the criteria to the extent as the clinicians. Yet, the two sets of raters produced very similar structures, suggesting that their groupings were not derived from clinical experience with the criteria, but were based primarily on their semantic meaning, as was intended.

STUDY II: DSM-III-R

Study I was conducted before the 1987 revision of the DSM-III was available, so one may ask whether a different structure would have emerged if the symptom list had been based on the revised symptom pool, or if the new symptoms had been included in the original task. As described earlier, however, symptoms from several alternative conceptualizations and diagnoses were included in Study I, and less than half (41%) of the symptom descriptors used were criteria from DSM-III Axis II alone (although an additional 22% were from Axis II as well as some other source). This suggests that the resulting structure may not be dependent on the particular symptoms comprising the DSM-III Axis II diagnoses. Furthermore, as previously stated, the specific items included in a semantic sorting task of this nature are less important than the assurance that the entire domain is well sampled. In this light, the more appropriate question to ask is whether the new symptoms can be incorporated into the resulting structure, or whether they involve novel symptom domains that were not included in the original set. This was investigated in a second study.

Method

Raters. Raters were eight professional psychologists (3 M.A. and 5 Ph.D.) and seven second-year graduate students. Twelve of the raters were the same as in Study I. The psychologists' average number of years of post-degree experience was 6.4 (STD = 5.8, range = 1–17).

Materials. First, each of the PD criteria used in DSM-III-R (APA, August, 1986 draft), including the appended diagnoses of Self-defeating PD and Sadistic PD, were reviewed by the author, together with four psychology graduate students. Fifty-four criteria that all five reviewers agreed were identical (or virtually so) to the original DSM-III criteria were eliminated from further consideration. The remaining 75 symptoms (or their component parts, as in Study I) were typed on separate 3 × 5 index cards; 58 symptoms were from the 11 main categories, and the other 17 from the appended diagnoses. As before, examples were included only if they were sufficiently broad, and did not simply describe a specific behavior. Second, a complete list of symptoms comprising each of the 22 factors identified in Study I was prepared. The symptoms were grouped by factor without any identifying labels, and the factor groups were arranged in a random order.

Procedures. Raters were presented with the set of cards in random order, and asked to "place each card with the group that you feel it fits best. These groupings should be made on the basis of similarity of meaning, not on the basis of any theoretical system or empirical correlation. If you cannot decide between two groups, write the item on a blank card and place it in both groups, but please try to keep such items to a minimum." This option was used for only nine cards altogether, less than 1% across all raters.

Because part of the purpose of Study II was to investigate the possible existence of symptom categories not previously seen, raters were also instructed, "You may find that some of the cards do not fit into any of the groups. Take these cards and make your own groupings with them. You may also consider a Miscellaneous group.'' The raters were free to place as many cards as they deemed appropriate into these new or miscellaneous symptom categories.

Results and Discussion

The results indicate that the DSM-III-R criteria can largely be incorporated into the overall structure identified in Study I. As mentioned, 54 (42%) of the 129 total symptoms were judged to be identical to existing symptoms by a group of five reviewers. Moreover, all of the 75 new items were placed by more than half the raters into one of the 22 factors, and 68 (91%) were placed by at least two thirds of the raters into the existing structure. The seven items that failed to meet this two-thirds criterion were all from the two provisional diagnoses, Self-defeating PD (3 items) and Sadistic PD (4 items). Thus, despite extensive revision in both the symptom pool and their organization into diagnostic categories, the domain covered by Axis II in DSM-III-R is quite comparable to that of its predecessor, with the possible exception of these two controversial categories. Symptoms from these categories are considered separately for the following analyses.

Specific correspondence was clearly found between most of the 112 remaining DSM-III-R criteria and the 22 identified factors; representative items are included in Table 9.2. In addition to the 54 identical items, which were all from the 11 primary diagnoses, another 39 (35%) were placed in the same factor by more than half the raters, and an additional 11 items (10%) were placed in the same factor by at least a third of the raters. The former level of agreement is comparable to that found in Study I for moderately strong markers of a factor (e.g., a loading of .60 or higher), and the latter level to that for less prominent markers (e.g., .40 to .60). Thus, 104 of the 112 primary DSM-III-R criteria (93%) could be specifically incorporated into previously identified symptom categories at approximately the same level of agreement that was originally used to determine the groupings. This is only slightly lower than the 96% classification rate obtained in the original study.

It should be noted that four raters created their own symptom groupings (ranging from two to four items) with the new primary symptoms, but no consistent categories emerged. Finally, five raters produced a miscellaneous category, but no item was included by more than two raters. Thus, with some inevitable minor disagreement, the primary items of the new symptom pool can be incorporated into the basic symptom categories derived from previous conceptualizations of the domain of personality disorders.

One of the goals of the Axis II revision committee was to reduce symptom overlap between diagnoses (B. Pfohl, personal communication, November 8, 1986), and it appears that this goal has been at least partially attained. The average number of DSM-III PD diagnoses per symptom cluster was 2.6 (range = 1–5), while the corresponding figure for the DSM-III-R primary diagnoses is 2.0 (range = 0–4). Thus, any given symptom group is now shared, on the average, by fewer PD diagnoses than previously. This may help to reduce the percentage of patients receiving multiple diagnoses.

Provisional Diagnoses.   Less comparability and agreement were seen with regard to the provisional diagnoses. One third (⅓) of the symptoms from Self-defeating PD were grouped with the same category by over half the raters, whereas one half (⅛) of those from Sadistic PD were so placed by at least one third of the raters. Moreover, six raters proposed a Sadistic/Sadism category, and three items were placed by at least one third of the raters in this cluster. Similarly, five raters spontaneously created and variously labeled a Self-defeat-ing, Martyring, Intrapunitive, or Masochist category, and two items were consistently placed in this group. Three more items were split between the created Self-defeating category and one of the pre-existing 22 groups. It is also likely that if these categories had been among the defined groups presented to the raters they would have been used more frequently. In sum, although about 40% of the items comprising these new diagnoses were placed with some consistency into one of the pre-existing categories (compared to 93% of the primary items), their proposed addition would appear to expand the domain of personality disorder symptoms beyond previous conceptualizations.

GENERAL DISCUSSION AND CONCLUSIONS

In this chapter I have presented a conceptual structure of symptoms in the general domain of personality disorder. It is sufficiently comprehensive to include criteria from 11 DSM-III diagnoses and their DSM-III-R revisions, as well as a number of alternative conceptualizations of personality disorder and diagnoses that have been hypothesized to be PDs, but that are currently considered clinical syndromes (e.g., Dysthymia). The more radical DSM-III revisions—the provisional categories—appear to expand this structure somewhat. If, on the basis of other empirical evidence, these categories are eventually fully included in (or the clinical syndromes conclusively excluded from) the domain of personality disorder, it will be necessary to revise the structure accordingly. However, even if this were to happen, the large majority of the symptom factors would be unaffected.

It is important to remember that these factors represent raters' semantic group-ings of criteria relevant to personality disorder, not a structure empirically de-rived from patient ratings. As mentioned in the introduction, identification of semantic clusters does not itself shed any light on whether the domain of person-ality disorders is best described dimensionally or categorically. However, the results do provide a framework for the development of a dimensional approach to the assessment of personality disorder, and provide some support for the potential utility of viewing the domain from this perspective. Thus, just as was done in normal personality research, now that the basic synonym groupings of the domain have been identified, it is necessary to create measures for these factors. For example, the identified dimensions provide a systematic framework for the development of self-reported symptom scales, peer (e.g., spouse) rating scales, structured interviews, or clinicians' ratings of the symptoms relevant to personality disorders. It is hoped that researchers interested in personality disorder will use these identified dimensions to help develop a variety of measures for the assessment of this domain. Using such measures, one can then address the (ultimately more important) question of how these symptom clusters are ordered in individuals from various points of view (e.g., self, peer, clinician). It will then also be possible to compare how the structure of personality disorder is similar and different from that of normal personality. Thus, these dimensions represent the first step toward empirically derived structures of personality disorder symptoms, and also provide a bridge to related areas of research.

In the realm of self-report, development and psychometric evaluation of a set of personality trait scales specifically designed to measure the identified dimensions is underway. Preliminary analyses indicate that the raters have made many more conceptual distinctions than can be measured empirically through self-report. Because self-report measures are usually more finely differentiated than peer or clinicians' ratings (Tellegen, 1986), the resulting scales may represent the limiting case of what can be measured in the domain. Again, this is very similar to the results found in normal personality, where smaller conceptual factors are subsumed by larger, more general empirical factors; for example, Extraversion includes both Dominance and Affiliation, which in turn can be subdivided into more homogeneous content subscales. In the domain of personality disorder, Self-centered Exploitativeness may converge with Antisocial, Hypersensitivity may converge with Suspiciousness, and Emotional Coldness may converge with Social Isolation. Thus, the prospect of developing a set of scales to measure the domain in a comprehensive and systematic manner appears promising. These would then provide the foundation for a full-scale clinical comparison of the dimensional and categorical approaches to assessment of this domain.

ACKNOWLEDGMENTS

Preparation of this article was supported in part by National Institute of Mental Health Grant 1 R03 MH41618-01A1, and by an SMU Provost's Research Administration Grant to the author.

A portion of this paper was presented at the 1986 Andrew Woods Symposium and Meeting of the Iowa Psychiatric Society, November, 1986, Iowa City, IA.

I am grateful to David Watson for his comments on previous versions of this manuscript, and to Lisa Binz, Jay Leeka, Leah Odeneal, Cathey Soutter, and Doreen Voirin, for assistance in the data collection and entry.

Correspondence concerning this chapter should be addressed to Lee Anna Clark, Dept. of Psychology, Southern Methodist University, Dallas, TX 75275-0442.

REFERENCES

Akiskal, H. S. (1984). Characterologic manifestations of affective disorders: Toward a new conceptualization. *Integrative Psychiatry, 2,* 83–96.

Akiskal, H. S., Hirschfeld, R. M., & Yerevanian, B. I. (1983). The relationship of personality to affective disorders. *Archives of General Psychiatry, 40,* 801–810.

Akiskal, H. S., Rosenthal, T. L., Haykal, R. F., Lemmi, H., Rosenthal, R. H., & Scott-Strauss, A. (1980). Characterological depressions—Clinical and sleep EEG findings separating 'subaffective dysthymias' from 'character spectrum disorders.' *Archives of General Psychiatry, 37,* 777–783.

Allport, G. W., & Odbert, H. S. (1936). Trait names: A psycholexical study. *Psychological Monographs, 47,* (1, Whole No. 211).

American Psychiatric Association. (1980). *Diagnostic and statistical manual of mental disorders* (3rd ed.). Washington, DC: Author.

American Psychiatric Association. (August, 1986). *DSM-III-R in development* (2nd draft). Washington, DC: Author.

American Psychiatric Association. (1987). *Diagnostic and statistical manual of mental disorders* (3rd ed., Revised). Washington, DC: Author.

Benjamin, L. S. (1974). Structural analysis of social behavior. *Psychological Review, 81,* 392–425.

Borkenau, P. (1986). Toward an understanding of trait interrelations: Acts as instances for several traits. *Journal of Personality and Social Psychology, 51,* 371–381.

Buss, D., & Craik, K. (1983). The act frequency approach to personality. *Psychological Review, 90,* 105–126.

Buss, D., Craik, K. (1984). Acts, dispositions, and personality. *Progress in Experimental Personality Research, 13,* 241–301.

Buss, D., & Craik, L. (1987). Act criteria for the diagnosis of personality disorders. *Journal of Personality Disorders, 1,* 73–81.

Cantor, N., Smith, E. E., French, R. de S., & Mezzich, J. (1980). Psychiatric diagnosis as prototype categorization. *Journal of Abnormal Psychology, 89,* 181–193.

Cattell, R. B. (1945). The principal trait clusters for describing personality. *Psychological Bulletin, 42,* 129–161.

Cattell, R. B. (1946). *The description and measurement of personality.* Yonkers-on-Hudson, NY: World Book.

Cattell, R. B. (1965). *Scientific analysis of personality.* Chicago: Aldine.

Clark, L. A. (1989). The anxiety and depressive disorders: Descriptive psychopathology and differential diagnosis. In P. C. Kendall & D. Watson (Eds.), *Anxiety and depression: Distinctive and overlapping features* (pp. 83–129). New York: Academic Press.

Clarkin, J. F., Widiger, T. A., Frances, A., Hurt, S. W., & Gilmore, M. (1983). Prototypic typology and the borderline personality disorder. *Journal of Abnormal Psychology, 92,* 263–273.

Cleckley, H. (1964). *The mask of sanity* (4th ed.). St. Louis, MO: Mosby.

Conte, H. R., & Plutchik, R. (1981). A circumplex model for interpersonal personality traits. *Journal of Personality and Social Psychology, 40,* 701–711.

Eysenck, H. J. (1970). *The structure of personality* (3rd ed.). London: Methuen.

Eysenck, H. J., Wakefield, J. A., & Friedman, A. F. (1983). Diagnosis and clinical assessment: The DSM-III. *Annual Review of Psychology; 34,* 167–193.

Frances, A. (1980). The DSM-III personality disorders section: A commentary. *American Journal of Psychiatry, 137,* 1050–1054.

Frances, A. (1982). Categorical and dimensional systems of personality diagnosis: A comparison. *Comprehensive Psychiatry, 23,* 516–527.

Frances, A. J., & Widiger, T. (1986). The classification of personality disorders: An overview of problems and solutions. In A. J. Frances & R. E. Hales (Eds.) *Psychiatry Update: The American Psychiatric Association Annual Review, Vol. 5* (pp. 240–257). Washington, DC: American Psychiatric Press.

Guilford, J. P. (1952). When not to factor analyze. *Psychological Bulletin, 49,* 26–37.

Gunderson, J. G. (1983). DSM-III diagnoses of personality disorders. In J. P. Frosch (Ed.), *Current perspectives on personality disorders.* Washington, DC: American Psychiatric Press.

Hine, F. R., & Williams, R. B. (1975). Dimensional diagnosis and the medical students' grasp of psychiatry. *Archives of General Psychiatry, 32,* 525–528.

Hogan, R. (1985, August). *What every student should know about personality psychology.* G. Stanley Hall Lectures presented at the 93th Annual Convention of the American Psychological Association, Los Angeles, CA.

Hogan, R. (1986, August). On the origin of the "Big 5." In W. T. Norman (Chair), *What are the basic dimensions of personality?* Symposium conducted at the 94th Annual Convention of the American Psychological Association, Washington, DC.

Horowitz, L. M., Post, D. L., French, R. deS., Wallis, K. D., & Siegelman, E. Y. (1981). The prototype as a construct in abnormal psychology: 2. Clarifying disagreement in psychiatric judgments. *Journal of Abnormal Psychology, 90,* 575–585.

Horowitz, L. M., Wright, J. C., Lowenstein, E., & Parad, H. W. (1981). The prototype as a construct in abnormal psychology: 1. A method for deriving prototypes. *Journal of Abnormal Psychology, 90,* 568–574.

Kass, F., Skodol, A. E., Charles, E., Spitzer, R. L., & Williams, J. B. W. (1985). Scaled ratings of DSM-III personality disorders. *American Journal of Psychiatry, 142,* 627–630.

Kendell, R. (1975). *The role of diagnosis in psychiatry.* Oxford: Blackwell.

Kiesler, D. J. (1982). The 1982 Interpersonal Circle: A taxonomy for complementarity in human transactions. *Psychological Review, 90,* 185–213.

Liebowitz, M. R., & Klein, D. F. (1981). Interrelationship of hysteroid dysphoria and borderline personality disorder. *Psychiatric Clinics of North American, 4,* 67–87.

Loevinger, J. (1957). Objective tests as instruments of psychological theory. *Psychological Reports, 3,* 635–694 (Monograph No. 9).

Mann, A. H., Jenkins, R., Cutting, J. C., & Cowen, P. J. (1981). The development and use of a standardized assessment of abnormal psychology. *Psychological Medicine, 11,* 839–847.

McCrae, R. R., & Costa, P. T. (1985). Updating Norman's "adequate taxonomy": Intelligence and personality dimensions in natural language and in questionnaires. *Journal of Personality and Social Psychology, 49,* 710–721.

Norman, W. T. (1963). Toward an adequate taxonomy of personality attributes: Replicated factor structure in peer nomination personality ratings. *Journal of Abnormal and Social Psychology, 66,* 574–583.

Norman, W. T. (April, 1967). *2800 personality trait descriptors: Normative operating characteristics for a university population.* Unpublished manuscript, Department of Psychology, University of Michigan, Ann Arbor, MI.

Penna, M. W. (1981). Classification of personality disorders. In J. R. Lion (Ed.), *Personality disorders: Diagnosis and management* (pp. 10–31). Baltimore: Williams & Wilkins.

Perry, J. C., & Klerman, G. L. (1978). The borderline patient: A comparative analysis of four sets of diagnostic criteria. *Archives of General Psychiatry, 35,* 141–150.

Presley, A. S., & Walton, H. J. (1973). Dimensions of abnormal personality. *British Journal of Psychiatry, 122,* 269–276.

Shepard, M., & Sartorius, N. (1974). Personality disorder and the International Classification of Diseases. *Psychological Medicine, 4,* 141–146.

Tellegen, A. (1985). Structures of mood and personality and their relevance to assessing anxiety, with an emphasis on self-report. In A. H. Tuma & J. D. Maser (Eds.), *Anxiety and the anxiety disorders* (pp. 681–706). Hillsdale, NJ: Erlbaum.

Tellegen, A. (1986, August). What are the most general dimensions in self-report? In W. T. Norman (Chair), *What are the basic dimensions of personality?* Symposium conducted at the 94th Annual Convention of the American Psychological Association, Washington, DC.

Tyrer, P. (1986, November). *Subject or informant: Who best to assess personality?* Paper presented at the 1986 Andrews Wood Symposium and Meeting of the Iowa Psychiatric Society, Iowa City, Iowa.

Tyrer, P., & Alexander, J. (1979). Classification of personality disorder. *British Journal of Psychiatry, 135,* 163–167.

Tyrer, P., Alexander, M. S., Cicchetti, D., Cohen, M. S., & Remington, M. (1979). Reliability of a schedule for rating personality disorders. *British Journal of Psychiatry, 135,* 168–174.

Tyrer, P., Cicchetti, D., Casey, P. R., Fitzpatrick, K., Oliver, R., Balter, A., Giller, E., & Harkness, L. (1984). Cross-national reliability study of a schedule for assessing personality disorders. *Journal of Nervous and Mental Disease, 172,* 718–721.

Tyrer, P., Strauss, J., & Cicchetti, D. (1983). Temporal reliability of personality in psychiatric patients. *Psychological Medicine, 13,* 393–398.

Watson, D., & Clark, L. A. (1984). Negative Affectivity: The disposition to experience aversive emotional states. *Psychological Bulletin, 96,* 465–490.

Watson, D., & Tellegen, A. (1985). Toward a consensual structure of mood. *Psychological Bulletin, 98,* 219–235.

Watson, D., Clark, L. A., & Tellegen, A. (1984). Cross-cultural convergence in the structure of mood: A Japanese replication and a comparison with U. S. findings. *Journal of Personality and Social Psychology, 47,* 127–144.

Widiger, T. (1982). Prototypic typology and borderline diagnosis. *Clinical Psychology Review, 2,* 115–135.

Widiger, T., & Frances, A. (1985). The DSM-III personality disorders: Perspectives from psychology. *Archives of General Psychology, 42,* 615–623.

Widiger, T., & Kelso, K. (1983). Psychodiagnosis of Axis II. *Clinical Psychology Review, 3,* 491–510.

Wiggins, J. S. (1973). Personality and prediction: Principles of personality assessment. Reading, MA: Addison-Wesley.

Wiggins, J. S. (1979). A psychological taxonomy of trait-descriptive terms: The interpersonal domain. *Journal of Personality and Social Psychology, 37,* 395–412.

Wiggins, J. S. (1982). Circumplex models of interpersonal behavior in clinical psychology. In P. C. Kendall & J. N. Butcher (Eds.), *Handbook of research methods in clinical psychology* (pp. 183–221). New York: Wiley.

Winokur, G. (1972). Depression spectrum disease—Description and family study. *Comprehensive Psychiatry, 13,* 3–8.

Winokur, G. (1973). The types of affective disorder. *Journal of Nervous and Mental Disease, 156,* 82–96.

Yerevanian, B. I., & Akiskal, H. S. (1979). "Neurotic," characterological and dysthymic depressions. *Psychiatric Clinics of North America, 2,* 595–617.

Author Index

Subject Index